THE FATE
OF AFRICA'S
DEMOCRATIC
EXPERIMENTS

THE FATE
OF AFRICA'S
DEMOCRATIC
EXPERIMENTS

ELITES AND INSTITUTIONS

Edited by Leonardo A. Villalón
and Peter VonDoepp

INDIANA UNIVERSITY PRESS   BLOOMINGTON AND INDIANAPOLIS

This book is a publication of
Indiana University Press
601 North Morton Street
Bloomington, IN 47404-3797 USA

http://iupress.indiana.edu

Telephone orders 800-842-6796
Fax orders 812-855-7931
Orders by e-mail iuporder@indiana.edu

The paper used in this publication meets the minimum
requirements of American National Standard for Information
Sciences—Permanence of Paper for Printed Library Materials,
ANSI Z39.48-1984.

Manufactured in the United States of America

Library of Congress Cataloging-in-Publication Data

The fate of Africa's democratic experiments : elites and institutions /
edited by Leonardo A. Villalón and Peter VonDoepp.
p.   cm.
The book originated in two linked panels at the Meetings of the
International Studies Association (ISA), held in Chicago in February 2001
and at a second meeting at the Univ. of Kansas in Oct. 2001.
Includes bibliographical references and index.
ISBN 0-253-34575-8 (alk. paper) — ISBN 0-253-21764-4 (pbk. : alk. paper)
1. Africa—Politics and government—1960–   2. Democracy—Africa.
3. Elite (Social sciences)—Africa.   I. Villalón, Leonardo Alfonso, date-
II. VonDoepp, Peter, date-
JQ1875.F38 2005
320.96—dc22

2004030445

1   2   3   4   5   10   09   08   07   06   05

CONTENTS

Contents

PREFACE

The character of African politics changed substantially in the early 1990s. Reflecting the combination of international and domestic pressures for change, familiar political tendencies began to wither as novel movements and processes reshaped and reconfigured African political systems. One of the most visible manifestations of these changes was a wave of apparent democratic transitions on the continent. Whereas "democracy" was largely a token phenomenon during the 70s and 80s, by the 1990s, a large number of African states were undertaking experiments in democratic rule.

More than a decade since these novel democratization processes emerged, the time is more than right to evaluate the fate of Africa's democratic experiments. How have new democratic regimes evolved since they made their apparently successful transition to multiparty politics? To what extent have these regimes actually represented viable "democracies"? And, most importantly, how do we account for the varied experiences of those countries that initially took steps to follow the democratic path? By focusing on the roles of elites and institutions in shaping the subsequent evolution of democracy in ten African countries that made initial transitions, this volume attempts to address these questions.

The book originated in two linked panels at the meetings of the International Studies Association (ISA), held in Chicago in February 2001. We gratefully acknowledge the support of the ISA in helping to bring together the initial group of scholars whose individual work and provocative interchange at that conference inspired the development of this edited volume. In the wake of the Chicago conference, we organized a second meeting at the University of Kansas in October 2001, which was attended by all of the contributors to this volume. This highly productive conference-workshop was made possible thanks primarily to the support of the University of Kansas's African Studies Resource Center, and we are deeply grateful to its director, John Janzen, and program coordinator, Khalid al-Hassan, for their enthusiastic support. We are also thankful for support from the College of Liberal Arts and Sciences and the Office of International Programs at the University of Kansas, and in particular to Associate Deans Joane Nagel and Paul D'Anieri. The interested participation of the terrific Africanist community in Kansas helped make the meeting a significant success.

We owe several other debts to institutions that supported this project. The University of North Texas Department of Political Science graciously supported travel costs required for the project, while the Office of the Vice President for Research and Technology provided funds to support the activities of a research assistant. We also acknowledge our gratitude to the colleagues and staff of the University of Florida's Center for African Studies.

The editors are also grateful for the assistance and contributions of several individuals who have aided this project at various stages. At the original meeting of the participants, Professor Dwayne Woods of Purdue University offered thought-provoking comments that helped us to refine the approaches used in this book. The Kansas meeting benefited from the participation of several individuals who served as discussants and facilitators: Elizabeth MacGonagle and Garth Myers of the University of Kansas, and Kisangani Emizet of Kansas State University. We have also been helped along the way by several research assistants, including Martin Willhoite, Adam Kiš, and Dean Haddock. Perhaps most importantly, we wish to acknowledge the patient support of Dee Mortensen and her colleagues at Indiana University Press.

Finally, we are grateful to Michael Bratton and Nicolas van de Walle, whose initial study of democratization in Africa, *Democratic Experiments in Africa: Regime Transitions in Comparative Perspective* (1997), provided the foundation on which this study was pursued. While differing in terms of methodological approach, we see our own work as an effort to continue and extend their contributions to the study of African democracy.

THE FATE
OF AFRICA'S
DEMOCRATIC
EXPERIMENTS

1 | Elites, Institutions, and the Varied Trajectories of Africa's Third Wave Democracies

Peter VonDoepp and Leonardo A. Villalón

In the early 1990s, Africa was swept by an apparent wave of democratization that generated dramatic changes in the political map of the continent. Pressed by novel international demands for "good governance," and confronted by newly emboldened domestic voices for change, regimes in virtually every African country were forced to undertake political reforms in the name of democracy. From the outset, it was quickly apparent that the nature of these changes would be highly varied. In some countries, political reform was quite limited, as long-standing autocrats developed new strategies for holding power in the altered national and international contexts brought forth with the fall of the Berlin Wall. Still other cases degenerated into tragic patterns of state collapse and civil violence, after initial pressures for political liberalization had surfaced (see Reno 1999; Villalón and Huxtable 1998).

Yet in a select number of countries, democracy appeared to make significant inroads. Most often, this was witnessed in the successful conducting of multiparty "founding" elections that brought new elites to power (Bratton 1998). These initial advances offered at least limited hope that democratic regimes might emerge, survive, and even prosper on a continent that heretofore had proven inhospitable to them. Indeed, the apparent successes of these transitions called into question certain earlier assessments suggesting that the prospects for democratic development in Africa were dim (Huntington 1984; Jackson and Rosberg 1985a). Breaking the pervasive pattern of authoritarian and personal rule of the previous two decades, by 1994 a significant number of countries in Africa had made transitions and were undertaking what Michael Bratton and Nicolas van de Walle (1997) labeled "experiments" in democratic rule.

More than ten years since the inauguration of these new democratic experiments, students of African politics confront the important and intriguing challenge of assessing and explaining the fates of the continent's "third wave" democracies. To what extent did these changes actually constitute democratic transitions? How durable have been the democratic regimes that emerged in the early 1990s? What is the character of those democracies that endure into the present day? And perhaps most importantly, how do we make sense of the varied experiences of these countries that, at least initially, took parallel steps along the same democratic path? As even the casual observer of African affairs must recognize, Africa's third wave democracies have realized widely differing degrees of success and/or failure. The time is right to comparatively analyze the course and progress of democratization experiments on the continent.

This volume is dedicated to undertaking this challenge. It comparatively examines the fates of ten countries—a distinct and important group consisting of those that initially appeared to make successful democratic transitions during the early 1990s. The set of countries under examination are highly varied. They represent Portuguese-, French-, and English-speaking Africa and are geographically dispersed across the continent. They represent countries that have received considerable attention in Africanist scholarship, but also several that are understudied. Most importantly, writing over a decade after the "third wave" swept Africa, we see extreme variations in the extent to which anything resembling a functional democratic system persists in these countries. Yet, together they represent those countries that, at the start of the decade, constituted a newly emerging democratic trajectory on the continent. Our task is to illuminate the forces and processes that have shaped the varied experiences of these regimes.

In addition to focusing on a clearly defined set of countries, this volume also uses a distinctive analytical approach to explore these countries' experiences. In a purely formal sense, democracy can be characterized as a system in which institutions constrain the behavior of political elites. Building from this premise, the central focus of this volume is to pinpoint and highlight the varied evolution of relations between elites and institutions in Africa's new democracies. Studying the interactions between elites and their institutional environments, we maintain, provides an effective starting point for understanding the experiences of these regimes.

In terms of the actual case studies in the volume, the emphasis on elites and institutions provides a framework both to *describe* regimes comparatively and to *explain* their specific experiences. With respect to the former, interactions between elites and their institutional environments reveal a great deal about the character of contemporary African democracies, thus providing a basis for characterizing these regimes. The extent to which elites variously follow, break, bend, or subvert governing institutions provides some testimony as to how effectively democracy is operating in these contexts. In turn, the explanatory exercise that emerges from this assessment concerns why elites have made particular choices with respect to democratic institutions. Here, institutions themselves become part of the explanation. As several of the cases indicate, the character and performance of institutions have very real consequences for the fates of democratic regimes. In some cases, institutional arrangements have given elites important incentives to support the democratic system; in other cases, they have undermined possibilities for elite habituation to democratic rule.

In short, then, this book offers analyses of a crucially important set of countries that present theoretically intriguing prospects for comparative inquiry. In so doing, it takes a distinct perspective, one that places elites and institutions at the center of analysis. By undertaking substantive examinations of these cases from this perspective, it aims to illuminate the forces and processes that are affecting the fate of democracy on the African continent.

Africa and the Study of Democratization

In its empirical and geographic focus, this book addresses a major gap in the literature on democratization. To date, the bulk of research on democratization has involved investigations of the experiences of countries in Southern Europe, the former Soviet Bloc, and Latin America. Indeed, even comprehensive, cross-continental investigations have tended to overlook Africa's experience with democracy. Diamond's (1999a) work, devoted to assessing the quality and prospects for democracy worldwide, for example, incorporates very little material dealing with African cases, drawing much more from the experiences of Latin American, Eastern European, and Asian countries. Where the African experience is considered, disproportionate attention is focused on South Africa, a relatively unique case within the African context. Similarly, Linz and Stepan (1996), in their comprehensive study of democratic transitions and consolidation, make only passing reference to Africa's third wave democracies, practically suggesting that these cases have only limited relevance to the larger investigation of democracy.

The lack of attention to Africa would appear to reflect a significant level of pessimism about prospects for democracy on the continent. And, indeed, to the extent that one is guided by the political science literature on democratization, one might presume that there is little basis for hope about Africa's democratic experiments. This is especially true of the tradition of scholarly work that attempts to identify the preconditions and supportive elements that are necessary for democratic development. Most of what this literature advises about democratization seems to suggest its unlikelihood in Africa. While scholars at times recognize that the prospects for democratization in Africa should not be understood solely in terms of whether conditions resemble those of other countries or regions at the point when those areas democratized, the available knowledge has long suggested that democracy will encounter severe difficulties in Africa.

Consider the importance of key political variables. The work of Linz and Stepan (1996), for instance, highlights the importance of what they call "stateness" as a necessary precondition for democratic consolidation. As articulated in their discussion, this variable has two components. First, it entails a basic agreement on the boundaries of citizenship. Echoing the sentiments raised earlier by Dankwart Rustow (1970), they suggest that questions of "who are the people" must be answered before developing a political system in which "the people" can govern. A viable national political community is necessary to generate the political stability required for democratic development. Secondly, "stateness" involves the presence of a viable state organization with the capacity to enforce laws, collect taxes, and effectively govern the population and territory. Without a state that has these capacities, Linz and Stepan argue, "there can be no democratic governance" (1996, 18).

As most students of African politics recognize, stateness is in many respects the central problem that has confronted the continent's political systems. As Jackson and Rosberg (1985b) so aptly put it, while African states obtained juridical statehood at independence, the empirical dimensions of statehood have been woefully lacking. Decades of arbitrary personal rule have actually made the problem worse. Even in new democracies, basic social support for state authority—the legitimacy that might evoke some level of voluntary compliance—remains evanescent. State bureaucratic structures and administrations remain fundamentally weak in terms of their ability to "project power," as Herbst (2000) has more recently argued. As such, the first challenge faced by many newly elected leaders in Africa has been to rebuild state authority and capacity. Whether democracy can endure where these are not in place at the outset is an open question.[1]

Analyses that focus on economic considerations also suggest fundamental difficulties for African democracies. Recent work by Przeworski and his collaborators (1996; Przeworski and Limongi 1997) is especially instructive in this regard. As their extensive cross-national research indicates, democracies born in poor settings are quite unlikely to survive. Democracies with per capita incomes below $1,000— a category which includes nearly every democracy in this study—have twice as high a chance of "dying" from one year to the next as democracies in countries that have per capita incomes ranging from $1,000 to $2,000. Moreover, as these studies suggest, poor economic performance in the post-transition period bodes poorly for democracy. Considering that five out of the ten new democracies reviewed in this volume averaged negative annual per capita growth from 1993 to 2002, there are even further grounds for pessimism.[2]

And there are still other reasons to be less than hopeful about Africa's democratic prospects. The cultural legacy of colonial and post-colonial authoritarian rule has done little to inculcate the social capital and civic culture that many scholars— from Almond and Verba (1963) to Robert Putnam (1993) or Larry Diamond (1999a)—have viewed as critical for democratic success. Much the same, the international climate for nascent democracies has shifted. Whereas the early 1990s saw international players—notably Western governments and international financial institutions—openly supporting democracies, by the close of the decade, outside efforts to promote democracy in Africa had backtracked.

While much existing scholarship raises doubts about the prospects for democracy, this nevertheless poorly justifies the lack of attention to African cases in the literature. Indeed, we maintain that the marginalization of African cases does a tremendous disservice to the study of democracy, and particularly in the post–third wave international context in which insights on African experiences with democracy can contribute greatly to our larger understanding of the phenomenon. As the cases examined in this book demonstrate, new African democracies present a wealth of empirical data from which to critically explore the conventional wisdom about the factors affecting processes of democratization. These cases, first of all, present rich opportunities to evaluate the relevance of the many proposed "preconditions" for democratic transitions. And, to foreshadow somewhat, the cases described in this book raise very fundamental questions about the received wisdom from that literature—a point raised by Michael Chege in his conclusion and by Bruce Magnusson in his chapter on Benin. Or consider, for example, the question addressed by several chapters in this volume of how variations in constitutional frameworks make democratic stability more or less likely. Are tendencies found in other parts of the world also operative in the African context? Or are expected patterns in the relationships between institutions and outcomes reworked and reshaped in the African context? One might expect that the terrain of African politics could affect expected relationships in unforeseen ways, suggesting the need to nuance and refine existing theories. The diversity of institutional forms in new African democracies thus offers opportunities to investigate these central questions.[3]

Beyond this, the African cases can at times suggest different kinds of factors that are not adequately addressed in the existing literature. One theme presented in some of the case studies in this volume, for example, concerns how internal dynamics within new ruling parties affect the character of democratic transitions. (See the cases of Mozambique or Malawi especially in this regard.) Other studies indicate how international actors can unwittingly undermine both state responsiveness and political stability. Understanding how these variables operate in African contexts can inform perspectives of democratization processes in other settings.

More fundamentally, investigating the African cases may actually generate some rethinking of conventional concepts used in the study of democracy. Consider how "democracy" itself has been conceptualized. Frequently, the literature treats democratization as a discrete process with a specified end. In this sense, countries are evaluated on the extent to which they are more or less democratic—that is, progressing toward the specific objective of consolidated democracy. Taken as such, many of the African cases might be categorized as "feeble," "tenuous," or "quasi" democracies—modifiers that have been variously used to capture their limited and problematic character.

As Herbst (2001) has argued, these kinds of labels are themselves problematic because they assume that African democracies are "somehow on the road to democracy and that they have simply been stalled or temporarily delayed" (358–59). Indeed, a closer look at the African cases indicates that placing them on the spectrum of more or less democratic does little to illuminate the important patterns and developments that are actually occurring. As becomes evident through the case studies in this volume, most new African democracies are limited in the extent to which democratic principles of fair contestation and open participation are effectively operative. Moreover, many of them exhibit tendencies that raise questions about their long-term viability. But to simply label them as "quasi" or "limited" fails to capture the essence of what is happening on the ground in these polities. In many African countries, substantial liberalization has occurred as old edifices have collapsed, and a new architecture of politics is being both contested and configured. The rules of the political game (both formal and informal) have changed in a manner that opens up new possibilities for political and civic action; expectations on leadership are different, as rulers must increasingly justify their hold on power with reference to the performance of their government; and the discourse of political life reflects the salience and currency of the normative principle of democracy.

What is witnessed in some sense is what has been described by others (e.g., Diamond 2002; van de Walle 2002) as hybridity—situations in which elements of democracy and liberal politics operate in contexts where neopatrimonial and authoritarian tendencies also remain. While recognizing these latter tendencies is important, the present patterns also suggest that the chances of newly liberalizing African countries returning to their point of departure—the manifestly authoritarian regimes that typified the political landscape in the 1970s and 80s—is quite unlikely. If democracy seems difficult, the liberalization of politics in Africa seems irreversible.[4]

Acknowledging this complex reality illuminates the shortcomings of contemporary conceptualizations that distinguish different polities as simply being more or less democratic on a single theoretical continuum. Our consideration of the African cases aims to shed light on the multiple and complex dimensions of the ongoing struggles and movements that constitute democratization, and at the same time to remind us that, as Herbst argues, hybridity may itself be an equilibrium situation (2001, 359). The static concepts of much of the literature on democracy miss an enormous amount of detail about the ongoing tensions between liberal politics and illiberal tendencies. Indeed, in a fundamental sense, the African cases require us to reconsider the very notion of "democratization" as a discrete phenomenon. While much of the literature presents the phenomenon in terms of the relative degree of progress in moving toward a given end, the changes that have occurred under the banner of democratization in many African cases are, in fact, far more complex and less easily categorized.

There is, in short, much scholarly leverage to be gained by a close consideration of the African cases. They may help to demonstrate the theoretical limitations— or strengths—of the established canon of received knowledge on "what makes democracy work." They can also help to illuminate the importance of factors that have received only limited consideration in the literature. And they may bring us to reconsider the adequacy of the conceptual repertoire used in theoretical discussions of democracy.

The Cases and the Question of Democracy

In the most comprehensive analysis of democratization in Africa in the early 1990s, and notably one that set the parameters for much of the ensuing discussion of democracy on the continent, Michael Bratton and Nicolas van de Walle (1997) examined the variations in African responses to the pressures for political liberalization that coalesced in the late 1980s and early 1990s. In this exercise, they elaborated a typology that categorized African countries on the basis of the different *outcomes* of the processes of change. Reproduced in table 1.1 below, their typology highlights both that the "third wave" had an extraordinarily wide impact on Africa and that its consequences were highly varied, ranging from dramatic failures to significant successes. Most important for our purposes here are the "successes"—those countries that fall under the category of "democratic transitions." Between 1990 and 1994, all of these countries developed basic institutions of electoral competition and participation and elected new governments by means of these institutions. Collectively, this set of countries represents the empirical focus of this book, what we here call Africa's "third wave democracies."

The categorization offered by Bratton and van de Walle thus provides the basis for the selection of cases included in the volume. Using their framework, we have included in our study *only* countries that underwent completed "democratic transitions" from 1990 to 1994. In an effort to expand the basis for comparison, we have sought to be as inclusive as possible in this respect. Thus, excluding only the small island republics and the very special cases of post-apartheid transitions (Namibia, South Africa, and the linked and rather unique case of Lesotho), *all* of the significant cases on Bratton and van de Walle's list of "successes" are represented in the volume. This includes some much-understudied countries, and more generally ones whose collective experiences shed important light on our understanding of democratization processes.

At the outset, it is important to acknowledge several potential hazards in using this conceptualization. One immediate issue concerns whether or not the countries in Bratton and van de Walle's category of "democratic transitions" actually underwent distinct processes of change in response to democratic pressures that surfaced in Africa in the early 1990s. That is, did those countries in fact merit being placed in a category that distinguished them from other African countries? The basis for placing a country in that category concerned the character of founding elections. In these countries, founding elections were held that were widely regarded as free and fair, with outcomes accepted by the losers of such contests. Yet the focus on elections as the metric of democratic success can itself be problematic, running the risk of committing the "fallacy of electoralism" outlined by Schmitter and Karl (1991). Recognizing this fact, Bratton and van de Walle are quite open about the limited character of the transitions that did occur, acknowledging the tenuous character of their list of "democratic transitions." And indeed, candid observation a few years later might lead one to suggest that their typology of "outcomes" was premature, one that did not necessarily reflect the conclusion of a clear process, but perhaps only a snapshot of one brief moment in an ongoing period of transition and flux.

Complicating this issue further is the accumulating evidence, which suggests that undergoing a "democratic transition" in the manner described by Bratton and

Table 1.1. Bratton and Van de Walle's Typology: "Transitions Outcomes, Sub-Saharan Africa, 1994"

Precluded Transitions	Blocked Transitions	Flawed Transitions	Democratic Transitions
Liberia	Angola	Burkina Faso	Benin
Sudan	Burundi	Cameroon	Cape Verde
	Chad	Comoros	Central African Republic
	Ethiopia	Côte d'Ivoire	Congo
	Guinea	Djibouti	Guinea-Bissau
	Nigeria	Equatorial Guinea	Lesotho
	Rwanda	Gabon	Madagascar
	Sierra Leone	Ghana	Malawi
	Somalia	Kenya	Mali
	Tanzania	Mauritania	Mozambique
	Uganda	Swaziland	Namibia
	Zaire	Togo	Niger
			São Tomé
			Seychelles
			South Africa
			Zambia

van de Walle was not even a necessary step to placing a country on the path of subsequent democratic development. The implied significance of their categories is not only that they distinguished between the outcomes of transition processes in Africa but also that they provided information about which countries were headed in a democratic direction. However, subsequent developments indicate that some countries in their categorization that did not undergo "democratic transitions" are today more appropriately labeled democratic than those that did. Returning to the table above, for example, we can note that Ghana and Tanzania were considered "blocked" and "flawed" transitions in 1994, whereas Congo-Brazzaville and the Central African Republic (both included in this volume) fell under the "democratic transitions" category. Yet in the current era, it is the former that might more plausibly be labeled "democratic."[5] More recently Kenya, considered in 1994 to be a "flawed transition," appears with the 2002 election of Mwai Kibaki to the presidency to have moved significantly into the democratic camp.

Though the situation is clearly more complex than that suggested by Bratton and van de Walle's typology, it nevertheless is also true that this categorization of initial responses to democratic pressures has important heuristic value. Cognizance of the electoral fallacy should not lead us to commit the anti-electoralist fallacy, suggesting that elections never matter (Seligson and Booth 1995; cf. Bratton 1998, 52). While a focus on elections as the measure of democratization can be problematic, it is equally problematic to assume that there were not important differences between those countries that experienced free and fair founding elections and those that did not. The fact that these countries witnessed effective founding elections indicates that significant changes had occurred in the polity.

Moreover, despite the fact that subsequent developments indicate that countries that experienced blocked or flawed transitions could still undergo significant democratic development, our comparative focus on solely those countries that experienced initial success has an important analytic basis. Few would question that, in 1994, the countries that we examine in this book did in fact represent a unique phenomenon. At that time, all of these countries had selected leaders using new rules of the game—competitive multiparty elections—that had been elaborated during their respective transition periods. That is, they had each experienced a new distribution of power among political *elites,* and this had occurred via new democratic *institutions.* Including only these countries thus enhances the comparative basis of our project, allowing us to examine the subsequent variations among these "like-cases." What happened beyond their initially similar starting points and why have they evolved in the manner that they have? What have been the varied fates of these African experiments with democracy?

An additional complicating issue concerns the very labeling of the phenomenon represented by these countries as "democracy." In this sense, the issue is less whether these countries represent a distinct category than whether the label for that category is appropriate. In terms of conventional usage and connotation, democracy clearly implies some enhanced level of control by the citizens over the political decisions that affect their lives.[6] To be sure, even in the most established democracies, the extent to which reality approximates this ideal is subject to question (see Lindblom 1977; Bourdieu 1998). Yet in Africa's new democracies, the democratic label is decidedly more problematic. All of Africa's new democracies exhibit major shortcomings in the extent to which their transitions actually transferred power to the citizenry. As numerous critical observers have pointed out, citizens in these societies often remain quite unable to influence policy decisions, let alone to hold elites to more effective standards of accountability (Ake 1995; Mkandawire 1999; Olokushi 1999; Englund 2003; Dowd 2001). Indeed, certain chapters in this volume echo this sentiment (see the case of Madagascar in this regard). As such, from a normative angle, to speak of "democracy" may appear somewhat naive or, worse still, disingenuous.

Clearly, there are limitations in the extent to which popular control of elites has existed in these regimes. And yet we should not also understate the possibilities for greater citizen control that are embedded in the new political frameworks of these new democracies. Each of the countries that underwent a successful democratic transition adopted a set of institutions that in principle held the *potential* to generate more accountable styles of governance, and it would be quite unwise to dismiss the existence of such democratic institutions as meaningless over the longer term. To the extent that democracy, at least in a formal sense, is a system in which elite behavior is constrained by institutions, the installation of these new regimes opened the door to more substantial and far-reaching processes of democratization. Echoing Giuseppe DiPalma (1990), Mozaffar (1998) has argued that:

> To produce democracy is to craft institutions. To craft institutions is to design rules that, in the first instance, authorize the restrained exercise of power in public life by both the governors and the governed. And to the extent these rules also encourage accommodation, compromise, and tolerance of diverse opinions, protracted functioning democracies produce rather than reflect a civic "political" culture (Karl and Schmitter 1991) in which emancipatory projects might evolve. (83)

As the recent political histories of Senegal or Ghana (or indeed Mexico, to move beyond Africa) demonstrate, formal yet imperfect or incomplete democratic institutional regimes can, over time, evolve into systems that are more substantively and meaningfully democratic. As such, the fate of the new democracies—however incomplete or purely formal they might appear in their original incarnations—is of central importance to all who hope for the evolution of more accountable systems of government on the continent. The survival of these systems is a prerequisite to obtaining the kind of popular leverage that can hold elites accountable to the people writ large.

From their apparently similar beginnings at the start of the 1990s, the ten countries examined in this volume have evolved in politically varied ways. It is these variances that we seek to illuminate and explain in the volume. Most fundamentally, we are concerned with the relative successes and/or failures of these countries with democratic rule. While this might be understood in alternate ways, the conceptualization that we adopt here posits democracy as a system of government where elite behavior is controlled by institutions, and thus leads us to focus our attention on the relationship between elites and institutions. Our primary emphasis in assessing the experiences of these countries, in turn, is to question the extent to which their new institutions have continued to constrain the behavior of elites along "democratic" lines. Conversely, we also ask whether and to what extent these institutions have been marginalized, manipulated, or destroyed by elite action.

Focusing on this relationship allows us to examine several important dimensions of the experiences of Africa's new democracies. First, a central issue concerns the question of survival versus breakdown. In a select few of the countries under review, fragile experiments met "quick deaths" (Schedler 1998) as key elites opted to jettison democratic institutions that generated outcomes contrary to their preferences, or that more generally limited their capacity to aggrandize power. Civil conflict and returns to authoritarian rule were the unsurprising results in these situations. In most other cases, however, elites opted to leave the rules of the game largely intact (despite frequent efforts to minimize their effects), and basic democratic institutions have endured to the present day. Thus several of the authors in the volume devote considerable attention to detailing why specific regimes have either endured or collapsed.

In and of itself, however, the question of survival versus breakdown is somewhat limited. Most of the countries that underwent "completed transitions" in the early 1990s have minimally preserved the basic form of democracy. As such, other important dimensions of their experiences deserve attention. For one, countries have varied in the extent to which elites have engaged in behaviors that threaten to subvert democratic institutions. Zambia's democracy, for instance, has been typified by high levels of political violence and tension. Threats of military intervention, rumors of extralegal behavior by opposition politicians, and even suspected assassinations of government opponents have marred political life since the onset of democracy. By contrast, countries such as Benin and Malawi have—to date—largely avoided such tensions.

Yet another dimension concerns the extent to which government, and executive power in particular, has remained effectively constrained by political institutions. Mozambique provides an example of a new democracy where presidential power has remained very much in check. Unique dynamics within the governing party have limited the capacity of the executive to change or bend the rules of the democratic game in his favor. Madagascar, on the other hand, has witnessed a wholly different situation. Owing to presidential manipulation of key political institutions, checks on executive power have been largely nonexistent. This has created the situation described by Richard Marcus in his chapter as "legitimized autocracy." Thus, despite the fact that these two countries are significantly similar in that the basic form of democratic institutions has remained intact since their respective transitions, they are marked by important differences in how effectively these regimes have restrained executive power.

The case studies are thus devoted to examining such dimensions of each country's experience with democracy. By its very nature, this study involves a considerable amount of "thick description," with in-depth analyses that detail the complexities and nuances at work in each country, and which thus serve to illuminate the gray area depicted by labels such as "quasi," "virtual," and "illiberal." As we have argued, one of the important aspects of political changes occurring in Africa concerns the multiple tendencies at work and the diverse hybridities that typify contemporary politics. New regimes may be liberal and democratic in the sense of employing basic institutions and formal practices, but in other ways their democratic nature may be severely qualified. In some regimes, elections have limited impact on the distribution of power in the polity. In others, executives are constrained in only a limited sense. And, in many, informal, "neopatrimonial" practices, as opposed to formal rules, remain the modal form of governance. It is specifically these kinds of multiple tendencies that the volume seeks to address. Attempting to illuminate the hybrid character of political life in Africa, the case studies assign themselves to unearthing the messy complexities actually at work in this important set of Africa's third wave democratic experiments.

Elites: Definitional and Conceptual Issues

As should be apparent by now, we view elites as primary authors of the various outcomes witnessed in the new African democracies under investigation. Their choices and behaviors represent a primary focus of inquiry for the case studies in the volume. Our emphasis in this respect thus deserves further specification, and some justification. This is especially true in that our focus on elites situates this work quite distinctly within some of the larger conversations and debates in the literature on democratization.

One important preliminary issue concerns the question of how we define and conceptualize "elites." This study distinguishes itself from the sociological tradition that examines patterns of elite dominance in the political process (see, e.g., Mills 1959; Pareto and Finer 1969; cf. also Putnam 1976, 3–5). In this tradition, elites are conceptualized as a particular social *stratum,* relatively homogenous and self-perpetuating, which dominates the political process. From that perspective, the key analytical project concerns the investigation of how this group perpetuates its hold on power via the subordination of other classes or groups, and what consequences ensue. An important line of research on African politics and society has extended this tradition in an effort to highlight how processes of social stratification in Africa shape the political and developmental fortunes of the continent (see Fatton 1992; Bayart 1993; Chabal and Daloz 1999).

By contrast, our attention to elites concerns their roles as *individual political players.* As such, this study remains only marginally concerned with how elites, as a particular stratum, engage in a project of domination over subordinate classes. We focus on elites as a discrete set of political actors and explore how their decisions and behaviors shape national-level political fates. Our conceptualization thus resembles, and to some extent borrows from, the work of Burton, Gunther, and Higley, whose study of democratic consolidation in Latin America and Southern Europe similarly emphasizes the decisive role played by political elites. For these scholars, elites represent "those persons who are able . . . to affect national political outcomes regularly and substantially" (1992, 9). By "regularly," the authors specify that elites have the ability to influence political life in a relatively routine manner. Individual assassins, for example, would not qualify. "Substantially" delineates the extent of potential influence available to these persons. As individuals, they have the power to shape the very character of national political life.

In African contexts, the individuals who possess this kind of power over outcomes represent a relatively narrow set of people—indeed, so narrow that for quite some time the study of "personal rule" was a major analytical perspective in the study of African politics (Jackson and Rosberg 1982). Depending on national circumstances, such elites could include politicians who command substantial resources and followings, leaders of major ethnic groups and civil society organizations, and ranking individuals in military and government bureaucracies. In the substantive chapters that follow, however, it is the first-named, the key politicians (both governing and opposition), who obtain the bulk of analytical attention. As the authors of the various chapters detail, it is these individuals, perhaps more than any other elites, whose actions have shaped their respective countries' experiences with democratic rule.

The emphasis on elites situates this project specifically within the large and growing literature on democracy and democratic consolidation. Within this literature, there are differences in the kinds of issues that obtain emphasis. Some authors very clearly downplay the role of elites, arguing that other variables are more critical in determining the success and/or failure of democracies. In so doing, they build on a long tradition of scholarship that has emphasized how cultural, structural, and economic forces have shaped the prospects for democratic development (Lipset 1959; Almond and Verba 1963; Moore 1966; Rueschemeyer, Stephens, and Stephens 1992). Diamond (1999a), concerned with the "determinants" of democratic consolidation, provides one recent example. While not overlooking the importance of political elites, he privileges the role of a supportive, mass political culture and says that the development of civil society is critical. Przeworski et al.'s (1996; Przeworski and Limongi 1997) extensive cross-national work, while taking a different line of argument from Diamond's, similarly de-emphasizes the role of elites. Their analysis emphasizes institutional variables as well as economic factors that are critical to democratic longevity. Finally, Linz and Stepan's (1996) work highlights the complex array of factors that combine to create a supportive environment for democracy: a viable state, the rule of law, civil society, and the presence of an "economic society," among others.

These studies, of course, do not argue that the actions of elites are irrelevant. The issue is one of emphasis—most of these studies treat elite actions as secondary to other factors that affect the fate of democracies. Part of the reason for this may be related to the scope of the scholarship. Most of these projects deal with a large sample of countries whose experiences with democracy extend beyond the recent past. These inquiries focus on national economic or cultural factors in an effort to build generalizations about the variables that affect democratic longevity and success. Importantly, as we have already noted, virtually all such studies suggest the unlikelihood of democracy in Africa, indicating that perhaps other frameworks might more effectively illuminate the varied experiences that are today evident.

Yet, for the African countries that underwent democratic transitions in the early 1990s, such structural analysis is of very limited utility. These cases are marked by their distinctly transitional character. Patterns of interaction remain highly fluid, institutions are untested, and the efficacy of the democratic political process is undetermined. To be sure, in the long term, other variables, especially cultural and economic ones, may have a significant impact on how well these regimes perform or even on their very survival. However, as other scholars have specified, in highly uncertain and fluid periods, elite actions deserve special attention as the primary variables shaping political trajectories (Linz 1978; O'Donnell and Schmitter 1986; Bunce 2000). For Africa's new democracies, the key issue at present concerns how elites have responded to regimes—the degree to which they have supported or undermined the new democratic institutions put in place only a few years earlier.

In emphasizing the role of elites, this work thus builds upon an alternate, rich, and well-developed tradition in the study of regime change and democracy. The classic statement on the importance of elites in democratization processes is found in the work of Dankwart Rustow (1970). In contrast to other scholars of the day who emphasized the cultural or sociostructural bases of such processes, Rustow maintained that the creation and sustaining of democracy needed to be understood in terms of the choices of key political actors. In his view, the implementation of a democratic system hinged on conscious decisions of "a small circle of leaders" (1970, 356). Likewise, "habituation" (or consolidation) processes depended on the acquiescence of elites to the rules of the democratic game. Following Rustow, the work of Juan Linz on the *breakdown* of democratic regimes also pinpointed the importance of elite actions. Although processes of breakdown were shaped by structural factors, in the final analysis the fates of these regimes were connected with actions of "relevant actors" and ultimately "failures of leadership" (Linz 1978, 10–12). More recent work has built on these perspectives to explore how elite-level dynamics affect important phenomena such as the outcomes of transition processes (Karl 1991) or levels of regime stability over time (Field and Higley 1985; Burton, Gunther, and Higley 1992; Case 1996). As all of these studies effectively illuminate, varying patterns of elite interactions have important consequences for national-level political situations, and more specifically for the prospects for democracy.

Explaining Elite Behavior:
Normative and Analytical Dimensions

Two important theoretical concerns emerge from this emphasis on elites. The first is the issue of how "the people" figure into our analyses. Given its focus on democracy, one might question the fact that this volume devotes the bulk of attention to elites rather than to the popular experience and its role in these new regimes. To be sure, it is highly important to examine how average citizens in new African democracies experience, engage in, and even shape the political sphere. Of special importance is attention to the question of how members of the mass public can develop the inclinations and means to more effectively access and influence political officials at the level of the state; that is, how can average citizens make democracy work for them? Recent work by many of the scholars in this volume has examined precisely these kinds of issues (Marcus 2001; Posner and Simon 2002; Simon 2002; VonDoepp 2002a).

Attention to elite-level dynamics should be viewed as complementary to these types of concerns. Indeed, from an analytical perspective, questions of whether and how national democratic institutions operate may in fact be necessarily prior to those focusing on the substantive quality and depth of democracy. And in examining the high politics of democratic institutional operation and stability at the national level, the focus on elites is absolutely required; ultimately, it is elites who shape whether these new regimes will survive and how they will develop. Because we are concerned with these types of regime-level questions, we narrow attention to the key players in the political process.

This does not imply that "the people" are wholly left out of the analyses in the chapters that follow. However, the role that they play in these new democracies is very much an empirical question, and authors of the case studies vary in the extent to which they consider average citizens as significant. An implied theme that emerges from several of the chapters in the volume is that the popular classes have played a fairly limited role in shaping the actions of elites. Chapters on Congo-Brazzaville and the Central African Republic suggest that elites in these countries have operated with only limited consideration of popular expectations—or have even been able to neglect them. By contrast, several other chapters emphasize various ways in which citizens have affected the experiences of these regimes. Some, for instance, focus on the role of elections. These serve as critical moments when average citizens exert important collective influence on elites, both legitimizing their rule and providing messages about their relative strengths. In a different vein, chapters on Niger and Benin highlight how questions of popular "representation" have figured in the design of central governing institutions in these countries. In turn, these institutions have had an important impact on the relative successes of these two new democracies. Finally, Madagascar's experience after the country's third presidential election suggests that popular upsurges, in response to elite-level machinations, can shape the course of democratic development in important ways.

The second theoretical concern is more analytical in nature. As elite choices and behaviors represent a primary issue for investigation in the volume, we confront the fundamental issue of how these choices and behaviors can be effectively interrogated and explained. Raising this question goes to the very heart of our analytical objectives. If the experiences of these democracies are shaped by elite actions, how is it that we make sense of those actions?

The literature on democracy presents different perspectives on this issue. That is, different answers emerge with respect to the question of why elites make certain choices and engage in particular behaviors. In somewhat simplified terms, three alternate, meta-theoretical perspectives can be delineated. The first treats elite choices and behaviors in a largely *voluntaristic* manner. In this respect, the kinds of actions that elites take with respect to democracy remain relatively unproblematized. Linz's (1978) description of the breakdown of democratic regimes offers a clear example of this kind of approach, focusing much more on what elites do than on the question of *why* they make certain choices. Indeed, in highlighting the "failures of democratic leadership," Linz indicates that the collapse of democratic regimes might have been avoided if key players had pursued other available options. A similar emphasis emerges in DiPalma's (1990) prescriptive essay, *To Craft Democracies*. The tone of this work is that governing elites have a range of choices about the kinds of rules and norms that operate in new democracies. This is especially important because these norms and rules affect opposition decisions about whether to subvert or work within the democratic system. The key task for leaders, then, is to make intelligent choices that enable democratic survival.

A second perspective focuses more on the *normative environment* in which elites make decisions. In this view, elite behavior with respect to democratic institutions is related to habits and attitudes developed over time. Burton, Gunther, and Higley (1992) emphasize that patterns of democratic stability and endurance reflect "attitudinal consensus" on the rules of the game among key players. This involves not only normative support for political institutions, but also a willingness to see "politics as bargaining," rather than "politics as zero-sum." Certain conditions, such as a prolonged crisis or the possibility for face-to-face bargaining, make "elite settlements" about democracy both possible and durable. By contrast, situations where elites are "disunified" bode poorly for democratic stability. Levine's (1978) investigation of democratic consolidation in Venezuela offers a somewhat similar view. A process of political learning over a long period of violence and instability culminated in a normative consensus among key political actors about the formal and informal rules of the game. The re-emergence and consolidation of democracy, he argues, hinged on the "development of common norms of behavior among Venezuelan political elites" (84).

The third perspective on elite behavior highlights the *strategic considerations* of elites. Rather than viewing elites' choices as the product of norms or attitudes, they are understood as the outcome of the rational calculations of actors seeking to advance their interests. Certain elements of this approach are evident in the earlier work of Dankwart Rustow. For him, democracies emerged not as a result of the rise of democratic norms, but when circumstances "tricked, lured, or cajoled" nondemocrats into democratic behavior (1970, 344). The extent to which actors were able to achieve "success" through democratic institutions, in turn, increased their willingness to operate within such a framework.[7] A more recent and definitive example of this approach is found in the choice–theoretic arguments of Adam Przeworski (1991). In his framework, the specific interests of elites, as opposed to attitudinal consensus, are the operative mechanism of democratic survival. The survival of the system reflects equilibrium "of the decentralized strategies of all the relevant political forces" (26). In this sense, democracy endures when the interests and calculations of the key players stimulate them to work within or comply with the system, rather than to subvert it.

In the case studies that follow, all three of these approaches can be discerned, as authors variously emphasize how elite agency, normative commitments, and rational calculations have affected the experiences of these regimes. This eclecticism reflects our understanding that, while each of these three approaches sheds some insights into elite behavior, in the real, complex world of given political systems, the motivations and actions of elites are never simply reducible to one theoretical perspective. *Within any given case, elites make choices of their own, but they do so within constraints established by the normative and cultural context, and taking into account their own strategic considerations.* As such, rather than attempt to situate cases within a single intellectual framework, chapter authors effectively begin with the empirical—

the actual experience with democracy in the country under review. Thereafter their task has been to explain the patterns and behaviors revealed, using the theoretical perspective that they feel most effectively illuminates the case. The consideration of the cases themselves thus constitutes an ongoing dialogue on—or a comparative examination of—the relative importance of human agency, the cultural environment, and rational calculations of key elites.

While approaching their material from different macro-theoretical frameworks, the analytical foci of the chapters overlap in important ways. Specifically, authors address similar kinds of issues when assessing the factors affecting these new democracies. As the reader of the case studies will observe, as authors examine and interrogate the actions of elites with respect to democracy, they raise questions about broadly similar kinds of explanatory factors. To be sure, when accounting for distinct patterns of democratic development in different countries, authors at times emphasize the significance of factors specific to given cases. In some cases, for instance, the size and composition of the elite sector is itself a crucial variable as it helps to determine the possibility for elite bargaining and consensus-building. In others, ethnoregional dynamics are a central determinant of the interactions among key players. The status and activities of the military also emerges as a central concern in a number of instances. The military still represents a critical variable in African politics, but as the case studies demonstrate, the anti-democratic nature of military interventions can no longer be assumed.

This said, there are certain factors that stand out as commonly relevant to shaping elite behavior in Africa's new democracies. Considering the cases as a whole, four such factors emerge as centrally important: (1) economic factors, (2) the role of international actors and organizations, (3) political culture, and—of special relevance to our analytical focus—(4) the impact of political institutions.[8] Collectively, the case studies illuminate and evaluate the salience of these critical variables. After discussing the first three below, we elaborate our view on political institutions in a separate section.

Economic Factors

As indicated above, economic factors have long been considered one of the key determinants of democratic development. Recent research has provided ongoing support for this contention (Przeworski and Limongi 1997). Building on this premise, many Africanists have maintained that economic conditions in society will affect the prospects for Africa's new democratic regimes (van de Walle 1997; Ndegwa 2001). From this perspective, one of the real challenges for new regimes has been to overcome economic crisis and generate growth in a manner that cultivates legitimacy for the new regime. As Bratton and van de Walle articulate, "crisis will continue to undermine the legitimacy of any political regime" (1997, 239). Failure to address economic crises will increase the fragility of new democracies. As will be seen, the question of economic conditions in society figures in many of the studies in this volume. Forrest's chapter on Guinea-Bissau, for example, emphasizes how ongoing economic struggles played into decisions by the military to intervene to subvert the relatively dysfunctional democratic regime that was installed in 1994.

Beyond the question of economic conditions, however, lies the more immediate issue for our purposes of how economic factors affect elite behavior. In this sense, the analytical lens focuses less on broad questions of economic performance and material conditions in society than on the relationship between economic resources and the actions of the key players with respect to democracy. The role of economic resources can be understood on two levels. The first concerns the *distribution* of resources among key political players, and more specifically, how that distribution affects the balance of power among elites. Some authors demonstrate how certain democratically elected governments have been able to control a disproportionate share of resources in domestic economies—giving them income streams and rent-seeking opportunities. In turn, control over resources translates into political advantage as incumbent elites obtain the ability to dispense patronage, run viable party organizations, and mount effective campaigns. Enfeebled domestic opposition in this context has little capacity to shape the political agenda, and the resulting context can create problems for ongoing democratic development. On the one hand, such a situation can increase political apathy and frustration with democratic institutions, increasing the probability of opposition defections from the democratic game. On the other hand, it may lead to a situation where incumbent governments can disproportionately shape the course of institutional and political development in the new democracy.

The second issue concerns the *nature* of resources available in the domestic political economy. One important point that emerges from recent literature is that the kinds of resources available in domestic economies have an impact on the incentives and choices available to key actors. Catherine Boone (1998, 2003b), for example, maintains that different types of political economies facilitate alternative approaches to building political authority. Owing to differences in the extractive demands placed on leadership, peasant-based economies are more likely to witness the development of rural–state institutions than economies with plantation or extraction enclaves. In the latter situations, leaders can eschew conventional strategies such as cultivating legitimacy and building state institutions, instead building power through the control of markets for portable resources. This point is supported by William Reno's (1999) work on "warlord politics"—virtually all of his cases are economies based on extractive or plantation enterprises. Overlapping with this perspective is recent literature on the onset and duration of civil conflicts, in Africa and elsewhere. A consistent finding from cross-national studies seeking to locate the correlates of civil strife is that the presence of portable resources is clearly associated with such conflict. These resources provide both the means and the motives for key players to engage in violent strategies (Collier and Hoeffler 1998; de Soysa 2000).

These kinds of arguments have direct implications for the investigation of the fates of Africa's democratic regimes. The literature suggests that in those contexts where portable resources are available to elites, the range of strategic alternatives will be greater. So, too, will be the motives for holding and acquiring power. This in turn may diminish the likelihood of democratic survival. Hypothetically, opposition elites will be more likely to engage in extralegal tactics that can disrupt and derail democracy. Similarly, governing elites will be more likely to jettison democratic institutions and practices. To the extent that they control streams of income from portable resources, leaders obtain limited power to ignore international donors who condition aid disbursement on respect for democracy and human rights. Several chapters bring attention specifically to these issues, examining how the interests, capacities, and actions of key elites are shaped by the resources that they control.

International Actors

The impact of international actors on elite behavior represents a second factor that requires consideration. Like economic considerations, this is also an issue to which Bratton and van de Walle (and others) devote attention. In their view, the contribution of donors and Western governments to the survival and consolidation of new democracies should not be exaggerated. This is true despite the rhetoric of Western donors and the seemingly important role that aid conditionality might play in shaping the decisions of key players about whether to retain or subvert democratic institutions. To be sure, as Bratton and van de Walle detail, donors have sanctioned African militaries that have intervened in new democracies; and they have actively discouraged elected leaders from manipulating democratic rules in their favor. At the same time, the support of donors for democracy is not as stark as might be assumed from their rhetoric, and indeed other goals may be more decisive in shaping their interactions with African states. As such, they have not been consistent in pressuring authoritarian regimes and in some instances have actually enabled the efforts of authoritarian leaders seeking to entrench their holds on power (1997, 243).

Many of the authors in this volume are concerned precisely with the broader issues that Bratton and van de Walle highlight in this respect. Accepting that Western governments and donors can shape the actions of elites and hence the prospects for democratic rule, the authors detail empirically the specific kinds of roles that these actors have played. As becomes evident, the impact of these international actors varies considerably from case to case. In some instances, their interventions have appeared to be supportive of democratization processes. In both Malawi and Zambia, for example, donors pressured incumbent governing elites who sought to manipulate electoral processes. In others, however, their role has been quite problematic. Clark, for instance, indicates that the actions of the French government may have encouraged some elite players in Congo-Brazzaville to undermine the civil peace that underlay the fragile democratic experiment there. In a slightly different manner, Mehler's description of democracy in the Central African Republic describes how donor actions may have unwittingly encouraged members of the opposition to engage in political violence. This reminds us that the role of international actors is itself conditioned by local circumstances that deserve to be highlighted in each of the respective cases.

Elite Political Culture

A third issue is the role of elite political culture or what might be called "learned norms and patterns of behavior." Attention to this issue recalls the focus on normative environments that writers such as Levine (1978) and Burton, Gunther, and Higley (1992) emphasize in their work. The basic premise is that elite actions reflect what Aaron Wildavsky (1987) once described as "mediating mindstuff"—the subjective frameworks that shape values, filter information, and establish the cognitive repertoire of potential courses of action.

What types of subjective factors warrant attention in this regard? The chapters that follow suggest that three overlapping issues deserve consideration. The first concerns the values of key elites. For example, to the extent that democratic institutions are not viewed as a "good" in and of themselves, the likelihood of elites investing in those institutions is limited. Clark's chapter argues that liberal democratic institutions have practically no reference point in the history of Congo-Brazzaville. As such, the cultural repertoire of political action has not supported behavior governed by democratic rule. Another important value in this regard might concern elite approaches to political dissent. Simon's chapter on Zambia argues that intolerance of critical political viewpoints has represented one of the impediments to democratic consolidation—leading in some instances to the use of authoritarian tactics to silence opposition in political and civil society.

Second, the question of political habits is of importance. In this sense, the focus is less on what elites view as normatively good than on the received cultural guidelines for how one conducts oneself in political life, what Robinson (1994a) describes as the "culture of politics" or what Schatzberg (2001) has labeled the "moral matrix of legitimate governance." One theme that emerges in Bratton and van de Walle's work is the persistence of "big man" tendencies in new African democracies—a theme echoed in Schatzberg's discussion of paternal metaphors in African politics. The neopatrimonial character of post-colonial African politics has left a perception that political success and even personal survival are linked to effectively elevating oneself above other political players and institutions. Consistent with this received wisdom, certain newly elected leaders and party heads have operated with excessive focus on consolidating their own status and position of power. To be sure, the effort to retain power is to be expected. But the means through which that goal is pursued may reflect less the most viable strategy than learned ideas about how one holds power. The example of Alfonso Dlhakama in Mozambique stands out in this regard. His own political weakness has in some sense been exacerbated because of his failure to change his own personalist leadership style of Renamo—a guerilla organization that became an opposition party with Mozambique's transition to democracy.

A final subjective factor is the normative basis of elite interactions and, in particular, the learned expectations that various political players have of each other. As Greif (1994) effectively demonstrates, cultural expectations about how other actors will behave condition the strategic calculations and behavioral choices of all the players in a particular game, thus shaping outcomes or equilibriums. His analysis of two different medieval trading societies clearly suggests that variations in such expectations can lead to very different paths of economic and political development. We might similarly expect that culturally inherited "expectations of others" would condition the choices and behaviors of key players in new African democracies.

Owing to past experiences with zero-sum politics, and perhaps reflecting the "big man" logic just described, political trust among key players is quite low in many new democracies. This might help to explain why opposition elites in Zambia failed to mount a collective challenge to the incumbent Movement for Multiparty Democracy (MMD) government in 2001—leading, as David Simon details, to an election in which the winner received only 30 percent of the vote. As key opposition elites trusted each other no more than they did the incumbent regime, none would accept a secondary position to achieve the larger goal of displacing the MMD. The same issue might explain the dangerous buildup of militias in Congo-Brazzaville. Conditioned to expect the worst from one another, key elites in some sense experienced a classic security dilemma. The result was a preemptive attack by government forces on opponent militias, leading to the civil conflict that brought the Congolese democratic experiment to a close.[9]

In short, political culture in the form of values, habits, and conditioned expectations can play an important role in guiding elite actions with respect to democratic institutions. Variously emphasized in different cases, consideration of such issues illuminates how the subjective plays a role in shaping the fates of these democratic experiments.

Comparing the Relationships of Elites to Institutions

The main focus of this volume is on the relationship between elites in different countries and the democratic institutions put in place at the time of their respective successful transitions. Our set of cases is defined by the common fact that they all experienced the creation of regimes premised on the idea that the behavior of principal political players should be channeled by democratic institutions. A successful democratic consolidation, in turn, is one in which elite behavior remains fully bounded and guided by rules and norms embedded in those institutions. While arguably none of the cases explored in this volume meet these stringent criteria, there is also considerable variation in the extent to which they approach them. At one extreme, we find cases (such as Congo-Brazzaville or the Central African Republic [CAR]) in which the relationship was defined by the complete rejection and ultimate subversion or destruction of the initial institutions by political elites. More commonly, we find a middle ground in which elites have continued to be to some extent constrained by institutions, but in which they also find ways to manipulate, circumvent, or neutralize them to varying degrees.

It is these variations in how elites have responded to new democratic institutions that we seek to examine in detail in the case studies. We have argued above that there are many motivations for elite actions. Thus one primary concern of this volume is to attempt to sort out the varying factors—economic, cultural, strategic, and others—shaping the relative willingness of elite actors in each country to accept democratic institutions of any form.

We also want to suggest that, at least in part, one other important factor explaining the varied relations of elites to institutions must be the form and nature of the specific institutions themselves. Institutions of democracy vary in many ways, including in the relative distribution of power to elite groups. Some institutional arrangements are more easily seen by elites as providing safeguards for defending their interests. Some institutional configurations structure incentives for collaboration, while others push more toward conflictual politics. Some institutions unify and concentrate power, while others fragment authority. To varying degrees in different cases, we argue, variations in the specific institutional configurations of democratic experiments in Africa are in themselves an important part of the explanation for elite responses in the post-transition phase, and hence to the relative survival of democratic elements in these political systems.

In emphasizing the importance of these institutional factors, the chapters and the volume as a whole build on important trends within the literatures on both African politics and democratization. Prior to the watershed events of the early 1990s, investigations of political life in Africa tended—quite rightly—to downplay the significance of institutional factors vis-à-vis personalities, and "personal rule" was the dominant prototype of African political systems (Jackson and Rosberg 1982). In the context of political opening and liberalization of the 1990s, however, this earlier de-emphasis began to be called into question as the various experiments in political reconfiguration suggested that institutions required renewed attention (Widner 1994; Bratton and van de Walle 1994, 1997). More recent research on Africa has argued, for example, that political institutions can play an important role in the development of ethnic identity (Posner 1998), the stability of post-conflict regimes (Ottaway 1999), party systems (Mozaffar, Scarritt, and Galaich 2003), and the success of electoral processes (Sisk and Reynolds 1998; Gyimah-Boadi 1999a). Yet the systematic, comparative study of the impact of institutional choices on African democracies has been rather limited.

Attention to African institutional choices and democratic experiments is all the more important, given that much of the theoretical literature on democratization has clearly highlighted how institutional choices affect the prospects for democratic stability and even consolidation. One of the more important debates along this line has been that concerning the impact of the choice of presidential systems in Latin American democratic transitions, and the relative merits of presidential—as opposed to parliamentary—systems (see Linz 1996a, 1996b; Mainwaring and Shugart 1997; Power and Gasiorowski 1997). Other scholarship, particularly that examining the Eastern European cases, has drawn attention to the impact of variations in electoral institutions (Lijphart 1996a, 1996b; Linz and Stepan 1996). Among the more notable impacts of these variations is their effect on the nature of political party development and, in turn, on the extent to which players can play winner-take-all as opposed to coalition-building games. Electoral systems also affect the extent to which cultural identities translate into political identities, arguably one of the most important factors affecting the stability of newly inaugurated democratic systems in plural social contexts. (In the African context, see Reynolds 1995a, 1995b; Barkan 1995; Mozaffar 1998; Mozaffar, Scarritt, and Galaich 2003.)

Building on these themes, a central concern of this volume is to examine how the configuration of institutions in new African democracies has itself affected the nature of elite choices and behaviors vis-à-vis those institutions. As is true of the set of newly democratizing countries in Latin American and Eastern Europe, Africa's third wave democracies of the early 1990s varied widely in terms of the type of institutional arrangements in place, and in how they have operated subsequently. Many Francophone African countries, for example, adopted institutions that closely mimic those of the French Fifth Republic, in which executive authority is divided, thus generating the possibility for gridlock between presidents and assemblies. Yet we also see that variations within this French-style framework, along with other factors shaping elite behavior, have resulted in varying experiences with this institutional model. Countries have also varied in terms of the forms through which representation is achieved, with some systems opening the possibility for political polarization to a significantly greater degree than others. Similarly, there are important variations in the nature of other critical institutions, such as judiciaries, electoral commissions, and the structures of ruling parties.

Evaluating the role of these institutions, the case studies in this volume take as a point of departure one of the key insights from the growing literature on institutions in other democracies: the impact of institutions cannot be reduced to the isolated effect that one particular type of institution tends to produce, but rather these must be studied in interaction with each other. Thus, rather than look at one specific aspect of potential institutional variation (e.g., presidential versus parliamentary regime types), individual cases consider instead the dense network of institutions that together comprise "institutional complexes." Mainwaring and Shugart's (1997) major contribution to the long-running debate on the effects of presidentialism in Latin America is especially instructive in this regard. A central point of their volume is that while institutional choices certainly *do* matter, the analysis of the ways in which they do so must be heavily contextualized. In addition, small variations in institutional configurations, timing in their elaboration, and the interaction of different institutional choices may all prove determinant in any given case. The careful comparison of the complexity of individual cases, therefore, emerges as the most useful methodological strategy for examining such issues, and we adopt it here.[10] There is thus no intent in the chapters that follow to assess in abstract terms such questions as whether semi-presidential systems produce any given macro outcome, or to make pronouncements on whether majoritarian or proportional-representation electoral systems are "better suited" to Africa. The choice of such institutions clearly matters, but it matters in ways that are highly dependent on the socio-political context and on the weight of other factors affecting elites' orientations to these institutions.[11] The analyses frequently suggest that the significance of institutions can only be evaluated through interaction with the choices of state elites who attempt to manipulate them in such a way as to serve their interests.

As such, the chapters in this volume focus on what might be termed context-specific institutional questions. One issue that receives attention in many cases concerns the forces that have shaped the adoption of the specific institutional configurations that operate in these new democracies. These include:

- The kinds of institutional configurations that were left in place at independence, and their subsequent fate or evolution
- The ongoing impact of the colonial legacy in terms of the European reference models of elites pursuing democratization, and the resulting mimicking of the models of the former colonizer
- The lessons learned from previous historical experience with institutions (such as in Benin and the semi-presidential model)
- The unintended consequences of institutions elaborated in neopatrimonial contexts and preserved at the transition (such as Malawi's judicial system)
- The legacy of single-party dynamics on successor parties in the new contexts (e.g., Mozambique's parties)

Beyond this—and following much of the literature described above—the case studies examine *whether and how* the specific configuration of institutions that characterize any given case have shaped its experience with democracy. In some, the specific choice of institutions is central to the analysis. The cases of Benin and Niger, for example, highlight how these countries' differing acceptance of a French-style constitutional framework influenced their respective levels of subsequent political stability. Also of central importance in this respect is how different mechanisms for representation (i.e., electoral systems) have affected levels of political polarization as well as the capacity of elected leaders to govern. Other chapters underline the importance of specific institutions. The case of Malawi highlights the extent to which effective judicial institutions have shaped the interests and behavior of key political players. In Mozambique the internal dynamics of the ruling party, as shaped by its institutional legacy, help to explain the limits on executive authority.

Finally, in other cases, as we will see, the central argument is that the institutional configuration is rather insignificant in terms of the fate of these democracies. Chapters investigating Congo-Brazzaville, Guinea-Bissau, the CAR, or Zambia place relatively little explanatory emphasis on the impact of institutional configurations. That is, in these cases other factors shaping elite behavior, such as those listed above, would appear to trump the specifics of any given institutional configuration.

In this regard, then, *the extent to which institutions matter is itself a variable.* This point, in fact, is an important element of our approach, and one central point of comparison among the cases. We ask, that is, not only: "What variations in the experiences of democracy can be explained by varying institutional factors?" but also: "What factors explain variations in elite willingness to accommodate to democratic institutions?" We are interested, that is, *both* in how different institutional complexes have shaped democratic politics and in how different political contexts have shaped the prospects for democratic institutions to survive.

Institutions in this sense are thus seen less as causal, independent variables with clear consequences and more in terms of their dialectical interaction with elites as potential objects of manipulation, which, in turn, shape subsequent political interactions. In each case, then, we are concerned both with the extent to which institutions shape elite behavior (from virtually no effect to a high degree of effect) and with how elites in themselves deal with institutions. Institutions are mechanisms for distributing power and authority, and they are potential resources as well as dangers for given actors. They also constitute the rules that key players must live by, manipulate, or subvert. We thus need to ask how institutional interactions themselves reshape elite perceptions of their own goals and what is required to realize them, as well as how elites in turn reshape institutions to serve their interests.

In sum, then, this volume aims to learn from, and in turn enrich, theoretical discussions concerning the impact of institutional factors on democratic stability and survival—a major area of debate and concern for comparative political scientists since the early 1990s. Beyond this, the structure of the volume is embedded in an important methodological consideration for the approach to these issues. In contrast to efforts to identify and isolate relatively few causal variables to explain complex phenomena (such as democratic survival) in large numbers of countries, we highlight the value of structured, comparative-case analysis. If in fact—as our contributions suggest—outcomes are highly contingent, political, and shaped by the interaction of complex clusters of variables, only in-depth case analysis that is also sensitive to these theoretical concerns can fully account for the variations we have observed. We offer here important data on African cases for this theoretical work.

NOTES

1. It bears mentioning that Linz and Stepan (1996) also emphasize that prior regime type affects the prospects for democratic consolidation. In this regard, the prospects for Africa's democracies appear even dimmer. Sultanist/neo-patrimonial systems, from which Africa's new democracies have emerged, offer a very poor inheritance to successor democracies. Economic society is underdeveloped, civil society is atomized, and state bureaucratic structures have been enfeebled by decades of mismanagement, clientelism, and corruption. In this sense, the historical legacy arising from Africa's authoritarian past is especially problematic for Africa's democracies.

2. Source: World Bank World Development Indicators. Available at http://devdata .worldbank.org/dataonline/.

3. Some of these questions are inspired from a roundtable discussion, "The Relevance of Democratic Theory for African Politics," at the 2001 Meeting of the African Studies Association, Houston, Texas. Comments by Nicolas van de Walle were especially instructive in this regard.

4. Several of these points are more elaborately argued in Leonardo Villalón, "Constructing and Reconstructing Political Space: Africa in the Age of Democracy," presented at "Africa at the Turn of the Century," a conference held at the Centro de Estudos Africanos, Instituto Superior de Ciencias de Trabalho a da Empresa, Lisbon, Portugal, September 20–23, 2000.

5. In this regard, it is instructive to compare Bratton and van de Walle's typology with subsequent Freedom House Annual Country Ratings, available at http://www .freedomhouse.org/.

6. Recall, for instance, Dahl's notion that "democratic theory is concerned with processes by which ordinary citizens exert a relatively high degree of control over leaders" (1956, 3).

7. Importantly, Rustow also argued that the emergence of democratic norms could ensue from this process.

8. Of note, all of these are highlighted in the final substantive chapter of Bratton and van de Walle's (1997) work in which they delineate the factors that will affect the future of Africa's new democratic regimes.

9. Attention to this issue also recalls important arguments by Fukuyama (1995) about the importance of trust in developing complex organizations and institutions. It also speaks to Putnam's (1993) claims about the role of social capital in making democracy work.

10. It may merit noting that, as in this volume, the Mainwaring and Shugart book reaches these conclusions by means of a set of complex comparative-case studies to assess the validity of broader generalizations.

11. See Mozaffar, Scarritt, and Galaich (2003) on this point as well.

2 | Repetitive Breakdowns and a Decade of Experimentation

Institutional Choices and Unstable Democracy in Niger

Leonardo A. Villalón
and Abdourahmane Idrissa

In contrast to most other African countries, Niger never enjoyed even the brief mirage of a multiparty democracy before the 1990s. In spite of an intense party competition within the colonial context in the 1950s, under the regime of Hamani Diori the consolidation of single-party rule and the personalization of power had already begun—with French collusion—even before independence in 1960 (Charlick 1991, 40–62). Diori's reign itself was ended in 1974 by a coup that brought to power a military regime under Lieutenant Colonel Seyni Kountché. Kountché attempted to capitalize on a boom in uranium export prices to consolidate power via the elaboration of a corporatist state apparatus, but his regime otherwise represented significant continuities in terms of its authoritarian nature (Robinson 1991).

Although Kountché always presented his rule as a *régime d'exception,* whose eventual goal was the re-establishment of "republican" (i.e., democratic) institutions, it was only after his death in 1987 that the first tentative steps toward the liberalization of politics were undertaken by his successor, Ali Saïbou. The "constitutional normalization" launched by Saïbou, however, was intended as a carefully controlled process under the tutelage of a hierarchically institutionalized single party, never described by the regime itself in terms of "democratization" (Charlick 1991, 76).

And yet despite this bleak history, and like much of Africa, Niger found itself caught up in the worldwide "wave" of pro-democracy agitation and protest in the early 1990s. Unable to master the situation, Saïbou was obliged in 1991 to agree to the holding of a National Conference, a turbulent affair, but one that managed to establish "democracy" as the sole legitimating standard for subsequent regimes. What has particularly distinguished Niger even in Africa, however, has been the extraordinary turbulence of the effort to actually meet that standard, and the dramatic swings in a decade-long, political roller coaster ride. A count of the decade's major events reads like a litany of chaos: four republics, and hence four constitutions with presidential or semipresidential regimes; three transitions of six, nine, and eighteen months; one National Conference and a Committee on Fundamental Texts; one Forum for Democratic Renewal; one Technical Constitutional Committee; a Consultative Council of Elders; three constitutional referenda and eight other national elections; four heads of state and one president of a High Council of the Republic; four National Assemblies; nine prime ministers; at least one hundred and fifty ministers; one civilian coup d'état; two military coups d'état; one electoral boycott; one strike by the president and one strike by parliamentarians; one campaign of civil disobedience; and one dissolution of the National Assembly. All this has taken place against a background of armed rebellions and communal and rural conflicts (Idrissa 2000). Niger's unending experimentation over the decade of the 1990s has produced a wealth of empirical grist for the theoretical mills of political analysts who are concerned with the question of democracy in Africa.[1]

The country's recent turbulent history of democratic experimentation suggests much, in terms of our thinking, of what the "democratic wave" has meant south of the Sahara. In many ways Niger has presented a puzzle to political analysts attempting to catalogue the effects of this democratic wave on the continent. In the mid-1990s, the country appeared to many to be among the successful cases of democratic transitions, and in the most comprehensive effort to date to explain the variations in African "democratic experiments," Bratton and van de Walle classified it as such.[2] The extraordinary political difficulties that marked the new regime from its inception, however, and its denouement with a coup in 1996, quickly led to the country being invoked instead as an example of the limitations of democracy in Africa, variously signaling to some scholars that it was the end of the democratic wave, and suggesting to others the corrective proof of the premature nature of earlier optimistic pronouncements about the inevitability—or even the possibility—of African democracy.

And yet by the end of the decade the country surprisingly found itself once again debating and approving a democratic constitution, holding elections deemed largely "free and fair," and inaugurating a new—this time the fifth—republic. This latest "transition," however, is if anything even more puzzling and difficult to label. In many ways it appears to be simply a replay of the events of 1992–93, carried out under virtually the same circumstances, with a barely modified set of rules and a remarkably similar cast of actors and political parties. Has the country come full circle, back to the point of departure? Or have we witnessed instead an evolution to a new experiment with greater chances of success? Contemporary Niger, it seems, vividly illustrates what may be emerging as the most interesting and somewhat paradoxical reality of the democratic question on the continent: the extraordinary persistence of a democratic ideal in the face of the manifest extreme fragility of the democratization project.

The label of "democracy" in Niger (and by extension in much of Africa), we will argue below, must at best still be used with caution. Yet clearly the political game being played in the past decade differs markedly from the rules that defined politics in the first three decades of independence. Close consideration of the Nigerien experience suggests that an understanding of the consequences of the period of political change on which African countries have embarked, and the attendant social transformations, requires a more nuanced analysis than has been provided by measures of the relative success or failure of "transitions to democracy." Political struggles in the country have been dominated by questions concerning the distribution of power both among elites and between elites and populations, all under the rubric of democracy. This has been played out at two levels: first, as debates among political elites—*la classe politique*—about the formal institutions of democracy and struggles for their control; and second, in the struggle between elites and mass social groups concerning the substance of democracy as a normative model.

Many scholars of democracy have argued that, in Guillermo O'Donnell's formulation, "the installation of a democratically elected government opens the way for a 'second transition,' often longer and more complex. . . . from a democratically elected *government* to an institutionalized, consolidated democratic *regime*" (O'Donnell 1994, 56). Alternatively, however, O'Donnell has noted that two other scenarios are possible: a democratic government may oversee a regression to authoritarian government, or it may stagnate as a non-institutionalized "delegative democracy," maintaining procedural democratic elements but not consolidating the substance of democracy. Niger's initial transition to an elected democratic government, by contrast, did not produce any of these outcomes: neither consolidation, nor collapse, nor the persistence of a non-consolidated, "delegative" democracy. Rather, from the perspective of a decade, the country might best be characterized as having engaged in a virtually continuous process of transition.

The paradox of Niger's instability along with its seeming extraordinary commitment to an elusive democracy can only be understood in terms of the reconfiguration of political forces in the crucial juncture of the early 1990s,[3] especially by the process of the National Conference and by twin aspects of its legacy. On the one hand has been the rise to prominence of a civilian political elite, which is fatally divided about the sharing of power and the institutions for doing so. On the other hand, this elite has demonstrated itself to be fundamentally united around a shared normative conception of democracy, but one which places it at odds with strong social forces that have themselves been created and politicized by the period of democratic experimentation. In this chapter, we focus primarily on the first of these aspects: the nature of the elite struggles and the institutional debates that have produced this turbulent history. The second issue, the clash of world-views that has grown out of the politicization of social—notably religious—groups as response and reaction to the efforts at democratization, can be only briefly evoked below. This focus is merited, we would argue, in that the effort to end authoritarianism in Niger in the early 1990s must in fact be seen primarily as a power struggle among elements of an urban elite, and not as a popularly driven uprising against the regime.

From an Authoritarian Legacy to a Democratic Agenda

As in neighboring Benin and Mali, from which the model was borrowed and the inspiration drawn, the National Conference in Niger represented a significant rupture with the past (Eboussi-Boulaga 1993; Robinson 1994b). It grew, however, out of a preceding period of prolonged agitation by politicized social groups, particularly students and labor unions, in a context of intense economic crisis, indeed virtual economic collapse. And this agitation, in turn, had emerged in response to the tentative political liberalization ("*décrispation*," as it was dubbed by the Nigerien press) started by Ali Saïbou after Kountché's death. While unwilling to relinquish power, Saïbou had attempted a legitimization of his beleaguered regime by initiating a return to a constitutional order of "democratic one-party rule" under the *Mouvement Nationale pour la Société de Développement* (MNSD). The new constitution was approved by referendum in October 1989, inaugurating what was declared to be the "Second Republic." In accordance with its provisions, Saïbou then had himself approved as president by a reported 99.6 percent of voters, and the ninety-three deputies to a National Assembly presented as a single list by the MNSD were similarly "elected" by 99.52 percent.

This experiment, however, was to be short-lived. Within less than two months the Saïbou regime was faced with massive protests in response to its efforts to impose the structural adjustment reforms demanded by the International Monetary Fund (IMF) as preconditions for continued financing of the bankrupt state (Gervais 1995). Most vociferously, the national student association, the *Union des Scolaires Nigériens* (USN), protested against proposed cuts in the budget for higher education and limits in the recruitment of graduates into the civil service. If there was a clear turning point in the regime's capacity to maintain control, it came with the violent repression of a student demonstration in Niamey on February 9, 1990, in which at least three—and perhaps many more—students were killed.[4] The days and months that followed witnessed the most massive social protests and strikes in the country's history, with upward of 100,000 people periodically demonstrating in the streets of Niamey. By midyear, the first independent newspaper in the country's history, *Haské,* began publishing. Its critical and independent editorial line immediately centered on a call for a National Conference and the elaboration of a multiparty democratic system.

By November 1990, Saïbou was obliged to agree to holding a National Conference, but there followed several months of maneuvering concerning control of the process. In January of 1991 the major labor union federation in the country, the *Union des Syndicats des Travailleurs du Niger* (USTN), once part of the state's corporatist institution, dealt the regime a major blow when it renounced its official link to the MNSD. Continued protest and agitation, further fueled by popular anger and demonstrations against Niger's participation in the American-led coalition in the 1991 Gulf War, eventually tipped the balance in favor of the opposition forces, which were able to dictate the terms for convening the conference. What is particularly salient about this period, however, is the nature of the social forces that managed to gain the political upper hand, and thus set both the agenda and determine the eventual shape of a democratic system in the country. The massive mobilization of Nigerien "civil society" demanding the installation of a democratic system was in fact an overwhelmingly urban phenomenon of "modern" social groups intent on furthering their interests.

The compromise between the government and the opposition entailed the convoking of a preparatory commission to set the terms for the National Conference, a commission whose composition was effectively dictated by the opposition (Raynal 1993, 58–68). Its sixty-eight members thus included only seven representatives of *le pouvoir,* defined to include both the totality of state institutions and the MNSD. Workers (the USTN) and students (the USN) were each also awarded seven seats, along with seven to be shared by the country's employers' unions. Each of the other legal labor unions not affiliated with the USTN as well as each of the eighteen officially recognized political parties were to have two seats. These political parties had proliferated in the initial period of legalization, and as there had not yet been any electoral test of their relative strengths they were all treated equally. It was apparent, however—as proved to be the case—that the vast majority of the parties were built around small groups of urban intellectuals,[5] with little or no resonance among the masses of the Nigerien population. No seats on the commission were foreseen for any of the important official associations—notably those of women, traditional chiefs, and Islamic groups—whose political power had been tied to their roles in the corporatist state structures. The glaring fact that the commission initially included only one woman, however, provoked an unprecedented set of protests by women's groups, who were able to secure the addition of six women to the commission.

Not surprisingly, this commission set in place a National Conference with a similar distribution of power, although with a significantly expanded membership of 884 voting delegates, plus an additional 320 "resource persons" with no voting powers. Once again unions, students, and the parties of urban intellectuals reserved for themselves the lion's share of representation. Thus *le pouvoir,* the USTN, the USN, and the employers' unions were each accorded 100 seats. Officially recognized parties received fourteen, and each independent labor union two seats. This time the official national associations were also given a token representation, with two seats each. Among the non-voting "resource persons" were sixty-four representatives of the "rural world," forty from the army, and thirty from the state administration, along with a number of individuals named on a personal basis.

Considering the composition of these institutions, one longtime observer of Nigerien politics noted shortly after the conference: "One is led to wonder about the representativity of the conference when we see that the representatives of the 'rural world' have no vote, the representation of such important associations as that of women and of traditional chiefs is limited to two delegates, while the USN has one hundred delegates and each party has fourteen. This division would appear not at all to reflect the sociological realities of a country whose population is 82 percent rural, where women represent 51 percent of the population (and 47 percent of the economically active population), in which the level of school attendance peaks at 29 percent (of which 1 percent is in higher education), and which has a lively and respected traditional chieftaincy" (Raynal 1993, 61).

The Nigerien National Conference must thus be understood as a seizure of the political agenda, in the context of the crisis of the early 1990s, by a civilian elite comprised of people in the modern (nonagricultural) and formal sectors of the urban economy.[6] Given its composition, a primary theme of the conference was a critique of the years of military rule, and the establishment of an unquestionable norm of civilian rule, to be decided by democratic contestation of an electoral process. Indeed, the proceedings of the conference concentrated on discrediting the mismanagement of politics by the military and the MNSD regime, and effectively marginalized them from the discussion of the country's political future during the subsequent transition.[7] The norm of multiparty electoral democracy that was embraced by the conference as the sole legitimating criterion for any government has endured as one central component of its legacy.

Two other themes, similarly, continue to define the conference's impact on the Nigerien experiment. The first is the insistence by those groups who led the transition—namely, students and unionized workers—on their right to organize, strike, and demonstrate in defense of their corporate interests. These groups have tolerated no questioning of what they claim as entitlements to their jobs, wages, and scholarships. As a result, significant discussion at the conference was devoted to denouncing structural adjustment programs and stressing a refusal to accept the dictates of international financial institutions. This legacy has plagued every subsequent government throughout the decade. As governments have found themselves obliged to seek outside fiscal support—and submit to the conditions under which this is provided—students and unions have repeatedly paralyzed the economy and shut down the educational system in defense of their perceived rights. The second theme, less visible at the time but with important longer-term consequences, concerns the notion enshrined by the National Conference that what was meant by *democracy* in Niger was to be built on the prevailing international, dubbed "universal," conceptions of individual rights and liberties and the nature and role of the state in assuring these. These, in fact, are clearly rooted primarily in the Western (especially French) tradition, and leave no room for alternative conceptions, popular though they may be, the most significant of which in Niger is religious. The marginalization of religious groups from the conference thus ensured at the time that the principle of the secular state was seen as a nonnegotiable element of Niger's democratic model, with enduring consequences for its acceptance by large social categories.

The National Conference set in place a transitional government, with the mandate of writing a constitution and a number of related "fundamental texts," to enshrine these principles in the institutions of the "Third Republic" that was to follow. Saïbou was allowed to stay on as president, but in a purely ceremonial role. Real power during the transition was, instead, to be shared between a government, headed by a prime minister, and a fourteen-member, transitional legislative body designated the *Haut Conseil de la République* (HCR). An international civil servant in the regional civil aviation organization based in Senegal, Amadou Cheiffou, was asked to return to Niger as prime minister. And André Salifou, a professor of history at Niger's sole university, who had in addition presided over the National Conference, was elected president of the HCR. None of these three individuals was to be eligible to stand for president for the post-transition government. The transition was to prove tumultuous and marked by numerous controversies, and had to be prolonged by several months. By the end of 1992, however, a new constitution had been drafted, which was approved by referendum on December 26 of that year, thus preparing the groundwork for elections and the inauguration of the Third Republic.

Institutional Experimentation and the Long Transition

The norm of electoral democracy that has defined the "third wave" everywhere necessitates a choice among a variety of institutional models, each with consequences for the functioning—and even the survival—of democratic systems. As new systems have been put in place, there has emerged a growing interest among political scientists concerning the impact of alternative institutions. Electoral systems, naturally, have been central to much of this debate, and there has been some preliminary attention to this in Africa (Barkan 1995; Reynolds 1995b; Mozaffar 1998). Although there has been a rich and insightful debate about the impact of presidential systems in Latin America (O'Donnell 1994; Linz 1996a, 1996b; Mainwaring and Shugart 1997), the choice of regime type—parliamentary, semi-presidential, or presidential—has, however, received virtually no systematic analysis in the context of African democratization.

Part of that lack of attention must be attributed to the fact that, despite the consequences, the choice of regime institutions elicited very little debate in the transitions of the early 1990s. In virtually all of the Francophone countries, including Niger, the choice was made by default: the institutions of democracy were to be modeled on the semi-presidential system of the French Fifth Republic and the French constitution of 1958. Thus Jibrin Ibrahim points out that the Nigerien constitution of the Third Republic "was copied on the liberal democratic model and strongly resembled the constitution of the French Fifth Republic" (Ibrahim 1999, 196). Indeed, like others in former French colonies, it was in many respects virtually identical. This tendency has been so striking that in a 1999 book on the constitutions of Francophone Africa, two French scholars are able to discuss constitutional provisions across many countries as if they were discussing a single constitutional system. They note in justification that in contrast to the "great diversity of political regimes" that had existed in Africa some years earlier, following the "process of democratic transition beginning at the end of the 1980s, a certain unity has been recreated. More or less everywhere one finds the same institutions, more or less identical means of naming officials, and very comparable relations of power" (Cabanis and Martin 1999, 187).

In a discussion of alternative democratic institutions and their consequences, Giovanni Sartori has suggested that semi-presidentialism based on the French model—with power shared between a directly elected president and a prime minister and government arising from a legislative majority—has a number of positive consequences, in contrast to the opposing difficulties of purely parliamentary or presidential regimes (Sartori 1994). Certainly, as the debate on presidentialism in Latin American has shown, it is too simple to generalize broadly about basic models, about whether any particular regime type per se is good or bad. In fact, the devil is clearly in the details; the actually functioning of any given system in a given country is conditioned by a number of other factors, including most significantly electoral and party systems. A close look at Niger certainly suggests that the regime type must be considered in context, but the experiences of the country in terms of experimenting with semi-presidentialism is also quite instructive, and suggests many problematic elements to that model.

Niger's Third Republic, inaugurated with such sound and fury, was to last less than three years, and was to be marked by constant, turbulent political instability. These difficulties had many causes, but it is indisputable that democratic institutions on the French model were central to the Third Republic's troubles. In assigning shared power to both a president and a prime minister, but in making the prime minister responsible to the legislative body, the "spirit of the constitution . . . assumed the necessity of a parliamentary majority to govern" (Ibrahim and Niandou-Souley 1998, 157). Even in France, where many had also made the same assumption until the first experience of "cohabitation" from 1986–88, this aspect of the constitution has proved problematic.[8] In Niger the choice of electoral system was to complicate this further.

In the interest of assuring wide representation to parties and to minorities, and in a context of initial democratization and the attendant proliferation of a multitude of parties and social groups seeking to make their voices heard, there has been a tendency in Francophone Africa to choose electoral systems likely to maximize the representation of groups. In Niger the choice of electoral system was much debated, and given the voice provided to the large number of parties in the National Conference and the transition, a system likely to guarantee wide representation to many parties was eventually agreed on (Illiassou and Alou 1994). The Nigerien electoral system created to choose the eighty-three deputies to the National Assembly involved the election of seventy-five deputies by a system of proportional representation in eight variable member districts ranging from four to fourteen seats, with no minimal threshold specified and a quota (Hare) electoral formula. Particularly in the larger districts (five of the eight have ten or more seats), this system easily favors the representation of smaller parties. In addition, and complicating things further, in response to pressure from representatives of small ethnic groups, and with the ongoing rebellions in much of the north of the country as backdrop, a further electoral provision provided for the election of the remaining eight deputies from small single-member "special districts," intending to ensure the representation of these minorities.[9] The electoral system thus strongly favored the emergence of a highly fragmented legislature, with many parties represented. In the context of a semi-presidential system with an assumption of a need for a parliamentary majority to govern, the institutions of the Third Republic suggested difficulties from their inception.

As the prolonged transitional period reached its end in late 1992 and the presidential and legislative elections approached, two clear dynamics in party politics began to emerge. One was the effort by virtually all of the other recognized parties in the country to join forces in attempting to keep the MNSD, the renewed heir to the single party of the short-lived "Second Republic," out of power. The MNSD in fact appeared to enjoy a potential electoral advantage, which raised fears in its rivals, both because of its strong national organization and because of a growing popular nostalgia for the stability of the military regime in the wake of the tumultuous National Conference and transition period. Thus from the beginning and throughout the Third Republic, "the essence of national democratic practice in Niger was effectively reduced to a concerted effort at sidelining the MNSD from the corridors of power in spite of the fact that it always emerged as the single biggest party in all of the competitive elections that were held in the country" (Ibrahim and Niandou Souley 1998, 145).

The second dynamic introduced by the advent of electoral competition was a reconfiguration of the ethnoregional balance of power in the country. Both Diori and Kountché, heirs to the French colonial legacy of promoting their community, represented the dominance of a Zarma (or Songhay) political elite over the majority Hausa population of the country. Although Kountché had promoted the development of Zarma merchants to parallel the powerful Hausa merchant class, he had nevertheless carefully balanced political appointments in an effort to manage the ethnic issue. This balance was to be upset with the advent of the transition. The ethnic issue was to make itself felt most significantly early on in the struggle for leadership of the MNSD following Saïbou's resignation as party president in the period leading up to the National Conference. The eventual victory in that struggle of Mamadou Tandja—who is of mixed Mauritanian, Kanuri, and Fulani parentage but originates from the predominantly Hausa southeast of the country—over a scion of the Zarma ruling elite within the MNSD, Adamou Djermakoye, "saved the MNSD from being reduced to a Zarma ethnic party" (Ibrahim and Niandou Souley 1998, 151). It simultaneously provoked, however, a major split as Djermakoye withdrew to form his own party, the *Alliance Nigerienne pour la Démocratie et le Progrés* (ANDP). The party that was most closely identified with Hausa interests, and especially with the important Hausa commercial class, was the *Convention Démocratique et Sociale* (CDS). Yet the ambiguity of this ethnic link merits emphasizing. The CDS's president, Mahmane Ousmane, considers himself of Kanuri ethnicity, and the party's first vice-president, Sanusi Jackou, is of Tuareg origin. And yet it was possible for two inside observers to argue that "Hausa identity has however never been a narrow 'ethnic' issue and as such, these leaders are as Hausa as anyone else" (Ibrahim and Niandou Souley 1998, 152). The rise of this ethnic dimension, therefore, should be seen not so much as an ethnicization of politics as a breaking of an ethnic domination, and the creation of a multiplicity of regional power bases, aligned with different group interests.

These dynamics were to shape the results of the first contested multiparty elections in Niger's history. Twelve parties competed in the legislative elections of February 14, 1993, and nine of the parties won seats. The MNSD won the single largest share, but it fell short of a majority with twenty-nine of eighty-three seats. Taking fourteen seats in its power base in the regions of Zinder and Maradi, the CDS won a total of twenty-two seats. Two other parties, the *Parti Nigerien pour la Démocratie et le Socialisme* (PNDS) and the ANDP, received respectively thirteen and eleven seats, with the remaining eight seats distributed among five small parties.

Two weeks later the first round of the presidential elections was held, with eight candidates competing. Again the MNSD's candidate, Mamadou Tandja, emerged with the single largest number of votes at 34 percent. Having failed to win an absolute majority, however, a second round was necessary against his closest rival, Mahmane Ousmane of the CDS, who had received 26 percent of the vote. In the month intervening between the two rounds, the anti-MNSD forces, which comprised all of the other significant parties in the country, banded together to form an alliance called the *Alliance des Forces du Changement* (AFC) to compete against the MNSD. In a move of doubtful constitutionality, which was to produce problems later on, Ousmane promised shares in the political pie, notably the positions of prime minister and of president of the National Assembly, to the leaders of the PNDS and the ANDP, the two other significant candidates in the elections. The fragile coalition held, and on March 27, 1993, Ousmane was elected president of the Third Republic with 54 percent of the vote. As table 2.1 shows, strong regionalist orientation of all of these elections is suggested clearly by a look at the vote distribution across the country in the presidential elections.

The first government of Niger's Third Republic took office on April 16, 1993, signaling for many the country's successful transition to democracy. Having been obliged to promise much to hold the coalition together, it was the largest government in Niger's history, with eighteen ministries and ten state secretaries. From the beginning the alliance was marked by tensions over the distribution of prebends, mostly posts within the administration, leading the Nigerien press to speak of a political *wasoso*, a Hausa term suggesting a scramble to get as much as one can. The complete bankruptcy of the state, with civil servants owed several months of salary in arrears and student scholarships unpaid, likewise increased the pressure on the alliance from the beginning.

In fact, the entire experience of the Third Republic was to be marked by an unending series of political tensions and a virtual incapacity to govern through the democratic institutions that the country had adopted. Protesting from the beginning against the pact made in the period between the two rounds of the presidential elections, which it labeled as amounting to buying support, the MNSD refused to play a loyal opposition's role in the National Assembly, and by early 1994 engaged in what it called a campaign of "civil disobedience." In addition, the rela-

Table 2.1. Niger Presidential Elections, 1993

Candidate	1st round total	% in highest district	% in lowest district	2nd round total	% in highest district	% in lowest district
Tandja (MNSD)	34.2%	53.5	19.2	45.6	67.4	25.0
Ousmane (CDS)	26.6%	63.7	04.7	54.4	75.0	32.6
Issoufou (PNDS)	15.9%	40.8	06.1			
Djermakoye (ANDP)	15.2%	43.4	01.8			
Others	8%					

tionship between the president and the prime minister was fraught with tensions about the relative powers of each.

The tensions came to a head in September 1994, leading Mahamadou Issoufou to resign as prime minister, and his PNDS party to withdraw from the AFC, in protest against what he portrayed as Ousmane's appropriation of powers. Ousmane attempted to woo the MNSD, or a faction within it, to form a new majority, but when his efforts were unsuccessful, he responded by appointing a minority government under a close ally, Souley Abdoulaye. The French semi-presidential model that Niger had adopted, however, clearly is based on a presumption of a parliamentary majority for the government, and in any case provisions allowing for a vote of no-confidence brought down the minority government just eleven days later. Faced with no other option, and gambling on his ability to blame the opposition for the impasse, Ousmane dissolved the National Assembly in October 1994, just eighteen months after it had taken office, and called for new elections in early 1995. The results, however, varied little from those of 1993 (table 2.2).

While the results by party were virtually identical, the politics of elite alliances had changed significantly given the PNDS's break with the AFC and its alliance with the MNSD. This new alliance was striking in that it brought together two parties with a history of bitter ideological disagreement; the PNDS's background and strength was in the Nigerien left wing, long the major foe of the MNSD's military forebear. Joined by two other small parties—the Union des patriotes démocratiques et progressistes (UPDP) and the Parti progressiste nigerien/Rassemblement démocratique africain (PPN/RDA)—with one seat each, the MNSD coalition thus held a narrow majority of forty-three of the eighty-three seats. Faced with the obligation of appointing an opposition prime minister, Ousmane continued to try to dominate the process by appointing his own choice to the post, rather than the person proposed by the majority. The MNSD refused to accept this, and in Feb-

Table 2.2. Niger Legislative Elections, 1993 and 1995

Party	1993 (%)	1993 (no. of seats)	1995 (%)	1995 (no. of seats)
MNSD	34.9	29	34.9	29
CDS	26.5	22	28.9	24
PNDS	15.7	13	14.5	12
ANDP	13.3	11	10.8	9
PPN-RDA	2.4	2	1.2	1
UDFP	2.4	2	0	0
UPDP	2.4	2	1.2	1
PSDN	1.2	1	2.4	2
UDPS	1.2	1	2.4	2
PUND	0	0	3.6	3

ruary the majority's nominee, Hama Amadou, took over the post and named a new government.

With neither side willing to cede powers, and given the ambiguities of the constitution and the lack of precedent in sharing power, the experiment in "cohabitation" in Niger led almost immediately to institutional paralysis. As both president and prime minister went "on strike," refusing to carry out duties prescribed by the constitution for the normal functioning of the government, a near-total breakdown in constitutional procedures resulted. It was apparent to many that the institutional choices on which the Third Republic had been founded were at least in part responsible for the crisis, and by the middle of the year "most political observers in the country were of the view that some drastic institutional changes were necessary if the entire democratic experiment was to survive" (Ibrahim and Niandou Souley 1998, 165).

With no end to the impasse in sight, on January 27, 1996, the military stepped into Nigerien politics once again, in a coup that dissolved the institutions and ended the experiment of the Third Republic. Unlike in the past, however, the coup leaders, led by Colonel Ibrahim Mainassara Baré, insisted that the military had no intent to rule, but only to oversee the fixing of the constitutional problems and a quick return to democratic civilian rule. The Baré coup marked the return of the military to power, but it is significant that Baré always attempted to portray the coup as a continuation of the democratic process that had started with the National Conference, only intended to fix some of its problems, and never as a return to the military regimes of the past.

It is noteworthy that immediately following the 1996 coup, many politicians welcomed the event as an acceptable solution to an institutional impasse, effectively accepting the army's depiction of itself as an arbiter in the political process. Thus Mohamed Bazoum, who had served as minister of foreign affairs in the MNSD government before the coup, agreed initially to stay on to serve in Baré's government, explaining that "the political crisis born of the dysfunction of the republican institutions was inevitably leading the country towards an untenable impasse." The coup, he initially suggested, could thus be seen as a "salvation, intended to endow the country with more appropriate political institutions."[10] Even the deposed leaders of the Third Republic took a similar attitude; overthrown president Mahmane Ousmane and two former prime ministers, Hama Amadou and Mahamadou Issoufou, all made public appearances on television in which they called for a modification of the Third Republic's institutions, thus in effect lending legitimacy to the coup's publicly stated rationale.

Moving on this stated goal quickly, Baré convoked a "National Forum for Democratic Revival" (*Forum National de Renouveau Démocratique*), which was to be headed by a "Council of Wise Men" (*Conseil des Sages*) under former president Ali Saïbou, with the mandate to propose a new regime. The Nigerien press referred to the commission as the "National Conference–bis," but, unlike the earlier effort, its proceedings were carefully controlled by the military, a fact also readily recognized by the critical press.[11] The central issue that the Forum was to address was the choice of new political institutions, expressed in terms of regime type. Baré made no secret of his strong preference for a "presidential" system, the option that ultimately was adopted. It is significant, however, that this system was in fact still a variation on the French model. The major difference between the institutions of the Third Republic and the "presidential" model favored by Baré lay in a clearer separation of powers. The new model granted the directly elected president no right to dissolve the National Assembly, and at the same time gave the National Assembly no means of censuring the government, which was to be headed by a prime minister appointed by the president. While this was portrayed primarily as a reaction against the impasse of the previous regime, it bears noting that this model was also to have the effect of granting significantly greater powers to Baré himself.

The military government found itself under extreme pressure from international actors to "restore democracy." The United States in particular activated a provision of a law that required an immediate disengagement and the cutting off of all aid to any government coming to power through the overthrow of an elected regime.[12] In response to these pressures the "transition" process was shortened and rushed, and the new constitutional referendum held on May 12, 1996 was approved by an alleged 92.5 percent, although with a low turnout of some 35 percent. The new "Fourth Republic" was thus born, slightly more than three years after the inauguration of the Third.

Presidential elections were set for July of the same year. Reversing his previous stance as a neutral arbiter intending to step aside, Baré resigned from the military and announced his intention to run as a candidate. Yet there was an initial perception that the election would in fact be competitive, and deposed President Mahamane Ousmane himself, along with other central political figures of the Third Republic, also announced their candidacy for the presidential election. It is striking and significant that the top four candidates in the 1993 presidential elections— including the deposed Ousmane, calling himself a candidate for "re-election"— were again in the lineup, running against the leader of the coup that had overthrown them. In addition to Ousmane, these included Tandja Mamadou (the top vote-getter in the first round of the 1993 elections), Mahamadou Issoufou (the first prime minister of the Third Republic), and Moumouni Adamou Djermakoye (first president of the National Assembly in the Third Republic).

Early returns on election day seemed to suggest that the electoral bases of each of these Third Republic politicians remained largely intact. As these results came in, moreover, it became clear that Baré's candidacy was doomed. Announcing that the independent national electoral commission (the CENI) had compromised its impartiality, Baré abruptly stopped the counting of votes in the middle of the process, dissolved the CENI, and appointed a new commission to complete the counting. Although the CENI refused to recognize its dissolution, the military forcibly took control of the process. Voting was extended into a second day, and Baré ultimately was declared the winner by the new commission. On August 7, 1996, Baré had himself inaugurated as the first president of the "Fourth Republic."

Legislative elections were then scheduled for November 1996. The new "opposition," now including all of the major parties of the Third Republic, stipulated their conditions for participation in these elections, prime among them being the reinstatement of the CENI and the annulment of results of the presidential election. The parties, allied to form a "Front for the Restoration and Defense of Democracy" (*Front pour la Restauration et la Défense de la Démocratie,* FRDD), undertook a period of constant agitation. Despite efforts at negotiation no compromise was found, and the majority of the FRDD eventually boycotted the elections, leaving Baré's newly created party, the *Union Nationale des Indépendants pour le Renouveau Démocratique* (UNIRD), to win fifty-nine of the eighty-three seats. In December 1996 a new government was named with another prominent Third Republic politician, Amadou Cissé, as prime minister. Most international actors refused to recognize the elections and hence did not recognize the new government (although, tellingly, France was among those that did), and there followed a period of constant FRDD agitation, with ongoing clashes, protests, strikes, and military mutinies. What is most noteworthy about this period is the extent to which students, labor, and the press were capable of defending the gains they had made during the National Conference and the striking incapacity of the Baré regime to fully repress this resistance.

In the context of this standoff between Baré and the opposition, the FRDD eventually declared itself willing to abandon its demands for new presidential elections, but retained its insistence on the dissolution of the National Assembly and the organization of new legislative elections. The fact that the Fourth Republic constitution included no provision for dissolving the National Assembly once again led to a political stalemate. When a prominent Nigerien jurist proposed a referendum as a means of doing so, the French sent the vice-president of the French National Assembly, himself a well-known jurist, to Niamey to study the situation. He eventually pronounced his opinion, which was that the assembly could *not* be dissolved, eliciting a strong debate in the press (Idrissa 2000, 52–55). Protests continued, and in an effort to gain some legitimacy Baré dismissed the government in November 1997, naming a new one under Ibrahim Hassan Maiyaki as prime minister. The change had little effect, and as scheduled local elections approached, the FRDD maintained its hard line on conditions for participation, including the restoration of an independent CENI. The elections were finally held in February 1999, in a disastrous context of obvious manipulation and intimidation. Full results were only announced two months later, and by then the Baré regime had clearly exhausted its room for maneuvering in the effort to legitimate itself.

In an event reminiscent of General Sani Abacha's "mysterious" death in Nigeria a year earlier, the military sought its own solution out of this impasse. In what was officially proclaimed an "unfortunate accident," Baré was shot dead by members of his own presidential guard as he prepared to board a flight at the Niamey airport in April of 1999. The head of that guard, Major Daouda Mallam Wanké, was pronounced head of state, and immediately announced a nine-month transition, to take place under a military "Council of National Reconciliation" (*Conseil de Réconciliation Nationale, CRN*). The National Assembly and other institutions were dissolved and the Fourth Republic's constitution was suspended. In a move that clearly demonstrates the limited objectives of the coup, Maiyaki was kept on as prime minister along with much of the previous government. While there was a widespread sentiment of relief in Niger that Baré was gone, the CRN immediately found itself under the same pressures as previous governments. Various governments in the region, joined by the French, pushed hard for an inquiry into Baré's death. And, as had been the case for the past ten years, there was no end of agitation by "civil society" groups, workers' strikes, student demonstrations, and more, each group mobilized primarily around economic demands. In May 1999, for example, the faculty at the single university went on strike, demanding payment for five months' arrears of 1997 salaries, one month of 1998 salaries, and three months of 1999 salaries. Under pressure from all sides, the CRN announced it would shorten the transition process, and hastened to do so.

The result was an immediate resurgence of the institutional debate; should the country return to the "semi-presidential" system of the Third Republic, or maintain the "presidential" one of the Fourth? While the post-1993 experience had suggested the dangers of the semi-presidential model, the subsequent Baré regime raised fears over permitting the concentration of power. One Nigerien academic in a revisionist mood, reacting to the strong consensus *against* semi-presidentialism just three years earlier, suggested that the Third Republic's institutions were "not as bad as some claim," and suggested that the failure of the Third Republic had been one of politicians and not the system (Niandou Souley 1999). Echoing this viewpoint, former prime minister Hama Amadou proclaimed that "a presidential regime is a regime of gridlock [*régime de blocage*] which does not foresee mechanisms for resolving crises," and a leading Nigerien academic published an article making a similar argument in the independent newspaper, *Le Républicain,* under the title: "*Pour la démocratie et contre le régime présidentiel.*"[13]

Wasting no time, in May 1999, a Technical Committee was named and promptly proposed that a choice be made between the two previous systems. A Consultative Committee of eighty members was then asked to make a recommendation on the issue, quickly revealing a major split in elite opinion on the matter; the initial committee vote was split forty-one to thirty-nine in favor of a return to a semi-presidential system. Unwilling to accept such a divided recommendation, and frustrated with the tone of the debate, the CRN issued an ultimatum to the parties to find a consensus position. The eventual counterproposal included a large number of innovations, such as a five-year "National Unity Government," adding a second chamber (Senate) to the legislature, and a series of new "national commissions." The proposal was widely decried in the press as a transparent effort to create jobs for all politicians. Impatient with the process, the CRN rejected the new proposal outright and opted instead to impose a return to a semi-presidential system. The political parties were left with little choice but to accept the decision, and on July 17, 1999, Niger's fourth constitutional referendum in a decade approved the new constitution, but with little enthusiasm (the official turnout was approximately 30 percent). Most importantly, the new constitution of the Fifth Republic was virtually identical to that of the Third Republic, with only some minor revisions in the form of provisions intended to mitigate conflicts in cases of cohabitation.

Despite the public and political attention devoted to the institutional debate, the options presented were in fact variants of the French democratic model, all involving dual executive authority. In addition, and despite talk of changing the electoral system used for legislative elections to some variant of a majoritarian "first-past-the-post" system, the same system for electing representatives to the National Assembly was in fact maintained. Alongside the deputies elected by proportional representation in the eight districts, the electoral code maintained a number of "special circumscriptions." Originally envisaged as a temporary measure to ensure the participation of ethnic minorities in the democratization process, these have found themselves institutionalized in subsequent regimes. Politically, no government has been willing to change this system, despite the significant distortion introduced by reserving eight of eighty-three seats (or almost 10 percent) for populations totaling approximately 2 percent.

Under this system, the Wanké regime moved quickly to organize elections, in two rounds for the presidency, first on October 17, 1999, and then, simultaneously with legislative elections, on November 24. The lineup evoked strong feelings of *déjà vu* among observers of Nigerien politics.

Mahamane Ousmane (CDS), Tandja Mamadou (MNSD), Mahamadou Issoufou (PNDS), and Moumouni Adamou Djermakoye (ANDP)—the top four vote-getters in the elections of 1993, and the four who ran against Baré in 1996—were joined by the former president of the transitional HCR of 1992–93, André Salifou (UPDP), and by a newcomer named Amadou Djibo Ali (of the new *Union des Nigeriens Independants*, UNI) to contest the election. The first-round results quickly reduced the field to three serious contenders: With a virtually identical score to that of 1993, Tandja Mamadou of the MNSD received 32.3 percent of the vote. Unlike 1993, Issoufou was to place second, this time narrowly edging out Ousmane by 22.78 percent to 22.52 percent. In contrast to 1993, however, the anti-MNSD bloc did not hold, and Ousmane eventually lent his support to his erstwhile rival, Tandja

Mamadou, who was elected "first president of Niger's Fifth Republic" by 58.89 percent. These results were roughly paralleled in the legislative elections, which assigned seats as follows:

- MNSD:38 seats
- CDS:17 seats
- PNDS:16 seats
- RDP:8 seats
- ANDP:4 seats

With the CDS now joined in a governing coalition with the MNSD, a new government was named in early January 2000, with the veteran politician Hama Amadou becoming prime minister. The PNDS, joined by several other parties, was to comprise an official parliamentary opposition.

Elite Continuities and Ruptures

As this complicated history demonstrates, Niger's efforts to install a democratic system have been marked by intense institutional debates, and it is hard to escape the conclusion that institutions have had a marked political impact. But it is also quite striking upon closer examination that these fierce debates revolve around choices to be made from a relatively limited menu: all are based on a model of liberal electoral democracy whose parameters are set by the range of variations on the institutions of the French Fifth Republic. The degree of "experimentation" in Niger should not be overstated. While it is certainly possible that the military interlude of 1996–99 will caution parties against behaviors likely to provoke crises like those that marked the Third Republic, it is also clear that the new institutions themselves present the same dangers.

Indeed, the institutions of the Fifth Republic are virtually identical to those of the Third; the most significant of the constitutional revisions, intended to address the institutional stalemate of the Third Republic, was the extension of the period during which the president could not dissolve the newly elected legislature from one to two years. This striking continuity in the face of the earlier difficulties was justified by the dominant argument within both the political class and public opinion: the failure of the Third Republic was explained not primarily as a failure of institutions, but rather as a failure linked to the behavior of politicians, *la classe politique*.

Considering the nature of that political class, a striking aspect of Nigerien politics is the extremely limited size of the relevant political elite, a fact underscored by the phenomenon of repeated elections, punctuated by coups, with the same individuals as candidates. Much of the variation in the functioning of institutions, and most of the country's political crises throughout the decade, result from shifts in elite alliances, not from shifting power bases. Indeed, there is a remarkable consistency in the electoral bases of the major parties throughout the decade. In contrast to Ibrahim and Niandou Souley, who have suggested that the AFC "lost" in 1995 compared to 1993 due to a failure to carry out campaign promises (Ibrahim and Niandou Souley 1998, 161), the electoral results by party in fact suggest quite the opposite: there was a remarkable consistency in the relative electoral strength of parties. Their varying fortunes in government are only the result of shifting alliances among them. And while the weight of the MNSD in the new government is somewhat reinforced relative to its position in 1993, the situation is otherwise quite similar in that the president must rely on a fragile legislative coalition to maintain a governmental majority. There is a clear potential for a new stalemate if party alliances were to shift and "cohabitation" again becomes necessary.

A similarly striking continuity throughout the decade has been the extent to which the forces that gained the upper hand in the process of the National Conference have been able to continue to drive the political agenda in the country. Every government since 1991, including the military regimes, has found itself in conflict with the same politicized social groups. Students, who see themselves as the initiators of the democratization process, joined by labor unions, have been constantly willing and able to strike and threaten government, while the stagnant economic situation has also meant that successive governments have been unable to meet their demands, and salary arrears continue to accumulate.

Given these continuities, how are we to characterize what has happened in Niger over the decade of the 1990s? After seemingly unending transitions, constitutions, and elections, which in many ways were aimed primarily at keeping them out of power—the new president and his party are the direct heirs to the single party of the pre-democratic period.[14] And they have been elected with a return to an institutional system that had not worked just a few years earlier, and under virtually identical circumstances. But at the same time a government has been elected in widely accepted elections, and has come to office promising (again) the rule of law and a respect of individual liberties. Is this a democratic transition? A clear answer is not apparent. Ultimately any answer would hinge on the definition of "democratic transition" that we applied, and thus becomes semantic. While we have certainly witnessed a set of remarkable and interesting political developments, the central question that remains is whether they entail a reconfiguration of power relations that will shape the political future of the country over the longer term. We would suggest that this is the theoretical question that we are challenged to pose in attempting to make sense of the democratic decade in contemporary Africa.

Most of the political science literature on African (or indeed other) politics in the "Third Wave" has treated democracy as the dependent variable, to be explained by other "causes." At this juncture, perhaps, there is a need to treat the "democratic wave" of the last part of the twentieth century as an independent variable, which has provoked its own consequences for political regimes around the globe. We must thus also ask what processes it has set in motion, and attempt to sort out the long-term consequences of these processes. To date, political scientists considering the question of democracy in Africa have focused primarily on counting "successes" and "failures" of transitions, usually defined in narrow terms of electoral turnover. The exhaustive survey by Bratton and van de Walle, an effort to catalogue "transitions" in terms of success or failure and then to explain these divergent outcomes, is ultimately limited in that the dependent variable ("successful" or "failed" transitions) is largely the result of dramatically overdetermined and idiosyncratic (i.e., "path dependent") processes, considered at only one brief moment in time (see chapter 1). Measuring African politics in terms of the relative success of "transitions to democracy" often hides more than it reveals. Rather, the more fundamental questions concern the effects of the efforts at transition—whether they succeed or fail—on the redistribution of power and the elaboration of rules concerning its disposition. If we are to seek a more comprehensive understanding of comparative political outcomes on the continent, we must attempt to understand variations in the politicization of social groups, in the elite groups who have driven democratic agendas and debates, and in the process that has reshaped the institutions of the state.

The urban and administrative elites who initiated the transition to democracy in Niger conceived it primarily as a means to end the authoritarian corporatist state and engineer their own rise to power based on a modern democratic republic. Having imposed the National Conference on the old regime, these elites were disproportionately represented in this forum, and subsequently they dominated the institutions of the Third Republic. The National Assembly of the Third Republic was largely composed of civil servants, teachers, and other Western-educated intellectuals. Yet it is also now clear that one outcome of the decade-long transition has been a gradual erosion of this dominance.

This is reflected in the changing profiles of elected deputies to the National Assembly. In contrast to earlier legislatures in Niger, major traders and merchants were widely represented in the Fifth Republic's first legislature. These merchants represent a very different social category from the intellectuals; while they control relative wealth they rarely possess significant education or technical skills in administration—indeed, many are illiterate. The dominance of the merchant class remained limited; thirty-six of eighty-three deputies elected to the first legislature of the Fifth Republic were merchants, while teachers, civil servants, and other Westernized intellectuals numbered some thirty-eight. This latter group thus continued to dominate the legislative activities of the Assembly, but they now needed to seek the support of the merchants, which significantly enhanced the latter's influence. In part the growing influence of this trading elite must be explained as a result of their wealth. They have contributed large sums of money to electoral campaigns and other party activities, and expect to be rewarded by the parties in return. But it is also clear that they benefit from broad popularity among segments of the populace. The dominance of the intellectual elite is thus eroded by the functioning of representative democratic institutions.

It is clear that despite all the acrimony and disagreement among the intellectual elite, there is an important degree of normative consensus that a liberal democratic model is the only legitimate option for the country's political system. But as the rising power of the merchant class suggests, to some extent, the democratic process itself limits elites' abilities to control the direction of political change. And there are seeds of potential challenges being sown in the process.

While elite consensus around the goal of democracy remains strong, it is important to look closely at what is embedded in this conception of democracy. In many ways it reflects the predominant international conception of democracy, including notions of individual human rights, secularism, and more. Faced with a society where these norms are in many ways alien, the "democratic" agenda thus largely entails a revival of what we might call the "transformative project" of the late colonial and early independence periods. That is, this notion of "democracy" includes much more than consulting the will of the people; it incorporates efforts at building a "modern" state and of engineering social transformations to conform to this effort. In effect, a debate about alternative forms of modernity has been opened up all over Africa over the past decade, with much more entailed than consulting "the people" about their will. Much of pro-democracy "civil society" is instead engaged in a project of trying to *transform* and *shape* that popular "will," yet divided over who will be in charge of the project.

The dilemma is that democracy also includes a discourse on the representation of popular will, and the elaboration of institutions that make representation possible. The liberalization that has accompanied democratization everywhere has produced an explosion of a wide variety of organized groups. Much attention has been devoted to the pro-democracy "civil society" groups—devoted to human rights, women, journalists, and others—but these have been accompanied by other manifestations of associational life. As one observer has noted in the Nigerien case, the political relaxation (*décrispation*) accompanying the "transition to a civilian, democratically elected regime has promoted an upsurge of popular ambitions and fostered the emergence of new forms of social protest," thus creating "a climate conducive to identity based politics" (Masquelier 1999, 224–25). Herein lies a latent potential for a significant gap between the elite conception of the modernity to be constructed and the conception held by other segments of the population. In Niger these have been manifested most notably in the rise of a religious opposition to the democratization project, and all that it entails. To date, the state elite has responded firmly in limiting the organizational capabilities of religious groups, but their potential should not be underestimated. To the extent that such groups elicit popular support, the state elite may find itself pushed to authoritarian reactions in the name of preserving democracy.[15] Institutions, and the uses elites make of them, will be a core determinant of the future impact of such social formations.

A onetime minister in Niger's Third Republic, M. Bazoum, suggested in the middle of the turbulent decade that "the future of democracy in Africa is at stake in Niger" (1997, 13). The comment is understandably overstated, yet it would also seem that the paradoxes of the ongoing democratization process in the country suggest important lessons for understanding the future configurations of power and politics resulting from Africa's responses to the "Third Wave."

NOTES

1. Despite this, it should be noted that Niger's politics are among the least studied on the continent. Among the relatively few scholars who have written on Nigerien politics one might note: Jean-Jacques Raynal, Abdoulaye Niandou Souley, Myriam Gervais, Jibrin Ibrahim, Robert Charlick, and Pearl Robinson. It bears noting, however, that little of this literature is in English, and much of it dates from the early 1990s.

2. Bratton and van de Walle (1997). See their table (120) for a categorization of African transition outcomes. *Africa Demos,* a publication of the African Governance Program of the Carter Center that monitored the progress of democratic developments in Africa for much of the decade, likewise listed Niger as "democratic" in its 1994 survey. *Africa Demos* 3, no. 3, 1994. Similarly, Myriam Gervais's case study of Niger in the volume edited by Clark and Gardinier (1997) is included in the section headed: "Cases of Peaceful Regime Change." It merits noting, however, that Gervais, like other observers at the time, were more cautious in their evaluation. See, e.g., Decoudras (1994) and Villalón (1996).

3. For a discussion of the notion of a "critical juncture," see Villalón (1998).

4. The government officially recognized three dead, although popular belief in Niamey in the early 1990s regularly put the figure as high as twenty.

5. The term "intellectual," in the Francophone African context, refers broadly to those with a secondary or higher French education, a demographically small group characterized by being significantly more Westernized in terms of outlook and expectations than the vast majority of their fellow citizens.

6. The World Bank, it merits emphasizing, estimates that some 70 percent of economic activity in the country is in the informal sector, and that agriculture makes up 40 percent of GDP and involves some 90 percent of the population. See the section on "Economy" in the entry for Niger, *Africa South of the Sahara 2004.*

7. Elements of the military, however, proved willing and quite capable of continuing to defend their corporate interests, as demonstrated by a series of military mutinies and arrests of political figures across the country and throughout the early 1990s. The difficulties of the Third Republic were to eventually provoke elements of the military to re-intervene in Niger, but it merits noting that even the Baré regime saw the need to quickly give itself a civilian cast.

8. Serious political debate raged in France preceding the legislative elections of 1986, with many analysts arguing that if the Socialists were to lose their majority, President Mitterrand would of necessity be forced to resign. His refusal to do so when that event in fact occurred, and the pragmatic compromise that was worked out with the government of the right that emerged, established in effect a new constitutional understanding in France of the possibility of "cohabitation."

9. A discussion of Niger's electoral systems under the 1992 and 1996 constitutions is available in Basedau (1999).

10. Interview with Mohamed Bazoum published under the title "L'Avenir de la Démocratie en Afrique se joue au Niger," *Démocraties Africaines,* no. 9 (Jan./Feb./March 1997). This is a journal of the *Institut Africaine pour la Démocratie* (Dakar). Bazoum resigned from Baré's government within three months, when it became clear that the new regime did not intend to quickly relinquish power.

11. See, for example, the editorial by Idimama Koutoudi of the independent *Le Républicain,* April 4, 1996, who noted that even the more outspoken of the partici-

pants in the National Conference were reduced to "military" (i.e., "yes sir") statements in Baré's Forum.

12. It may be of interest to note that U.S. embassy officials in Niamey were decidedly angry at the policy. Pointing to the many "exceptions" that the U.S. government regularly made to the law, many suggested that Niger's very weakness and lack of strategic importance made it a case where the United States could afford to pretend to stand on principle. Interviews with embassy officials by Villalón in Niamey, March 1998.

13. Hama Amadou's comment is quoted and discussed in this article by Bagoul Idaly, in *Le Républicain,* April 29, 1999.

14. This irony has led to the conviction among segments of urban intellectuals that the MNSD was ultimately behind both military coups, and that the party would not be satisfied until they had orchestrated their return to power.

15. For a case study of one situation that clearly demonstrates this danger, see Villalón (1996).

3 The Tribulations of a Successful Transition

Institutional Dynamics
and Elite Rivalry in Mali

Leonardo A. Villalón
and Abdourahmane Idrissa

Of the cases discussed in this book, Mali is among the countries that have most frequently been identified as democratic success stories. In a broad study of politics in Francophone Africa, for example, Victor Le Vine (2004) has included Mali as one of the rare "unqualified examples of successful democratic transitions." In many ways this qualification is well merited; based on a number of important dimensions, Mali's decade under President Alpha Oumar Konaré (1992–2002) provides a model of political stability for the region.

There are also significant limits, however, to the parameters of Mali's successes. In September 2002, shortly after the presidential and legislative elections, the Malian daily newspaper *Info-Matin* published a series of articles under the banner headline, "Political Crisis and Institutional Vacuum: The Republic in Danger!" (*Crise Politique et Vide Institutionnel: La République en Danger!*). While certainly one can suspect a bit of hyperbole from this source, in fact the articles point to some very real, potential difficulties facing Malian democracy. This chapter both examines the significant successes of Mali's transition and analyzes the dimensions of the country's tribulations. In particular, it examines how the institutional configuration that Mali adopted at the transition and how elite responses to the impact of these institutions created a troubling situation by the mid-1990s, and one which continues to bear the potential for future difficulties.

Institutionally, it is useful to compare Mali's democratic experiment to that of Niger (see chapter 2, this volume), a country with which it shares many common elements. At the time of their respective transitions in the early 1990s, both countries adopted a variant of the French semi-presidential system, including a direct presidential election requiring an absolute majority in two rounds. However, in terms of the legislature, upon which a governmental majority must be based in each case, the countries adopted different electoral systems. In Niger, an electoral system of proportional representation had the effect of fragmenting the party system in the legislature, resulting in no clear majority for the president's party and leading eventually to the stalemate and breakdown of the Nigerien Third Republic.

In Mali, by contrast, the legislature was elected by a majoritarian, winner-take-all system in multimember districts. This system thus had the effect of magnifying the victory of the single largest party, and in the "founding elections" of 1992 it did just that, producing a very solid majority for the *Alliance démocratique du Mali* (ADEMA) party of President Konaré. Widely recognized as free and fair, these first elections of 1992 thus produced a relatively strong and capable government, confirming for many Mali's early reputation as a "successful transition." Taking the lesson from the elections, however, the Malian opposition also quickly realized just how difficult it could prove to dislodge this very dominant party once established, and by the time of the second elections of 1997 Malian opposition parties were loudly denouncing the system as unfair and undemocratic.

The elections of 1997 were in fact plagued by enormous difficulties. After the first set of legislative elections was annulled by the Constitutional Court due to organizational complaints, the subsequent elections were all boycotted by the opposition, leaving ADEMA with the presidency and an overwhelming majority of parliamentary seats. The Malian situation in 1997 thus could be (and was) compared unfavorably to that of Senegal at the same time, where a nominally "democratic" system was built on institutional structures that ensured the seemingly perpetual dominance of one party.[1] Importantly, and in sharp contrast to Mali's image of success, it could be argued that in 1997 it did not in fact meet the basic criteria of many procedural definitions of democracy, including that proposed by Bratton and van de Walle, which requires competitive elections in which "all of the contestants accept the validity of election results" (1997, 13).

Dark clouds thus loomed on the horizon as Mali approached the third elections of 2002. The constitutional limit on two presidential terms produced a number of aspirants to succeed President Konaré, as well as significant tensions within the ruling party. In the months preceding the elections two scenarios seemed possible: (1) If ADEMA could find a consensus presidential candidate without splintering the party, a continuation of its dominance was likely. This continuity and stability, however, was almost certain to come at the cost of the continued "senegalization" of the system, with significantly eroded legitimacy as opposition elites decried the system as unfair and undemocratic. (2) If ADEMA splintered, the institutional configuration of the Malian republic opened up the possibility of a president elected in a second round, with no strong party base and thus facing a divided parliament with no majority support. The choice in the mid-1990s, it seemed, was between following the "quasi-democratic" path of Senegal (Villalón 1994) or risking the turbulence of Niger's Third Republic.

As it turns out, ADEMA's dominance did not hold, due to its own internal rivalries and the somewhat surprise candidacy of Amadou Toumani Touré, the famous "ATT," a military hero of the Malian "revolution" of 1991 that overthrew the old regime. ATT was in fact able to win election relatively easily in two rounds. But very importantly, given his lack of a strong party base of his own, the legislative elections that followed produced a parliament divided among a number of parties, and with no clear presidential majority. Major crises were avoided as ATT was able to parlay his wide popularity into broad legitimacy for his rule in the early years of his mandate. But it is important to note that this may well fade, and that the continued successful functioning of Malian democracy now hinges on elite willingness to work with a potentially difficult institutional system, and one that many have loudly denounced for years. It is this very delicate balancing that *Info-Matin* suggests may place the "republic in danger." And it reminds analysts that we would do well to be cautious in pronouncing the "consolidation" of even one of the most successful of the still-young democratic experiments in Africa.

In what follows, we present an examination of Mali's experience with democracy, suggesting three important points that characterize this particular experiment:

1. The "success" of Mali's first decade of democracy is a partial one; it has been marked by stability but not necessarily by legitimacy, a fact highlighted by the 1997 elections and their aftermath. That stability, in addition, was by no means the expression of elite consensus on the functioning of the democratic system in the country, but rather was based on the inability of the political opposition to mount a meaningful challenge to ADEMA, the party that ruled the country from the 1992 rounds of inaugural elections to the 2002 electoral cycle.

2. This mixed record—of stability but contested legitimacy—is a result of both the institutional setup adopted by the National Conference in 1991 and the play of political forces that emerged from the process of transition. The dynamics that have defined the attitudes of the elite, and which have shaped the organization of the party system, partly have their origin in elite responses to the institutional choices made at the time of the emergence of democracy in Mali.

3. The difficulties that characterized Malian democracy in mid-decade, and which seemed to portend further problems ahead, were sidestepped following the *alternance* of 2002 by the election of a charismatic president with unique political credentials. This situation, however, is clearly exceptional on many counts. The sources of these difficulties, and especially the unresolved institutional debates, are thus highly likely to re-emerge as central points of contention in the ongoing experimentation with democracy in Mali.

Prelude to a Democratic Experiment

When the Mali Federation uniting it with Senegal broke apart just months after independence in 1960, the former French Sudan kept the name and became an independent republic under the presidency of its most famous politician, Modibo Keïta. Keïta, a socialist who had been active in Franco-African politics in the post-war period, declared the country a single-party state under his *Union Soudanaise* party and embarked almost immediately on a series of "socialist" policy undertakings, notably the extensive nationalization of the economy. Relations with France, with which the Malian economy remained intricately tied, were consequently difficult. In 1962 Keïta took the radical step of withdrawing from the African Financial Community (CFA) whose common currency, the CFA franc, was tied directly to the French franc. The bold policy efforts were largely unsuccessful, and by 1967 Keïta was moving back to a closer collaboration with the French. Both the relative failure of his initial policies and the rapprochement with France won him new enemies. Threatened by the resulting political activism of social groups, in particular youth and students' groups, in November 1968 a group of young Malian army officers staged a coup d'état and instituted the regime that was to last for almost twenty-three years.

Lieutenant (later General) Moussa Traoré was named president of the military council that took control of the government, and throughout the next two decades he consolidated his version of personal rule with military backing. Although he did not totally abandon the state's official commitment to some form of "socialism," Traoré was able to establish better relations with France than his predecessor had done. His regime, however, was marked by periodic expressions of opposition from various social groups. At regular intervals students, civil servants, labor unions, and other such groups clashed with Traoré's rule, only to find themselves banned and their leaders arrested and occasionally killed or tortured. In 1976 the formation of a new, single party was announced, the *Union démocratique du peuple malien* (UDPM), which became the new instrument for Traoré's rule, never living up to the promise of its name.

Although challenges to Traoré's authority were never tolerated, in the early years of his rule he felt obliged periodically to promise a return to civilian government. And throughout his tenure he constantly resorted to pseudo-democratic gestures, namely formal elections, as a justification for his rule. In 1974 a referendum was held on a new constitution that, among other things, extended military rule for an additional five years. The official results indicated 99 percent of the voters approving the new constitution. Presidential and/or legislative elections (usually unopposed) were held in 1979, 1982, 1985, and 1988, with Traoré or his party never "winning" fewer than 98 percent of the vote by the government's count. Autocrat though he was, Traoré found it useful, or necessary, to maintain at least the trappings of democracy throughout his tenure.

During the course of the 1980s Malian politics were dominated by economic concerns. In 1981 a program of "economic liberalization" was initiated with prodding from the World Bank and Western donors. Despite severe drought conditions in the years that followed, particularly in 1983 and 1984, the program was pursued. Although Traoré's hold on power appeared to be well consolidated, socio-economic conditions worsened over the course of the 1980s. In response to increased popular protests, the government was obliged to suspend the implementation of portions of an IMF "austerity program" in 1987. Nevertheless, further economic reforms were undertaken the following year. As a result, by the end of the decade the country had experienced years of authoritarian rule and no improvements—indeed a decline—in the standard of living of the majority of its population. Faced with a declining economic situation and increasing political demands, Traoré made some modest concessions toward the end of the decade. In December 1989, however, the UDPM reaffirmed its longtime opposition to any multiparty system.

This legacy would seem to be a major contribution to the fact that, of all the West African countries that undertook democratic transitions in the 1990s, Mali had the bloodiest beginning to that process. In contrast to Benin, where President Mathieu Kérékou averted significant conflict by launching the first West African transition process himself, autocrats in neighboring countries refused to take this step. The more common pattern was rather one of organized civilian groupings clamoring for the initiation of a democratic transition, while autocratic rulers attempted to devise ways and means to thwart civilian groups and hold on to power, with varying results. This pattern was to mark Benin's northern Francophone neighbors. Niger and Mali can in many ways be considered twin countries; their sociocultural makeup and economic circumstances are very similar and their political histories are almost chronologically parallel. By 1991, the two countries were ruled by military corporatist regimes that were strikingly comparable. The difference, however, was that the founder of Niger's corporatist regime, General Seyni Kountché, had died four years earlier, and his much weaker and uncharismatic successor, Ali Saïbou, found himself eventually obliged to submit to the critics of his regime and relinquish power in the face of massive protests. In Mali, by contrast, General Moussa Traoré remained intent on retaining power in the face of growing popular discontent.

As elsewhere, this protest and criticism in Mali originated in the dissatisfactions of urban dwellers about the effects of the neoliberal economic policies that had been accepted in the 1980s. Imperato noted in 1991 that "the urban political class" in Mali had long benefited from "artificially low retail prices for domestically produced food, relatively early retirement from government service on good pensions, generous leave, and free health care and educational benefits for dependents" (26). Those "privileges" were curtailed or suppressed by policies forced on the government by IMF structural adjustment programs, triggering a defensive reaction of this "urban political class," comprised mainly of civil servants and students. Their unhappiness was built upon a broader historical critique of the Malian regime. Traoré's coup overthrowing Modibo Keïta in November 1968 had initially received popular support, but the promises of order and development that had legitimated

his government in the early years were quickly sunk in corruption and mismanagement. By the 1980s, there grew a sense among many Malians that his regime
was both detrimental to the country's well-being and un-reformable. The 1987 dismissal of Soumana Sacko, a finance minister hailed for his integrity, was widely interpreted as a clear sign of the regime's stagnation. The protests were therefore an
outgrowth of the sense that the ruling regime had led the country into an impasse,
compounded by economic hardship. And because, as Mané (1997) puts it, democracy was in the "*air du temps*" at that critical juncture, the protests quickly took the
form of pro-democracy movements.

In reaction to the development of democratic ideals, Traoré, like virtually all
other African autocrats confronted with the same situation, attempted to defuse
the movement. At a general meeting of the UDPM on June 26, 1990, Traoré delivered a speech warning Malians against the "dangers of multi-party politics" (Imperato 1991, 27). The party leadership, however, was unable to reach a consensus
on the issue, and deferred its examination to the party's planned "special congress,"
scheduled for March 28, 1991. In the meantime, in October 1990, three opposition political movements that were to become central actors in Malian politics were
created around democratic ideals: the *Comité nationale d'initiative démocratique*
(CNID, National Committee for a Democratic Initiative), the *Alliance démocratique
du Mali* (ADEMA, Democratic Alliance of Mali), and the *Association des élèves et étu-
diants du Mali* (AEEM, Association of Mali's Students and Pupils). The three groupings quickly united to form the *Comité de coordination des associations et organisa-
tions démocratiques* (CCAOD) and began agitating, seeking to mount pressure on
the UDPM before its special congress. The coordination proved very effective in
organizing massive demonstrations in Bamako in December of that year. Moreover,
its influence extended into the very machinery of the corporatist regime. In January 1991 the *Union nationale des travailleurs maliens* (UNTM), the labor union
theretofore linked to the ruling party as an element of the corporatist state,
launched a series of strikes. The democratic movement had taken control of the
unions through the UNTM's general secretary, Bakary Karambé, who like many
UDPM leaders had grown sympathetic to its goals. Most seriously for the regime,
the military was increasingly split between conservative supporters of Moussa Traoré and dissenters—such as the youthful Lieutenant Colonel Amadou Toumani
Touré.[2] These divisions started to erode Traoré's grip on power, although he appeared to believe that he still had room to maneuver, especially given the vested
interests of many in maintaining his rule.

Traoré's strategy for defusing the democratic movement was modeled on the
classical stick-and-carrot pattern, but was from the beginning more heavy-handed
than Saïbou's reactions in Niger. After having promised to install democratic institutions *within* the context of the UDPM, Traoré appointed General Sékou Ly, a
hardline soldier, as minister of the interior in reaction to the demonstrations afid
strikes of December 1990 and January 1991. Ly promptly proceeded to prohibit
political activities by CNID, ADEMA, and AEEM. His prohibition was not heeded,

however, and the policy only resulted in a bloody clash between students and the military on January 21 and 22, in which six students were killed and 232 people detained. In response, AEEM staged a bigger and more defiant demonstration in Bamako on March 22. The appalling outcome of the subsequent repression—some 150 dead and close to 1,000 injured—quickly led to the involvement of other segments of Malian society.[3]

The following day an estimated two thousand women demonstrated in front of the ministry of defense, again leading to further atrocities. On March 24, Traoré, after having tried to appeal to religious leaders for support, met with CCAOD representatives and made a number of concessions, including lifting the state of emergency, freeing political prisoners, and promising political reforms. These, however, were rejected as insufficient; holding him responsible for the killings on March 22 and 23, CCAOD representatives now demanded his immediate resignation.[4] In support of the demand, the UNTM labor union called for a general strike the following day. Importantly, figures from the top leadership of UDPM, namely the administrative secretary M'Bouillé Siby and the political secretary Djibril Diallo, publicly disassociated themselves from Traoré by calling for the establishment of a multiparty system. At this point, Traoré was perfectly isolated. Even his support in the army was failing him and there was thus no opposition when, on March 26, 1991, a group of military officers ended his twenty-three-year rule.[5]

The Making of a Model Transition

With Traoré's deposition the momentum toward the establishment of a democratic system quickly took shape. There were initial fears that the military action engineered by the then-unknown Amadou Toumani Touré (who was quickly to become popularly known as "ATT") would lead to the replacement of one military autocracy with another, but the rapid coordination between the *Comité de réconciliation nationale* (CRN) set up by the military and the CCAOD defused those apprehensions. Three days after the coup, a joint communiqué of CRN and CCAOD announced that municipal, legislative, and presidential elections would be held within the year and that CRN would proceed to abolish itself. The transition itself was to be administered by a Transition Committee, the *Comité de transition pour le salut du people* (CTSP), consisting of twenty-five members, of which ten were military and the remaining fifteen were civilians from the CCAOD. The committee was chaired by ATT.

Again in contrast to Niger, two distinguishing features of Mali's transition at this stage were to prove to be important: the role of the military, and the collapse of the old ruling party, the UDPM. Although in Niger the army was acrimoniously attacked by the civil associations that organized the transition, it was not nearly as discredited as the Malian army was at the eve of the transition. The main accusation directed at the Nigerien army was that it was tied to the ruling regime. The

Malian army, on the other hand, was held directly responsible for the massacres of March 22 and 23. In the days that followed public sentiment was so intense that soldiers, fearing assault by civilians, remained confined to their barracks. Even while plotting the coup against Traoré, ATT has colorfully recounted, he was obliged to wear an "old *boubou* [robe]" and drive an unofficial car to visit his accomplices, carefully avoiding the uniform that would have subjected him to popular ire (Touré 1994).

Yet the way the army deposed Traoré and then clearly showed that it was in favor of the democratic movement resulted in an overnight reversal of its terribly damaged image. The Malian army indeed quickly became more popular than the army could ever become in Niger, and hence played a key role in the transition's institutions. In a sense, this was due to ATT's behavior as the main leader of the coup, something for which he was widely hailed internationally. But as ATT himself explains, his exemplary behavior was also the most rational path to follow:

> Not only did the power that I held not exist, but everyone claimed it. If one is to believe the democratic movements, they are the ones who arrested Moussa [Traoré]. In the end, the legitimacy of this power was very wide, that is to say diffuse, and that's one reason why I chose not to stay. That is, it is true that the street had contributed to the weakening of Moussa. It is true that many people were entitled to something. The legitimacy of [the coup of] March 26 was contestable. For the well-being of our people, it was necessary to restore as quickly as possible an incontestable legitimacy. (Touré 1994, 45)

The quiescence of the Malian army afterward—again compared to the Nigerien—may also be construed, at a certain level, as a consequence of its tragic and then redeeming involvement in politics in 1991.

The actions of ATT had put the army, previously the mainstay of the corporatist single-party regime, on the side of the democratic movement and against the UDPM. This, compounded by Traoré's arrest and the virulent critique of his regime that followed in the wake of his trial, debilitated his party completely. In fact, the UDPM was officially excluded from the transition. It did not receive a seat in the Transition Committee and played no role in the National Conference that it was to organize; it was in short wiped out (at least temporarily) in Mali's public life. Transformed into political parties, and (again unlike Niger) with no need to unite in the face of a powerful ancien régime party, CNID and ADEMA soon found themselves rivals, as well as in competition with a number of new parties that quickly began to emerge.

The twenty-five-member Transition Committee played the key role in the transition process, and its composition was a direct product of the democratic movement and ATT's coup. In addition to the ten military representatives, the members of the committee came from organizations anointed by their struggle against the Traoré regime, with the two main movements that would become political parties—ADEMA and CNID—providing two members each. Three members were drawn from the labor unions, and three others from the *Association malienne des droits de l'homme,* the country's main human rights association. Other social groupings—including the Tuareg rebels—provided one member each. Soumana Sacko, the minister removed by Moussa Traoré in 1987, was called back to Mali from a post abroad to serve as chair. The Transition Committee drafted the texts that were to serve as the institutional framework that would form the basis of the workings of the National Conference. This framework included a constitution draft, an electoral code, and a charter for political parties. The Transition Committee also determined who would be able to participate in the National Conference, with the stated goal of being as inclusive as possible.

The National Conference, convened in July 1991, was divided up into special committees to discuss the issues on its agenda.[6] Additionally, it was charged with reviewing the draft texts prepared by the Transition Committee that would define the institutional structure of the new democracy. These were subsequently to be adopted without amendment. The Malian democratic experiment has been at times characterized as particularly innovative, and (as we shall note below) there is some truth to this perspective. Nevertheless, the central institutions of the democratic constitution were distinctly less innovative. Written by judicial experts whose legal culture was mainly French, the texts were very much inspired by the French system. In particular, the constitution replicated France's semi-presidential system, with a directly elected president who must share power with a prime minister drawn from a parliamentary majority. In this Mali represented a common trend in Francophone African transitions.[7]

The electoral system crafted by the Transition Committee grew out of a debate involving the goals of both ensuring the political power of the major parties and creating electoral opportunities for smaller ones. The electoral code made it easy for parties to be recognized, and indeed, by the end of the conference, forty-seven political parties had received approval to participate in the elections. At the same time, however, the main parties argued that it was imperative to produce stable governing majorities. Writing for the Institute for Democracy and Electoral Assistance (IDEA), Mozaffar (n.d.) notes that "the initial proposal for using the Two-Round System (TRS) in single-member districts was rejected, in order to diminish the influence of local notables and strengthen party control over candidates. Also rejected was a proposal from smaller parties for a PR [proportional representation] system, because of its anticipated potential for political instability. However, the adoption of the PR formula for municipal elections accommodated the smaller parties, most of which lacked national support and were regionally or locally based."

As we shall see, at the legislative level, the majoritarian electoral system that was adopted significantly disfavored smaller parties, with the partial exception of those with a strong regional basis. Deputies to the National Assembly were to be elected in fifty-five multimember districts of one to six seats. Candidates were to run on a party list, with a winner-take-all provision, and with an absolute majority required. In those districts where no party won a majority in the first round, therefore, a second round of elections would be held. The winner would take all of the seats for that district. Mozaffar (n.d.) notes that "it was thought that a Two-Round majority-runoff system for legislative elections would encourage coalitions in the second round between smaller and larger parties." As it turned out, however, the "winner take-all" party-list provision ensured that the legislative electoral system was favorable to the formation of a dominant party or a dominant coalition block.[8] The seeds of a major challenge to Malian democracy were thus planted by an electoral system that favored the allocation of a strong parliamentary majority to one party. Given the additional advantages of incumbency, the specter of an entrenched dominant party, as in Senegal, was to worry the losers of the first elections from the beginning.

This particular institutional provision—the majoritarian nature of the legislative electoral system in a context of a semi-presidential regime—would thus prove to have a major impact on the development of the democratic system in Mali. Within a semi-presidential system, the party composition of the legislature becomes crucial to defining the relations between the prime minister and the president, and hence to the functioning of the system itself. Differing legislative electoral systems, by producing very different party representations, will thus have a central impact on the system. As discussed in chapter 2, Niger's semi-presidential system in the context of a proportional representation electoral system, which encouraged the fragmentation of representation in the legislature, produced a situation that required coalitions to form a governmental majority. When a coalition "marriage of convenience" broke up a few months after the transition to democracy in that country, it was faced with a "cohabitation" between a president and a prime minister belonging to two different parties, and rather quickly led to institutional gridlock and a coup. In Mali, the majoritarian electoral system had very different results; by producing the domination of a single large party, it effectively eliminated the need for coalitions.

This result, however, cannot be attributed exclusively to the electoral system. It was clearly also determined in part by the dynamics of the party system, which itself grows out of its historical evolution as well as deriving from the institutional incentives found in the electoral system (Vengroff 1993; Vengroff and Koné 1995). At the establishment of the Transition Committee, only two formal political groupings were represented: ADEMA and CNID. Later, successful efforts were made to revive the *Union Soudanaise* (US-RDA), the party of the first president, Modibo Keïta, until his overthrow in the 1968 coup. But in this context, with Traoré's UDPM wiped out of the political scene and the military showing extensive compliance, ADEMA came to dominate the political stage. The reasons for ADEMA's dominance at this point are complex. Of importance, however, is that for much of the 1980s the party's charismatic leader, Alpha Oumar Konaré, had been involved in social and cultural politics that bestowed on him a significant degree of national prestige. Founder of the *Jamana* cultural and publishing cooperative in 1983, this respected scholar was highly instrumental in the crystallization of the democratic movement in the late 1980s, and several clandestine organizations came together under his leadership to establish what was to become ADEMA. Konaré's leadership was thus a key factor in ADEMA's success in gaining a firm national base as a political party. The party's eventual difficulties at the end of his presidency point to the fact that ADEMA's cohesion rested a great deal on the personality of its leader.[9]

Two other parties, CNID and US-RDA, appeared to have representative abilities at the national level. During the elections, however, CNID's abilities to draw voters quickly proved to be overstretched outside of Ségou, the regional stronghold of its leader, Mountaga Tall.[10] The US-RDA, on the other hand, revived not only its political pull but also its historical, internal ideological divisions, with a somewhat weakening effect. There were over forty remaining political parties, consisting of an array of small groups, many organized around individual figures. While a few presented ideological or programmatic platforms, others were purely opportunistic, and none presented genuine representative abilities outside of very limited locales.

In the early months of 1992, the constitution and other institutional texts were adopted by referendum (January 12), and all rounds of elections (municipal, legislative, and presidential) were held. Following the electoral system that had been agreed upon at the transition, the elections for municipal councils in January 1992 used a proportional representation system to elect large councils ranging from thirty-one to fifty-five members. In most cases, then, some 2 percent of the vote was sufficient to win a councilor seat. As expected, these elections broadly distributed councilor seats among participant parties, with some nineteen parties winning seats. Together, the three largest parties—ADEMA, CNID, and US-RDA—won 59 percent of the vote, but tellingly, none received a majority in any given council. These elections, nevertheless, emphasized the potential dominance of ADEMA, which received 28 percent of the vote to US-RDA's 17 percent and CNID's 13 percent, winning pluralities in thirteen of the nineteen municipalities.[11] These results provoked an immediate reaction from the other parties, which was to foreshadow later dynamics at the national level. The election of municipal mayors was to take place within the councils, on a majority vote. With very few councils in which any one party held a majority, parties were obliged to form local alliances within each council. Fearing ADEMA dominance, in many cases parties joined forces to keep it from winning mayoral positions. Thus while ADEMA won a plurality in all six "communes" (districts) of the capital city of Bamako, it was only able to elect a mayor in one.

As expected, ADEMA was considerably more advantaged by the majoritarian electoral system at the legislative elections, held in two rounds on February 24 and March 9. Twenty-two parties competed in the first round, though with very wide variations in terms of the number of districts contested; only two (ADEMA and CNID) presented lists in all 55 districts. The elections were nevertheless competitive, and only 11 of 55 districts (15 of 116 seats) were decided at the first round, with ADEMA winning 7 of those and placing first in 35 others. At the second round, ADEMA came out easily ahead of its major competitor, US-RDA, in all but 4 districts, eventually winning 74 of the 116 contested seats (or some 64 percent) to secure strong control over the National Assembly (see table 3.1).

A comparison with the results of the municipal elections gives a good indication of the extent to which ADEMA's dominance of the legislature was the result of the electoral system. Richard Vengroff (1994) has calculated that a proportional representation system like that used in the municipal elections would have given ADEMA only some 43 seats in a single round, and would have required a coalition of at least three parties to produce a parliamentary majority. In such a fragmented legislature, and with only an ADEMA plurality, one could well imagine a dynamic similar to that which took place during mayoral elections at the municipal level, with strikingly different consequences for the subsequent evolution of Malian democracy. In actuality, however, ADEMA's strong victory in the legislative elections raised immediate concerns among other parties. As Vengroff noted in 1994, "The possibility of the emergence of a one-party dominant government and the eventual drift to a one-party state is an obvious concern to both observers of and participants in the system" (1994, 37). Precisely these fears were to drive the behavior of opposition elites throughout the remainder of the decade.

Unsurprisingly, in the presidential elections held in April, ADEMA leader Alpha Oumar Konaré won a strong plurality of almost 45 percent in the first round. In the second round he overwhelmingly defeated Tieoulé Konaté, his rival from one of the US-RDA branches, which had emerged from a split in that party following the legislative elections (see table 3.2). Notably, Konaré's showing in the first round was stronger than his party's showing in the earlier elections, a fact no doubt attributable to his personal reputation and his extensive national campaign.

Thus, after an exemplary transition process and an open electoral competition, Mali entered a period of democratic government under a president who was to remain in place for a full decade. Yet, as we shall see below, the apparent stability of that period also belies major difficulties in the functioning of democracy in Mali, arising from challenges rooted in the electoral institutions discussed above and eventual elite disagreement on the democratic legitimacy of those institutions.

Tribulations: Majoritarian Institutions and Divided Elites

The Konaré presidency began on June 8, 1992, when ADEMA's leader was sworn in as the first president of Mali's Third Republic. Despite widespread international acclaim for the truly remarkable transition, in fact Konaré's presidency was immediately caught up in political and social turbulence, resulting in three different governments under three prime ministers in its first two years.

An immediate and potentially serious challenge was presented by a conflict in the northern Saharan region that pitted Tuareg rebels against both the Malian and the Nigerien states in the early 1990s. A complex and shifting array of militant groups and individual rebel leaders complicated any resolution to the conflict. Yet from the start of the transition, the Malian political elite sought to address the issue directly, including Tuareg representation in the Transition Committee and engaging in a long series of negotiations and peace talks. Though the remote region was to remain problematic in various ways, the successful political resolution of the Tuareg rebellion by the mid-1990s must be counted as a significant success of the Konaré government (Diarrah 1996, 41–63; Seely 2001).

A more intractable challenge, and one that has continued to plague Malian democracy, was the social crisis provoked by student grievances and demands. The politicization of the student movement has a long history in Mali (as, indeed, elsewhere in the region), but the role of the AEEM students' association in the overthrow of the Traoré regime placed this group at the center of national politics. Subsequently, this role has been used consistently to legitimate student political demands. Reacting largely to the neoliberal reforms begun under Traoré, which included reductions in student grants and subsidies, students placed the educational system at the center of Malian politics in the new democratic era, periodically shutting down Bamako with demonstrations and roadblocks. For the first three years following the overthrow of Traoré, no regular school years were completed in the country, and such problems continued periodically throughout the Konaré years. Following the transition, the continued radicalization of the student movement was fed by party dynamics, as opposition politicians with limited national followings exploited student demands to their own ends. As Diarrah has argued: "The acceleration of demographic pressures considerably restricts the room for maneuver of the leadership, which is compelled to adopt emergency measures. . . . Urban youth are therefore the ferment of the agitation that punctuates the current political evolution of most African states, including Mali. That social fringe also turns out to be the most courted by politicians unable to gain a hold in the countryside" (1996, 246–47).

Despite these challenges, under President Konaré the challenge of building a new democratic state was taken up seriously from the beginning of his presidency, and innovative measures were launched. Thus, for example, a measure of political relaxation was provided by an original democratic institution known as the *Espace d'interpellation démocratique,* which allows citizens to address grievances directly to government members (Wing 2002). Under the intellectual leadership of Konaré, the very public culture of the new regime broke significantly from past practice, and the urban landscape of Bamako was consciously crafted to reflect and promote a new awareness of Malian history (De Jorio 2003). Such initiatives introduced a real sense of reform and progress in the country, and though they seem to have been more appreciated abroad than at home, they must also partly account for the stability of the Konaré presidencies.

By far the most far-reaching and significant of the new measures launched by the regime was a massive decentralization project. Institutionally, this project may prove to be one of the most interesting aspects of Mali's experiment, although its full impact still remains to be seen. Decentralization as a political strategy was widely embraced—at least rhetorically—as a core part of the democratization process across West Africa (Boone 2003a). In Mali, however, the process was exceptional in terms of the ambitious extent of the project and its political centrality. As elsewhere, the issue was put on the political agenda by the National Conference, which mandated it for the first post-transition government. Seely (2001) has argued that the project to decentralize was driven politically by the Tuareg issue, although the depth of commitment to the project suggests that it has much deeper roots.

In January 1993 a commission on decentralization was put in place to plan and oversee the process, and its *chef de mission*, Ousmane Sy, quickly emerged as an articulate spokesman for a highly theorized argument about the imperative of decentralization for "democracy," "development," and, indeed, "modernity." The extent of state restructuring entailed in the project, and the consequent changes in relative power that would result, provoked a significant degree of resistance from within the government itself. Thus, rather quickly there was major opposition to the plan from high officials in the Ministry of Territorial Affairs (that is, the ministry of the interior) and even from within the president's close circle of advisors. Yet despite this opposition the project was pursued aggressively, and by the second Konaré presidency the internal struggle had been won politically by the advocates of decentralization: the key interior ministry was renamed the "Ministry of Territorial Affairs and of Local Collectivities," and the new minister was none other than Ousmane Sy. With some 702 local "collectivities" to be created, the implementation still presented serious difficulties. A number of local-level social conflicts erupted, for example, around the drawing of boundaries and the establishment of local governmental units.[12] While its ultimate fate is still uncertain, the decentralization project is certainly among the more striking institutional innovations of Mali's democratic experiment.

Despite the relative success of these original efforts, the most significant trend in the first Konaré presidency was the gradual emergence of a serious political crisis, rooted directly in the country's institutional setup and the dynamics that played out at the transition. In the face of the overwhelming ADEMA dominance of the Third Republic institutions, much of the opposition was to challenge their very legitimacy over the course of the 1990s. The institutional framework in Mali was to promote stability, but it also undermined its own legitimacy. Focusing on perceived failures of the 1992 electoral process, opposition demands centered initially on reforms to the electoral process. Among the major demands were the creation of an independent national electoral commission (CENI) and a revision of the electoral system, specifically the adoption of a proportional representation system. In the spirit of compromise and inclusiveness, these demands were taken seriously by the Konaré government, which established a committee to consider changes to the electoral code. The demands for the electoral commission were in fact conceded and the CENI created in due course, but despite much debate on the electoral system (a debate to be revived again late in the second Konaré presidency) there was to be no accord on this matter. Commenting on the difficulties of such an agreement, an advisor to President Konaré noted in 1995 that the problem lay in the fact that the form of the institutions unanimously agreed to in the heat of the transition were not intended to be permanent, but rather would be revisited at a later date. Any discussion of changing the institutions by a partisan government, however, immediately provoked cries of protest by the opposition, regardless of the government's intentions.[13] One might note, in addition, that a government that has emerged victorious from a particular institutional arrangement has little rational incentive to change it.

As the crisis of Malian democracy resulting from ADEMA's dominance of the Third Republic's institutions deepened, it was further complicated by two factors: the complex dynamics of the party system, and the logistical difficulties in managing the 1997 electoral cycle.

In the immediate wake of the transition, there were efforts by Konaré to build inclusive governments with representation of various parties. These, however, were largely unsuccessful, contributing to the instability of the early governments. Konaré's first prime minister, Younoussi Touré, a former director of the Central Bank of West African States in Mali, included in the government members of the US-RDA and a minor party, the *Parti pour la démocratie et le progrès* (PDP). The most strategic offices, however, were all allocated to ADEMA, and in July ADEMA's political secretary, Aly Nouhoun Diallo, was elected president of the National Assembly. These moves, which ADEMA defended as normal in the context of its clear, strong majority in the National Assembly, nevertheless outraged opposition parties, who saw them as an effort by ADEMA to entrench its dominance over the new democracy. Opposition deputies boycotted the vote in the National Assembly to protest their perceived lack of political influence. This boycott set the line of behavior that would become standard for the opposition during the remainder of the ADEMA government.

The strident social problems of the period further strained the capabilities of the government and ricocheted back to ADEMA. Thus the prolonged strike carried out by students in April 1993 ultimately led to the resignation of Prime Minister Touré. In an effort to defuse the growing protest against ADEMA's power, a successor who was not officially affiliated with any party was named. While the government formed by new prime minister Sékou Sow was still dominated by ADEMA, three ministries were allocated to CNID, US-RDA, and PDP. Another party, the *Rassemblement pour la démocratie et le progrès* (RDP), was also represented in this government. The Sow government adopted a neutral or nonpartisan stance, eventually being labeled the "government of the council of ministers" in the Malian press. This stance, however, frustrated some in ADEMA who saw no reason for a majority party to limit its own authority. In November, ADEMA's vice-president, Mohamed Lamine Traoré, resigned from his ministerial post amid complaints that the decision-making process was too dominated by Konaré, Sow, and the Council of Ministers. Tensions came to a head following the social problems produced by the 50 percent devaluation of the CFA Franc in January 1994, and the following month Sow himself resigned.

Sow was replaced by Ibrahim Boubacar Keïta, a central ADEMA figure and close associate of Konaré's, who was to remain as prime minister for the next six years. In many ways the rise of Keïta signaled the end of the effort to seek a multiparty government and the victory of those forces in ADEMA who wanted to assert the party's dominance. This move, however, precipitated a crisis inside ADEMA itself for control of the party, leading eventually to a schism. In September 1994 the new prime minister was elected to the presidency of ADEMA, securing his control over the dominant party. Chagrined by Keïta's election, prominent party members resigned to form the *Mouvement pour l'indépendance et la renaissance de l'intégration Africaine* (MIRIA) in December. ADEMA was not, however, the only party affected by dissent. In September 1995, a breakaway movement from the CNID formed the *Parti pour la renaissance nationale* (PARENA), which was to establish a political alliance with ADEMA in February 1996. In the meantime, members of the UDPM, the party of former President Traoré, succeeded in reviving it under a different name, the *Mouvement patriotique pour le renouveau* (MPR).[14] As various elite politicians attempted to secure their political bases, these dynamics and fluctuations became symptomatic of the Malian party system.

As a result, on the eve of the 1997 cycle of elections, the country counted sixty-three formally registered political parties, sixteen more than at the start of the 1992 cycle of elections. Nevertheless, ADEMA remained in a very strong position, which both the institutional configuration and its incumbency helped it to reinforce. The proliferation of the new parties, compounded with the volatility of the situation in the larger parties, created an uncertain and tense situation leading up to the 1997 cycle of elections as ADEMA sought to maintain its unity and the opposition feared the entrenchment of ADEMA dominance.

The problems were further aggravated by the fact that the elections were not well prepared. Although in the end there were no strong indications of systematic fraud, a host of difficulties and irregularities marred the process. These elections were to be the first held under the new code approved by the National Assembly in January, which included the creation of the CENI, the independent national electoral commission, to oversee the process. The first mission of the CENI was the enormous task of preparing, ordering, and transferring the electoral lists to voting locations throughout the country. The 1992 electoral lists had to be entirely updated, since the government had not managed to revise the electoral lists annually as had been mandated. The CENI included fourteen political party representatives (half for the majority party and the remaining seven distributed among the opposition parties), eight members from the government, and eight nonpolitical members. A number of debates, however, delayed the actual appointment of the members, and the CENI thus came into being only days before the first round of the legislative elections. Held on April 13, the first round of elections quickly turned out to be a management disaster. Although the electoral lists were ready in advance as specified by the electoral code, those available in polling stations were highly flawed. Overwhelmed, the chairman of the CENI authorized voters missing on the lists to vote with their ID cards, creating further confusion.

Opposition parties reacted harshly, promptly denouncing the fiasco as an attempt by the government to steal the election. United in a common front, they presented a series of extensive demands: they wanted the government to resign, the

CENI to be dismembered, the electoral process stopped, and a new discussion begun on restarting the transition. While recognizing the inadequacy of the elections, the government and the CENI nevertheless insisted that the second round should be carried out as scheduled. In the meantime the Constitutional Court annulled the results of the first round, feeding the opposition's claim that the electoral process was fundamentally flawed. The court decision, however, was based on findings of irregularities in the process, but not fraud, and it thus supported the government's position that the electoral cycle could be continued. In response the major parties of the opposition, united in a new "radical" opposition movement, the *Collectif des partis politiques de l'opposition* (COPPO), announced their intention to boycott the elections. When the elections were in fact held on July 20 and August 3, then, only ADEMA and PARENA campaigned, although the COPPO parties remained on the ballot and received some votes. Six minor parties also won seats and were eventually to join ADEMA and PARENA in parliament.

Announcing their intention to also boycott the presidential and municipal elections, the COPPO parties challenged the planned presidential elections, reiterating their demands for the cancellation of the entire electoral process, the complete revision of the voter's register, and the resignation of the government, which would be replaced by a transitional administration. These radical demands were listed in a petition filed in the Constitutional Court, but rejected. The presidential election was in fact held on May 11, opposing Konaré to only one challenger, May Mamadou Maribatou Diaby of the *Parti pour l'unité, la démocratie, et le progrès* (PUDP). Konaré won with 84.4 percent of the votes, which in the official results was increased to 95.9 percent through the discounting of votes cast for the candidates who declared their boycott. Though the presidential elections proceeded smoothly, Konaré's legitimacy was clearly undermined by the refusal of opposition parties to recognize them and also by the lack of any serious opposition. Although COPPO argued that the low voter turnout represented the success of their boycott appeal, in fact the turnout in 1997 was higher than the one recorded at the 1992 election, and there are many reasons to expect that Konaré would have won handily in any case.

In contrast to 1992, the legitimacy of the 1997 elections was seriously compromised by the consistent refusal of the COPPO parties to recognize their validity, and the strategy of rejection adopted by the radical opposition left little room for compromise. The Malian system thus found itself faced with a not-uncommon dilemma, based on calculated elite reactions to an institutional setting they do not dominate. A minority opposition that is in fact unlikely to win elections—whether because of the electoral system, a lack of support, or the advantages of incumbency—has little incentive to play the game and is better off staying out and denouncing the process instead. Once the radical parties had declined to abide by the decision of the constitutional court, they essentially adopted a logic of rejecting the legitimacy of the institutional context. The game is a dangerous one in that, in calling into question the institutional framework itself, the opposition left open only one alternative—a power showdown to secure its goals. It is not in fact difficult to imag-

Table 3.1. Malian Legislative Elections, 1992 and 1997

Party	1992 % of vote	1992 seats (of 116)	1992 % of seats	1997 % of vote	1997 seats (of 147)	1997 % of seats
ADEMA	48.4 %	74	63.8 %	75.3 %	128	87.1 %
US-RDA	17.6	8	6.9	*b*		
CNID	5.6	9	7.8	*b*		
PDP	5.1	2	1.7	*b*		
RDP	4.4	4	3.5	*b*		
UDD	4.4	4	3.5	*b*		
RDT	3.8	3	2.6	*b*		
PMD	2.7	6	5.2	*b*		
PSP	1.7	2	1.7	*b*		
UFDP	1.6	3	2.6	*b*		
UMDD	0.4	1	0.9	*b*		
Others	4.3	0	0	24.7 %	19	12.9

b = boycott

ine that a leader less committed to democracy than Konaré might have seized the opportunity to proclaim a state of emergency and begun to overturn the democratic spirit of the institutions.

In the wake of these boycotts, the second Konaré presidency was marked by what Malians called "the political vacuum." With the COPPO parties refusing to recognize his legitimacy, Konaré governed without any institutional opposition. At the same time, the radical parties devoted themselves almost exclusively to taking every opportunity to challenge the legitimacy of the government. Ibrahim Labass Keïta of the satirical newspaper *Le Scorpion* notes that "the parties of the COPPO coalition seize every occasion to denounce [Konaré's] bad re-election. They made it clear numerous times when meeting with foreign personalities, a behavior which disturbs the tenant of the Koulouba [presidential] Palace, who is now obliged to provide explanations of his re-election every time he meets foreign visitors" (April 4, 2002). The global result of this period was the declining legitimacy of the entire democratic system as the population grew disaffected with the behavior of all parties and political elites.

The only occasional opposition to ADEMA in parliament was presented by its official ally, PARENA. Most significantly, in 2001, PARENA leaders were instrumental in the failure, once again, of proposed reforms to the electoral code that would have introduced a measure of proportionality into the legislative electoral system. Significantly, the reasons invoked by PARENA to challenge the reform were directly tied to the question of the legitimacy of such an institutional change in a legislature overwhelmingly dominated by one party. PARENA leaders argued that such a major decision could not be made when the majority of the political class could not be part of the debate on the issue.

Table 3.2. Malian Presidential Elections, 1992 and 1997

Candidate	1992 first round	1992 second round	1997 (including vote for boycotters)	1997 official results (excluding vote for boycotters)
Alpha Konaré (ADEMA)	45.0	69.0	84.4	95.9
Tiéoulé Konaté (US-RDA**)	14.5	31.0	1.6*	
Mountaga Tall (CNID)	11.4		1.8	
Almamy Sylla (RDP)	9.4		1.0	
Baba Haidara (US-RDA**)	7.0			
Idrissa Traoré (PDP)	7.1		1.2	
Amadou Niangadou (RDP)	4.0		1.0*	
Mamadou Diaby (PUDP)	2.2		3.6	4.1
Bamba Diallo (indep)	2.0			
Others (1997)			5.8	

* Represents vote for different candidate from the same party.
** The US-RDA split into two factions, and two candidates ran in its name in 1992.

At the transition the Malian elite had chosen a majoritarian electoral system to offset the risks of instability incurred by electoral fragmentation. The objective was to provide larger parties the necessary majorities to produce a legislature capable of governing. What was not foreseen, however, was the instability of the party system itself. The majoritarian electoral system was thus ultimately both affected by and contributed to elite disunity about the institutional configuration of Malian democracy, resulting in boycotts and the constant splintering of the party system. The stability that came from ADEMA's ability to hold together and ensure its dominance during the Konaré years thus came at the cost of the rejection of the legitimacy of the system itself by much of the elite. As the country neared the end of Konaré's second mandate, constitutionally prescribed to be his last, uncertainties surrounding the future of ADEMA and rivalries among potential heirs to the party's leadership cast dark clouds over the future. In addition, given their boycott of the 1997 elections, the relative strengths of the various opposition parties remained largely unknown. In the context of this great uncertainty the political landscape of the 2002 elections proved once again to be highly fragmented.

The Return of ATT: Managing Institutions with Charisma

At the approach of the July 2002 legislative elections, Malians were faced with the task of electing 147 deputies out of 1,103 candidates registered on 387 lists presented by parties, coalitions, and independent candidatures. An additional 13 deputies would be elected by Malians abroad. The extreme partisan fragmentation undercut the logic of forming larger parties that might take advantage of the favorable electoral framework. A similar pattern of fragmentation marked the approach of the presidential elections, with 24 candidates managing to deposit the required sum (approximately $7,000 U.S.), thus becoming eligible to contest the election. In addition to a proliferation of splinter groups from various opposition parties, the internal rivalries that had long marked ADEMA led to its own divisions. In anticipation of his own candidacy, Ibrahim Boubacar Keïta had resigned as prime minister in 2000. Finding himself marginalized in the party due to the presidential ambitions of the new prime minister, Mandé Sidibé, Keïta left ADEMA to found his own party, the *Rassemblement pour le Mali* (RPM), in July 2001. Sidibé himself, however, was then challenged by another ADEMA baron, Soumaïla Cissé, who was chosen in January 2002 to be the party's presidential candidate. Sidibé then resigned in March and announced his intention to run as an independent candidate. With ADEMA thus fatally splintered, and following months of speculation as he continued to deny any intent to enter the race while simultaneously positioning himself to do so, a second independent candidacy was announced, that of Amadou Toumani Touré (ATT) himself. The hero of the deposition of Moussa Traoré in 1991 and of the management of the "exemplary" transition process quickly became the frontrunner.[15]

Given the long-held objective of all opposition parties to dislodge ADEMA from power, there was talk of presenting a single candidate to challenge the candidate of the incumbent party, but in the highly fragmented climate the project did not materialize. In the end, three of the twenty-four candidates in the race drew significant support: Amadou Toumani Touré, ADEMA's Cissé, and Ibrahim Boubacar Keïta. While ATT clearly ran first with some 28 percent of the vote, the other two candidates found themselves in a tight competition for second place. The initial count gave Cissé some 23 percent to Keïta's 21 percent, but Keïta challenged the results given irregularities that could have disadvantaged him. A recount under the supervision of the Constitutional Court did indeed find irregularities, yet it yielded results that left the ranking unchanged: while ATT's votes increased slightly to 28.70 percent, Cissé's decreased to 21.30 percent, positioning him a hairsbreadth ahead of Keïta with 21.03 percent. Keïta conceded defeat and, together with the other opposition parties, called for support to ATT. In fact, most commentators in

Mali and abroad have suggested that even outgoing president Konaré was in favor of ATT. Konaré did not make any explicit endorsement, but he showed only luke-warm support for ADEMA's candidate while publicly displaying his high regard for ATT. Unsurprisingly, ATT won the second round with 65.01 percent. Although officially an independent candidate, in the second round ATT was supported by a loose coalition of forty political parties centered around Keïta's RPM, and calling itself "*Coalition espoir 2002*."[16]

The legislative elections that followed in July 2002 essentially confirmed the weakness of the Malian party system, yielding a highly divided national assembly, but one in which the various parties were to espouse the idea of "consensual gov-ernance." The legislative election results thus showed how the highly fragmented party system could trump even the majoritarian logic of the electoral system. In the initial results, Ibrahim Boubacar Keïta's RPM, in alliance with a number of smaller parties, won forty-six seats. Along with CNID (thirteen seats) and its other partners in the "*Coalition espoir 2002,*" RPM thus gained control of a total of sixty-six seats. Opposing this bloc, ADEMA, which with forty-five seats had come in a very close second to the RPM, joined six minor parties to form the *Alliance pour la république et la démocratie* (ARD), with a total of fifty-one seats. The remaining seats were distributed among two minor coalitions and various nonpartisan candidates. Despite the party fragmentation, then, the majoritarian logic of the electoral frame-work would seem to have at least encouraged the creation of two large blocs, but these blocs had to accommodate the sprawling party system, including many par-ties with highly localized bases of support.

The legislative elections were not without their own flaws; the results in eight constituencies were eventually annulled, and by-elections were conducted in those districts. The ADEMA party benefited the most from this, emerging as the single largest party, with a plurality of 53 deputies in a parliament of 160 seats. Constant maneuvering soon appeared to be necessary in order for any real majority to emerge in the National Assembly. When President ATT announced his willingness to work with any constituted majority, a "presidential bloc" was created from a coalition of various smaller parties in an effort to provide him with parliamentary support, but this bloc lacked any obvious cohesion. This potentially fragile situation was held together by a professed ideology of consensual cooperation with the president, something seemingly possible only given ATT's charisma and personal prestige.

In the early years of ATT's presidency, the consensual ideology has worked to preserve political stability and to provide the president with legislative legitimacy. Besides ATT's charisma, two factors appear to have contributed to this remarkable situation. The first is the weakness of the parties themselves, who have managed to erode their own bases of support (as pointed out regularly by the Malian me-dia). None of the parties can thus now claim to be a mass party, and none count on the loyalty of a significant base that is willing to follow its lead. Secondly, given this weakness, and with the next round of elections still far off, there was no ra-tional incentive to challenge a prestigious incumbent whose integrity cannot be faulted. But the situation was also clearly problematic; "consensual government" does not appear sustainable in the long run in the context of a democratic institutional structure. Indeed, a significant political debate concerning the party system emerged in the early years of the ATT presidency.

On the surface, the debate is about responsibility for the seeming loss of legitimacy of the democratic process in Mali. On one side are those who hold the political elite, and particularly the party leadership, responsible for the erosion of legitimacy of the party system. They contend that the behavior of the elites during the difficult years between 1997 and 2002 explains the low electoral turnout and popular dissatisfaction. On the other side are those politicians who attempt to vindicate the parties. Thus the independent *Le Républicain* (April 21, 2004) published a scathing criticism of the politics of "consensus" that indicts both the president and the political parties. And the same month Ibrahim Boubacar Keïta delivered an impassioned defense of political parties at the *rentrée parlementaire*. "It is not democratic," he intoned, "to claim that the parties are done with their historic mission. It is false and dangerous to claim that they are now nothing more than a space for shady business. It is false and unfair to say this, for they still have a powerful role to play" (*Les Echos,* April 7, 2004).

At a more fundamental level, the debate addresses the central issue of the nature of this "consensus," questioning the political motives behind it. In his speech, Keïta thus hinted at a situation that indicates the hidden dynamics at play behind the smooth facade of the consensus: "No one has the right, for reasons of political opportunism or trafficking of influence, to use the consensual image of the head of state in order to gain a position in the political arena. If that was somehow encouraged, our fragile equilibrium will not survive. God forbid! Let it be known!" (*Les Echos,* April 7, 2004). This statement, in its seemingly ambiguous wording, is in fact quite clear in the context of Malian politics since the election of ATT. The people implicitly accused by Keïta are those using the notion of "consensus" to their own political ends. This would appear to particularly target the *Mouvement citoyen* (Citizens' Movement), an informal political association created in support of the president. And clearly Keïta's fear is that ATT himself is encouraging this movement.

The *Mouvement citoyen* is a formal expression of the entourage that helped to promote the "independent" candidacy of ATT in the elections of 2002. It describes itself as a spontaneous coming together of sympathizers, and subsequent supporters, of ATT's candidacy. Reflecting its emerging formalization, however, the Malian press began to refer to ATT as "the candidate of the *Mouvement citoyen*," implicitly treating the movement as a political party. And indeed, although in mid-2004 the grouping was not registered as a political party, it increasingly behaved as one, including activities that would seem to be intended to promote support for ATT in future elections. Yet in January 2003, appearing on a popular television show that was broadcast in the Bambara language (the Malian lingua franca), the new president reiterated his frequent claim that he did not have "the slightest intention" of creating a political party (*L'Indépendant,* January 10, 2003).

The key strategy used by the grouping is to recruit cadres from among other political parties who, while remaining affiliated to their own parties, nonetheless declare their support of ATT's actions and future candidacies. The strategy is threatening, and hence viewed as a "catastrophe" by official political parties who, in the words of Yaya Traoré and Mohammed Sacko (*Info-Matin,* January 16, 2004), have to find ways and means to "cope with the bloodletting from among their ranks." But the options for the parties are highly limited given the public professions of support for the current consensualism. Espousing any other position, especially for seeming electoralist concerns, is highly risky for any party. Paradoxically, as Traoré and Sacko point out, the only option available to the parties is to appeal directly to the president to request his support in sanctioning the co-optation strategies of what they refer to mockingly as "*la mouvance informelle,*" implying a vaguely defined sphere of influence.

Sambi Touré, the editor of *Info-Matin,* is more directly critical of the head of state. He accuses him of betraying his nonpartisan commitment, which is in any case impossible in a democracy, in accepting the support of the *Mouvement citoyen* (*Info-Matin,* March 11, 2003). In any case, it is clear that ATT's informal relations with the *Mouvement citoyen* work against the emergence of any clear majority in the National Assembly. Given the weaknesses of the political parties and the powers of the president, the key to the formation of a majority in the National Assembly appears to be in his hands, and the institutional relations between the presidency and the legislature thus appear to be at odds with the semi-presidential constitution. Since there is no majority, ATT has appointed governments from what he labels "personalities from civil society," without systematic regard to their political affiliation. While ATT may relish such independence, many in the Malian elite find it unhealthy for democracy. In his 1994 interview with *Jeune Afrique,* ATT espoused certain political principles that seem consistent with his current behavior—including the notion that men and women should be used according to their competence, and not out of political calculations. For Malian commentators such as Sambi Touré, however, this high-ground stance smacks too much of the military: "The principles and practices of democracy are a far cry from those of the army. . . . For Mali to become the model democracy he hopes for, General President Amadou Toumani Touré should accept as a 'democratic minimum' the free interaction of political movements and formations" (*Info-Matin,* March 11, 2003).

Indeed, in the first few months of 2004, the *Mouvement citoyen* took steps that seemed designed to transform it into a regular political party. In order to take part in the upcoming communal elections, it named a "constitutive group," rendering its leadership more visible. Two members of the current Malian government, Youth and Sports Minister Djibril Tangara and Minister for Mines, Energy and Water Ahmed Diane Séméga appear on the list of the "constitutive group." The group's official mission is to secure the necessary document (*récépissé*) that will allow it to present candidates under its own banner at the communal elections. Once such a step is taken, and although the *Mouvement citoyen* continues to claim that it is not a political party, it will be treated as such for all practical purposes.

Will the *Mouvement citoyen* become a large party—as its co-opting moves suggest is its intention—that will come to successfully compete with ADEMA and RPM? If not, how will ATT position himself as the independent candidate of an informal political association that acts, for all practical purposes, as a political party? Or on the contrary, could the *Mouvement citoyen* as a party come to establish a dominance over elected institutions much as ADEMA was able to do in the Konaré years? If it does so, will the legitimacy of those institutions again be called into question? Such issues will be shaped by upcoming electoral competitions, and will thus help to define the future of Malian politics. At stake in this democratic experiment is the normal, constitutional functioning of the governing institutions.

ATT's charisma and stature as hero of the revolution and transition may have postponed an institutional crisis—one whose potential was clearly demonstrated with the elections of 1997. There have been many successes in Mali's experiment with democracy, to be sure, and many lessons that can be drawn from the experience thus far. It is certainly possible, therefore, that creative solutions to the institutional dilemmas will be proposed. Nevertheless, the evidence of how elites have engaged with the institutional configurations of the Third Republic to date also suggests caution in pronouncing the consolidation of this remarkable experiment. Institutionally, in many ways, Mali's experiment with democracy remains ongoing.

NOTES

1. Indeed, unfavorable comparisons to Senegal were already being made well before the 1997 elections. Such comparisons were noted various times in interviews carried out by Villalón in Mali in 1995, 1999, and 2000.

2. Amadou Toumani Touré (ATT) was not himself directly connected with the democratic movement, however. Rather, his dissent was rooted in the military ideology of restoring order and reforming the state, and not by any adhesion to the democratic doctrine per se. In a lengthy post-transition interview with *Jeune Afrique* (Touré 1994), ATT voiced a sharp criticism of the democratic movement in Mali, especially of the fact that it masked personal interests and imported institutions unimaginatively from the West. But he added that, given the number of people who lost their lives to the ideals of that movement and the resulting unpopularity of the army due to their deaths, it was both ethical and pragmatic to endorse the democratic movement.

3. These figures are provided by Imperato (1991), but estimates of death casualties vary widely between 100 and 200, according to official or opposition counts (see Clark 2000). Clark adds that "there is no way to determine if people died at the hands of the armed forces or in the general chaos of the riots and demonstrations" (258).

4. Given the paradoxical role of the military as both reason for and catalyst of the "revolution," ATT's subsequent analysis of Traoré's responsibility in these events is of significant interest (Touré 1994). According to ATT, although Traoré should indeed be held responsible for the killings, these events did not unfold in the straightforward fashion presented by civilian politicians. Traoré, he notes, did not order troops to fire

on the demonstrators. In such situations, troops are trained to fire following a certain phased procedure. The duty of the higher command is thus the negative one of prohibiting the firing. The responsibility is in any case the same, but ATT's intention in providing that explanation was not to excuse Traoré but to provide a military explanation for an argument, paralleling a similar one concerning the February 1991 deaths in Niger, where the military leadership asserted that it was "responsible, but not guilty" of killing several students.

5. The process was more a deposition than a coup. Traoré was so isolated that, according to ATT (Touré 1994), no resistance was expected. The only practical difficulty he encountered in the removal of Traoré were the roadblocks that civilian protesters had erected in the streets of Bamako.

6. For a good discussion of the national conference, see Diarrah (1996, 26–37).

7. Thus Cabanis and Martin note that despite significant divergences in Francophone African constitutional forms after independence, the democratic movements of the early 1990s resulted in a re-convergence around the French model. "More or less everywhere," they note, "we find the same institutions, more or less identical means of appointment, and quite comparable relations between powers" (1999, 187).

8. For a more detailed discussion of the electoral system and its effects, see Vengroff (1994).

9. Thus Clark (2000, 261) writes: "the reputation of Alpha Konaré . . . assisted party candidates in municipal and assembly elections. . . . Konaré himself visited every part of the country during the elections. Other presidential candidates, focusing on the towns, delegated authority to colleagues, especially in the countryside, whereas Konaré undertook the campaign personally in both rural and urban areas. It is likely that the Malian people, particularly in the countryside, responded to seeing and hearing personally such a prominent Malian." Diarrah (1996, 229) similarly notes Konaré's "personal quotient" as a key aspect of ADEMA's political influence.

10. A descendant of El Hadj Omar Tall, the famed religious leader and resister to French colonization, Mountaga Tall claims a prestigious heritage. This appeal, however, proved to have a clear ethnoregional basis, limiting his influence at the national level. He nevertheless was to emerge as one of the most vocal and strident members of the "radical" opposition elite in the mid-1990s.

11. The detailed results of these elections and a discussion of all of the 1992 elections are available in Vengroff and Koné (1995).

12. The discussion of decentralization is based on interviews conducted by Villalón in Mali in 1995 and 2000. These included interviews in June 1995 with Ousmane Sy, then *chef de mission* at the commission on decentralization; Baba Hamane Maïga of the Ministry of Territorial Administration; and the late Seydou Mamadou ("Totoh") Diarrah, advisor on institutional issues in the president's cabinet.

13. Villalón interviews with Baba Hamane Maïga, head of the committee for the revision of the electoral code in the Ministry of Territorial Administration, and Seydou Mamadou Diarrah, June 1995.

14. The Supreme Court had twice rejected applications to revive the UDPM under its former name.

15. The splintering of ADEMA continued even after the elections. Thus Soumaïla Cissé, the party's candidate in 2002, left ADEMA in mid-2003 to create a new party, the *Union pour la république et la démocratie* (URD), to be led by one of Cissé's lieutenants, former prime minister Younoussi Touré.

16. It should be noted that again at the second round, the Constitutional Court had to intervene to redress irregularities, in this case giving Cissé more votes than he had actually received. His results (34.99 percent) were in any case vastly inferior to ATT's, but the reasons exposed by the Constitutional Court were serious, since they not only pointed at administrative flaws, as in 1997, but also at "fictitious voting stations," "fraudulent handling of figures," and other gerrymandering activities (*Afrique Express* 251, June 18, 2002).

4 | Democratic Legitimacy in Benin
Institutions and Identity in a Regional Context

Bruce A. Magnusson

According to the usual indicators of democratic success, Benin was not a good democratic prospect. It has, nevertheless, defied the odds since 1990. As a case, then, Benin presents us with some analytical problems. Because it violates most of the predictors of democratic transition as well as of survival, we could be tempted to dismiss it as an interesting anomaly. Yet, the consistency with which the Benin case violates social science predictions should lead us instead to ask different questions about these predictors, not necessarily about their overall comparative validity, but rather about what other factors might be missing. Rather than engaging in additional predictions about the long-term prospects of democracy in Benin or about how the Benin case conformed or did not conform to various benchmarks of democratization or consolidation, anomalous cases such as this should lead us to ask how it is that democracy as a regime type acquired the legitimacy necessary to survive what, according to the social science consensus, would appear to be almost insurmountable odds.

Two fruitful lines of analysis could help us in this endeavor. First, rather than examining regime institutions in isolation (e.g., presidential vs. parliamentary systems; proportional vs. single-member district electoral rules; federalism vs. centralism), it is crucial to examine the overall configuration of regime institutions, viewing it as an institutional effort to resolve fundamental problems of the distribution of power and accountability, which initially provoked regime change. In other words, first, for *what purpose* was this democratic regime constructed and in what domestic context? Second, the analysis of domestic regime change, legitimacy, and survival can also be embedded analytically into a broader regional and transnational context. Democratic legitimacy is as much an external as an internal matter, particularly for small, poor, relatively weak countries. Both of these tasks require a relaxation of the analytical boundaries between transition and consolidation, and also of the boundaries between internal and external politics.

Examining the relationship between elites and institutions is key to both of these analytical tasks. The first task suggests that the purpose behind the configuration of regime institutions is the result of deliberate choices made by elites in the pursuit of particular interests, whether these are personal, sectional, broader, principled national or normative interests, or some combination of these. It assumes that those crafting the regime understood that these institutions would regulate (constrain) behavior (their own as well as that of real and potential rivals) in particular ways. In the case of Benin, whose democratic institutions were not the result of decades or centuries of institutional accretion and re-molding, but rather the endpoint of an extremely limited one-year process of deliberation, elite choices and interests are featured in the construction of regime instruments that would in the future constrain elites' behavior and shape their understanding of political interests. At the same time, Benin had substantial experience in the drafting of failed constitutions, particularly during the 1960s amid the tumult of ethnoregional political stalemate and multiple military coups.

The second task, the analytical incorporation of regional and transnational contexts, suggests that opportunities and constraints are also a result of institutions and individuals outside the boundaries (or across the boundaries) of the state in question. For example, the regional economy of West Africa plays a large role in how cross-border, commercial networks define their interests and manage their businesses commercially and politically. Similarly, changes in the global economy and the re-focusing of French economic interests within the European Union help define a larger and less manageable set of institutional constraints on elite interests and behavior.

While these two tasks appear to be rather clear and uncontroversial, the difficulty arises in extending this kind of interactive approach to elites and institutions beyond the construction phase of the regime and applying it to the survival of the regime. After all, political history is replete with examples of leaders who were not constrained in the least by the formal institutions of their states, even as the formal facades of cabinets, parliaments, and courts were embellished. Inevitably, questions about how and why democracy survives leads to a richer analysis in which institutional constraints and elite choices are tempered, weathered, and structured by more amorphous and fluid factors such as norms, values, political culture, and legitimacy.[1]

Benin's Democratic Survival

Since the 1990 National Conference that peacefully abolished an eighteen-year-long military-authoritarian regime, Benin has emerged as one of Africa's democratic success stories. It has survived four scheduled National Assembly elections and three scheduled presidential elections. The first two presidential elections successfully removed the incumbents. Each National Assembly election has transformed the relative positions of the major political parties in the country, resulting in a rather low incumbency-survival rate. The constitutional separation of powers is a reality, as presidents and national assemblies alike have acquiesced to adverse rulings of the Constitutional Court. As of yet, no real institutional military challenge has threatened the new democratic regime. And, on the whole, economic liberalization has actually improved conditions in Benin—an economy growing an average 4.7 percent annually in the 1990s. Literacy rates, primary school attendance, health service access, infant mortality rates, access to clean water, and direct foreign investment have all shown improvements. Decentralization of authority in the social sectors, and in local affairs, continues to be a major challenge, but most parties are committed to decentralization. After many years of debate and tinkering, Benin held its first local level elections in seventy-seven districts in December 2002 and January 2003, finally implementing one of the primary recommendations, made by the transitional leaders more than a decade earlier, in favor of fundamental decentralization reforms. Electoral democracy has not precipitated any major outbreaks of ethnoregional violence, despite continuing (and sometimes major) procedural and technical electoral problems. The government generally conforms to most international human rights standards of basic political freedoms (e.g., freedoms of association, speech, and religion), although there have been breaches in law enforcement methods and occasional attempts to intimidate and bully what is otherwise an extremely active and independent press. Politically, Benin is generally ignored in the international press—perhaps one of the better indicators of success.

The Treachery of the Single Case

Even though we know better, were we to generalize from the Benin case, we might construct the following set of predictors for democratic success:

1. GDP/capita less than $500;
2. A relatively small middle class;
3. Colonization by the French;
4. No previous successful democratic experience;
5. Historically elevated levels of ethnoregional tension and inequality;
6. A history of multiple military coups (there were seven during Benin's on-and-off democratic regimes 1960–1972);
7. A political elite fragmented by deep regional and family antagonisms;
8. Lack of civic trust;
9. Economic dependence on a giant, but much less democratic neighbor (Nigeria), characterized by sometimes explosive politics; and
10. A less democratic (if not authoritarian) neighborhood (Benin's neighbors are Nigeria, Niger, Burkina Faso, and Togo).

Although the above list is in the spirit of tongue-in-cheek, it does serve as a good starting point for (1) understanding the limits of comparative predictors; (2) exemplifying the bewildering, seemingly consistent violation of nearly all mainstream predictors in this case; and (3) trying to understand why a case such as Benin (which seems to be relatively exceptional) may actually have quite a bit to teach us about some of the conditions under which new democracies might survive (or not fail).

How does legitimacy become attached to a regime type such as democracy? Where does it come from, and how is it maintained in an adverse economic and political environment?[2] This chapter will explore the two particular areas of analysis mentioned above that will contribute to the goal of understanding regime legitimacy. The first re-embeds the analysis of regime attributes and institutional design into *the purposes for which they were constructed,* asking how they have succeeded in addressing the problems of the predecessor regime as they were perceived at the time of transition, and whether they have been flexible enough as a totality to continue to address over time the fundamental issues of representation, distribution of power, and accountability of power. The purpose here is twofold. First, it reverses our tendency to privilege institutions as types (e.g., proportional vs. majoritarian) over the reasons they were chosen—that is, the purpose behind the institutional choice. Second, it takes account of the reality that institutions (e.g., electoral systems, presidential or parliamentary systems, unicameral or bicameral legislatures, and courts) are part of a broader institutional web of interactions and relationships referred to as "the regime." Isolating these interactions for the purpose of analysis makes it possible to ignore crucial regime attributes that govern these relationships and interactions. In any regime, the interactions among institutions are certainly as crucial as the internal mechanisms of particular institutions. It matters, for example, whether or not a system biased toward presidential-legislative conflict possesses a mechanism such as a Constitutional Court for mediating these regime-level disputes, just as much as it matters whether a legislature is elected proportionally or by single-member districts. These factors matter both for how a legislature operates internally and how it operates in relation to a president or a prime minister.

The second area of analysis is *the regional and transnational context within which democratization is taking place.* It must be assumed that institutions in weak states are the result of domestic choices that are also shaped by encounters with multiple, transnational flows—for example, flows of ideas and conceptual frameworks such as democracy, sovereignty, and capital, along with transnational institutions that carry them. It is simplistic to assume that elite choices are *determined* by these ideas and institutions, but they must in some way take them into account for reasons ranging from security to ideological consent. Ali Mazrui's conception of the African state as both "incorrigibly and rigidly *national*" and as "irresistibly *transnational*" is an elegant illustration of this idea, for neither of these processes is purely endogenous (1984, 289). In this respect, James Mittelman's perspective of democratization—as one element of a survival strategy in the context of globalization, regionalism, and marginalization—is especially suggestive (2000). Seeing democracy from the analytical standpoint of a "survival strategy" in a rapidly changing international and global economic and political context, rather than as an ideal to which populations may or may not strive, or as an ideal type to which regimes may or may not conform, necessarily changes the standards for "success," "consolidation," or even "legitimacy." The point is that one vantage point is not necessarily more correct, but that it can be analytically useful to multiply our vantage points. In fact, different vantage points are not necessarily mutually exclusive and may coexist comfortably on the ground. It is this simultaneity of perspective that leads us to one of the questions at the heart of democratic legitimacy: How does the international (and transnational) context affect the ways in which democracy takes hold in transitional countries? Most of us assume (correctly) that there is a connection between broad systemic change and domestic politics. Scholars almost always position the current wave of democratization in Africa "at the end of the Cold War," but the nature and processes by which this context is important internally is rarely examined as more than a newly permissive absence of constraint (or loss of Great Power interest) that permits the otherwise natural emergence of democratic institutions to take hold.

What are the relationships among structure, ideals, and strategy? What are the relationships among the structural, normative, and instrumental components of democracy? And, if we pay attention to these interactions, how do we evaluate democratic "performance"? The idea of "good governance," for example, promoted and financed by bilateral and multilateral donors, can be criticized on the one hand for its assumptions about democracy as the endpoint of modernization, and on the other hand for an economistic, utilitarian focus that serves the interests of transnational capital. From another vantage point, though, this notion bridges the gap between "democracy as ideal" and "democracy as survival strategy," pointing our attention to the agency of elites, civil society, and state bureaucrats. In addition, we should build on the extremely useful conceptual roadmap developed by Risse, Ropp, and Sikkink (1999) to analyze the socialization process of how transnational norms of democracy were appropriated and legitimized within transitional countries to help create the kind of political culture that delegitimizes non-democratic practices.[3] Key to their analysis is the idea that norms are useful strategic instruments given certain environmental and enabling contexts, and that a normative embrace (in this case, embracing human rights norms) is the result of the "institutionalization and habitualization" of instrumental and strategic politics. The analysis of norms (such as democracy, human rights, good governance, and accountability) as tools used within certain broader contexts to address particular problems, such as state survival or elite well-being, provides us with conceptual mechanisms to bridge the gaps between values and instruments during periods of structural change. This analysis also helps to illuminate the connections between transnational and international contexts and the purpose of institutional change.

The Context of Institutional Change

What were the problems that the Beninese tried to resolve through a transition to democratic regime institutions? A summary would include a redefinition of the public and private realms in the political economy; economic and political justice and fairness; accountability; ethnic and regional representation and participation in the elaboration of economic and political reforms; and the control of state violence (Heilbrunn 1993, 1994; Magnusson 1997).

By the late 1980s, Benin was reeling from the consequences of a bloated state and massive corruption. It also experienced a political stalemate—between the old guard of a self-described Marxist-Leninist revolution and the more pragmatic reformers in the regime, who sought accommodation with international financial institutions and a deeply cynical, disgusted public. By the end of the decade, bankruptcy of the financial system, unpaid salaries, public debt, and the imminent collapse of Benin's usually thriving informal sector, itself dependent on a working banking system and well-oiled patronage networks, set the stage for an almost complete collapse of the state itself. With labor unions and the civil service on strike, government offices emptied onto the streets, and the economy tanked.

While similar outcomes were visible across Africa, the explanation for Benin's particular crisis is entangled with a particular set of elite institutional choices prior to and following independence in 1960 (when it was the Republic of Dahomey). These choices aimed, on the one hand, to manage an economy deeply dependent on France and Nigeria, and on the other hand, to handle an internal political stalemate marked by rivalry among three deeply institutionalized, ethnoregional patronage networks (and political organizations), a north–south cultural division not unlike that of Nigeria's, with a resource-poor economy unable to meet the aspirations of a relatively large (and southern) educated elite.

It should be recognized that Mathieu Kérékou's Marxist-Leninist state (1974–89) was neither simply a revolutionary reflex nor a means by which to ensure northern domination over the entire country and its economy, even though these factors might have played some role in the establishment of the People's Republic of Benin (RPB) regime.[4] Like the democracy established in 1990–91, the institutions of the *Parti de la Révolution Populaire du Bénin* (PRPB) were the result of institutional learning and an effort to rid the country of ethnoregional political stalemate and the potential for civil war. The 1960s and early 1970s in Dahomey were marked by a stunning sequence of six successful military coups d'état (the first in 1963) and multiple civilian constitutional designs, which in 1970 culminated in a tripartite, ethnoregional elite pact closely conforming to what Arendt Lijphart would later call consociationalism (1977). Under this arrangement, the three regional leaders constituted a collective Presidential Council under which each would serve a rotating two-year term as "president," and in which each member possessed a policy veto. The purpose behind this regime was to avoid the perpetual political stalemates among the three ethnoregional political machines, none of which possessed a majority in the country. Following the first two-year rotation of power—from

Maga (a northerner and the country's first president from 1960–63) to Ahomadégbé (a Fon from Abomey)—Major Mathieu Kérékou seized power in 1972.[5] While the coup d'état was ostensibly aimed at addressing endemic corruption, it was no accident that this northern military officer waited until the end of Maga's rotation, and the beginning of Ahomadégbé's, to overthrow the council. Kérékou did not embrace Marxism-Leninism until 1974, following an extended internal debate between radicals and reformers about the best path to development and political consolidation.

In addition to the brief consociational interlude, Dahomey also experimented with both presidential and semi-presidential (similar to the French model) constitutional regimes and, of course, military regimes. Despite these numerous institutional models, the electoral systems for the legislatures when they existed remained rather stable. Although the various representative assemblies leading up to independence were based on multimember, winner-take-all, multidistrict formulas, those following independence reflected the national (and continental) worries about stability and unity. The country was "unified" into a single, plurality-take-all electoral district. The effect of this arrangement was to disenfranchise most of the population, permitting one or two ethnoregional groups to monopolize power at the expense of the others. President Kérékou abolished all political parties save his own, the PRPB, which permitted only a modicum of competition for representative seats through occupational lists rather than party competition.[6]

The centralization of power during the Kérékou era succeeded (at least temporarily) in badly damaging the ethnoregional political infrastructure, which, along with foreign domination of the economy, was defined as the enemy of the new Beninese regime.[7] The nationalization of the economy and the creation of dozens of state-owned enterprises (and new jobs) silenced the powerful labor and student unions that had been so successful in destabilizing previous regimes during Benin's seemingly perpetual economic crises and austerity programs. At the same time, the oil boom in Nigeria lubricated Benin's transshipment economy to such an extent that massive (and unwise) investments (and public debt) became attractive options to policymakers. The Kérékou regime was able to link an external threat of economic domination (*néocolonialisme*) with an internal threat of ethnic conflict (*féodalisme*) to create a powerful ideological basis upon which to construct an authoritarian, state-building, security regime undergirded by the buying off of the intellectual and commercial classes with state salary payments to an enormously expanded public sector.

The economic collapse of the late 1980s that resulted in the inability to pay salaries and the disintegration of the banking system was an effect not only of a generalized economic crisis across Africa but also of massive, rent-seeking activity and sheer looting by the governing elites (Westebbe 1994). So, while the purpose behind the establishment of Marxism-Leninism was in some measure guided by the desire to de-institutionalize ethnoregional competition and conflict, the choice of regime instruments eventually bankrupted the regime, providing the baseline for the new set of institutional choices to be made following the National Conference in 1990.

Despite President Kérékou's expectation that the National Conference would assist him in defining a new national purpose and institutional framework for governing the country, the declaration of sovereignty was completely unforeseen by the ruling elites, the National Conference participants, neighboring African states, and the international community. Carried live on the radio, the conference deliberations combined with uncertainty over whether the military would intervene produced a profound moment of national identity. When Kérékou eventually acquiesced and the military remained in its barracks, the National Conference, the subregion, and the population realized that they had witnessed a peaceful dismantling of an entrenched dictatorship or, from Kérékou's perspective, a "civilian coup d'état."[8] The appointment of an interim prime minister (Nicéphore Soglo), an interim governing body (the *Haut Conseil de la République* [HCR]), and the subsequent appointment of a new Constitutional Commission to write a new constitution occurred in a context of deep uncertainty over who and what would emerge as the new powerbrokers in Benin. With nearly fifty political parties, fragmentation of the old ethnoregional parties and patronage networks, and evident disarray of the discredited regime, outcomes were not at all predictable.

This point is especially important for understanding the kind of institutional choices that were made during the transition process. Three decisions were key and illustrate the concerns of the Constitutional Commission. First, the choice in favor of a strong presidential system, rather than the French model of semi-presidential, executive power-sharing, raised controversial questions about how much power should be vested in a single executive, especially given the recent history of dictatorship. Second, the extremely controversial constitutional recommendation to forbid anyone over the age of seventy from running for the presidency was an overt and ultimately successful effort to prevent ethnoregional leaders from the 1960s (especially Maga and Ahomadégbé) from monopolizing and polarizing the electorate once again.[9] Finally, the decision to create a Constitutional Court as the centrally important arbiter of constitutional conflicts between the presidency and the National Assembly was a clear recognition of major weaknesses in Benin's constitutional past, as well as a reflection of the lawyerly makeup of the commission.[10] Separately, the HCR's choice of a highly proportional system for electing the new National Assembly reflected an obvious break with the electoral history of the previous thirty years.[11]

Regime Purpose and Configuration

The Benin case helps to illustrate the utility of analyzing electoral systems as one element within larger webs of institutions, rather than as an isolated unit of analysis. Two such interrelated institutional networks are the focus of this chapter. The first is the set of formal regime institutions and the allocation of power among them. The second is the set of representative institutions or representative opportunities, which may be either formal or informal, including such domains as sector-policy advisory bodies, "traditional" life, professional interests, and internal security.[12] The legislative branch of government and the electoral system are members of both sets. Following the 1990 National Conference that ousted Mathieu Kérékou's eighteen-year-long Marxist-Leninist regime, Benin has experimented with multiple forms of political representation. These multiple forms and venues of representation in Benin have been crucial to the legitimacy of Benin's democratic regime. Each has responded to a particular problem of governance central to the collapse of previous governing regimes in Benin and has therefore been designed (or has developed more informally) to address historical problems of misgovernance. With that understanding, the focus here is more on the success or failure of these institutions to address the problems they were designed to solve, rather than more abstract indices of representativeness and effectiveness.

The National Assembly and the Electoral System

Benin's new constitution provides for a unicameral legislature. The initial electoral system established by the Constitutional Commission for the first National Assembly divided the country into six multimember districts (following provincial boundaries), providing for a total of sixty-four seats to be decided by proportional vote, with a threshold of a 5 percent party vote. Voters in each district would vote for party lists established separately in each district. Fearful of an electoral system that would revert to the conflicts of the 1960s, these arrangements were designed to encourage the proliferation of political parties and to discourage the consolidation of two or three ethnoregional parties.

Fourteen political parties won seats in the assembly in 1991, none achieving even one-third of the seats. Electoral support in each historically ethnoregional stronghold was fragmented into multiple parties, although parties associated with the leaders of the 1960s tended to attract substantial support. In order to govern the National Assembly, parties grouped themselves into pro-government, opposition, and independent *groupements,* whose membership tended to shift with a party's changing fortune within the governing coalition and the cabinet (Magnusson 1997, 170–73).

In 1995, eighteen political parties won seats in the Assembly under new electoral rules—eighty-three seats from eighteen multimember districts. The change in electoral rules came only after a lengthy national debate over the most appropriate electoral system. President Soglo, hoping to regain control over the assembly, lobbied for a single-member district plurality system. Popular criticism of the assembly focused on its urban bias and elitism. Most political parties (and most members of the National Assembly) supported a continuation of the proportional system. In order to accomplish the goal of bringing members closer to their constituencies while retaining proportionality, the assembly opted for a system that would triple the number of districts (and thus make them much smaller and more intimate) and increase the total membership by nineteen. Although there is evidence of the increasing consolidation of several regional parties, and only three parties were able to win seats in more than two of the six administrative regions, intra-ethnic regional loyalties remained fragmented. No party won more than 25 percent of the eighty-three seats (*Forum de la Semaine,* February 8, April 5, April 12, April 19, and May 31, 1995; *La Nation,* June 6, 1995). By contrast, the *Renaissance du Benin* party of former president Soglo captured nearly one-third of the seats in the 1999 elections, representing a widening regional influence in the south, at least, by one major party, even as other regional parties lost ground.[13] By contrast, the 2003 elections represented a consolidation of support for President Kérékou. The pro-government group (*Mouvance présidentielle*), composed of multiple (particularly northern-based) political parties, picked up the additional support of Adrien Houngbédji's Porto-Novo based party, giving Kérékou a substantial (if temporary) majority over the diminished opposition.

It is clear that the electoral system has achieved its purpose of supporting a multipartyism that has stymied the historical, three-way, ethnoregional deadlock, while guaranteeing representation not only of the major ethnic groups, but also of smaller groups.[14] The electoral system provides substantial incentives for dissident groups within the ethnoregional blocs to form their own political parties and gain representation either in the National Assembly or, even better, in the cabinet. Despite substantial fragmentation and bickering within the assembly, leaving it without a great deal of policy influence, the importance of this result to democratic legitimacy only really becomes clear when seen in relation to the other regime institutions—the presidency and the Constitutional Court.

Network of Formal Regime Institutions

Political scientists have a tendency to isolate particular regime institutions in comparisons, rather than analyzing how these institutions work together. In addition to trying to understand the advantages and disadvantages of particular types of electoral systems, historical context and positioning within a broader institutional configuration are critical dimensions for understanding how and why these systems may or may not work. For example, people in Benin have long memories of how important social and economic cleavages have been addressed or ignored in the past. From 1960 until the mid-1970s, reaching consensus on how to address perpetual economic crisis was impossible under a system of seemingly intractable ethnoregional deadlock. Under Kérékou's one-party regime, policy consensus was reached, but at the price of economic catastrophe, terrible human rights violations, massive corruption, and the eventual self-destruction of the regime. The Constitutional Commission and the HCR were faced with the task of creating a workable governmental system that would acknowledge ethnoregional aspirations for representation, while preventing both stalemate and renewed intervention by the military. In addition, it would require a fairly strong executive while incorporating credible mechanisms for ensuring the accountability of government officials to prevent egregious opportunities for corruption. A too-strong executive evoked memories of unbridled power, corruption, and human rights abuses. A too-weak executive and ethnoregional stalemate evoked memories of military intervention. Plurality electoral systems in the past had all failed.

While the executive under the new constitution has substantial powers, it must act in concert with the National Assembly for most policy matters, especially for enacting a budget. The National Assembly has substantial executive oversight powers, and when the opposition controls the assembly, these powers have been used. It is almost impossible with the multimember, multidistrict, proportional electoral system in place for the president's political party to control the assembly. Constant coalition-formation and maintenance is a necessity. Shifting alliances within the assembly are manipulated by the president through cabinet appointments, but both President Soglo (1991–96) and President Kérékou (1996–?) have had trouble sustaining either a constant or continuing majority coalition, although the latter has been more successful in consolidating his power in the National Assembly following his reelection in 2001.[15] Nonetheless, these shifting coalitions keep the assembly from developing any real policymaking power. At the same time, the cabinet reshuffles that result become a form of ethnic arithmetic in which no group is ever finally excluded from access to power and state resources.

When stalemates between the executive and legislative branches have developed, the Constitutional Court has taken on the role of arbiter during both the Soglo and Kérékou presidencies. The court established its public legitimacy soon after it was formed by a series of deadlock-breaking decisions against both the president and the National Assembly. These decisions were made according to the letter of the Constitution and were the very first instances in Africa of an independent court deciding against a sitting president. In many respects, the court as arbiter has superseded the historical role played by the military until 1972, and it has since only consolidated its public legitimacy in this role (Magnusson 1999).

A real tradeoff has developed between the relative inefficacy of divided government, that is, an opposition-controlled National Assembly, and the evidence of corruption during periods under both Soglo and Kérékou, when the pro-government coalitions controlled the assembly. Corruption, generally kept to a rather low level during the Soglo administration, intensified during the first three years of Kérékou's administration, rising to dramatic new levels (*Agence France Presse,* July 2, 1999; *La Nation,* no. 2274, July 7, 1999). With the further consolidation of Kérékou's control over the National Assembly following the 2003 elections, the independent and relatively unfettered press will serve as the corruption watchdog, a role it has had few qualms about in the past, revealing real and imagined malfeasance at all levels of government.

The guarantee of regional and ethnic representation (and therefore access to political and economic resources), in a legislature almost necessarily in opposition to or only loosely aligned with the executive, is politically salutary in a context in which a president symbolically represents one particular region, and in which conflict between institutions is effectively regulated by a fair arbiter other than the military. In addition, the gradual implementation of decentralization policies and the elections for local government councils further reduces the extremely dangerous zero-sum political dynamic that continues to afflict African countries. No traditional political grouping faces permanent exclusion from state access in a system in which the electoral opportunities are fluid and dependent on coalition formation. The structure of the system itself guarantees that no coalition will be permanent and that coalitions will remain unstable and weak. While such a system may appear to outsiders to be fragile and ineffective, it does respond to historical memories of exclusion, abuse of power, human rights violations, and corruption—the baseline, after all, of what democracy in Benin is being measured against, and the purpose for which it was constructed.

Network of Representative Venues

When we compare systems of representation, more often than not we focus on legislatures and electoral systems. As noted earlier, Benin's experience until the 1990s in this regard was not a particularly happy one, and even though the proportional, multimember-district system Benin has chosen is not particularly efficient, it does guarantee the representation of ethnic minorities and other communally based groups that would be shut out of a plurality-based, single-member-district system based on the U.S. model. But national legislatures are not the only venue for the representation of communities and interests. For example, the fluidity of party alignments in Benin has guaranteed that no group is permanently shut out of the president's cabinet, since both Soglo and Kérékou have been forced to periodically reconstruct a coalition to work with the National Assembly out of a variety of political parties not confined to any particular ethnoregional grouping.[16] Other extra-constitutional institutions have become important in providing representative space for interests not incorporated by the political parties, most notably in the domains of policymaking and policy implementation. National sector policymaking and the implementation of policy (particularly in the health and education sectors) are two such domains in which formal decentralization plays a key role in providing additional representative opportunities. The de facto (or informal) decentralization resulting from the inability of the state to provide or finance local infrastructure has also provided new opportunities for the representation of interests within local communities, particularly if the allocation of local resources is at stake. Participation in health centers, schools, road-building, and other infrastructure requiring local decision-making has become more vibrant as central state financing has declined.

Estates General (*États-généraux*)

One set of important venues for interest representation in Benin has been the series of national meetings, dubbed the *États-généraux*, to deliberate over specific sector policies. A subset of a whole range of advisory meetings that various leaders have called over the past forty years, the *États-généraux* have been an explicit effort since the National Conference to gather together a variety of interested groups in civil society to contribute to the formulation of specific sector strategies and policies (not unlike the model of the National Conference itself). Participants in these meetings include ministers, bureaucrats, and professionals directly involved in particular policy arenas (e.g., education, territorial administration); local officials; economic groups such as business leaders, farmers, and representatives of regional development associations; teachers and professors; labor unions; women's organizations; and human rights groups. The representation is more corporatist than party-based and reflects a continuing effort since independence to diversify political participation. The Kérékou regime, for example, used an explicit corporatist formula for representation in the Revolutionary National Assembly, abjuring political party and ethnoregional representation (Allen 1989). Since independence in 1960, different forms of these largely advisory bodies have been called on to air grievances, to advise on particularly thorny national questions, or to enhance the authority of whatever regime has requested advice, support, or criticism (Magnusson 1991).

While not incorporated in the constitutional rules of government, the National Conference did propose that a series of meetings of the *États-généraux* be convened, particularly to deal with conflict-laden issues in territorial administration (to help determine the shape and scope of state decentralization) and in the education sector, in order to formulate strategies to rebuild the vital infrastructure devastated by years of neglect and ideological mismanagement. In addition, during the first ten years of the democratic regime, leaders have summoned the *États-généraux* of the military, the judiciary, health, and the national economy to deliberate on policy. The actual record of these meetings is rather mixed, as one might expect. Certainly in the domains of education and territorial administration and decentralization, the proposals emanating from the meetings set the parameters of debate nationally and in the assembly. In other cases, such as the major meeting about the national economy called by President Kérékou, the impetus was probably more to create an atmosphere of national support for continued economic development and reform, or to internalize external conditions, rather than making real, creative policy recommendations. Nevertheless, whatever the motivation, this quasi-institutionalized mechanism of national representation has created at least the illusion, and at most the reality, of real civil society participation in national policymaking and governance. It also replicates on the national scale representations of generational, occupational, and gender interests that are often observable in governance at the local levels both by village chiefs and royal families.

Local Policymaking

Further reducing the stakes in national electoral contests, increasing decentralization of both policymaking and implementation has, in some cases, provided substantial local control over local resources. Given the financial constraints of a very poor country under the restrictions of IMF and World Bank programs, more and more responsibility for local infrastructure has been decentralized by default as well as by express policy. Local development associations created during the Marxist era as a mechanism for rural mobilization under the one-party framework have transformed themselves into especially vigorous tools for local development projects, agenda setting, and financial resources, while shedding the monopoly the PRPB exercised over them. In the north especially, the cotton boom has generated substantial new sources of local financing, and the development associations have informally taxed these resources for community benefits. While restricted during the Marxist period to one development association per district, the democratic transition has permitted the multiplication of such associations, often organized by political rivals. In fact, it was the Constitutional Court, in a ruling based on the African Charter of Human Rights, which forbade the Ministry of Interior from arbitrarily setting limits on the number, membership, and charters of these organizations (Magnusson 1999, 226–27). These have become an emergent political training ground at the local level.

In the health sector, new systems of local management and cost recovery programs have kept increasing amounts of money under local management. Local health councils are elected bodies at the small-district level, and are designed to ensure representation of elders, women, and youth. Local intellectuals such as teachers or agricultural agents often serve as officers on these councils. Funding is provided through a national generic drug cost-recovery program, in which sales of drugs (at much lower than name-brand prices) and minimal fees for medical services are kept at local levels for infrastructure and development purposes. A complex system of local, multilayered financial accountability has kept these accounts fairly clean. Remarkably, the local health councils often have substantially more resources at their disposal (often in time deposit accounts) than the local government itself. These funds have been fed back into community development, especially the health infrastructure, but also in providing energy assistance during oil shortages, and financing for road, school, and market repairs and maintenance (Magnusson 1997, 207–37).

In the education sector, too, local parent associations and their elected representatives are often forced to make do with meager national resources. With no source of funding such as exists in the health sector other than the state-set school fees, these organizations have much less to work with and find themselves organizing the community around work projects while combing local, national, and international nongovernmental organizations, as well as local health and government agencies, for support. School fees, at rates set by the national government, are occasionally modified upward by teacher-parent organizations in order to pay for needed maintenance. Parent associations, both in the administrative regions and nationally, have begun the difficult process of organizing themselves into a more cohesive interest group in order to make more coherent and powerful claims on the central government (Magnusson 1997, 237–70).

What has become clear, though, is that both by design and by default, the central government is less of an overt player in local communities. Local governments and sector institutions are no longer controlled by a single-party apparatus designed more for patronage purposes than policymaking and implementation. People are able to see the effects of local voting in these areas, and accountability at the local level is increasing as a result.

Policing is one area in which the process of ceding centralized state control to more representative institutions has encountered some real tradeoffs for regime legitimacy. With the contraction of the reach of the central state, the collapse of authoritarian institutions, and the concomitant devolution of authority to local government and traditional leaders, there has been a corresponding increase in crime, banditry, and more localized forms of insecurity. While militias organized around ethnoregional leaders, which emerged in places like the Republic of Congo, have not emerged in Benin, gangs and even quasi-legitimized neighborhood security organizations have, in some places, created the seeds of a semi-privatized security apparatus verging on organized crime. These may be associated with local political authorities, male youth groups, or religious groups in more traditional watchdog roles, which in certain circumstances have increased insecurity for other religious groups, women, and outsiders, particularly at night. Devolution and decentralization, therefore, are not always state-planned processes, but can also be the result of state incapacity. In cases where these processes result in locally planned and managed development and infrastructure investment, it is certainly positive for the legitimacy of the democratic regime. In cases where the result is increased insecurity and corruption by those who take advantage of the failure of state capacity to provide controls, its effect on the legitimacy of democracy is more problematic (Magnusson 2001).[17]

The National Assembly is one of several venues of representation in Benin, and depending upon where one sits, not necessarily the most important. Taken together, these venues represent an interlocking system of opportunities for representation based on region, ethnicity, occupational position, age cohort, gender, traditional status, level of education, and so forth. At the national level, historical experience generated a system based on inclusion, rather than exclusion. Local norms about how power should be allocated among groups and, just as importantly, norms about how power should be held accountable, have been vital considerations in legitimizing Benin's democratic institutions and, therefore, their survival.

Situating Benin in a Transnational and Regional Context

Small, weak states are particularly buffeted by their position in international and regional markets, associations, and political structures.[18] Benin has been both a victim and an opportunist in the regional, transnational game. Much of Benin's wealth is tied up in the transshipment trade in West Africa (Igue and Soule 1992). With family, business, and identity ties crossing borders in this part of Africa, national identity is not only a function of state power, but is constructed out of a panoply of internal and external ingredients. To the extent that national identity becomes bound together with "democracy," both take on a certain transnational character. Benin's position in the West African regional economy as a financial and trading center of multiple informal and formal economic networks lends democratic openness to a globalizing economy, with a certain regional utility that generates support from unlikely sources. Certainly the flow of Nigerian capital into the increasingly Nigerian-owned banking sector in Benin generates questions about the regional role of democratic and open regimes that require further research. Benin's security as a state and as a democracy is as dependent on its relationship with its regional neighbors and the international community as it is on the multiple insecurity dilemmas it faces internally (Job 1992, 11–35; Jackson 1992, 83; Ayoob 1995, 176–80; Magnusson 2001). Transnational networks of families, civic associations, NGOs, and businesses provide some protection from the hazards of economic dependence on Nigeria (and Europe), as well as from the hazards of local politics, but similar networks are also held responsible for deepening social insecurity regarding crime and the failures of state security forces.

Even if we embrace the idiosyncratic factor that elite choice and human agency will always add to institutional explanation, if we shift our focus from institutional configurations (and the relative stasis that the concept implies) to more fluid notions about *becoming* democratic, we can begin to explore what it is that becomes constitutive of democracy in regional and global contexts that are also somewhat fluid. This requires adopting an understanding of democracy and its survival as dynamic. Institutions are not democratic absent their agents; agents are not democratic absent their institutions. To what extent does national identity necessarily become co-constitutive with democracy and to what degree is a democratic identity bound up with structural and security factors (political economy, geography, demography, external and internal threats), in addition to institutional factors? If we can accept that national identity is in some measure a result of these situational variables, what role does national identity play in the survival of democratic institutions, and vice versa?[19] What follows is suggestive of the kinds of relationships it would prove fruitful to examine in more analytical depth, thus illustrating why there are no easy answers to the initial question of why democracy has survived in Benin and elsewhere, but not in other countries.

As a country dependent on its economic position as a major transshipment point, lubricating markets all over West Africa, Benin requires an increasingly open gate to its own markets, particularly as it reduces its economic dependence on France and seeks to increase its access to formal and informal markets in the region— especially in Nigeria, but also in the landlocked Sahel. What is true for goods to be traded is also true for the financial facilities necessary to move those products and the people involved in the vast trading networks that do the moving. The openness of democratic institutions and their accessibility to all (or most) social, ethnic, and regional groups enhances the effectiveness of the particular economic functions that Benin performs in the West African region. The value of transnational family, ethnic, religious, and commercial ties is especially important in this context, but raises important questions about national identity and domestic security.

National identity in Benin is a fluid and complex amalgam of many different internally and externally generated elements. A former French colony, the primary state language is French. Benin is a member of the official and unofficial Francophone community of states. Indeed, it hosted the 1995 *Francophonie* conference of states. At the same time, Benin has made a continuing effort to valorize the multiple languages indigenous to the country—ranging from an unwieldy and failed effort during the Kérékou era to force the teaching of local languages in the schools to more recent efforts to increase adult and child literacy in these languages, in addition to French. As a would-be lingua franca uniting not only the diversity of Benin, but the even more diverse former French empire, the French language also carries critical colonial and neocolonial baggage. In the aftermath of the 1994 CFA currency devaluation, Professor Guy Midiohouan, for example, in his critique of *francophonie,* states forthrightly that the prefix "franco- has become our castrator, our first reality, the beating heart of our cultures, the living source of our energies, the sublime crucible of our identities. . . . We must become conscious that in Africa we are first and foremost, not francophones as they seek to convince us, but Africans" (1994).[20]

Identity entrepreneurs, such as the historian Bio Bigou, are engaged in research and production of the recovered narratives of groups in Benin whose history was repressed, if not dismantled, during the colonial and postcolonial periods. Genuine pride for the National Conference and the model it established for peaceful transitions to democracy coexists uncomfortably with the less happy democratic transitions in the surrounding states—Togo, whose transition was aborted; Niger and the military coup ending its initial transition; the discredited Compaoré transition in Burkina Faso; and Nigeria's endless tumultuous efforts to find a workable democracy following the brutality of the Sani Abacha dictatorship. This rearticulation of the past, the celebration of Benin's religious traditions after a century of repression and the desire to create a genuine African democracy, lie at the heart of an emergent and vibrant national identity closely tied to the historical and cultural transformations of democracy.

The sheer complexity of relationships between Benin and its neighbors feeds not only a fluid sense of national identity through the security of familiarity, kinship, and finance but also reinforces identity through the national insecurity entailed by such proximity. Regime differences are a clear source of pride, as are cross-border family relationships through intermarriage; ethnic heritage; solidarity networks fused by university cohorts (in France and Senegal, for example) and social class; and common commercial relationships that crosscut all of·these. Political refugees from Togo and Nigeria in the early 1990s are blamed for an ever-increasing urban and rural crime wave. Drug gangs from Nigeria have been accused of using Benin's openness as a cog in the transcontinental drug trade. Nigeria, generally, is viewed as a dangerous place, and the source of most criminal activity, even as the commercial and kinship ties across that border remain one of Benin's most important economic resources.

Democracy, in this context, plays an ambiguous role. On the one hand, it is a source of pride and differentiation. Simultaneously, democracy (with Nigeria) is blamed for what is perceived to be a growing gap between the values of domestic harmony and the dangers on urban streets and rural highways. It is this ambiguity between democracy as a solution to public ills and democracy as a generator of new kinds of insecurity that remains unresolved. It is in the articulation of these various strands of public perception and intellectual effort with the continuing experimentation with democratic institutions that simultaneously create an "authentically" Beninese democracy steeped in its own particular context of power, representation, and accountability—a democracy whose more global institutional templates are forced to adapt, adjust, and incorporate. In other words, it is necessary to analyze democracies as purposeful and fluid responses to specific circumstances in a broader transnational and regional context.

How the Treacherous Single Case Might Yield Useful Questions

The choice of regime configuration, an electoral system, and choices about how representation (and power) should be allocated have emerged, in this case, as responses to historical experience. Because group exclusion, abuse of power, and uncontrolled corruption by the few were important factors in the collapse of the one-party state, elites found it necessary to address group threat reduction, ethnoregional distribution issues, and accountability if democracy was to survive following the transition. National purpose is a necessary baseline factor in analyzing the efficacy of an electoral system, as well as institutional choice, in a democracy. Proportionality might very likely have been a failure if, as in Niger and the Republic of Congo, power had been divided between a president and a parliamentary prime minister without a publicly legitimate arbiter such as a Constitutional Court available and capable of resolving institutional conflict. In Niger, the military intervened as arbiter. In Benin, institutional mechanisms were (for the first time in Benin's history) able to mediate the standoff between president and legislature, without recourse to extra-constitutional (military) solutions. In Niger and Congo-Brazzaville, the institutional configuration provided no such constraints on military intervention, but rather created the opportunity (if not the incentives) for military elites to ignore constitutional rules and to take power.

Formal representation in the National Assembly is only one element of a more complex network of representative institutions in Benin. Ethnoregional interests are gathered together in no other single institution. Structurally almost incapable of consistent and steady policymaking capacity, the National Assembly functions, when in opposition, as an important watchdog over executive action, while having some, but limited, influence over real policy. Instead, the kind of occupational and functional representation in the meetings of the *États-généraux* provides broad representative outlets for very different kinds of groups in the setting of public policy goals against which the more formal institutions of state will be measured. Locally, representation responds to decision-making mechanisms more resonant with traditional, local allocations of power—the representation of elders, women, and youth, for example, on the local health councils.

Historical contingency, formal regime structure, and the density of representational venues and opportunities all appear to be important factors supporting the survival of Benin's democratic institutions. All are deeply related to regime legitimacy. Since norms are clearest when they are violated, the abstractions of the normative dimension of democracy take on substantive shape when the public protests blatant abuses of power by the police, or when the press exposes outrageous levels of corruption, or when students ponder the irony that democratization has resulted in the fragmentation (and therefore increased the inefficacy) of their national union. But, democratic legitimacy is also about rewiring institutional machinery so that it operates according to new rules. It is, therefore, about procedure as well as norms, and the Constitutional Court has reinforced the idea that procedural rectitude is an indispensable piece of the puzzle of democratic legitimacy in Benin. Performance is important, too, but the legitimating resources of performance include much more than economic well-being. It is not only measured against the material failures of the past but also against the normative content that the idea of democracy holds in the minds of its citizens. The ability and will to dismiss electorally two consecutive presidents and, in 1995, 80 percent of the National Assembly, illustrates not only a performing democracy, but a reinvigoration of deeply held norms, and the procedures by which those norms hold officeholders to account.

It is a mistake, though, to ignore the regional and transnational context in which these experiments in democratic rule are being carried out. The transnationalization of national identity and its attendant norms and expectations must be related as well to Benin's position in the regional economy of West Africa. What this relationship is should certainly be a subject of further research, raising important questions about the role and influence of international and regional structure, transnational norms and processes, as well as the agency inherent in the extremely hard and frustrating work of democratic governance. Should the question really be, "Is democracy consolidated in Benin?" Or is the question, "Have the institutions of democracy created in Benin been able to address the fundamental political problems of representation and the distribution of power that have plagued Benin since independence?" Also: "What are the internal and external (and transnational) dimensions of democratic survival?" and "How is Benin's somewhat unique position as a regional trade and finance distribution center related to the survival of democracy in that country?" To my mind, the latter questions are the prior ones, and until we have a good handle on those, the question of consolidation is premature. While these are primarily institutional questions, they really cannot be answered without understanding the relationships among elite behavior, institutional choice, structural and normative context, and the constraints or opportunities those institutions subsequently place on leaders and publics. Survival, from this perspective, depends as much on (primarily) elite choices as it does on institutional incentives and constraints.

Finally, and with regard to the comparative indicators of democratization, the Benin case illustrates that anomalous cases can yield questions, such as those mentioned above, that may be useful for researchers to pursue in non-anomalous cases. Context is still crucial. If the complexity of formal and informal regime configurations as a purposeful response (rather than a template response) to specific historical and regional circumstances can help explain why democracy thrives in a country where "it should not," we might be well-advised to rethink our explanations for those cases that "fit" the models, or at least be quite wary about substituting variables for explanations.

NOTES

1. This is a point made in general in Green (2002), and in particular by Kurt Burch in his chapter in that volume, 69–72.

2. The concept of regime legitimacy is discussed in much more depth in Magnusson (1997).

3. In fact, the authors make the suggestion that their analysis of human rights norms could also be applied to democratization (38). On the importance of norms to democratic legitimacy, see Larry Diamond (1999a) and Magnusson (1997).

4. Although Kérékou took power in 1972, he did not create the Marxist-Leninist regime until 1974.

5. The Presidential Council under this constitution consisted of Hubert Maga, Justin Ahomadégbé, and Sourou-Migan Apithy. The presidency of the council was to rotate every two years. Hubert Maga filled the first two-year term, Ahomadégbé was to fill the second, and Apithy the third. Each had a power of veto over policy. Ahomadégbé was a member of the royal family from Abomey, the seat of the kings of the historical, expansionist, precolonial Dahomean state. Apithy was the leader from Porto Novo, the third of the ethnoregional seats of power (Ronen 1968; Decalo 1987).

6. The details of the various electoral systems over the years in Dahomey and Benin are discussed in part or in whole in Ronen (1968), Decalo (1987), Glélé (1969), Allen (1989), and Magnusson (1997).

7. In 1974, President Kérékou changed the name of Dahomey to the People's Republic of Benin (la République Populaire du Bénin), choosing a name of a regional precolonial power without the internal political overtones of Dahomey (at least outside of Nigeria).

8. Boulaga (1993) describes the religious, almost sacramental quality of these dramatic events.

9. Apithy had died by this time. This question was decided in the referendum on the Constitution. Voters could vote an unconditional yes, a modified yes (without the age-limit provision), or no.

10. The commission was led by Maurice Glélé, the respected constitutional scholar. Noudjenoume (1999) provides a more critical perspective on the drafting of the Constitution.

11. Electoral systems in Benin are in the domain of legislation and are not, therefore, specified in the Constitution.

12. By "traditional," I am referring to those aspects of everyday life that are generally referred to locally as traditional in contrast to those that are referred to locally as "modern." It is understood that this dichotomy is problematic, but it also expresses a common understanding of the duality of everyday life that finds deliberate expression on a daily basis.

13. It is clear that the coalition supporting President Kérékou lost its majority in the National Assembly, while the coalition supporting the Soglo machine gained substantially. Soglo's party, led by Mme. Rosine Soglo, captured twenty-seven of eighty-three seats, making it the largest party delegation.

14. Crawford Young (1976) discusses how differing ethnic configurations require different institutional management mechanisms.

15. Nicéphore Soglo, appointed by the National Conference as the transitional prime minister responsible to the HCR, was elected president in 1991, defeating Mathieu Kérékou (the former Marxist dictator) by a two-to-one margin. A "reformed" Kérékou, now committed to democratic institutions, defeated Soglo in 1996 by a lesser margin. Although Kérékou's coalition in the National Assembly suffered electoral setbacks in the 1999 National Assembly elections, his reelection in 2001 and the success of his coalition in the 2003 National Assembly elections have given him a rather clear policymaking majority, at least temporarily.

16. In the U.S. and European contexts, Krislov and Rosenbloom (1981) developed the concept of representative bureaucracies. Because of the clear connections between patronage and government ministers in African bureaucracies, the concept of representative bureaucracy becomes relevant to the ethnoregional arithmetic of presidential cabinets.

17. Note the similarities with youth-organized security systems in Tanzania (Abrahams 1989); more generally here, Brian Job (1992) and Mohammed Ayoob (1995) are especially suggestive.

18. See Magnusson (2002) for an expansion of this argument.

19. For more on the constructivist contribution to comparative politics generally, and on the role of identity in particular, see Green (2002).

20. This analysis is reminiscent of Ngugi wa Thiong'o's analysis of language politics in Kenya (1986).

5 | The Collapse of the Democratic Experiment in the Republic of Congo
A Thick Description

John F. Clark

The Congolese experiment with multiparty democracy that began in 1991 was ended in 1997 by willful human agents, who certainly understood that their actions would likely terminate the ongoing experiment.[1] On June 5, 1997, in the midst of a presidential election campaign for a contest then scheduled for late July, Congolese President Pascal Lissouba dispatched a unit of the army forces to the Mpila neighborhood of Brazzaville to arrest "certain associates" of his main rival, former President Denis Sassou-Nguesso ("Sassou"). Sassou was well prepared for the challenge, however, and his private militia successfully prevented his arrest or that of any of his partisans. Lissouba subsequently sent larger and larger contingents of military forces to arrest Sassou and disarm his militia, but these efforts were met by ever more numerous militiamen, who rallied to Sassou's defense from Mbochi-dominated parts of the city. Within days, the capital was engulfed in a full-scale civil war that soon spread to parts of the countryside over the ensuing weeks. The war proved frightfully resistant to the outside mediation of numerous parties. When Sassou returned to power through force of arms in October 1997, and with the support of foreign interveners, the Congolese experiment with democracy begun in 1992 was over.

In keeping with the primary goal of this volume, this chapter offers an empirical enquiry into the collapse of the Congolese experiment. The case of Congo stands in considerable contrast to most of the others presented in this volume. Whereas most of the others have hobbled along in some form or another, Congo's experiment (like that in the CAR) underwent a dramatic collapse in the midst of civil war. In the aftermath of the collapse, the country's former dictator has returned to power and run the country in an authoritarian manner. The elections that Sassou staged in 2002 were fraudulent and designed primarily to legitimate his continuing presence in power, and thus *do not* represent a return to genuine democratic experimentation. Whereas cases such as Guinea-Bissau and Niger subsequently renewed their experiments with democratic governance following military coups (that proved to be only a hiatus in democratic experimentation), Congo has not. Accordingly, it represents the most complete failure to make progress toward democratic governance of any case in this volume over the period under study.

Beyond the empirical goal of presenting an analysis of the failure of the Congolese experiment, this chapter also represents a statement on how researchers can understand—though not *explain*—the variable outcomes that follow the advent of democratic experiments. The analytical framework for understanding the outcome of democratic experiments is based on the conclusion that such outcomes are not foreordained, particularly not at any given moment in time. Careful theorists of democratic consolidation may have been able to make well-founded, educated guesses about the prospects of survival of the Congolese experiment over a specified period of time. The more ambitious of such theorists might even have ventured a probability. The same theoretical observers, moreover, would likely have assigned a similar probability to the likelihood of democratic survival for the case of Benin. As we know, however, the experiment with formal multiparty democracy begun in 1990 is ongoing as of 2004, having now survived three presidential elections with the constitution, rule of law, and basic public order intact.

The fact of the survival of Benin's democratic experiment should give us pause in considering the failure of the experiment in Congo. After all, Benin and Congo share a great many things in common: a former colonizer, intensive ("neocolonial") relations with the same former colonizer, and a pre-democratic past that was nominally Marxist-Leninist but actually authoritarian-military. Both states are also of small size and boast strong intellectual classes. Moreover, northern military officers ruled both Congo and Benin during the years of their "Marxist-Leninist" experiments, while there is a fundamental split between northerners and southerners in both cases. In both cases as well, northerners suffer from demographic inferiority and there is a legacy of social advantages to southerners. The survival of Beninese democracy in social conditions not so different from those of Congo thus makes the case far more intriguing than it would be otherwise. Meanwhile, two major differences between the two cases also stand out: first, Congo suffers from the "curse of resources" in terms of its petroleum endowment, a "burden" that Benin does not share; second, the institutional arrangements of Benin and Congo were different in a number of regards, especially in that Benin's did not allow the possibility of French Fifth Republic–style cohabitation. Each of these differences is explored below as possible keys to understanding the divergent outcomes in the Congolese and Beninese democratic experiments.

The above recitation of events leading to the demise of the Congolese experiment may seem to identify the actions of specific agents as the "cause" of democratic breakdown, but it really only identifies them as the *instruments* of democratic failure. Like all social agents, those who ended Congo's democratic experiment were embedded firmly in social and political contexts that shaped, channeled, and conditioned their acts. The dictum of Marx may be among the most hackneyed of social analysis, but no less shrewd for its overuse: "Men make their own history, but they do not make it just as they please; they do not make it under circumstances chosen by themselves, but under circumstances directly found, given and transmitted from the past" (1978, 595). Giddens, among others, has given over a considerable part of his career to fleshing out the idea, though his vocabulary sometimes obscures this basic fact. It is an inevitable starting point for the analysis of virtually any dramatic social event, be it Louis Napoleon's 1851 coup, Yelstin's attack on the Russian parliament in 1993, or Lissouba's decision to arrest Sassou in June 1997.

Those who study democratization, either in the "transition" or "consolidation" phases, are particularly likely to specify that one must be aware both of agents' choices and the structural frameworks of action; see Linz (1978, 4); Przeworksi (1986, 47); Przeworksi and Limongi (1997, 177); and Young (1999, 34). With regard to the specific problem of democratic breakdown, Juan Linz was perhaps the first to argue specifically that both agents and structures must be taken into account in understanding this specific social phenomenon. In his opening presentation of the problem, Linz at once acknowledges the element of free will in democratic survival or consolidation and the undeniable weight of socioeconomic circumstances in constraining the behavior of individual agents:

> In our view, one cannot ignore the actions of either those who are more or less interested in the maintenance of an open democratic political system or those who, placing other values higher, are unwilling to defend it or even ready to overthrow it. These are the actions that constitute the true dynamics of the political process. We feel that the structural characteristics of societies—their actual and latent conflicts—constitute a series of opportunities and constraints for the social and political actors, both [individuals] and institutions, that can lead to one or another outcome. (Linz 1978, 4)

In this case, too, then, one must pay attention to both agents' actions and their social contexts. One only need add that the actions that ended Congo's democratic experiment were hardly the first to be relevant to democratic survival. There were many occasions when the democratic experiment was severely threatened before June 1997, but it managed to survive. The actions of agents at those moments merit our attention, too, since they speak to both the motives and intentions of the key actors, and to the changing nature of social circumstances. Yet none of the socioeconomic conditions that Congo faced *forced* the agents to act as they did.

Some of those who engage in the scientific study of social phenomena, including democratic experiments, do generously allow that there is a place for the case study in the accumulation of our social knowledge (King, Keohane, and Verba 1994, 34–35). Moreover, such epistemological theorists assign the student of the case the apparently simple task of "analytical description"—that is, merely to identity the one variable that *explains* the outcome for the chosen case (ibid., 43–45). Those researchers who engage in the rigorous comparative work can then make use of the conclusions about the case to reach "scientific inferences" applicable to the social world in general. Unfortunately, it is often not possible to either identify one single variable that "explains" a case, or even to assign some quantitative value to the influence of various factors that coalesce to produce a given outcome. Those who study specific cases in great detail and during other long periods become particularly aware of this epistemological conundrum. In keeping with the spirit of Linz's position, this chapter will describe the actions of the individuals who destroyed the Congolese democratic experiment and will attempt to put those actions in their socioeconomic context. This paper will thus provide a kind of "thick description" of the failure of democracy in Congo.[2] Thus, while this chapter eschews the pretense of scientific explanation of the case, it attempts to provide the mature student of democratic experimentation with an understanding of the case's failure. More detail on the nature of the kind of description offered here comes at the conclusion of the following section, which briefly recounts the course of the Congolese democratic experiment in outline.

Historical Overview

A few succinct observations on the advent and demise of the Congolese experiment will set the stage for our discussion. Congo's experience with multiparty politics prior to 1992 was limited to a brief period at the end of the colonial era continuing into the first two years of independence. The Congo Republic did not exist, of course, as a distinctive territorial state until colonial times. During the colonial period itself, the country naturally did not gain experience with democratic norms or institutions. Although the colonial period ended with a French bequest of nominally democratic, multiparty institutions, metropolitan and local French authorities played a major role in the country's first legislative and presidential elections (Bernault 1996, 264–93). Before any subsequent (and freer) election could be held under the new constitution, Congo was already in the grip of "revolutionary" leaders who did not envision a short-term return to procedural democracy. Whatever the intentions of those who ended the nominal democracy of 1960–63, those who followed merely used revolutionary rhetoric as a cover for a succession of transparently authoritarian and military-dominated regimes.[3]

Congo's democratic transition issued from a political reform movement that gathered steam at the end of the Cold War, and culminated in a national conference from February to June 1991 (Clark 1993; Quantin 1997). Following the Beninese example, the Congolese national conference temporarily reduced the powers of the presidency to those of a figurehead. This step allowed President Denis Sassou-Nguesso, who had been president since 1979 under the one-party state, to remain temporarily in office. Meanwhile, the conference set up an interim government under the authority of André Milongo, a former international civil servant. This administration wielded real power during the transition. The conference also put in place the mechanisms to draw up a new constitution, duly approved in a referendum in March 1992. Under this new constitution, Pascal Lissouba, a former prime minister

(1963–66), political prisoner (1973, 1976–79), and UNESCO official (1980–90), was elected to the presidency in the second round of elections held in August 1992.

Over the course of its short life, the Congolese experiment with multiparty politics underwent a series of severe challenges. The first crises began in the transitional period. One involved efforts by the transitional government to rein in the army, accompanied by alleged coup plots; a second involved alleged cheating by the transitional government in the local and municipal elections of May 1992 (Clark 1997, 69–70). Soon after the election of Pascal Lissouba, however, a far more serious crisis erupted. This one was occasioned by the collapse of the president's coalition in Parliament. Lissouba had won the second round of the 1992 elections by forging a partnership with former President Sassou. Through this alliance, Lissouba not only won the presidency, but also controlled a majority in the assembly. His own *Union Panafricaine pour la Démocratie Sociale* (UPADS) party held thirty-nine seats and Sassou's *Parti Congolais du Travail* (PCT) held eighteen after the legislative elections; with the cooperation of some smaller parties, Lissouba's coalition achieved a majority in the 125–seat body. When Lissouba announced the formation of his first government in September, however, Sassou's PCT only received three minor cabinet posts. Insulted, Sassou bolted the coalition and made an alliance with Lissouba's strongest competitor, Bernard Kolélas. Kolélas himself had finished second in the presidential balloting, and his *Mouvement Congolais pour le Développement et la Démocratie Intégrale* (MCDDI) party had won twenty-nine seats in the assembly, the second-highest total. Rather than naming a prime minister from this opposition coalition, Lissouba dissolved the assembly and ordered the holding of new elections the following year.

The opposition did not concede to this "solution," however, and a major confrontation ensued. According to any honest reading of the constitution, Lissouba should have named a prime minister from the majority (opposition) coalition in the assembly.[4] When the opposition demonstrated outside the presidency in December, the first blood of the conflict was spilled. Lissouba's presidential guard eventually fired on the protesters, killing three persons. Towards the end of the year, the crisis was temporarily resolved when Lissouba was persuaded to appoint a "national unity" government, headed by a neutral prime minister. Congo's new multiparty system had just survived its first test, though not very gracefully.

The re-run of the legislative elections in May 1993 marked the beginning of a far more serious crisis, Congo's first "civil war." In the presence of numerous international observers, Lissouba's new coalition of his UPADS and many smaller parties (the "Presidential Domain") won a total of sixty-two seats in the assembly. With eleven seats still undecided because of a lack of majority in the first round, it was clear that Lissouba had won a majority. Citing "monstrous frauds and irregularities," however, the opposition rejected the results of the election.[5] At this point, Congo's notorious militia groups made their first appearance on the scene (Bazenguissa-Ganga 1994). A militia group loyal to opposition leader Kolélas (the "Ninjas") took control over the neighborhoods of Bacongo and Makélékélé, those largely populated by the Lari people whose champion was Kolélas. This militia began to purge the neighborhoods of Diata and Mfilou of those who came from the southern regions. These neighborhoods were populated mainly by residents from Niari, Bouenza, and Lekoumou ("Nibolek"), the regions that had overwhelmingly supported Lissouba in the elections. When the second round of voting was held on June 6, the opposition boycotted. In the aftermath of these elections, which were later struck down by the Supreme Court, the fighting between Kolélas's Ninjas and the government forces nearly reached the point of civil war. Meanwhile, however, cooler heads had organized major mediation efforts by neutral Congolese political figures, international diplomats, and Gabonese president Omar Bongo throughout the months of June and July. On August 4, these efforts reached fruition in the Libreville Accords, which arranged for the arbitration of the disputed seats by a special international jury and specified procedures for the re-run of elections to fill the unresolved seats (Zartman and Vogeli 2000, 273–76).

In October, elections were rerun for the eleven seats in which no majority was gained in the first round of elections. The results yielded three more seats for the Presidential Domain and eight more for the opposition coalition. The three additional seats gave the Presidential Domain an undisputed majority in the assembly. This development caused the opposition groups to boycott the opening of the new assembly session, and led to a renewal of violence in the streets. The violence was even worse this time, with further rounds of ethnic cleansing and incredible violence aimed at the representatives of rival ethnoregional constituencies. The worst of the killing took place between November 1993 and January 1994 when Lissouba finally ordered the shelling of the Bacongo and Makélékélé neighborhoods. During this round of fighting, like that in May–July, former president Sassou and his Cobra militia mostly stood on the sidelines.

In the case of this conflict, it was entirely the Congolese themselves who restored peace, chiefly through an interregional committee in the assembly, composed of deputies from the two warring sides (Zartman and Vogeli 2000, 278). By January 31, the basic accord was in place, and peace returned gradually to the country, though marked with specific outbreaks of violence. In January 1995, Lissouba reached a new agreement with Kolélas, then his key opponent, in which the latter's party, the MCDDI, gained cabinet posts, including the interior ministry, in a new government named by Lissouba. Relative peace prevailed in Congo from the middle of 1994 through the first months of 1997, at which time the start of the next presidential election campaign got underway.

Sadly for Congo, the 1997 re-election campaign proved to be the context in which the country's shaky civil peace—and democratic experiment—was destroyed. The fragile peace of the campaign was first broken in the northern region of Cuvette, from whence hailed two former Congolese presidents: Sassou and Joachim Yhombi-Opango, the latter of whom had joined the Lissouba government in 1993 at the height of the first electoral standoff. In early May, when Sassou sought to be carried into Yhombi's hometown of Owando on a ceremonial chair of the kind reserved for chiefs, violence broke out between Yhombi's (mostly Kouyou) supporters and Sassou's (mostly Mbochi) bodyguards (Pourtier 1998, 18). A bout of fighting between the supporters of Yhombi and Sassou in the towns of Oyo and Owando ensued, leaving several persons dead. Before the fighting got out of hand, however, outside mediators again intervened. In this instance, UNESCO director-general Federico Mayor persuaded the feuding politicians to sign a pledge to refrain from any further violence during the campaign on May 31.

Although the advocates of peace in Congo surely breathed a sigh of relief when this accord was signed, their hopes were soon dashed. On June 5, 1997, government forces surrounded Sassou's residence in Mpila with a mission to arrest two of Sassou's associates implicated in the Owando violence and to seize the arms of the Cobras. Since Sassou's Cobras had already organized the residence as a virtual armed camp, however, the arrests could not be effected, and fighting broke out. This fighting soon spread to the surrounding neighborhoods, and eventually to all of Brazzaville. What followed was a four-month-long civil war between Sassou's well-armed militia, on one side, and the government forces that remained loyal to Lissouba, as well as to his own militia, on the other (Clark 1998a). Kolélas (and his militia) initially remained neutral, and Kolélas even tried to mediate the dispute. Lissouba finally persuaded him to join his government in September. Before his forces could have any impact on the stalemated war, however, a more important intervener had joined the fray: the Angolan armed forces. In apparent revenge for Lissouba's embrace of UNITA, Angola sent thousands of its troops into Congo on behalf of Sassou, allowing him to seize the country's key installations in October 1997.

Having seized control of the capital through foreign assistance, Sassou slowly consolidated his grip over the rest of the country during the following years. He employed both neo-patrimonial cooptation and raw force to achieve this objective. His efforts to put a legal gloss on the new regime began with a conference, the *"Forum sur la Réconciliation Nationale,"* which he organized in January 1998. This conference put in place a transitional legislature of carefully vetted supporters, leavened with a sprinkling of "moderate opposition" defectors. The real opposition, composed of Kolélas's and Lissouba's main supporters, remained in exile outside the country. Uprisings in the southern regions of the country in late 1998 provided Sassou with the pretext to send in his reorganized army, supported by Angolan troops and Rwandan Hutu mercenaries (Le Pape and Salignon 2001). The opposition forces signed a ceasefire agreement in December 1999 that amounted to a virtual surrender. It was only in this war—the most devastating in Congo yet—that Sassou consolidated his grip over the country's southern regions. In 2001 the Sassou government drew up a new constitution that prevented exiled politicians from seeking office and placed most political power in the hands of the president. This new constitution was nominally debated during that year in a process euphemistically called the *"Dialogue National Sans Exclusive"* (Open National Dialogue) and adopted through a public referendum in January 2002. Sassou won an overwhelming victory in the presidential elections in March, following the withdrawal of the only significant opposition figure shortly before the election on grounds that the elections were rigged. In equally dubious elections, pro-Sassou parties won a majority of seats in the new parliament in the legislative elections held in May and June 2002. The turnout was markedly low in all of the regions and urban districts known to be hostile to Sassou. In this classic way, Sassou put a veneer of democratic legitimacy on a regime that depended heavily on French diplomatic and financial support and on Angola's continuing military presence.

The key questions raised by the failure of the Congolese experiment are three-fold. First, how much freedom of action did the individual agents have in the actions they took that bore on the trajectory of the democratic experiment? Second, which structural contexts exerted the most influence on the actions of the major state agents? And, third, how did the various structural contexts of the democratic experiment interact with one another to support or undermine the prospects for democratic consolidation?

To address these questions, the sections below describe and evaluate the significance of six sociopolitical contexts of the Congolese democratic experiment. These include the institutional context, the economic class context, the ethnoregional context, the neocolonial context, the military context, and the politico-cultural context. Each of them helps us to understand the overall context of political actions that caused the Congolese democratic experiment to unravel decisively in June 1997. While the number of contexts is regrettably large, none can be dismissed in a full consideration of the events surrounding the democratic collapse. In understanding the end of Congo's democratic experiment, the primary challenge is to specify these sociopolitical contexts and the linkages among them. Each section also considers how much each structural context constrained the freedom of action of the key agents. The final section offers a summary judgment on the freedom of action of these agents and discusses which structural conditions were most important in prompting the actions that led to the democratic collapse.

The Institutional Context

In keeping with the key theme of this volume, the analysis of the collapse of Congo's democratic experiment begins with attention to the institutional structure. In general, for societies with well-developed socioeconomic classes, the key institutional challenge for transitional democracies is to find a formula that allows for a (perceptually) equitable distribution of national income among all classes. For Congo, and most other African states, the key institutional challenge is to provide for an equitable distribution of political power and economic resources among a plurality of ethnic or ethnoregional groups (Mozaffar 1995). The introduction to this volume explores many other specific facets of the linkage between institutional choice and the fate of democratic experiments.

Aside from the theoretical literature, several other cases in this volume provide prima facie evidence for the importance of institutional arrangements. Perhaps the most striking institutional problem faced by all of the former French colonies included in this study is that most adopted constitutions with structural similarities to the constitution of the French Fifth Republic. Specifically, this French constitution provides for a division of executive powers between an independently elected, republican president and a prime minister appointed from within the majority bloc of parties in the legislature. This arrangement has led to "cohabitation" between opposing presidents and prime ministers in such African states as Niger, as it has within France itself. In the case of Niger, the legislative elections of January 1995 produced a majority in the National Assembly opposed to the leadership of the president, Mahamane Ousmane (Gervais 1997, 104). The subsequent standoff between the new prime minister and President Ousmane led to the first collapse of the democratic experiment in Niger (see Villalón and Idrissa, this volume). Since Congo's first post-transition political crisis was also linked to the looming prospect of cohabitation, institutional arrangements do seem to be one likely culprit for the failure of democratic consolidation there. The fact that Benin's democratic experiment has survived under a constitution that does not allow cohabitation strengthens this suspicion.

As in other cases, the most important part of the institutional structure for Congo was the politico-legal framework erected by its new, multiparty constitution, put in place in 1992. The adoption of this constitution lies precisely at the intersection of structural conditions of Congo's past and the choices made by the political class at the "critical juncture" of Congo's transition.[6] On the one hand, the shape of Congo's new constitution reflects one of many critical choices made during the whole period of democratic experimentation, a choice that also bore directly on the final outcome. On the other hand, after the moment of its adoption, the Constitution became part of the structural context for political action. Other relevant institutional arrangements include the division of powers between the central and local governments and the nature of the electoral system for the selection of deputies to the National Assembly (neither of which is specified in the Constitution).

There is no denying that the provisions of the Constitution became in 1992 the axis upon which the first critical decision of Congo's new, multiparty government turned. The nature of executive authority provided for in the Constitution reflects both the influence of the French experience on the Congolese political class and that class's authoritarian ("presidentialist") instincts. Three articles of the Constitution are directly relevant to the relationships among the president, parliament, and prime minister. Article 75 specifies that the president is to name the prime minister who "issues from the Parliamentary majority in the National Assembly" (La Constitution 1992, 45).[7] The provision in Article 80 states that:

> When the equilibrium of the public institutions is upset, notably in case of a sharp and persistent crisis between the executive and the Parliament, or if the Assembly twice rejects proposed governments in the space of a year, the President of the Republic may, after consulting the prime minister and the President of the National Assembly, pronounce the dissolution of the National Assembly. (Ibid., 53)

Finally, Article 123 endows the National Assembly with the power to "disapprove" the policies of the prime minister, in which case the latter must submit his resignation to the president.

These articles specify the legal context in which Lissouba made his first critical choice as president. Lissouba had been elected president through an alliance between his own political forces and those of former President Sassou-Nguesso, who had finished third in the first round of voting for the Congolese president. Kolélas had finished second in the first round, and hence stood against Lissouba in the second round. In this context, Sassou endorsed Lissouba's candidacy and urged his supporters to vote for Lissouba, which they did in large numbers, allowing Lissouba to achieve a 61 percent majority. Had the coalition of political forces led by Lissouba and Sassou held together, Congo's democratic experiment might have gotten off to a reasonably good start. In the event, Sassou and the PCT were greatly dissatisfied by the number and quality of the posts that they were offered in the first cabinet suggested by Lissouba (Parti Congolais du Travail 1992). As a result, the PCT bolted the coalition and joined forces with Lissouba's other main opposition bloc, the *Union pour le Renouveau Démocratique* (URD), led by Kolélas. This new coalition voted no confidence in Lissouba's choice for prime minister, who came not from the (new) majority bloc in parliament, but from his own party. Lissouba responded in October by declaring the parliament dissolved and calling for new elections. When the new opposition coalition rejected these moves as illegal, Congo saw its first episode of post-transition political violence. Security forces killed three persons marching in a peaceful protest in December 1992. This in turn led to a charged political standoff between Lissouba and his opponents, and to the appointments of rival "governments" in early 1993.

Lissouba's moves violated both the spirit and letter of the Congolese Constitution. First, the Constitution required him to name a prime minister "issuing from the parliamentary majority," which he failed to do. Secondly, his choice for prime minister was rejected by the assembly not twice, but only once (though there *was* a "sharp and persisting crisis" among the branches of government). While a "cohabitation" government in Congo would have been unwieldy, Lissouba never even gave it a chance. His determination to rule with a firm majority in parliament, regardless of constitutional provisions, was the first major choice that undermined the rule of law and the democratic experiment in Congo. Nothing in the constitution, or in his political situation, however, forced Lissouba to act as he did; rather, his dissolution of the assembly was a purely self-regarding political act aimed at consolidating his own power. He could easily have appointed a prime minister from within the opposition coalition and continued to rule as the constitutionally sanctioned president.

When the rerun of the elections took place the following May and June (1993), Lissouba's coalition won by the narrowest of margins, gaining control of sixty-four seats in the 125–member assembly. Both branches of the opposition coalition protested against the alleged fraud in the first round of these elections, and they boycotted the second round, which allowed Lissouba to secure his majority. Unlike the 1992 elections, those in 1993 did not receive the sanction of a well-staffed delegation of international observers. Lissouba's moves again violated the spirit of a democratic political process. These disputed elections began a second round of civil violence that came close to all-out civil war. The fighting during this period was primarily between Kolélas's "Ninja" militia and army units loyal to Lissouba.[8] In August, the two sides signed an accord in Libreville reaffirming their commitment to the 1992 Constitution and deploring the recent violence. The accord put in place a mechanism to arbitrate in the districts where the electoral outcomes were disputed and set a date for a re-running of the second round of the elections (Zartman and Vogeli 2000). As noted above, though, a second round of fighting ensued.

There is a case to be made that the confrontations of 1992–94 poisoned Congo's political atmosphere and made subsequent efforts to consolidate democracy impossible. After all, the militias assembled during this period never disappeared and ended up fighting each other again in 1997. Yet the fragile peace that was achieved in 1994 and sustained throughout 1995–96 suggests otherwise. The conflict of 1997 was a fresh one generated by a different political dynamic, namely Lissouba's fears that he would either lose the elections or lose a military contest to Sassou if the elections were challenged. Unlike the original conflict of 1992, this had nothing to do with the nature of the Congolese Constitution. Moreover, a different constitutional structure would not logically have made for a different outcome. Consider the counterfactual idea that the Congolese constitution might have provided for a prime minister elected by the assembly (as in Niger), rather than one appointed by the president. Would such an arrangement have made a difference in the trajectory of the Congolese democratic experiment? While no one can know for sure, logic—as well as the Nigerien case itself—suggests that it would not have made a difference. Indeed, even a constitution that provided for no prime minister whatever would have made no difference. Under any arrangement, Lissouba would have faced a difficult re-election campaign in 1997, just as President Soglo of Benin did in 1996, and there is no reason to believe that a different constitutional arrangement would have altered his behavior.

If the division of executive power seems to have made little difference in the outcome of the Congolese democratic experiment, what was the impact of the system for the election of deputies to the assembly? Magnusson argues in his study of democratic survival in Benin (chapter 4) that the country's two post-transitional electoral systems each served to prevent the emergence of large ethnoregional blocs in the assembly. Both systems produced representation for a larger number of smaller parties in the assembly following the 1991 and 1995 legislative elections. This, he argues, muted some of the ethnoregional rivalries the country might otherwise have known. Congo's legislative electoral system also had multimember districts (International Foundation for Elections Systems 1998, 196), but these were operationalized as single-member circumscriptions. Two rounds of voting determined a single winner for each circumscription, and thus Congo's legislative elections had no element of proportionality. Nonetheless, the results of the 1992 elections were not so different from those of Benin. Lissouba's UPADS won only 31 percent of the legislative seats, versus 23 percent of seats for Kolélas's MCDDI and 16 percent for Sassou's PCT. As in Benin, no party controlled more than one-third of the legislative seats, and about 30 percent of the legislative seats were occupied by independents or small, local parties. The system thus offered enough flexibility to prevent the domination of large ethnoregional blocs, had the political class chosen to operate it in that fashion.

As in Benin, local institutions and offices might have served to reduce the winner-take-all aspect of Congolese political competition. The meager attention paid to local institutions in the 1992 constitution reflects the strongly *étatist* traditions that Congo inherited from France. Nonetheless, Article 170 of the constitution did specify that "local collectivities" would "enjoy administrative, patrimonial, financial, economic, cultural and social autonomy." Moreover, at the outset of his presidency, Lissouba frequently emphasized the importance of decentralization of power, in keeping with the contemporary calls for such by international financial institutions. And in fact, local institutions did play a most important role in healing the wounds of the 1993–94 fighting: in mid-1994 Kolélas became mayor of Brazzaville, and Jean-Pierre Thystère-Tchicaya, leader of the fourth-largest party in the assembly, became mayor of Pointe Noire, the country's second city (Clark 1997a). No such role could possibly satisfy former President Sassou, however, and the pace of decentralization in general was too slow in Congo to have much impact in defusing the highly charged political atmosphere.

To be sure, Congo's political institutions might have been more wisely fashioned. Most notably, a number of somewhat vague phrases in the constitution might have been made clearer. Yet the main reason for the failure of Congo's institutions was that the political class, and especially the president, showed precious little regard for the rule of law. There was no serious effort to develop Congo's new political institutions and make them work. And had these institutions been crafted in a different way, other problems would have arisen. For instance, had the National Conference fashioned a forthrightly presidentialist constitution, like the one Congo has now, Lissouba would have even more easily accumulated all political power for himself. This would hardly have ensured a better ultimate outcome for the ill-fated Congolese democratic experiment.

The Economic and Class Contexts

The distribution of income and resulting class divisions within Congo represent a second context in the collapse of Congolese democracy. In most ways, socioeconomic stratification in Congo resembles that in many other developing states: income is more inequitably concentrated at the top than in developed societies, and those at the bottom endure a just-above-subsistence standard of living. In a small population of less than 3 million, infusing a certain amount of petroleum-revenue money into the economy has had the effect of raising the overall level of income in Congo, but also has caused the distribution to be even more skewed.

In analyzing the effects of Congo's petroleum income, one should first note that it did not cause the country to become industrialized, despite some efforts of the regimes of the 1970s to bring about this outcome. As a result, Barrington Moore's (1966) dictum of "no bourgeoisie, no democracy" seems entirely relevant to Congo. Yet one should also note that such proto-democratic states as Mexico, India, and Senegal have only very small, fragile bourgeois classes, though democratic institutions seem recently to have been strengthened in all three cases. Since the nonexistence of a classic bourgeoisie does not seem to preclude the development of proto-democratic institutions, our attention is drawn toward the relationship of income distribution and democratic consolidation (or non-consolidation).

One scholar has drawn a specific connection between misdistribution of income and political violence in Congo by pointing to the existence of the "political militia" (Bazenguissa-Ganga 1994, 1999). The 1997 civil war was not the first outbreak of civil violence during the period of the multiparty experiment. Following the 1993–94 conflict, Bazenguissa-Ganga (1994) argued that the existence of a large urban lumpenproletariat provided the socioeconomic basis for the militia. This same militia fought the 1997 civil war and was a direct instrument in ending the democratic experiment. By implication his work suggested that civil violence in Congo resulted directly from the lack of formal employment or other opportunities for alienated youth in Congo's stagnant economy.

In reply, one might point out that the mere existence of such a lumpenproletariat is in itself insufficient to explain this outbreak of violence in Congo. Many other countries of the world, including deeply impoverished states such as Bangladesh, have even larger and more marginalized social classes. Such classes are prompted (or not) to civil violence depending on a range of other social stimuli that may (or may not) drive them into the employ of unscrupulous warlord-politicians.

Moreover, the nature of the Congolese economy affected the prospects for democratic consolidation in ways more complex than is suggested by this type of analysis. To understand these effects, one must consider primarily how oil income has affected income strata and the gaps between these strata in the Congolese case. Petroleum income has been infused into the society in a way that has had diverse effects on these strata. To begin with, a certain fraction of the oil wealth was simply diverted (stolen) by members of the political class, who directed the money mostly into their foreign bank accounts.[9] This sort of diversion also widened the income gaps between a tiny slice of the political class with direct access to oil money and the population at large. This observation reinforces the valuable analysis of Bazenguissa-Ganga.

Another fraction of the oil wealth, however, was used to employ an ever-growing stratum of public functionaries in Congo. The size of the civil service grew from 3,000 at independence to some 85,000 in the early 1990s (Clark 2002b, 33). This "class" supported a far larger group, mostly in their extended families, at an above-average level of income. The employees of public enterprises and of the public service enjoyed a much higher income than Congo's peasants and domestic service workers. In effect, this form of distribution of oil wealth created in Congo a "bureaucratic bourgeoisie," or non-industrial middle class, which might have become a solid basis for democratic consolidation. Some of the oil wealth even trickled down to still lower strata. The relatively large middle class in Congo was able to pay for a variety of services from the uneducated portions of the population, providing extra paid labor for this group. State expenditures on health and education were also higher in Congo than in the non-oil states of the sub-Saharan African region. As a result of the diffusion of oil money into Congolese society over a long period, the country achieved the status of a "Medium Human Development" country according to the UNDP's Human Development Index score. Among the countries studied in this volume, Congo was the *only* one to achieve this relatively developed status (UNDP 1998, 129–30), and the achievement owes in part to the impact of oil money on the country's economy.

Nonetheless, the net, or overall, effect of Congo's oil wealth on the country's prospects for democratic consolidation was decidedly negative. As Ross (2001) has demonstrated, petroleum-producing poor countries are much less likely to experience democratization than states not saddled with the "curse of resources." Ross's study effectively reviews all of the previous literature on the impact of high levels of resource income on political development, and it statistically demonstrates the connection between authoritarianism and such incomes. Interestingly, however, most authoritarian states with high petroleum revenues have never experimented with democracy at all, so this literature has only modest value in understanding the Congo case. Thus the three "causal mechanisms" identified by Ross as the links between high petroleum income and continuing authoritarianism all have to do with the prevention of democratic transitions (Ross 2001, 332–37), and *not* with the collapse of democratic experiments. Among large-scale oil producers in sub-Saharan Africa, only Congo, and more recently Nigeria, have had genuine democratic transitions since 1991.

Yet the Congo case strongly suggests that proportionately high petroleum revenues served to create an adverse environment for democratic consolidation, just as they tend to impede democratic transition universally. One can discern the negative impact of oil revenues in the failure of the Congolese democratic experiment in two temporal frames: first, oil revenues helped to create a society that was materially and psychologically ill-prepared for democratic consolidation over the long period during which oil has been exported from Congo; and second, oil dependency served to undermine democratic consolidation in more specific ways during the period of democratic experimentation itself.

Over the long term, Congo's oil revenues caused the society to become one of the most heavily urbanized in sub-Saharan Africa. During the high-oil-price periods of the 1970s and early 1980s, huge numbers of former peasants were drawn into the cities to take advantage of the wealth of the oil boom (Achikbache and Anglade 1988). As a result, some 61 percent of Congolese lived in urban areas by 1998, a percentage second only to Botswana among African states (World Bank 2000, 232–33). Once detached from their rural social milieus, such elements were loathe to return to a rural life. Yet urban incomes declined after the mid-1980s because of the drop in oil prices, the growing debt burden that consumed an ever-growing portion of oil revenues, and the reforms demanded by the International

Financial Institutions (IFIs) in exchange for debt relief. Thus, petroleum incomes lured the Congolese into the urban areas, especially Brazzaville, but then did not provide for the economic sustenance of these internal migrants. The presence of a large, dissatisfied urban population put tremendous pressure on the Congolese government to satisfy economic needs in a way not experienced by more rural African states, like Malawi (15 percent urban), Mali (29 percent urban), or Niger (20 percent urban) (World Bank 2000, 232–33).

Another long-term effect of oil revenues was to make virtually all categories of Congolese workers dependent on the state for their economic welfare. Unlike in Benin, where a large, independent commercial class thrives, in Congo virtually all formal-sector workers are employed by the state as functionaries or parastatal workers. In turn, as Moore argued, a true bourgeoisie is more likely to support democratic consolidation than members of state-dependent classes. This phenomenon is partially psycho-cultural and partially material: on the one hand, reliance on the state for social and economic cues is an inheritance of French colonialism, absorbed into the political culture and reinforced by the petroleum boom; on the other hand, it has produced material conditions (classes) that erode the ability of any Congolese regime to endure economic shocks.

The more near-term effect of oil revenues on Congo's prospects for democratic consolidation is to be found in the performance of the state's economy during the years of the democratic experiment. As Przeworksi et al. (1997, 298) have recently demonstrated, economic performance after a democratic transition is vitally important for the prospects of democratic consolidation at all levels of development. Their statistical evidence shows that high levels of economic growth and moderate levels of inflation is the combination that most enhances prospects for democratic consolidation. In this light, a comparison of Congo and Benin is telling: Congo averaged *minus* 3.2 percent economic "growth" for the five years between 1993–97, while Benin averaged 4.2 percent growth.[10] The awful performance of the Congolese economy certainly soured the Congolese population on the Lissouba regime and left them disappointed with democracy in general. In turn, part of Congo's poor performance depended on the low, stagnant prices for oil on world markets following the end of the Persian Gulf War, and the country's virtually stagnant production levels in these years (as well as rampant corruption and the impact of the 1993–94 Congolese war). In this way, oil dependency made the task of democratic consolidation more difficult for Congo's political class as a whole.

A final manner in which Congo's oil income conditioned its prospects for democratic consolidation was by complicating its delicate, troubled relations with France. This problem is explored in a separate section, below. In sum, the impact of oil revenues on Congo's democratic prospects was mixed, but on balance negative. While such revenues did help Congo to achieve "lower middle class" status in the economic hierarchy of world states, they also created a population dependent on the state, and a state dependent on external revenues for its functioning. In turn, oil revenues precluded the kind of healthy symbiosis between society and state that is characteristic of functional democracies.

The Ethnoregional Context:
Cultural Pluralism and Political Confrontation

If those on the left instinctively turn to class strata as a source of understanding Congo's recent traumas, those who subscribe to a modernization theory prefer to emphasize the country's ethnic cleavages. Indeed, the prima facie nature of the recent civil wars in Congo suggests that ethnic divisions, and not those of class, represent the main impediments to development and democracy, built as it is on the foundation of civil peace. After all, ethnoregional militias, not parties representing class strata, have fought the wars that have wracked Congo since 1993.

There is no denying that the differing cultural habits of various ethnic groups at the village level, and also habits strongly featured among the older generations, are defining features of peoples' identities in Congo. For most rural and many urban Congolese, their sense of socio-cultural standing derives from belonging to distinct ethno-cultural communities. Congolese observers, even those who are fiercely nationalist, are perhaps more willing to recognize this reality than are Western ones (e.g., Nsafou 1996, 223ff.). Some even forthrightly ascribe specific, distinguishing characteristics to the representatives of various regions or cultures (Baniafouna 1995, 220–21).

The sources and consequences of ethnoregional identity are more contested than their existence, however. While some Congolese observers are more likely to attribute the politicization of ethnicity to the impact of colonialism, others acknowledge that colonial authorities actually tried to suppress ethnic conflict (Thystère-Tchicaya 1992, 92). This view recognizes the fundamental precolonial differentiation among the peoples of the region and the potential for conflict among them. Still, it was colonial authorities in Europe and Africa who drew the lines on the map, dividing ethnic peoples into multiple states and lumping together groups with historical animosities. In the wake of this fundamental act, one can scarcely imagine the sort of public policies that would have eliminated the potential for ethnic contestation in society over the ensuing decades. As for the consequences of ethnoregional differentiation, few Congolese find it to be the *root cause* of the successive civil wars that racked the country during the 1990s; rather, the large majority attribute ethnoregional violence to thirst for power by the political class, which stimulated such violence for short-term political advantage.[11] Academic analysts, whether of Congolese origins (Bazenguissa-Ganga 1999) or otherwise (Frank 1997; Sundberg 2000) generally share this view.

Ethnoregional contestation *has* been a signal feature of Congolese politics at every historical point where political groups have been able to compete for political access or privilege in the country's history. In keeping with the "instrumentalist" view of ethnic identity, however, the coalitions of ethnoregional forces have shifted over the various periods. In the early postwar period (1946–56), the southern Vili were pitted against the Mbochi group of the north, with other regional ethnicities supporting their co-regionalists. A second juncture for ethnoregional mobilization was the period of colonial decoupling between 1957 and 1960. During that time there was civil violence surrounding the elections of 1957 and 1959, pitting the Lari of the region surrounding Brazzaville (Pool region) against the northern Mbochi (Bazenguissa-Ganga 1997, 59–64). Subsequently, under the one-party regimes, it was a continuing preoccupation of the succeeding rulers to suppress open ethnic and ethnoregional struggles over access to power and the wealth of the state. Indeed, the one-party state that Congo endured from the mid-1960s to 1991 was justified partly on the basis of the need for "national unity." While all of the postcolonial regimes have engaged in ethnic patronage and balancing in the government, each ruler has also depended on an essential cadre of co-ethnics at the center of his regime.

With the opening of political space in Congo at the time of the National Conference in 1991, leading to the implementation of a multiparty system, the ethnoregional character of the nascent political parties was soon apparent. Three political groupings emerged at that time. The old single party from the "Marxist" era, the *Parti Congolais du Travail* (PCT), became a vehicle for the ambitions of former President Sassou and his Mbochi/northern supporters. The numerous and politically active Lari people from Brazzaville and the Pool region were represented by Kolélas and his *Mouvement Congolais pour le Développement et la Démocratie Intégrale* (MCDDI). Finally, a variety of different ethnic peoples from the regions of Niari, Bouenza, and Lekoumou ("Nibolek"), including many Kongo, coalesced under the leadership of future President Lissouba and the *Union Panafricaine pour la Démocratie Sociale* (UPADS). Lissouba himself is from the Nzabi, a non-Kongo group. The election results from the 1992 presidential elections and 1993 legislative elections leave no doubt that the voting followed an ethnoregional pattern (Clark 1997a, 71–73).

The civil war of 1993–94 pitted an ethnoregional militia organized by Kolélas against both loyal elements of the national army and Lissouba's own private militia. The fighting was characterized by the ethnic cleansing of neighborhoods and attacks on civilians because of their ethnicity, as revealed by Friedman and Sundberg (n.d.) in a horrifying report on that war.

The civil war that ended the Congolese democratic experiment in 1997 initially pitted the militia of Lissouba against that of Sassou, with elements of the national army defecting to the Sassou camp. Kolélas kept his militia out of the fighting until September 1997, when he made the ill-fated decision to join with Lissouba. Their combined forces were defeated shortly thereafter when Angola intervened in the 1997 Congo War, breaking the stalemate, and returning Sassou to power (Clark 1998b). Like the previous civil war, that of 1997 involved ethnic murder and the ethnic cleansing of neighborhoods by the various militia groups in specific sections of Brazzaville City and along the Congo-Ocean railway.

Despite these bracing realities, it is not enough to assume that ethnoregional differentiation in the society made social conflict inevitable. One does see a pattern of increasing ethnoregional conflict or actual fighting throughout sub-Saharan Africa in those countries that adopted multiparty systems in the early 1990s. Examples include Congo, Zaire, Rwanda, and Chad, among others. Yet one should also notice that such countries as Tanzania and Zambia moved to multiparty systems *without* engendering actual ethnoregional conflict, even if tensions arose among such groups. Smith's (2000) impressive empirical work actually suggests that "the relationship between political liberalization and ethnic conflict is the reverse of what the common assumptions would predict" (21). Namely, his study argues that liberalization actually reduces ethnic conflict, controlling for all other variables.

As for Congo, Frank (1997) cogently argues that the lines of ethnic conflict in Congo could not have been foreseen by the advent of multiparty politics in the country. Indeed, in the fighting of the late 1950s, the groups of the south and center of the country were united against those of the north; but in the 1993 war, residents of the capital representing two groups from the south fought each other. The ethnoregional coalition assembled by Lissouba was particularly unlikely, containing as it did a great multiplicity of ethnic groups scattered across half of the country. Hence, the ethnic "structures" of Congo hardly seem to have made civil war there inevitable. The structures exist more in the minds of Congolese political thought than in the actual cultural practices of various groups. Thus, the ethnoregional identity of groups has been constructed by ethno-political entrepreneurs. On this issue, the actions of elites certainly mattered more than the structural "givens" of the pre-transition situation.

The Neocolonial Context

A great many Congolese intellectuals and ordinary citizens regard the country's neocolonial status as critical to the fate of Congo's political trajectory in general and its democratic experiment in particular (e.g., Nsafou 1996).[12] Likewise, some European observers blame France for Congo's civil conflicts of the 1990s. Notably, Verschave (1998, 309–17) implicated France both in the 1997 civil war that ended Congo's democratic experiment and the even bloodier civil war that followed in 1998–99 (Verschave 2000, 15–69).

In theory, Congo underwent a purifying revolution in the late 1960s and 1970s that should have severed, or at least transformed, the country's links with the former (French) metropole. Congo's radical, nominally Marxist leaders in the 1960s and 1970s claimed that they had broken France's neocolonial grip on the Congolese economy, and even the psychological ties of dependency. Congo's growing links with the Soviet Union, Cuba, and China during these years superficially bolstered the claim. In reality, the putatively self-reliant "Marxist" regimes of Marien Ngouabi and Sassou I (1979–91) continued to rely on France for both economic and security assistance. France remained Congo's foremost trading partner throughout the "radical" period, and the state-owned French oil firm Elf-Aquitaine took the lead in developing Congo's oil resources. More embarrassingly, Sassou's regime was even sending Congolese officers and NGOs to France for training in the early 1980s, in the period before the onset of *glasnost* either in the Soviet Union or elsewhere in the Marxist world (Decalo et al. 1996, 112).

Yet Franco-Congolese relations are not the outright case of dependency that many believe; the real relationship is far subtler and slightly more balanced. It is perhaps better characterized as a case of international "patron-client" relations than one of outright dependency. While French officials can certainly manipulate Congolese politics through the levers of debt and the oil industry, Congo can also blackmail the French government into keeping the aid flowing by threatening to "play the American card" in the oil arena. The Lissouba regime momentarily managed to limit and constrain French influence over it partly by gaining American support in the Franco-American rivalry that played out in central Africa during the early 1990s. Hence, while a structural relationship between France and Congo certainly exists, and conditions the possibilities for political change in Congo, that relationship does not *determine* those possibilities.

These considerations are relevant specifically because of the manner in which the Lissouba regime (and hence, the Congolese democratic experiment) ended in October 1997. During the 1997 war, both sides sought sources of arms from outside the country. While the Lissouba regime bought arms openly on the world market, Sassou was forced to resort to illicit means of financing and acquiring arms. According to numerous sources, elements of the French government provided financing to Sassou and facilitated the flow of arms to him inside Congo during the critical weeks of the war (Verschave 1998; Clark 1998b; Clark 2002a). Some French networks, including the Chirac presidency, openly backed Sassou in the war, which raises two questions, one empirical and one analytical. The empirical question is whether these arms really determined the outcome of the war, and thereby the fate of Congolese democracy. The analytical question is whether the actions of Sassou's French supporters during this period should be seen as the inevitable result of a structural relationship or as a gamble of scheming politicians who might have made other choices.

The best answer to the empirical question is that France's actions were not directly responsible for the collapse of the Congolese democratic experiment. There is no gainsaying that the French president acted in a narrowly self-interested and capricious manner after the start of the 1997 war. After the war had begun, some of the same contacts made sure that Sassou had continued access to the arms he needed to fight the war, some of which were shipped through Gabon (Verschave 1998). But it was the start of the war itself, and not French policies afterward, which sealed the fate of the Congolese democratic experiment. No matter which side had prevailed in that war, peaceful electoral politics was certainly ended by the war itself. Had Lissouba's forces prevailed, there is no reason to believe that they would have, or even *could have,* organized free and fair elections in which Sassou would have been a participant. Of course, one might take the view that French agents *encouraged* Sassou to prepare for the war of 1997, rather than face elections. While such a suggestion is far from outrageous, it must be recalled that it was Lissouba who launched the war against Sassou, not the reverse. Moreover, Lissouba initiated the war in the context of a recently concluded peace agreement that followed the May 1997 events in Owando.

In a broader sense, French hostility to the Lissouba regime in the aftermath of the 1993 "Oxy" affair did help poison the environment for the consolidation of democracy in Congo.[13] The signals sent by France in 1993–97 may in this way have exacerbated Lissouba's paranoiac and controlling tendencies, but they did not rob him of his free will. The choice made by Sassou to prepare for war—and not elections—in 1997, and the choice Lissouba made to launch the war, were not inevitable ones despite the self-interested and meddling behavior of France.

The Military Context

Another logical structural impediment to democratic consolidation in Congo may have been intervention in political processes by the military. African polities are notoriously coup-prone, and a great many African civilian governments have been displaced by armed elements of the state. In many cases, African populations have cheered the end of corrupt and ineffective civilian regimes. Rare are the civilian regimes that can successfully "tame" the armed forces (Decalo 1998). Just as frequently, of course, groups in the armed forces have overthrown other military regimes in Africa. Less well appreciated by outsiders is the role that armed forces sometimes play in setting the stage for democratic transition. Yet this was the case with Mali during the recent wave of democratic transition across sub-Saharan Africa: the Malian armed forces overthrew a dictatorial regime and set the stage for democratic elections (Clark 1995). Unfortunately, perhaps, the role of the military of Niger has been more typical; in that case, the military overthrew an elected civilian regime in 1996 when the constitutional system produced a president and prime minister of different parties who could not work together (see Villalón and Idrissa, chapter 2 of this volume).

Interestingly, however, the professional military does not seem deserving of direct culpability for the end of the democratic experiment in Congo. Although the Congolese army had more than adequate pretexts to end the experiment on many occasions, it did not. The fact of the army's forbearance is all the more remarkable given that the Lissouba regime clumsily interfered in army affairs on many occasions.

The generally good behavior of the army throughout the years of the democratic experiment began during the transition. As the opposition gained momentum in displacing the authoritarian regime of Sassou I (1979–92), Chief of Staff Jean-Marie Michel Mokoko issued a public statement affirming that the army would not move to suppress the civilian opposition. He later reiterated this statement at critical moments in the process (Clark 1993, 62).[14] General Raymond-Damas Ngollo also played a role congenial to the establishment of civilian rule during his years as minister of defense (1990–95). Subsequently, there was a major standoff between the army and the transition government of Prime Minister André Milongo (July 1991–August 1992), during which time Sassou remained nominally president. This crisis began with rumors of a coup circulating in the government, followed by a heavy-handed effort of Milongo to dismiss senior army officers and replace them with his own loyalists. When a committee of the transitional parliament investigated, however, it determined that the coup rumors had been fabricated as a pretext for the military shake-up (*Africa Confidential,* March 6, 1992, 5–6).

There was, of course, potential for an enormous structural problem with the Congolese army inherited by post-transition regime, namely the large percentage of northern, particularly Mbochi, officers in the bloated top ranks. The ethnic makeup of the officer corps reflected both the colonial preference for northern officers and, more especially, the long period of rule of northern army officers. Lissouba, who had come to power with a solid base of support from "Nibolek," certainly did not trust these officers to do his bidding. For this reason, Lissouba allowed his overzealous minister of the interior, Martin M'Beri, to organize separate militias (the "Zulu" and "Aubevillois"), loyal specifically to the regime, for use in putting down revolts in early 1993. Indeed, as Lissouba had recognized, when he faced a rebellion by Bernard Kolélas's Ninja militia in 1993–94, the regular army was most reluctant to use heavy weapons to crush them (Clark 1997a, 74). It only did so reluctantly, and with some units defecting. Lissouba dismissed Mokoko in July 1993 in the midst of the first Congolese war and appointed a replacement from his own region. In the subsequent two years, he replaced groups of senior officers in the army who hailed from the north. In January 1995, yet another blow to the prestige of the army came when the minister of defense, General Raymond-Damas Ngollo, was replaced by a civilian. But none of these steps provoked a coup d'état.

Finally, one should note that the blow that ultimately ended the democratic experiment, Lissouba's attempt to arrest Sassou in June 1997, did not start with the army. Rather, Lissouba chose loyal units to carry out his arrest order, but they failed due to resistance by Sassou's own militia. Perhaps Lissouba himself can be faulted for not suppressing the partisan militia sooner, but had he tried to do so, he likely would have only started the civil war sooner. The ethnoregional militia organized by the political barons fought Congo's civil war, and terrorized the population, not the regular army. Thus, the professional soldiers and officers of the Congolese army cannot be directly faulted, though the army did make strong demands of the civilian government and protected its interests during the period of the democratic experiment.

The Political Culture Context

Perhaps the most encompassing "structural" feature of the Congolese polity that bore on the prospects for democratic consolidation is that of pre-transition political culture. In general, political culture is persisting and durable without being immutable or static. It can certainly change, but it is far more likely to change incrementally, with the permeation of new modes of political behavior into the popular consciousness occurring over long periods of time. New, experimental institutions of political control and decision-making that gain credibility for their fairness and effectiveness are among the most important instruments for changes in political culture. At the level of elites, on the other hand, the culture of politics can sometimes—though rarely—undergo more rapid change at the moment that a critical juncture in politics is reached. Hence, in evaluating the impact of political culture on democratic experiments, one should consider any changes brought about by the traumas of the transition, as well as the prevailing nature of political culture before the start of the democratic experiment.

One fundamental caveat about political culture is that widespread indifference or lack of knowledge regarding democratic practices at the mass level does not necessarily preclude either adherence to democratic procedures among elites or gradual change in mass loyalty to democratic norms. This is important to note because some scholarly work suggests otherwise. Schaffer (1998) has ably demonstrated that ordinary Senegalese often have in mind decidedly non-democratic ideals when they use the French term *"démocratie"* and the Wolof term *"demokaraasi."* But what matters in Senegal is that, first, the country's citizens understand perfectly well that they can affect political outcomes by participating in the voting ritual, and that they do so; and, second, that elites follow formal democratic procedures in choosing and installing new leaders. A great many Americans may feel disenfranchised under the country's current constitution, and indeed, their political freedom may be circumscribed in specific ways both by constitutional structures and by social values (e.g., racism). Large swaths of the American population have scarcely more understanding of, or appreciation for, democratic norms than do the Senegalese as a whole. Nonetheless, enough Americans—and apparently enough Senegalese— take formal democratic procedures seriously enough to participate in voting and return or reject parties that express differing values. Brilliant though Schaffer's work is, it clearly suggests that the roots of Senegalese democracy were exceedingly shallow, and that one could not expect sustained political evolution in a democratic direction in Senegal. Yet the trajectory of political events in Senegal between 1998 and 2002 suggests that there *are* possibilities for democratic institutionalization in Senegal despite the limits on the population's understanding of and commitment to democratic practice.

In analyzing the political cultures of African societies, Chazan (1994, 69–76) has suggested that one can usefully trace the origins of present-day political values in African societies through three distinct periods: the precolonial, the colonial, and the "anticolonial" (1945–60). Over each period, cultural values and institutions have mutually evolved and set the stage for the prospects for political change in the ensuing era. For those studying democratization in African societies in the 1990s, it is sensible to add the era of postcolonial authoritarianism to the list of periods since this most proximate period bears directly on the prospects for democratic consolidation.

In the case of Congo, no dynamic of progressive institutions reinforcing the liberal aspects of the political culture has ever been created. In general, proto-democratic institutions such as mass consultation, independent judiciaries, or checks on arbitrary rule were not common in precolonial African societies, as some Africans themselves have acknowledged (Simiyu 1988). There are of course some celebrated exceptions, like the institution of the *kgotla* (assembly) in the Tswana society of southern Africa. In the precolonial kingdoms that inhabited the political spaces of the contemporary Congo Republic, however, including the Tio, Vili, and Kongo kingdoms, among others, few such institutions emerge from the observations of historians and anthropologists (Vansina 1990; MacGaffey 2000). Accordingly, there are few indigenous institutions that could be recalled by Congolese in the process of building a modern democracy.

Some scholars analyzing the traumas of Congo in the 1990s have in fact started with the slave trade in their narratives of Congo's contemporary agony (e.g., Nsafou 1996). In the minds of these authors, the slave trade is really only a preamble to the advent of colonialism itself, distinctive though the periods are in the minds of historians. They form a whole complex of historical contact with Europeans that led to loss of pride, humiliation, feelings of inferiority, and other profoundly negative changes in identity.

As for the period of colonial rule, Congo endured a variety of colonialism that stands out for its brutality and arbitrariness even when compared with the harsh experiences of other colonized African societies. For the first three decades of colonial rule in Congo, the administration of the state was handed over to private "concessionary" companies, which ruled in return for access to human and natural resources. These concessionary companies carried out a forthright and nearly unrestrained exploitation of these resources for the benefit of the company and the larger metropole (Coquery-Vidrovitch 1972). The utter savagery of the mode of rule in this period can only be compared with that in the "Congo Free State," where King Leopold and his rubber-extracting agents erected an unspeakably brutal regime of control. Congo and the other parts of French Equatorial Africa endured thirty years of pillaging and utterly alienating treatment by the concessionary companies that inevitably precluded the development of liberal values or institutions. Of course, the degradations of colonialism do not link directly with the events of mid-1997. Rather, they are mediated by the creation of other, intermediate social conditions that created the environment for democratic failure in Congo. Nonetheless, it is striking that so many Congolese intellectuals perceive themselves to be virtual prisoners of a colonial past that inevitably shapes contemporary political values and institutions. Unfortunately, their perspective has the unintended consequence of absolving contemporary actors for the misdeeds they commit for purely selfish purposes.

In the subsequent period, between about 1925 and 1945, Congo experienced a more "normal" form of French colonial rule, but this experience did scarcely more to inculcate the leadership, let alone the population at large, with democratic values. As a result, Congo had no record of contact with democratic or proto-democratic institutions before World War II, and the development of liberal values was equally absent. Senegal provides some prima facie evidence that a different experience over the colonial period might have had some lasting impact in the contemporary era.

Senegal's experience of quasi-democratic practice in the legendary "four communes" surely represents a vital legacy for the contemporary experiment with multiparty politics that has recently yielded a case of peaceful *alternance*.

Many African states gained valuable democratic experience during the anti-colonial phase of their political evolution after 1945, but the impact of such tutelage in Congo was limited. Particularly after the independence of such Asian states as India, North Vietnam, and Indonesia, it became clear to all of the European colonial powers (except Portugal) that the end of colonialism in Africa was near. In the case of France, moreover, Charles de Gaulle had specifically promised the African colonial elites a larger measure of participation in their own self-government as a reward for rallying to France during the grim days of Nazi occupation. The exact modalities of this participation began to be debated between the French government and the local colonists in Congo immediately after the war (Bernault 1996, 94). It would continue to be debated and refined until the moment of independence in 1960.

While promising in theory, the real value of the experience in inculcating democratic values during the 1945–60 period was limited. Notably, the local colonists interfered perpetually in the process, manipulating events to ensure the emergence of their own African favorites. Naturally, they found ambitious Congolese elites willing to serve as their agents while posing as the repositories of indigenous aspirations (Bernault 1996, 135–80). The electoral politics of the era was resolutely ethnoregional, a pattern abundantly encouraged by the local Europeans. This tendency was strengthened when vigorous "anti-colonial" movements failed to appear.

Given this pattern in the late colonial period, it is not surprising that the first leader of independent Congo to emerge was both an ethnically animated political baron and a loyal lieutenant of French neocolonial interests. The very limited "nationalist" credentials of the Abbé Fulbert Youlou were strictly limited by his Lari particularism, on the one hand, and his willingness to serve French regional interests on the other. Unable to rally a regionwide, "national" following, Youlou relied on his Lari base in the Pool region and manipulation of the political processes to achieve power (Bernault 1996, 234–60). Ensconced in power, he could not find a voice to rally the diffuse peoples of Congo to his side in any truly national endeavor, be it national development or support of decolonization elsewhere in Africa. Instead, he played Machiavellian games of ethnic counter-balancing at home and supported the Tshomé secession in Congo-Kinshasa. Given the revolutionary Zeitgeist of the era, and his ineptitude in playing these games in the manner of Houphouët-Boigny, Youlou's regime lasted a scant three years before evaporating in the face of three days of violent street protests in 1963, now commemorated as *"Les Trois Glorieuses."*

Congo seemed to lurch from one form of banal, alienating authoritarianism to another. In some regards, the subsequent period of rule by Alphonse Massemba-Débat (1963–68) represented a political opening. The new regime momentarily embodied the popular aspiration of the people to exercise political freedom and to stand up to the West. Moreover, there was initially political space for a variety of political ideologies to be voiced. It quickly evolved, however, into another form of social domination by a new set of self-regarding elites. Most importantly, the new regime instituted the *Mouvement National de la Révolution* (MNR) as the only legal political party, effectively cutting off the hope for political pluralism, real debate, and criticism of the new regime.

The follow-up regimes of Presidents Ngouabi (1968–77), Yhombi-Opango (1977–79), and Sassou I (1979–92) maintained even less space for free political expression than had the previous two. These regimes were in place during the nominally Marxist-Leninist period in which the *Parti Congolais du Travail* (PCT) was the sole legal party (after 1970). All three used the mechanism of the PCT and the dogma of "democratic centralism" to suppress any meaningful political dialogue. Each of the three regimes was very much a personal one, set up first and foremost to maintain power for the rulers. Each of the three successive rulers was a ranking military officer as well, so that each regime also appropriately bears the label "military." The main PCT organs functioned as an alternative source of authority and legitimacy. The National Assembly went out of existence altogether between 1968 and 1973, and when it was brought back as the *Assemblée Nationale Populaire,* it functioned as a rubber-stamp body of carefully selected political loyalists. During the 1970s and 1980s, the most important elements of the civil society, including labor, women, youth, and the professions, were co-opted (loosely) into the state through organs set up by the PCT. Needless to say, the emergence of liberal political values in this climate was out of the question.

Thus one can see that very few elements of Congo's pre-transition past helped to set the stage for a democratic consolidation in the 1990s. At the moment of transition in 1992, the country had virtually no past experience with the functioning of liberal institutions, such as a vigorous civil society, a free press, or an independent judiciary, not to mention genuine political competition for office. In this sense, the Congolese environment was most unpropitious for the rooting of democratic politics in the 1990s. Even some of the barons of the old regimes now seem to concede that the "Marxist" regimes only perpetuated the intolerance and anti-democratic "mentality" inherited from colonialism (Obenga 1998).

Structures, Elites, and Choice in Congo's Democratic Experiment

By way of conclusion let us return to the three questions that were posed above regarding the findings that a study such as this one should reach: (1) How much freedom of action did the individual agents have in the actions they took that bore on the trajectory of the democratic experiment? (2) Which structural contexts exerted the most influence on the actions of the major state agents? (3) How did the various structural contexts of the democratic experiment interact with one another to support or undermine the prospects for democratic consolidation?

The answer to the first question is that the key actors in the quest to consolidate Congolese democracy actually had a considerable range of choice. If a democratic mode of rule is to survive, to become deeper, and eventually to be consolidated after a long period of autocracy, the first and heaviest burdens of leadership fall squarely on the newly elected president and, secondarily, on the outgoing ruler from the authoritarian period. In this test of leadership both Lissouba and Sassou failed miserably. Had each of these political figures behaved better—in a more tolerant, patient, and selfless way—the Congolese democratic experiment might still have failed. It could have been ended by a frustrated army general, an angry mob of citizens, or by foreign plotters. Had it ended in such a way, then one would be right to place the blame on structural factors outside the control of the key political principals. In fact, however, it was ended precisely by the knowing decisions of President Lissouba, who acted in a careless, reckless way in pursuit of his own power and ambitions. The blame lies equally with Sassou, who prepared for war, and sought to provoke a military confrontation. Lissouba only fell directly into the trap set for him by taking the decision to launch the war against his longtime rival. No one and nothing forced Sassou to organize his followers into an armed militia after his electoral defeat in 1993, and no one and nothing forced Lissouba to launch the military operation on the morning of June 5, 1997.

This position needs to be defended against a number of obvious rejoinders. In choosing a leader with as much lust for power and poor judgment as Lissouba, did the Congolese political class (in fostering Lissouba's initial re-emergence on the political scene) and the Congolese people (in favoring Lissouba in his final election) reflect their fundamental inability to choose leaders who would operate by democratic rules? In reply, one may say at least two things. First, Lissouba did not initially seem to be such a terrible choice as leader before and during his election in 1992. Although his record from the 1960s was certainly replete with many political transgressions and human rights abuses, few major Congolese leaders had clean hands in this regard. Moreover, his former political experience, his long exile in the West, and his superior education made him an obvious candidate for office. Few could have known in 1992 that his record would prove to be so bad. Second, populations thought to be in possession of more sophisticated and pro-democratic political cultures often show themselves to be scarcely more able in choosing political leaders. The mere mention of names such as Richard Nixon or James Traficant should suffice to make the point with an American readership.

Secondly, one might object that one or the other of the two Congolese leaders identified as having failed to provide leadership were *forced* to act as they did. In excusing their nefarious actions during the 1990s, the supporters of the two Congolese politicians have often suggested as much. Sassou's supporters maintain that the veteran Congolese ruler *had* to organize a militia, lest Lissouba use the national army and his own militia to irrevocably consolidate his power; meanwhile, Lissouba's supporters maintain that the ex-president *had* to master Sassou's militia before the 1997 election in order to ensure that the poll could take place without violence. Both sets of arguments are specious and evidently self-serving. Sassou had already begun to organize his own militia before the onset of violence in the 1993–94 war. And Lissouba had tolerated the existence of Sassou's militia up until the eve of the 1997 election and had agreed to an accord to have peaceful elections only days before he dispatched troops to arrest Sassou.

One can imagine other ways in which the Congolese democratic experiment might have ended. Lissouba might have been forced by IFIs to institute economic policies that would have provoked massive public riots. In such circumstances, the army might have seized power. Likewise, the army might have decided to seize power as Lissouba replaced northern officers with military cadres from his own region. Or, alternatively, Lissouba might have faced a spontaneous outbreak of ethnic fighting among different population groups at the grassroots, generating a chain of events leading to his fall from power. Under any of these scenarios, one would have felt Lissouba, and possibly Sassou, to be mere prisoners of events. But no such scenarios as these actually transpired in Congo. Rather, all of the major crises the country faced were generated by the political principals themselves.

With regard to the structural constraints on successful democratization in Congo, one should begin by acknowledging the limits of Congo's possibilities. That the Congolese polity would have emerged in the 1990s as a fully endowed European multiparty democracy, complete with widespread respect for human rights and relatively transparent political processes, is virtually unthinkable. Only the naive could have expected such an outcome. Such a political situation would indeed have to wait for a wholesale structural transformation of the Congolese economy and society. But the outcome envisioned by more hopeful but realistic observers would have resembled something like that in Benin, that is, a polity with the formal mechanisms for *alternance* of presidential leaders intact and with an opposition voice in parliament. Accordingly, it is not enough to point to the structural improbabilities of democratization in Congo to explain its failure there. The country's political class could have opted to keep playing by the democratic rules in a formal way for a bit longer, and that might have led over time to a more real democracy.

In reviewing the array of overlapping structural conditions described above, political culture emerges as the most basic and determinative of the ultimate outcome. Three of the other structural features of the Congolese polity, in fact, could easily be seen as subsets, or elements, of the country's political culture: the institutions the country's leaders chose during and immediately after the national conference reflected the cultural inheritance of French colonialism; the influence of the military in government was also an inheritance of colonial rule, passed down through the military regimes of the postcolonial era; and the habit of ethnoregional thinking and politics merely reflected the patterns that emerged in the late colonial era and persisted afterwards in the practice, if not the rhetoric, of every postcolonial regime that followed. Yet, intriguingly, it was *none* of these specific aspects of political culture that directly explains the Congolese outcome. Rather, it was the more general habits of the political class rooted in their psychology of politics that doomed the Congolese democratic experiment. Specifically, the personal lust for power and lack of respect for the rule of law in the chosen behaviors of the key leaders doomed the Congolese democratic experiment.

While the socioeconomic conditions certainly represent a daunting challenge to the establishment of viable, multiparty institutions, they did not contribute directly to a causal chain of events as some believe. While it is true that the militia members recruited from among the urban unemployed were a chief source of social disorder, one should remember that every society has its thugs. Even in relatively industrialized societies, such as Germany in the 1930s or Argentina in the 1970s, sadistic authoritarian rulers have little difficulty recruiting the necessary brigands and torturers to terrorize society. Moreover, it was not a mob of angry workers who brought down Congolese democracy, as with the angry mob that brought down the Youlou regime in 1963. While Congo also experienced a painful economic contraction in the early 1990s, the economic pain felt by ordinary Congolese was largely disconnected from the choices of Sassou and Lissouba that finally tore apart Congolese society and destroyed the democratic experiment.

Although the authoritarian habits of the political class were most directly responsible for this failure, these habits were tolerated by the larger population. Only a firm psychological resistance to such forms of rule deeply embedded in the population can stymie the would-be authoritarian predators present in every society. For now, Congo's population lacks such resistance to authoritarian modes of rule. Hence, when the politicians were ready to act to serve their narrow, ethnoregional and clan interests, they found willing collaborators among the population. If the politicians had not been confident of such collaboration, their behavior might have been better. Given this lack of a culture favorable to democracy, it is remarkable that the army did not assert itself even more vigorously as some point, for such an assertion would have likely met with social resignation.

Yet even despite the fearsome obstacle of Congo's political culture, the politicians might well have acted differently than they did; indeed, to suggest otherwise is to absolve those guilty of unspeakable crimes of responsibility for their actions. Certainly, no Congolese politician could have behaved as a European politician and hoped to survive. For instance, some initial reliance on an ethnoregional basis of support was probably inevitable (Frank 1997). Yet Congolese politicians certainly had some scope to play the game either ruthlessly or with a modicum of fairness. There is very little to admire in the record of Lissouba as president between 1992 and 1997. Had he made genuine efforts to develop the economy, even via a mere handful of improvements, he would have stood a fair chance of re-election in 1997. Instead, he allowed his ministers to loot the public treasury virtually unchecked and to scheme against his opponents, rather than concentrating on possible positive contributions to social development.

The choices of Sassou during the delicate moment of democratic transition and afterward were no more productive of civil peace and the entrenchment of democratic values. Most fundamentally, Sassou turned his Mbochi-manned presidential guard into a personal, private militia (the Cobras). This group of fighters was removed to his hometown of Oyo for most of Lissouba's presidency, where they trained and collected arms, sometimes by theft, preparing for a future armed conflict. Even though Sassou was able to travel freely within and outside Congo, he kept his militia intact. Given the very small ethnoregional basis of support that Sassou could bring to any election, he spent more of his time preparing for war than he did for participation in elections. Nothing compelled Sassou to behave in this way other than his own thirst for power.

Finally, the nefarious behavior of the influential French (and Gabonese) players in the Congolese civil war of 1997 can also been seen as a choice, rather than as a structural inevitability. As noted above, Sassou spent many months in Paris maintaining his contacts with French officials and agents of Elf-Aquitaine. Many of these doubtless hoped that Sassou might one day return to power in Congo (as Mathieu Kérékou did in Benin). It remains uncertain to what extent they encouraged him in any bid to retake power. In the event, Lissouba gave him the pretext he needed by seeking to arrest him on the eve of the election. Hence, while the choices of these outsiders were an important permissive cause of the war, they did not impose on Lissouba or Sassou any compulsion to *begin* a devastating war. By the time of Angola's intervention in October 1997, all prospects for the revival of the democratic experiment in Congo were long extinguished.

Ultimately, the elements of structure and agency in the demise of Congolese democracy are inextricably entangled. Likewise, the structural elements of the Congolese context are deeply enmeshed. Although the political values (culture) of elites and the population are identifiable as a key element of the structural situation, there is no gainsaying that the political culture is in turn a product of the country's colonial history and postcolonial economy. The political setting of Congo in 1992 was doubtlessly one in which even fair and high-minded individuals would have found it difficult to nurture a democratic opening. It also bears repeating, however, that the individuals in question were not high-minded, and that they never gave the multiparty system a chance of success. One can only hope that if Congo ever faces another, similar opportunity, those who emerge from the electoral process will be more inclined to act with equanimity, fairness, and good judgment than those who stepped onto the stage in 1991.

NOTES

1. For a somewhat more detailed recitation of these events, see Clark (1998a).

2. The term "thick description" comes, of course, from Geertz (1973). Although the sort of description offered here for the failure of Congolese democracy may not be exactly the kind Geertz had in mind, it is based on the same epistemological premises: that one cannot truly "explain" social phenomena with the same precision that one could bring to the study of natural phenomena, but that one can understand them by providing a detailed description of the social context in which individual action takes place.

3. John Wiseman's sarcastic characterization of these regimes as varieties of "kindergarten fascism" was not entirely inappropriate (Wiseman 1990, 605).

4. Article 75 states that the president of the Republic "names the prime minister coming from [issu de] the parliamentary majority in the National Assembly." On this point, see more below.

5. Opposition spokesperson cited in *Marchés Tropicaux et Méditeranéens* (MTM), May 21, 1993, 1321.

6. On the concept of critical junctures in the political trajectories of African states, see Villalón and Huxtable (1998). The adoption of a new constitution that significantly reorders the political space of a country, altering the prospects for its major political actors, represents one typical type of critical juncture for any state.

7. It is notable that under the Nigerien constitution of 1992 the prime minister was elected by the Assembly, and not appointed by the president.

8. According to knowledgeable sources whom I interviewed in June 2002, however, Sassou backed the military challenges of Kolélas's militia by transferring arms to the militia and providing financial backing.

9. As one result of such diversion, Sassou-Nguesso lived in opulent style as an exiled politician in Paris in the early 1990s, and was able to support his sizable militia during these years out of power.

10. Over the same period, Congo's average annual rate of inflation was 16.3 percent while Benin's was 12.3 percent. In this regard, both states' economies were heavily affected by the 50 percent devaluation of the CFA franc in January 1994. Data compiled from EIU, *Country Report: Congo,* and EIU, *Country Report: Benin,* various years.

11. This observation is based on more than thirty interviews conducted in Brazzaville in May and June 2002.

12. For a full exploration of the question of France's role in the end of the Congolese democratic experiment, see Clark (2002a).

13. The "Oxy" affair refers to Lissouba's negotiation and subsequent abrogation of a deal with the American company Occidental Petroleum. In exchange for the deal, which displaced France's Elf-Congo, Lissouba allegedly received $150 million that he subsequently used to support his backers in the 1993 legislative elections.

14. This stance of the army helps explain why Sassou gave up power in 1991, though he was willing to use extreme violence to re-take it in 1997.

6 | The Shaky Foundations, Adverse Circumstances, and Limited Achievements of Democratic Transition in the Central African Republic

Andreas Mehler

This chapter deals with the difficulties of reforming a neopatrimonial regime within the context of high levels of inter-elite distrust and political militarization. In 1993, the Central African Republic (CAR) obtained the distinction of having undergone a "successful" democratic transition. From that period to 2002, democracy survived (barely) in an environment punctuated by high levels of instability, engendered by outbreaks of political violence and extralegal efforts to take power. In October of that same year, the formal experiment with democracy appeared to collapse as "politics" degenerated into open and bloody confrontations between forces loyal to the president and those of his former chief of staff. When the rebels took the capital Bangui in March 2003, they were greeted by joyous inhabitants, but the prospects for civil peace—let alone democracy—remained bleak.

The experience of the CAR is important to consider for a number of reasons. In the first place, it clearly suggests that in a climate where political violence and high levels of state criminalization are the norm, democracy's survival is highly unlikely, and prospects for its development are dim. Both of these conditions have typified the CAR since the onset of democratic rule in 1993, and both of them helped to poison the political environment in a manner that made the prospects for elite consensus on the "rules of the game" highly unlikely. Second, the case of the CAR helps to demonstrate how certain practices at the level of the state act as independent variables that increase the likelihood of democratic decay and breakdown. These include, in particular, the politics of exclusion, an intolerance of consensus politics, and the use by the political elite of tactics outside the legal institutional framework of governance (the latter is similar to the situation in Guinea Bissau observed by Forrest; see chapter 11 of this volume). In this sense, institutions figure less importantly than the actual political dynamic engendered by state actors seeking to maintain and increase power. Finally, the case brings attention to the role of international actors in shaping the experiences of new democratic regimes—especially those potentially prone to breakdowns in civil peace. The failure of the international community to apply a sensitive policy for promoting democracy and peace, despite numerous and costly efforts to this effect, represents an important piece of the puzzle when seeking to make sense of the CAR's trajectory since 1993. The role of the international community in the CAR contrasts its role in Mozambique, as described in chapter 10 by Manning, this volume.

The primary analytical insights set forth below derive from a historical analysis of the experience of the CAR since 1993. In offering this historical narrative, I not only attempt to "tell the story" of the CAR's democracy, but offer certain analytical themes that help to make the CAR's difficulties with democracy more comprehensible. One especially important theme concerns the chronic tensions between the principle of consensual and inclusive politics and the practice of zero-sum and exclusionary politics. The former was the norm during the period of transition from authoritarian rule; the latter has been the modus operandi of the state elite during the democratic era. Yet another theme focuses on the recurrence of domestic crises threatening to undermine democracy and the problematic efforts to resolve these crises. Frequently, violence in domestic political conflict has been mediated through international intervention. Yet although international actors have recurrently asked for the restoration of the accommodative balance symbolized by devices of inclusive politics, this request was not conducive to any kind of "structural stability."[1] Finally, as indicated above, the historical overview suggests that attention to institutions is less important than a focus on other factors shaping the character of elite interactions. Of central importance in this regard is the role and emergence of a climate of distrust that has been engendered by state criminalization, the exercise of exclusionary politics, and recurrent political violence. This climate has made prospects for democracy quite untenable.

The chapter begins by describing the environment in which democracy in the CAR has been implemented. I devote attention, first, to the larger social, economic, and historical contexts of the country, and then proceed to describe certain of the key organizational actors in the country. My goal here is to offer a picture of the stage on which elites have interacted to shape the experience of the country. The overview of the experience of the CAR then follows, representing the primary analytical section of the paper. Corresponding to the historical development of the country since 1993, I focus first on the initial institutional and behavioral dynamics that characterized the early phases of democratic rule. As will be seen, patterns of political violence and state criminalization established themselves very clearly at this time. I then proceed to analyze the political dynamics surrounding the second elections in the country and the subsequent outbreak of conflict in 2001. I complete this historical overview with a short synopsis of the country's degeneration into political violence in 2002. A concluding section seeks to place the experience of the CAR in a larger perspective.

The Settings for Democracy

At the outset, it is necessary to present the environmental dynamics that set the stage for the actions of primary players in the decade 1993–2003. This includes attention to both the larger contextual circumstances underpinning political interactions and the makeup of the key organizational actors in the polity.

The Larger Context

While all political actors in the CAR have clearly had some autonomy of action, they have had to live with major constraints as well. One issue for immediate consideration concerns the relatively limited politicization of society as a whole in the CAR. The country has some 3.6 million inhabitants scattered over 623,000 square kilometers of the national territory. However, the state is considered to be a fiction in large parts of the country (Bierschenk and Olivier de Sardan 1997). The political arena is confined nearly exclusively to the capital Bangui, the country's only nerve center. There, the country's elite is estimated at 300–400 persons only.[2] In addition, although the CAR is a multiethnic state, ethnic identity has become a salient political cleavage only relatively late (in the 1980s). A common language (Sango) can be used to bridge divisions, and the memory of the "founding father" Barthélémy Boganda is a strong uniting factor among the elite and the people. One consequence of these features is that political life has been narrowly focused on the capital. For example, during the last decade the CAR has experienced recurrent scenes of violence close to civil war, but this has been largely limited to Bangui, where most civil servants are based and suffer from extended salary arrears. Large parts of the country have not experienced large-scale confrontations, and there is no "necessity" for degeneration into a downward spiral of violence.

While this is not the appropriate place to go into details of the CAR's economic structure, certain issues do deserve attention. The CAR budget has depended heavily on two sources: diamonds and foreign aid.[3] Both of these have shaped the political experience of the country insofar as they have been the primary ingredients of a particular political economy, which favors rent-seeking elites who have been prone to employ criminal activities to beef up their incomes (Misser and Vallée 1997; Bayart, Ellis, and Hibou 1997). Diamonds constitute the most important export commodity, consistently accounting for 40–55 percent of export revenues. However, diamonds leave the country legally only at a rate of 33–50 percent of real production. Although the diamond sector alone could lead the state out of the persistent financial crisis that underlies social malaise, under current circumstances the situation confirms the thesis of "resource curses" in Africa.[4] Despite the mineral riches of the country, the state itself has remained poor and in a constant fiscal crisis, which has resulted in salary arrears for civil servants, one source of political instability in recent years.

For decades the French were the primary source of foreign aid, ready to inject money into the system because they valued the geopolitical situation and the two military airports at their disposal. This began to change in the early 1990s. It bears noting that although the state has been extremely dependent on economic and military support from the outside world (and for a long time this meant France alone), the CAR leaders have all followed versatile foreign policies. This indicates that governing elites have had some room for maneuvering, despite the constraints imposed by external dependence.

Finally, the political legacy of the CAR has some bearing on the current experience with democracy. The country experienced years of an erratic, autocratic leadership under "emperor" Bokassa, but it experienced as well a (short) period of multiparty democracy (1979–81) when the rest of the continent was largely ruled autocratically. Thus, lessons from previous historical experience with institutions are diverse and partly contradictory. This becomes evident in an overview of the political history of the country leading into its current democratic era.

The former French territory Oubangui-Chari became independent on August 13, 1960, as the Central African Republic (CAR). The founding father and president of the "Conseil de Gouvernement," Barthélémy Boganda, who dominated precolonial politics, died in a mysterious plane accident in 1959, eight days before the last colonial elections. His closest aides, Abel Goumba and David Dacko, immediately engaged in a power struggle. This was won by Dacko, who had the backing of the French administration (Mehler 1999a). He arrogated the leadership of Boganda's Mouvement pour l'Evolution Sociale en Afrique Noire (MESAN) and engaged in legal action against Goumba and his breakaway faction. Dacko, who automatically became president of the Republic with the onset of independence, suppressed constitutional liberties in 1960 and forced the creation of a presidential one-party system as soon as 1962.

On December 31, 1965, the Dacko regime was toppled by Colonel Jean-Bédel Bokassa. The constitution was suspended and the National Assembly dissolved. Bokassa introduced an autocratic rule with some erratic ingredients; two alleged coup attempts in 1969 and 1976 were pretexts for a series of executions. Bokassa declared himself president for life in 1972. It was in that period that Ange-Félix Patassé became his prime minister (1976). Subsequently, Bokassa decided to introduce a monarchist constitution, and he changed the name of the country to the Central African Empire. In a glamorous act of self-coronation, Bokassa became emperor on December 4, 1977.[5]

After serious allegations of human rights violations in connection with schoolchildren demonstrations,[6] France, which retained prime importance by maintaining two military bases, decided to overthrow the Bokassa regime and reinstall Dacko. This took place in 1979. Dacko introduced a multiparty system with a presidential constitution. Irregularities in the 1981 presidential elections led to calls for annulment by opposition parties, civil unrest, and finally the postponement of legislative elections. Widespread discontent and the suspension of political parties was the pretext for the bloodless coup d'état of General André Kolingba on September 1, 1981. He suspended the constitution again and ruled with a military junta until 1985. In 1986, Kolingba introduced a new presidential constitution, adopted by a nationwide referendum. Membership in the new united party, the *Rassemblement Démocratique Centrafricain* (RDC), was voluntary.[7]

One especially notable feature of Kolingba's rule was a turn to a very particularistic style of politics. For political support, he increasingly relied on members of his own ethnic group, the Yakoma (a segment of the "river" populations). This was particularly visible in the recruitment patterns for the armed forces. In 1987, semi-competitive elections to parliament were held (as were municipal elections in 1988). But the two main opponents, Goumba and Patassé, boycotted these elections since their parties were not allowed to compete. They called for the re-establishment of the abrogated 1981 Constitution that would have led to a multi-party system.

It was only in 1990 that the pro-democracy movement (trade unions, human rights activists, intellectuals, and parties) became especially forceful. In May of that year, a letter by 253 prominent citizens asked for a National Conference similar to that installed in Benin months earlier. Initially Kolingba refused, detaining several prominent opponents. He then named a prime minister with the visible aim of not being held accountable for management errors. Only belatedly did he accept the principle of free elections, agreeing to hold them in October 1992. In the runup to the national elections, serious budget constraints led to salary arrears for the civil service and subsequently to strike actions and demonstrations that were violently suppressed (Tiangaye 1991).

By the time of elections, Kolingba's political capital was in short supply. When several irregularities occurred in some cities, the elections were suspended by Kolingba and the results annulled completely by the Supreme Court, probably because of a foreseeable defeat of the incumbent. The international community now pressed Kolingba to share power with his main opponents by introducing a collective *Conseil National Politique Provisoire de la République* (CNPPR) as an administering body, naming a "Mixed Electoral Commission" with representatives of all political parties (and the administration) and appointing one of his competitors as prime minister.[8]

New elections were held in August 1993. Kolingba came in fourth after Patassé, Goumba, and Dacko in the first round. Subsequently he tried to modify the electoral code as well as alter the composition of the Supreme Court. But all major donor countries firmly opposed this step, and Kolingba gave up his plans. The runup to the second round of elections offered some auspicious signs for the democratic future of the country. For example, Goumba and Patassé signed a joint declaration assuring each other the acceptance of any outcome.[9] In the second round Patassé was elected president, defeating Goumba, in a largely free and transparent election, with the former taking 52.5 percent of the votes and the latter 45.6 percent.

Notably, voting behavior showed a clearly regionalist pattern, suggesting the emergence of ethnic politics as a significant feature of the political landscape. Patassé and his support came essentially from the neglected, but relatively densely populated, northwestern part of the country. However, in the first round of the 1993 elections, Patassé's support was not confined to the northern part of the country; and, indeed, he did make some inroads in several southern prefectures. But his competitors' support was largely confined to their home regions without securing substantial support in the northern prefectures.[10] The second round reinforced this trend. Although Dacko and Kolingba did not formally voice their support for Goumba, the remaining southern candidate, a transfer of votes from Dacko and Kolingba to Goumba clearly took place.[11]

Another important aspect of these election results was that Patassé won only in seven of seventeen prefectures. Compromises with his political opponents seemed therefore unavoidable. Moreover, in the less closely followed parliamentary elections, his party, the *Mouvement pour la Libération du Peuple Centrafricain* (MLPC), gained a simple but not absolute majority of seats in parliament and therefore had to look for coalition partners.

Organizational Actors in the Elitist Game: Political Parties and Civil Society

The main political parties of the Central African Republic are the MLPC, the RDC, the *Mouvement pour la Démocratie et le Développement* (MDD), and the *Front Patriotique pour le Progrès* (FPP). All of these were tied to political veterans (Patassé, Kolingba, Dacko, and Goumba). The conflictual relationships these parties have had with each other at different phases of recent history have reflected disputes between these elites as they have jockeyed among themselves for power.[12]

The former single party RDC was known as a party of influential opportunists, knit together by the common aim to remain in power. Kolingba's ethnic group, the Yakoma, was prominent in the party, yet the membership extended substantially beyond that circle. The cult of personality around the then-unpopular Kolingba visibly harmed the RDC's electoral chances. In contrast, Patassé's MLPC, in existence since 1981 (longer than the RDC), was better organized and had a large number of party militants predominantly originating from the northwestern part of the country.[13] Goumba, on the other hand, relied on an alliance of smaller parties (*Concertation des Forces Démocratiques,* CFD). This decentralized formation was not able to provide him with a solid backing.

The electoral victory of Patassé in 1993 had several consequences for parties. The MLPC itself came under direct control of Patassé. Yet although Patassé successfully crushed this resistance to his paramount advantage within the MLPC, rivalries between concurrent party circles persisted.[14] The losing parties on the other hand did quite poorly in the aftermath of the elections. The RDC suffered the immediate setbacks of being ousted from power. Supporters of the RDC were soon removed from their positions in the state apparatus and from lucrative positions in the parastatal sector and replaced by (essentially) MLPC supporters. Subsequent trials against notables of the RDC and, later, the persecution of the Yakoma as a whole gradually turned the RDC into a martyr organization and into a perceived monoethnic (Yakoma) party. Goumba's alliance split after the elections. Although he tried to consolidate his own party, the FPP, he was gradually reduced to an intellectual critic with some strong backing in his home region of Ouaka.

Beyond this, parties emerged or gained salience in the aftermath of the elections. Dacko, who had relied on a highly personalized campaign machine during the elections, formed the MDD. Although the party did not produce a coherent program, it profited from the memory of the two phases when Dacko was in power (early 1960s and 1979–81) and when the CAR economy was better off. Next to those main forces, certain parties created during the transition period—such as the versatile PSD, the FC, or MLPC's partners *Parti Libéral Démocrate* (PLD) and *Convention Nationale* (CN)—obtained national political significance in the period that followed the 1993 elections.

Civil society is a problematic term when it comes to labeling a group of actors that might claim political significance in the CAR. Most of the associational realms in the country cannot claim autonomy from the state. What are here subsumed under "civil society" are public actors without personal political ambitions.[15] This very small civil society was particularly active (and effective) during the core transition phase (1990–93). Trade unions, journalists, students, and human rights activists played a crucial role in bringing down the "*ancien régime*" and in organizing the elections of 1993. After the transition, however, only the *Ligue Centrafricaine des Droits de l'Homme* (LCDH, human rights league) and the *Union Syndicale des Travailleurs Centrafricains* (USTC, one of four labor unions) were actively involved in politics.

Patassé and the Onset of Democracy: New Game and New Rules

One clear hope at the outset of Patassé's rule was that certain political patterns established during the transition would persist. The character of political interactions during the transition period seemed to bode well for the democratic future, as most of the major players both voluntarily and involuntarily engaged in practices that appeared to bespeak their acceptance of the democratic rules of the game. Kolingba, for example, had been forced to manage the country in a consensual and inclusive way by governing in conjunction with the CNPPR. In addition, the key actors at least appeared to accept the principle of mutual coexistence, as indicated by Patassé's and Goumba's pre-election declarations that they would accept the result of the elections regardless of outcome. In the first weeks after his election, it seemed that Patassé might carry this spirit forward. Several parties, for example, were involved in the first government, in particular the followers of the third-placed Dacko.

Very soon, however, it became apparent that there would be no embrace of an inclusive, much less a positive-sum, approach to politics. Instead, Patassé displayed a limited acceptance of compromise and even a willingness to engage in dirty politics to advance his power. Political style thus changed dramatically—and not necessarily for the better—with "democracy's" installation.

This was evident, in one respect, in Patassé's behavior vis-à-vis other political actors. In the second half of 1994, Patassé undertook judicial actions against several former ministers and assistant ministers charged with various crimes (desertion, theft, corruption). Already in March of that year, Kolingba was relieved from his military rank (general) and prohibited from leaving the country. Rumors of a planned overthrow by the Kolingba clan were constantly fuelled by the inner circle around Patassé. Additionally, Patassé now removed virtually all Yakoma from important and "juicy" posts in the public sphere. This happened with some outcry in the case of the state-owned oil company PETROCA and the radio and television services. Two hundred members of the presidential guard (mainly Yakoma) were dismissed or shifted to the army. Fourteen out of the sixteen prefects were changed. The RDC complained about a "witch hunt" against it.

More fundamentally, Patassé's rejection of consensus politics was evident in his approach toward the institutions governing democratic decision-making. His approach to the national electoral commission indicated troubling signs in this regard, as he refused to reinstall a mixed commission for some by-elections. A mixed commission was the norm established during the transition period leading into national elections, and it was demanded by the opposition after Patassé came to power. Thereafter, his approach to the drafting of the new constitution revealed the extent to which he was willing to ignore other political actors to obtain a constitution that suited his interests. Notably, however, despite the fact that Patassé invested heavily in creating a system of constitutional rules to his liking, the extent to which those rules have actually mattered remains an open question.

From a comparative perspective, the process of institution-crafting/constitution-making can be more or less inclusive, as well as more or less efficient. In several other young African democracies the elaboration of a new constitution involved relatively inclusive processes. These included the use of constitutional assemblies (Namibia, South Africa), a referendum followed by a provisional constitution and a revision by an impartial Constitutional Review Commission (Malawi), national conferences (Benin, Congo, Mali, Niger), a "national forum" (Madagascar) or other forms of consensus-building as part of a General Peace Agreement (Mozambique).

The opposition in the CAR asked for exactly these kinds of consensual processes. In contrast, however, Patassé sought to minimize the inclusion of his political opponents. He began by installing a technical committee that was charged with creating a draft text of the constitution.[16] Thereafter he called for a conference (*Assises nationales de concertation*) that would then discuss the new text. The newly appointed prefects, trade unionists, church leaders, and representatives of nongovernmental organizations (NGOs) and political parties were all invited. Following the conclusion of the conference, the draft would then be adopted by a national referendum.

Primary opposition emerged during the "conference" phase of this process. One major problem was that the conference was only given a short time span during which they could discuss the draft. The opposition's specific grievances concerned, on the one hand, the modalities of preparation for a constitutional referendum. It was to be organized and administered by the Ministry of Territorial Administration, rather than by a mixed electoral commission.[17] On the other hand, they were also concerned with the content of the constitution as developed by the initial technical committee. Their disputes focused in particular on the length (six years) and number of presidential terms,[18] the weak position of the prime minister (Articles 37 and 38; see below), and the aim to "regionalize" the country (Article 99) with elected regional assemblies (some opposition parties claimed that the outcome would be a "balkanization") (Tag 1996). Since Patassé offered no hope for compromise on these points, most political parties left the conference early.

Despite the problems of the conference, Patassé proceeded with the referendum. In the runup to the vote, five parties represented in the government (including Dacko's MDD) pleaded with the public to vote "no." Other major parties—the FPP and RDC—called on the population to boycott the referendum. Clearly working in Patassé's favor was the fact that public media programs barred the opposition's viewpoints. In the end 82.1 percent of the voters said "yes" (and 17.2 percent said "no"), but only 45 percent of those registered participated in the referendum. Given that only half of the potential voters had approved the constitution, this appeared to be an inauspicious start for the new republic.

As approved on December 28, 1994, and promulgated on January 14, 1995, the constitution contains several notable features from a comparative perspective. The text provides for a semi-presidential system with a strong president and a weak prime minister. The president functions as the "incarnation of national unity," oversees respect for the constitution, fixes the major orientations of the nation's politics, names (and suspends) the prime minister, acts as the chief of the executive, presides over cabinet sessions, has tremendous legislative powers, is authorized to dissolve the National Assembly. In addition, he can initiate popular referendums on important bills and other issues (Articles 21–35). The prime minister, by contrast, is just the head of government; "he conducts and co-ordinates the government's action" and only by delegation of the president does he have the right to call on the administration (Article 37). "At any moment" he could be dismissed by the president or following a vote of no confidence in the National Assembly (Article 38). The constitutional rights of the National Assembly are comparatively large (autonomy in internal affairs, parliamentary immunity, large definition of the domain of the law, frequent oral question sessions, possibility of parliamentary inquiries; Articles 46–65). The judiciary has a strong constitutional stance with guaranteed independence and the impossibility of transferring judges (Articles 75, 76). However, in practice the judiciary proved to be subject to pressures, understaffed and underfunded, not accessible to the population, and lacking possibilities to enforce the law.

The attention to the content of the constitution returns us to one of the primary questions raised in this volume: What is the relationship between the behavior of elites and the institutional frameworks that have governed these countries since their democratic transitions in the early 1990s? Several chapters in this volume indicate that institutional frameworks have had a significant impact on the trajectories of new democracies (see especially those by Villalón and Magnusson). Yet others highlight that institutional factors are less important than the neopatrimonial tendencies that continue to underpin elite behavior (see chapters by Clark and Simon in this regard). With respect to this question, the evidence suggests that institutions have been somewhat less important in the CAR. Notably, the constitution was certainly inspired by, but not comparable to the French model, where the prime minister has clearly more prerogatives. Some observers would clearly advocate the adoption of such a system as a means of overcoming the "gridlock" resulting from French-style semi-presidentialism (as in the Niger case)—though, to be sure, concentrating overwhelming power in the hands of a "democratically elected autocrat" was certainly not more conducive to democracy.

However, in light of the regular breaking of the law, the more fundamental question one must ask was whether the constitutional framework adopted to govern the new democracy was relevant at all. The country has until now lived through twelve constitutional changes and major amendments since independence.[19] A French author observed in 1983:

> The real meaning of Constitutions for the public life of the country is questionable. The ones of 1959 and 1964 have both survived only for 18 months, the one of 1976 was never applied and the one of 1981 had no time to be applied. In less than a quarter of a century the CAR has lived more than 15 years under provisional regimes. . . . And even when a Constitution existed, its respect barely seemed to be the chief worry of the government. (Raynal 1983, 815)

Today, the significance of the constitution is more ambiguous, but no less open to question. Opposition parties, who were originally opposed to the new text, referred to it constantly in their struggle against Patassé's excesses (for example, in the crisis in 2001); so at least it can be considered a "political resource" amongst others.[20] In addition, in the late 1990s the parliament was largely believed to fill its constitutional role of criticizing government action. On the other hand, President Patassé used his informal networks more extensively than his constitutional prerogatives to govern; for example, he established personal advisors who effectively took decisions in place of government ministers. Thus, to borrow from Von-Doepp and Villalón's introduction in chapter 1 of this volume, institutions were much more "potential objects of manipulation, which, in turn, shape subsequent political interactions."

Moreover, it quickly became evident that institutions played only a limited role in the fundamental political dynamic in the country. Elites interacted with one another and jockeyed for power and position, but the constitutional framework was less important in this process than more purely political factors. This becomes especially evident as we review two important tendencies that established themselves very early on and subsequently became defining features of the democratic experiment. The first is the periodic outbreak of political and military conflict. The second is the persistence of a somewhat crude and rapacious neopatrimonial practice bespeaking what others have described as the "criminalization" of the state.

The Mutinies in 1996–97
and the Militarization of Politics

In 1996–97, three army mutinies undermined the country's stability. While a particular situation in the security sector formed the background to these mutinies, they also need to be understood within the context of the larger political environment of Patassé's presidency. To some degree the mutinies were reactions by previously favored groups in the face of an increasingly autocratic, exclusionary, and even threatening state leadership. This said, at an analytical level, the root causes of the mutinies are somewhat less important than an understanding of how they shaped subsequent political developments. As will be seen below, the mutinies not only established a precedent for civil-political violence, they also poisoned the political environment in a manner that made democracy's preservation appear very unlikely.

By the end of 1995, Patassé's rule had resulted in the alienation of the old elite, who, although completely sidelined politically, still retained considerable potential to violently disrupt the political order. The president had shown that he was not prepared to respect his own laws and instead would use means outside the legal framework. The opposition parties were in a state of shock and had hardly gained experience in using the new institutional setup for promoting their interests.

The first mutiny, April 1996, was indirectly tied to Patassé's displacement of former beneficiaries of Kolingba's regime. We have seen that Kolingba was the first head of state who openly "ethnicized" politics in favoring his fellow Yakoma tribesmen. With the electoral success of Patassé, the situation was reversed and Yakoma had to leave important posts, being replaced by fellow "northerners" close to Patassé. But it was rather in response to arrears in their wages (three–four years) that some 250 soldiers took to the streets and protested. They demanded as well an exchange of the army leadership. After clashes in which several were killed, some of their corporatist demands were met. Only one month later the second mutiny erupted, this time involving 500 soldiers, who claimed that the promises made were not fulfilled and that certain strategic decisions (for example, the transfer of one regiment dominated by Yakoma to the countryside) were unacceptable. France intervened militarily, and this time forty-three people were killed.

Negotiations aided by a French army general resulted in the formation of a new inclusive government. Four members of the RDC as well as four ministers representing "civil society" were included. The former CAR ambassador to Paris, Jean-Paul Ngoupande, was appointed prime minister on June 6, 1996. He enjoyed some support by the opposition and immediately asked for more prerogatives, which Patassé was not willing to concede.

Violence returned once again in mid-November. Eight hundred rebels were involved, and this time they had political aims as well, demanding the resignation of the president. One son of Kolingba was involved in the third mutiny, but it remained unclear whether his father backed the uprising. The confrontation clearly had become more dangerous after Patassé had created his own party's militias a few months earlier. Now it was perceived as a threefold conflict: between the old and the new regime; between armed supporters of two important politicians; and, finally, between two still vaguely defined ethno-regional groups, as most "southern" opposition parties increasingly sided with the rebels. France was now dragged into the confrontation, despite the distance between governments in Paris and Bangui. French troops ultimately were considered to be a conflict party themselves after engaging overtly in military operations (Mehler 1996, 1997). France then pushed for mediation by four African presidents who flew in directly from the Franco-African summit in Ouagadougou (Mali's Konaré, Gabon's Bongo, Chad's Déby, and Burkina Faso's Compaoré). The efforts of the presidents led to the signing of the Bangui Peace Accord on January 25, 1997. The agreement provided for the deployment of an inter-African military mission, *Mission Interafricaine de Surveillance des Accords de Bangui* (MISAB).[21] Despite some bloody skirmishes and organizational shortcomings, MISAB played a constructive role, especially in collecting arms from combatants. Mali's ex-president and chief mediator, Amadou Toumani Touré, brokered the entry of mutineers into the government on April 7, 1997. A suspicious murder of three rebels led to the temporary suspension of the opposition's participation in government in May 1997. An inclusive government was re-established on September 1, 1997. The MISAB mission was later replaced by a U.N. mission, *Mission des Nations Unies en RCA* (MINURCA) (Mehler 1996, 1997, 1998; Faltas 2001). What the peacekeepers could not prevent was a tentative "ethnic cleansing" that took place in parts of the capital, Bangui. Some neighborhoods became completely ethnically homogeneous.[22]

Attention to these initial conflicts is important on one level because they reveal the extent to which violence has been endemic to the CAR's experience with democracy. As will be seen, periodic outbreaks of conflict have continued in the CAR; the events of 1996 were in this sense a forerunner of things to come. In addition, it is important to recognize that these conflicts and the character of their resolution had certain very negative effects on the political climate in the country—effects that undermined the subsequent prospects for both democracy and the preservation of civil peace. In this regard, the role of the international community in these conflicts deserves specific scrutiny. For in many regards the activities of international actors—despite intentions—may have contributed to the poisoning of the political environment.

In the first place, the character of conflict settlements, as promoted by international actors, amplified the tension between the principle of accommodation and the practice of exclusionary and privatized politics. International actors continuously asked for a broader representation of the radical and partly violent opposition in government. And at some point, something close to the objective was achieved: the mutinies of 1996–97 led to the inclusion of some rebel leaders in governmental responsibility as brokered by the U.N. and other mediators. Patassé felt compelled, as well, to include some opposition members in his government.[23]

However, the co-optation of individual opposition members cannot be compared to the establishment of the inclusive regime embodied in the *Conseil National Politique Provisoire de la République* (Provisional National Political Council of the Republic) after the annulled presidential elections in 1992. In that instance, all presidential candidates (with the exception of the "stubborn" Goumba) were represented. In 1996–97 Patassé was able to handpick which members of the opposition would be included in the government. At the same time Patassé extended the informal power of the presidential bureaucracy, with several advisors playing a bigger role than the heads of the ministerial departments. It was clear that decisions were not taken in cabinet meetings, but instead informally, in near-secret circles. Donors, the opposition, and even the MLPC criticized the expensive duplication of structures (Fengler 2001).

Thus, what appears to have occurred with these conflict settlements was a temporary and cosmetic acceptance of inclusive politics, resulting largely from international pressure. The practice of inclusion did not however result in any real participation in the decision-making process. Indeed, it seemed to involve more of an extension of rents to those elites with the power to disrupt civil peace. That the National Assembly later decided to give substantial pensions to former presidents Dacko and Kolingba serves as testimony to this.[24] Such pensions were clearly a bonus for renunciation of violence.

In the second place, a dangerous precedent was established in the resolution of these conflicts. A lesson learned by local actors was that the threat of violence could be instrumentalized to get material rewards. For example, the rebels were immediately accepted as a negotiation partner and concessions were quickly made— much quicker than those made to the civilian opposition. Exerting violence proved a means to garner international attention, which, at least at first sight, proved rewarding (Mehler 1999b). One message emanating from this situation was that those losing out in the redistribution of prebends should retain their capacity to sustain conflicts. This would preserve their capacity to come back to the "dining room."[25]

Third, the settlements did little to deal with the fundamental distrust and expectation of violence that characterized political interactions. The distrust created was such that an elite consensus around the "dining table" was no longer at hand— a problem that would endure throughout Patassé's tenure in office. As such, it comes as little surprise that the security aspects of the Bangui agreements were much more difficult to implement. The main stumbling block was the dissolution of the continuously beefed up *Forces Spéciales de Défense des Institutions Républicaines* (FORS-DIR). Only in the beginning of 2000 did Patassé agree to dissolve this unit allegedly responsible for serious human rights abuses and replace it with the much smaller *Unité de Sécurité Présidentielle* (USP)—which was made up of 400 troops instead of 1,600.

Finally, the conflict environment had deleterious effects on the party sector of the CAR polity. In particular, the conflicts served to undermine the legitimacy and viability of the organized partisan opposition to Patassé. This is shown by how the conflict affected interparty organization. In the mid-1990s, several new political parties had emerged, most of them created by disaffected followers of Patassé and Kolingba.[26] These parties, along with others with deeper historical roots, constantly looked for coordination frameworks in an effort to create an organized oppositional bloc to the government. In response to this, several of these parties—the FPP, MDD, PSD, FC, and the *Alliance pour la Démocratie et le Progrès* (ADP)—formed a *Conseil Démocratique des Partis de l'Opposition* (CODEPO) in 1995. The stated common goal of CODEPO was "the maintenance of democratic achievements." The overall strategy was disputed. In contrast to Kolingba at his time, the new president doubtlessly had popular legitimacy, so the efficient mixture of general strikes and demonstrations of the early 1990s could not be advocated as easily. On the other hand, CODEPO could claim that Patassé never behaved like a democrat.

With the mutinies in 1996–97 and, most especially, the divergent tactics of the member organizations during the crisis (accepting or rejecting violence as political means; accepting or rejecting being part of an enlarged government), mutual mistrust increased and CODEPO disintegrated. Subsequently, a new, loosely coordinated body emerged, the "group of eleven" (G-11).[27] Kolingba's participation in the alliance, however, undermined the civic and democratic credentials of the group. Since Kolingba was at least indirectly linked to the mutineers (through his son), Patassé could easily claim that "the opposition" had sided with the rebels. While the alliance allowed increased oppositional leverage in parliament, it clearly lost credibility as a pro-democracy forum.

Beyond this, the outbreak and progression of the mutinies complicated the strategies of the political parties. Military opposition was evidently more effective. And without openly approving violence, the sympathy of most parts of the civil opposition gradually turned to the rebels. But militarization also meant ethnic polarization; no opposition party could claim a mediating role during that time of crisis. The opposition as a whole was quickly amalgamated with the "river" populations;[28] this occurred despite their claim to be a bulwark against the "tribalization of politics" engendered from above by Patassé. As such, the very simple explanation of politics as competition among ethnic groups clearly gained momentum. A new alliance in 1999, the *Union des Forces Acquises à la Paix* (UFAP), tried to overcome that interpretation, with very limited success. Parties thus became victims of the violence.

Criminalization of the State

The second tendency that emerged concerned the visibility of what others have described as the "criminalization of the state" (Bayart, Ellis, and Hibou 1997, 39).[29] Criminal acts are difficult to prove by Africanist research (and usually do not constitute the field). Hard evidence is of course difficult to come by; by their very nature these practices are designed to be clandestine. However, overlooking the widespread perception that white-collar crime was rising in the CAR would be wholly problematic. To do so would ignore what many perceive to be a definitive tendency within the political practices of the new democracy.

Moreover, the effects of this tendency on democracy should not go unstated. For one, the perception of widespread corruption by office holders undermines popular perceptions of the probity of the offices. Extralegal activity is viewed as the norm, thus diminishing the salience of the formally prescribed rules of the game. Moreover, this sends messages to other state officials to themselves engage in petty rent-seeking. The administrative operations of the state suffer accordingly. In addition, as seen below, criminalization injures relations with donors, holding the potential to effectively sacrifice the flow of funds into public treasuries for the sake of preserving income streams into private coffers. Finally, criminal acts contribute to an economy of violence that, as we have seen above, undermines the chances of a successful democratic transition.

Much of the criminalized activity in this regard revolves around the trade of export commodities. The main export commodity, diamonds, is smuggled outside the country for some 60 percent of its value, according to official sources. This could even be a conservative estimation.[30] Some 160 "*collecteurs,*" who organize the "manual" exploitation (with shovel and water pump), all have possibilities to arrange for circumventing the publicly accredited purchase offices and engaging in illegal trafficking of the stones, because the frontiers are long and badly controlled, and the customs officers are notoriously corrupt.[31] Through different tracks, the CAR diamonds end up on the market in Antwerp.

It is important to note that Patassé himself and one of his sons were active in the diamond trade; three diamond companies belonged to Patassé's clan. The picture in other sectors is not necessarily different: over 500,000 hectares of forest were assigned for concession to a company in which a presidential advisor held 50 percent of the shares. One of Patassé's former prime ministers was in the gold business. While the CAR exported officially 38 kilograms of gold in 1997, this must have been only a small percentage of the overall production.[32]

To be sure, it is sometimes difficult to distinguish between the purely commercial and the purely criminal. It is publicly acknowledged that politicians engage heavily in commercial activities. Patassé himself did not hide that he had commercial interests in different sectors (forestry, agriculture, cement, and diamonds).[33] Yet the blurring between the private and the public is quite evident. An eyewitness recalls that at a meeting of the cabinet the finance minister made the president aware that the treasury was (once again) empty. Patassé offered the finance minister to make a personal loan to the public purse (nothing is known about the conditions, but he asked for a receipt).[34] The negotiations with a South African investor (later mentioned by a U.N. panel of experts on the exploitation of resources in the Congo), who wanted to introduce an "industrial" exploitation of diamonds, were conducted directly by the president's office. Patassé used the company's plane for his provincial tours. Patassé also made an Angolan businessman the CAR's ambassador to the United Nations (after receiving CAR nationality); the same man was offered a diamond concession in the west of the country.

Patassé, of course, was not the first leader of the CAR to use such techniques. Bokassa, for instance, had a diamond-purchase office during his reign. Kolingba was known for his excellent relations with the Lebanese business community. Some Lebanese gained CAR nationality and even had influential posts in the *parti unique*. They received big public contracts without due tender processes (mainly in the construction sector).

The protection of dubious commercial practices is easy when the judiciary is not independent. The newly appointed judges apparently acted under political pressure. Some nominations clearly followed party (and ethnic) affiliations.[35] However, even though the ruling elites seemed to control the judiciary, it remained risky to engage in criminal activities: the growing distrust of the international community has negative consequences for the flow of aid, and the blackmail potential from former partners in crime must be taken into account. The former minister of mines, Charles Massi, founder of the opposition FODEM party, launched an open letter in the international press with allusions to commercial affairs of the closer "entourage" of the president. He did this when the regime put him under house arrest in view of charging him for embezzlement of funds. His strategy was successful in the short term. He was released, and the plans not to acknowledge Massi's party were dropped. He won a mandate in the parliamentary elections in 1998 and enjoyed parliamentary immunity.

Parallel to the machinations at the high levels of the state, a whole "culture of impunity" has gained ground. The poor equipment and provisions of lower-level administrative offices contribute to this culture. For example, a *sous-préfet* usually has no administrative vehicle, but he needs to tour his administrative zone, so he is forced to requisition vehicles. And in the context of widespread poverty, the owner of the vehicle is a member of the local elite, sometimes a well-known smuggler. Given the local ethos it is difficult to sanction the same person the next time he is breaking the law.[36]

Elections in 1998 and 1999

The severe crises in 1996–97 and the tendency toward criminalization of the state, resulted in the growing inter-elite distrust, setting the conditions for parliamentary elections in late 1998 and presidential elections in 1999. The parliamentary elections saw a comeback of Kolingba's RDC as it won 20 seats in the 109–seat parliament. Patassé's MLPC secured 47 seats, suggesting the need that, like five years earlier, he would have to form a coalition with other parties. Despite the close result, however, Patassé felt no need to compromise with his political opponents. Instead, he secured a majority in parliament by buying over opposition and "independent" members of parliament. The opposition parties, many of whom felt that they had actually defeated Patassé, were furious (Mehler 2000).[37]

The individual opposition members co-opted in the government were forced by their parties to resign (one resisted). Opposition members of parliament boycotted the sessions for about two months. Ignoring this, President Patassé asked Anicet Georges Dologuélé, hitherto a finance minister respected by the Bretton Woods institutions, to form a new government. Inclusiveness—something the United Nations pressed for constantly—was no longer the order of the day, and this was one important precursor of a severe crisis in spring 2001. There is no doubt that Patassé's utter disregard of other potent political actors could only build up distrust. With hindsight it might be said that Patassé's behavior in this crucial period resulted in a potentially fatal blow to democracy. By 1999, he had split the population between supporters and followers. While favoring the former, he tried to exclude the latter from all areas of public life. This exclusionary policy caused a strong, conflict-escalating trend.

Presidential elections in 1999 exacerbated this trend. Successful organization of the elections was regarded as a main condition for the phasing out of the mandate of the MINURCA mission. The date of the elections was postponed two times, mainly due to "gaps" in the voting register. As in 1993, a mixed electoral commission was responsible for the organization, but clearly no continuity in management was safeguarded. Only a small number of the acting commissioners were involved in the elections in 1993 and this lack of experience accounted for several irregularities. As in 1993, the organization heavily depended on outside support in delivering election material to remote places. Airlifting was done in 1993 by the French air force; in 1999, U.N. machines were used. This fact sheds some light on the limited "sustainability" and "ownership" of democracy in the CAR.

The candidates' names were familiar. In addition to Patassé, there were the same candidates from the 1993 elections (Kolingba, Dacko, and Goumba); other leading opposition figures (Lakoué, Ngoupande, and Massi); and independent candidates (Henri Pouzère, Joseph Abessolo, and Fidèle Ngouandjika). The weakness of the opposition was underlined as the UFAP did not manage to unite around one single candidate. A formal arrangement to desist in favor of one common candidate for the second round was signed, but it turned out to be useless. Similar to the situation in Zambia, the ultimate failure to displace Patassé can be partly attributed to the inability of opposition members to cooperate. The climate of distrust hindered any purposive collective action to that end.

Tense situations preceded voting day. Patassé drew heavily on Chinese support during his election campaign (including their provision of trucks, motorcycles, and bicycles). During party rallies, confrontations between the MLPC and RDC cost the lives of at least two persons in Bangui. In three *sous-préfectures,* the vote took place only three days after the official date, due to technical problems. In Paris and Libreville the registered voters could not vote. Even before the official result could be announced, the opposition claimed to have been cheated and produced a list of irregularities. It called for resistance against an "electoral coup d'état."

The 200 international observers deployed by the United Nations, the European Union, and the Francophonie association came to a different conclusion and declared that all frauds and irregularities were not of a kind to affect the overall result.[38] The observers lauded the participation rate of 56.4 percent. Ultimately, the constitutional court declared Patassé the winner in the first round with 51.6 percent of the votes, followed by Kolingba (19.4 percent), Dacko (11.2 percent), and Goumba (6.1 percent).[39] The fact that Patassé only barely received an absolute majority raised some suspicions. However, the large distance between Patassé and second-place Kolingba made clear that he would have won with a high degree of probability in an eventual second round. That insight finally motivated the opposition to accept defeat after some days of hesitation.

The results were in fact clear. Patassé conserved and extended his massive backing in his home region (and in parts of Bangui); Kolingba was on the rise, which augured badly for democracy in the CAR; Goumba lost ground; and the ambitious younger candidates still had a long way to go. The ethno-regional cleavage had solidified.

As with the other elections held in the CAR (1993 and 1998), those in 1999 passed the basic test of being acceptable in terms of the procedures followed and the relative fairness of the process. Subsequent events reveal, however, that effective elections are not a sufficient condition for stability; for the circumstances of post-electoral arrangements were quite problematic. Indeed, one important and, in the end, dangerous result of the rather smoothly organized 1999 presidential elections was that MINURCA could regard its mission as being accomplished and was replaced by a small governance support unit, the *Bureau des Nations Unies pour la Consolidation de la Paix en RCA* (BONUCA). There was an assumption that, with those elections, the CAR would return to stability, but it was soon proved wrong. The unusually successful MINURCA mission apparently ended too soon; different U.N. organs were to try to save at least part of those accomplishments during the crisis in 2001 (see below). The Swiss foundation Hirondelle took over Radio MINURCA with the help of some bilateral donors (and the UNDP) and established the radio station Ndeke Luka.[40] Worse was to come.

The Remilitarization of Politics

In the period following the 1999 elections, politics in the CAR have witnessed a dangerous remilitarization of political life. The conditions leading to this process reflected themes already established in this chapter: a climate of extreme distrust among key political actors and groups, exclusionary and even authoritarian tendencies from the state, and uncertain signals and problematic actions by international actors. The outcome was ultimately the undermining of the democratic system itself.

The central event in this process of remilitarization was a full-fledged and violent coup attempt on May 28, 2001. Rebels stormed strategic buildings in the capital Bangui. Fighting raged in several parts of the city, but loyalists eventually regained control with the help of Libyan troops and Congolese rebels. The respite from violent and conflictual politics, however, would prove to be short-lived.

Several issues formed the backdrop to the coup attempt of 2001. On one level stood the deteriorating condition of civil and political rights in the country. Already before the presidential elections of 1999, severe human rights violations had increased. Both the president of the Human Rights League and a trade union leader were harassed and beaten by elements of the remodeled presidential guard. After the presidential elections, the problematic human rights situation remained unchanged. Parliamentary and extra-parliamentary opposition was restricted in some basic freedoms. Opposition and civil society figures were prohibited from leaving the country. Extralegal executions were the order of the day as an *Office centrafricain de répression du banditisme* took over the fight against criminality. Its commander, Louis Mazangue, gained a dubious reputation for shooting suspected criminals when they were caught stealing a second time. Finally, the private press was harassed. In late 1999, *Reporters sans frontières* issued an official protest note after four editors were summoned by a military tribunal in the context of a local massacre in Kolingba's home region (Dimbi).[41] Patassé now accused the press of inciting rebellion and ethnic hatred.

In the same period, tensions among the primary political players worsened considerably. In parliament, an impasse over the distribution of posts in its bureau triggered a complete, but passing, boycott of plenary sessions by a united front of fifty-two opposition members of parliament in late 1999. A motion of no confidence against the government was introduced by forty-five opposition members of parliament only a few weeks later—with no success. A second motion of no confidence in April 2000 was linked to new corruption allegations against some ministers. In an interview with the Paris-based weekly *Jeune Afrique,* Patassé threatened the majority of the initiators of the vote of no confidence with court action (*Jeune Afrique/L'Intelligent* 2052, May 9–15, 2000). Their aim, he claimed, was to sabotage the good relations between the CAR and the Bretton Woods institutions. The vote of no confidence later failed.

Tensions continued when Patassé's MLPC accused an opposition party, PUN (*Parti de l'Unité Nationale*), of working on plans to overthrow the government in a violent coup d'état. The PUN's leader Ngoupande and FODEM's leader Massi responded with reports of massive intimidation. A new youth movement began to erect barricades in Bangui in November 2000. Precipitated presumably by the mysterious deaths of ex–prime minister Jean-Luc Mandaba and his son, the *Flambeau Centrafricain* (FLAC) engaged in street battles with the police. The FLAC asked Patassé to resign. Patassé immediately hinted at contacts among FLAC, PUN, and the FODEM leadership. A later demonstration by the opposition that December was dissolved violently.

The political turmoil was accompanied by social unrest. Beginning in September 2000, the trade unions called continuously for action to protest against twenty-nine months of salary arrears. Once again the trade unions showed a remarkable ability to mobilize their members. A call for a general strike was effectively imple-mented in December. Patassé seemed to take note and finally dismissed his frequently criticized prime minister, Dologuélé. It is particularly telling to re-read the explana-tions of the influential president of Parliament, Dondon Konambaye, with regard to the delayed sacking of the prime minister in March 2001:

> I think we should let Dologuélé bring in the cash. . . . Keep him there so that what he has negotiated effectively comes in, so that he wipes out a good part of the wage arrears. And then, when the situation is back to normal, he can be replaced and the person who takes his place will not have so many difficulties; if not, they will stop everything. . . . He has negotiated with the Bretton Woods institutions, with the European Union, with our bilateral partners. I do not favor that Dologuélé should be eternally there. No! It is a question of opportunity.[42]

This was the regime's main concern: securing the development-aid rent.

Still, an explosive mixture of strikes, youth protests, and political-ethnic po-larization was brewing. After a short pause in strikes, the trade unions resumed the civil servants strike in May 2001. This was the situation when the attempted coup d'état took place in May 2001.

The specific progression of the coup attempt took place as follows: Rebels stormed the presidential residence and tried to control the nerve centers of the city, particularly the radio station. Fighting raged in several parts of the city. The army chief of staff, Abel Abrou, and the commander of the gendarmerie, the dreaded General François N'Djadder Bedaya, were shot, but no other major objective of the rebels was achieved. The loyalists regained the upper hand in the following days, supported by at least 300 troops of the rebel leader Bemba from the neighboring Democratic Republic of Congo and by Libyan forces. Kolingba publicly claimed that he orchestrated the rebellion, which reinforced the interpretation as a Yakoma uprising.

In the period that followed the uprising, retaliatory acts targeted all affiliated with Kolingba. This included his personal contacts, the RDC, and the Yakoma in general. Militia groups affiliated with Patassé, for example, "eliminated" several sym-pathizers of Kolingba. Bangui's southwestern districts of Bimbo, Petevo, Fatima, and Bruxelles, where the mutineers were hiding, were the targets of intense shelling. The total number of casualties was officially established at 57, but the num-ber of deaths might have exceeded 500. The RDC deputy for Bangui 5, Théophile Touba, was murdered, apparently after being tortured. Sylvère Omisse, a member of the Constitutional Court, was killed as well, probably because he had a name that sounded Yakoma (although he was not). Kolingba himself went into hiding (and was later exiled to Uganda). Persecution of Yakoma families began, houses in specific parts of the capital were destroyed (360 alone in the neighborhood of Ouango), and 80,000 inhabitants fled to the countryside or, predominantly, crossed the river Oubangui to the Congolese town of Zongo.[43] Some important personalities close to Kolingba (and some of his relatives) found refuge in the French

embassy. The assaults on the Yakoma and the RDC later took place from an institutional context. The parliament's chairman Dondon Konamabaye called the Yako-
mas "tolerated foreign elements" and advocated the dissolution of the RDC. Patassé
clarified that the decision to dissolve the RDC could only be taken by the judiciary. However, his Minister of the Interior suspended the RDC for several months
only a few days later. It was only rehabilitated in late 2002.

The initial response suggested that a rather simplified interpretation of the rebellion was at work, as Kolingba, the Yakoma, and the RDC were demonized as
the source of the conflict. However, a later judicial investigation of the rebellion
revealed that the matter was more complex. A "mixed judicial enquiry team" was
set up in June 2001 with the mission of investigating the rebellion. The investigation was conducted with great zeal by a commission headed by Chief Prosecutor
Joseph Bindoumi, and it led to the surprising indictment of Defense Minister Demafouth, who was accused of siding with the rebel leader Bemba in order to get
rid of Patassé in a potential second coup. About one hundred arrests were ordered
in the course of these investigations, which contributed to an atmosphere of suspicion and fear.[44] Disciplinary action was also taken: some 120 civil servants, most
with Yakoma names, who fled the country were sanctioned by their respective ministries. The national radio broadcast a list of about 200–300 names of soldiers who
did not report back to their barracks, most of them again with Yakoma names. A
highly regarded lawyer close to the RDC was arrested after questioning the legal-
ity of the Bindoumi commission.

Soon the Bindoumi investigations caused an atmosphere of general suspicion,
extending well into the MLPC itself. Patassé decided to dissolve the national coordination of party officers in October after it was suggested that Kolingba had accomplices within his own party. In turn, the first vice president of the parliament,
an eminent party member, was arrested amongst others.

A greater challenge lay ahead, however. This appeared with the dismissal and
later accusation of the chief of staff, General François Bozizé, who was implicated
in a new coup plan.[45] Bozizé refused to accept an arrest warrant, defected with
about a hundred troops, engaged in street battles in the northern neighborhoods
of Bangui (traditionally supporting Patassé), and moved to the north of the country. After taking weapons from several gendarmerie barracks and engaging in a
number of skirmishes, possibly involving additional Libyan troops and aircraft as
well as "recently recruited young members of a pro-government militia,"[46] Bozizé
went into exile in Chad.

This new escalation complicated the political game substantially. First, Bozizé
was a well-known supporter of Patassé, who stemmed from the Gbaya ethnic group.
His prosecution endangered the unity of Patassé's power base. Second, since the
Chadian authorities granted exile to him (probably motivated by their fear of being confronted with Libyan troops to the north and the south in an increasingly
uneasy relationship with its powerful neighbor), the regional security system began to affect Bangui once again. Hectic diplomatic activity in early December 2001
included Libyan-led initiatives in the framework of COMESSA (Community of

Sahelo-Saharan States), putting forward the idea of a peacekeeping force, and a Gabon-led initiative in the framework of CEMAC (Economic and Monetary Community of Central Africa) focused on dialogue processes. A small peacekeeping force from Sudan and Djibouti was deployed in February 2002.

Any normal political life of a young democracy was effectively destroyed by the military involvement of 2001. After the May coup attempt, the personal security of several political leaders was compromised. Ngoupande, Massi, and Pouzère all claimed to be targeted—this despite the fact that they had voiced their loyalty for the regime in the immediate aftermath of the rebellion. Trade unions halted their strike actions after being blamed for creating the pretexts of turmoil while their main motivations had not changed. The use of arms thus caused important "collateral damage" to this important actor of Central African democracy: each mutiny or coup attempt followed demonstrations organized by the trade unions (with the exception of the first Bozizé revolt). Their legitimate grievances could no longer be voiced without suspicion.

In short, the political climate had deteriorated so considerably that the entire vocabulary of democratic governance—loyal opposition, civil society, rule of law, tolerance of dissent—was wholly inapplicable. The "learned expectations that various political players have of each other" (see the introduction by VonDoepp and Villalón, chapter 1, this volume) all nurtured distrust. The hope of returning to a constructive democratic "game," with all players accepting the rules, seemed naive and distant. This was confirmed by the events stretching from October 2002 to March 2003.

The Collapse of Civil Peace: October 2002 to March 2003 (and Beyond)

Bozizé's troops came back to Bangui with a surprise attack on October 25, 2002. Heavy fighting once again involving Libyan troops and up to 1,000 fighters of the Congolese rebel organization *Mouvement de Libération du Congo* (MLC) on Patassé's side destroyed parts of northern Bangui. At one point, up to 150,000 inhabitants of Bangui and the immediate vicinity had fled their homes and taken refuge in safer suburbs in the south or in the bush. The pro-government forces fought back against the rebels. In contrast to earlier crises confined to Bangui, the countryside— particularly the towns of Damara, Bossangoa, and Bozoum—had now become a theater of combat. The MLC fighters were subsequently accused of raping, looting, and killing some 150 Chadian cattle herders. This new escalation was preceded by recurrent skirmishes on the Chad-CAR border and diplomatic activities attempting to reconcile both countries and find a political solution for the Bozizé-Patassé confrontation.

This time the opposition, now divided between some exiled leaders apparently in close contact with Bozizé and the *Co-ordination des Partis Politiques d'Opposition*

(CPPO), a new common platform under the leadership of Lakoué, did not condemn the attack. It accused Patassé of treason (failing to respect his oath of office obliging him to "assure the protection of people and goods") and abuse of authority. It called for a withdrawal of Libyan and MLC troops. The CEMAC peacekeepers effectively replaced the Libyans at the end of the year 2002, but the contingent was far too small to guarantee peace. The CPPO organized some impressive demonstrations, but Lakoué had to go underground when he was accused of subversion. Patassé offered a "national dialogue without exclusion" at New Year's Eve, but only gradually received support for the idea. The president was completely isolated, the country devastated, and democracy in shambles when a surprise attack by Bozizé's troops (helped by Chad) led to the downfall of the government.

Patassé was at a COMESSA summit in Niger. Upon his return he could not land, was forced to fly to Cameroon, and finally took exile (again) in Togo. Bozizé suspended the constitution and named a new cabinet that included most opposition parties, with Goumba as vice-president (in order to profit from his image as a spotless politician). A National Transitional Council (CNT) as an all-party body was introduced to serve as interim legislative body.[47] Patassé claimed that he remained the legitimate president, but he did not receive any outside support. To the contrary, the CEMAC leaders recognized the new regime early on. Patassés party (MLPC) split—with one faction eager to cooperate with the government. The postponed national dialogue was held from September 15 to October 27, 2003, resulting in a sober assessment of the country's situation. Despite numerous statements of forgiveness[48] and reconciliation, the climate of distrust continued.

The new government soon found it hard to pay salaries, particularly since GDP contracted by 7 percent in 2003 and outside budgetary support remaining suspended. With no proper accounting for government revenue and expenditure, the chaotic situation of state finances deteriorated while lawlessness in rural areas continued. Widespread banditry was attributed mostly to the "liberators" (Bozizé's supporters of northern or Chadian origin).[49] Despite numerous admonitions to behave like "ATT" (see the chapter on Mali by Villalón, this volume), Bozizé soon showed ambitions to stand as a candidate for presidential elections scheduled for early 2005. In February 2004 the CNT condemned the government for illegality and malpractice. This marked the end of the period of its broad public endorsement. On the positive side, the temporary commonality of interests between pro-Kolingba and pro-Bozizé forces may help to overcome the steady "tribalization" of politics, but both rebel movements have committed serious human rights violations themselves and can hardly be taken for democrats. Perspectives are bleak.

▼▼▼▼

The new confrontations in 2001–2003 represented a heavy blow to the high hopes for a democratic society expressed during the first phase of the transition. Notably, however, the democratic process might already have broken down with the presidential elections in 1999. By that time the balance sheet suggested democratic failure: the positive achievements of Central African democracy—repeatedly acceptable quality of elections, a more or less working parliament, and the survival of opposition parties under poverty conditions—are by far overshadowed by the negative elements—state decay, militarization, civil war, the bending of rules.

The terrible fate of democracy in the CAR can be explained in different ways. First, the redistribution of prebends under Patassé created powerful losers. Parts of those losing out retained military power and felt compelled to go beyond mere threats to achieve their aims. This was not a necessary outcome of the democratization process, but was brought about by Patassé's and Kolingba's behavior. Second, the president was not able to establish himself above the political class but followed a self-interested policy, using dubious means outside the legal framework. Third, opposition parties were not able to channel very real grievances into the formal political process, and they were not able to form a solid civilian alliance against autocratic tendencies. Fourth, civil society as a whole was not able to broker a sustainable peace. It was not able to drive the democratization process any further than the transition in 1993. In particular, trade unions were not able to channel material grievances into the formal political process without being exploited by the advocates of violence. A "deepening" of democracy did not happen.

Finally, the international community failed in that same respect. The reduction of the aid flow from the outside had a clearly negative effect. What was the lesson for the CAR elites? Optimists in the Bretton Woods institutions believed that the "swamp" would be dried out in the course of structural adjustment; since the development rent would disappear, elites would be "reasoned." However, skeptical voices were proven right when they claimed that the habitual resource flow worked like a drug. And like drug addicts, the elites going through withdrawal felt a necessity to provide themselves cash wherever they could get it and no matter how, including the increase of criminal activities—illegal trafficking, money laundering—and violence. A more politically attuned approach would have included support for a gradual process of reforming neopatrimonialism. The role of the international community in Mozambique has been crucial in permitting a rather smooth transition (see Manning's contribution, chapter 10, this volume). In the CAR, a more sensitive approach would have included an appropriate analysis of the political actors and institutions and the option of selective, yet substantial support (the "democracy bonus"). It would not have drastically cut assistance to the government while it would have established controls of illegal activities. But how much democracy and what pace of structural adjustment is (if at all) possible under the dominant political style of neopatrimonialism?[50] Here the answer must come from other African examples; the CAR case is not conclusive.

The room for maneuvering was certainly always small; the risks of civil war, anomie, or a return to authoritarian rule are more real than ever. Who could even talk about democracy in the CAR in early 2005? The situation was first and foremost a situation of fear.

NOTES

1. According to a frequently cited definition, "structural stability is to be understood as a term denoting a dynamic situation, a situation of stability able to cope with the dynamics inherent in [emerging] democratic societies. Structural stability could thus be defined as a situation involving sustainable economic development, democracy and respect for human rights, viable political structures, and healthy social and environmental conditions, with the capacity to manage change without resort to violent conflict" (Commission of the European Communities 1996). For an elaboration of the argument, see Andreas Mehler (2002).

2. Interview by author with a sociologist in Bangui, August 23, 1998.

3. *"La RCA est un pays sous serum,"* said a UNDP official in Bangui, August 24, 1998, during an interview by the author. In rough translation, this idiom implies that the RCA is a country on an IV.

4. There is a body of literature on this issue that could be more systematically used to understand variations of democratic transitions. See Ross (2001) and Clark (2002).

5. The material borrows from Mehler (1999a).

6. Bokassa was suspected of being directly involved in the murder of schoolchildren who had refused to wear obligatory school uniforms sold in his own stores. Equally, allegations raised of acts of cannibalism could not be verified.

7. See again Mehler (1999a).

8. First, Timothée Malendoma, founder of the *Forum Civique* (FC); later, Enoch Dérant Lakoué, *Parti Social Démocrate* (PSD).

9. See Goumba/Patassé, *Déclaration Commune,* Bangui, September 9, 1993 (unpublished mimeograph); and see also the reaffirmation between both rounds in Goumba/Patassé, *Déclaration Commune,* Bangui, September 25, 1993 (unpublished mimeograph).

10. Goumba in Mbomou, Haut-Mbomou, Haute-Kotto; Ouaka in the east; Mambéré-Kadey in the west; Dacko in Lobaye, Ombella-Mpoko, and in parts of Bangui; and Kolingba in Basse-Kotto.

11. Much of the above discussion draws from Mehler (1999a).

12. Main confrontations occurred between Dacko and Goumba in the 1960s, Patassé and Dacko in 1981, Kolingba and Dacko in 1981, Patassé and Kolingba in 1982 and 1986 (attempted coups), Goumba and Kolingba 1990–93, and Patassé and Kolingba/Goumba since 1993. There is a hidden conflict between generations at work, and it may be that some hope is permitted when finally the "old guard" will step down.

13. This includes the Sara-Kaba and Gbaya ethnic groups.

14. This came to light prominently during the 2001 crisis; see below.

15. Personalities entering the two governments of Prime Minister Dologuele in 1999 who had no party affiliation are therefore not part of this category, although they claimed they belonged to the civil society.

16. Constitutional maneuvering was observed in Zambia as well; see chapter 9 in this volume on Zambia by David Simon.

17. The text of the constitution is reprinted in *Afrique Contemporaine* 1995, 61–79.

18. The president can be elected for a second term (Art. 23); there was no interim arrangement, which meant that Patassé could effectively head for three consecutive mandates.

19. Beginning with an important revision in 1960 and a second in 1962. It con-

tinues: 1964 one-party system (new constitution); 1966 abolition of the constitution, replaced by a provisional text; 1974 Bokassa declared president for life; 1976 monarchy; 1979 provisional constitution; 1981 new constitution; 1985 text dismantling the military junta; 1986 new constitution; 1992 transitional rules; 1995 new constitution.

20. In 1996, the MDD filed a complaint at the Supreme Court regarding infringement of the Constitution by Patassé. The Supreme Court postponed its ruling for an indefinite period since it would fall under the competence of the not-yet-existent Constitutional Court provided by the new Constitution (which was established only in 1997).

21. Troop contingents came from Burkina Faso, Chad, Gabon, Mali, Senegal, and Togo; logistical support came from France.

22. Some of this material draws from Mehler (1999a).

23. Another ambiguous effect of the international peacekeeping mission was that the already-weak state lost the responsibility to care for the physical security of its citizens, after most social welfare issues were already "internationalized" and cared for by agencies of development assistance. Positive effects can be observed for the media landscape: MINURCA established its own radio (Radio MINURCA) in 1998, with the primary aim of promoting peace and reconciliation. The impact of such an independent source of information was remarkable. Credible and neutral information countered the wildest rumors that spread throughout the country. Radio MINURCA broadcast programs on civic education, potentially an effective tool in the democratization process, and particularly for the preparation of the 1998–99 elections.

24. This occurred on October 30, 1997.

25. The CAR example is in line with the argument by Bratton and van de Walle (1997), who claim that a transition from neopatrimonial rule is prone to a violent abortion because of the tendency of the democratically elected new president to distribute according to neopatrimonial logic, but this time not to the same circle of persons.

26. One of the most influential ones was the *Parti de l'Unité Nationale* (PUN) of Ngoupande. A particular case is the *Forum pour la Modernité* (FODEM) by ex-agriculture and mining minister Charles Massi (see below).

27. Notably, without the PSD, but including RDC.

28. "River populations" is a collective term for groups living in the Oubangui Valley, including the Mbaka, Sango, Yakoma, and other ethnic groups.

29. Already in 1993 Patassé was accused of having used embezzled money for financing his election campaign ("*affaire crédit mutuel d'Angoulême*"); Patassé denied having knowledge about the source of this money, but finally paid it back. A good number of other such affairs have come to light in recent years and rumors continue to circulate.

30. See *Africa Consulting* (1999). Some of the interviews backing this study were conducted by the author in August–September 1998.

31. On corruption of customs officers, see *Le Citoyen* (Bangui), August 28–29, 1998.

32. Interviews in Bangui, August–September 1998.

33. Patassé himself confirmed: "*Je fais des affaires au vu et au su de tout le monde. Je donne ainsi l'exemple à mes compatriotes, au lieu de vivre à leurs crochets. En Afrique, la tradition veut qu'un chef ait des ressources. C'est le réflexe d'un Africain digne* [I do business in a way visible for all. I thereby give the example to my fellow citizens instead of living at their expense. In Africa, tradition requires that the chief have resources. This is the reflex of a dignified African.]," quoted in *Libération,* April 9, 1998. More interesting information about Patassé's links to a famous French rightist extremist can be found in the same article.

34. Interviews in Bangui, August 1998. Patassé confirmed this in a recent interview in *Jeune Afrique*, April 22–28, 2002 (*"plus d'une fois, il m'est arrivé d'avancer de l'argent au gouvernement* [More than once I have had to lend money to the government.]"). Additionally, he claimed that his rivals would all be his debtors.

35. Interviews in the CAR, September 1998.

36. Interview with a *sous-préfet*, September 4, 1998.

37. Especially in the "Koudoufara affair" (member of parliament elected on a PSD ticket).

38. Reuters, September 24, 1999.

39. For other candidates the results were as follows: Pouzère (4.2 percent), Ngoupande (3.1 percent), Lakoué and Massi (1.3 percent each), and Ngouandjika and Abessolo (0.9 percent each).

40. See http://www.hirondelle.org for background information (accessed September 9, 2004).

41. Those were Faustin Babou/*Colline de Ba-Ubangui,* Cordose Meillot/*Le Démocrate,* Jude Zosse/*L'Hirondelle,* Maka Gpossokoto/*Le Citoyen.* See accounts under www .sangonet.com (accessed November 22, 1999).

42. See *L'Hirondelle* (Bangui), March 15, 2001, *"Interview exclusive accordée au journal L'Hirondelle par le Président de l'Assemblee Nationale Luc Apollinaire Dondon Konamabaye"* (translation by Andreas Mehler). The interview addresses rumors about Konamabaye's ritual tasks in the "entourage" of Patassé, as well.

43. According to the Italian NGO COOPI, 70,000 had returned by the beginning of September (see *Agence France Press,* "La situation humanitaire se normalise à Bangui," September 6, 2001). However, roughly 1,000 armed men remained in the DRC. In December the UNHCR signaled the presence of a total of 23,000 Central African refugees in Zongo (see UNHCR briefing notes, "Afghanistan, Ministerial Meeting on Refugees, East/Horn of Africa, Central African Republic," December 4, 2001). The refugees still considered their return premature. They listed preconditions ranging from the rehabilitation of their houses to a guarantee for their safety back home. In April 2002, some 6,000 refugees remained in the DRC.

44. Former minister and presidential advisor Alfred Poloko was one of the first VIPs arrested in this context. He was extradited by the embassy in Chad, where he had fled. Demafouth was only cleared from his charges in October 2002. By contrast, Kolingba, Massi, and twenty-two others were condemned to the death penalty in August 2002.

45. After the killings of N'Djadder and Abrou, the arrest of Djemafouth, and the sacking of the remaining "security ministers," Bozizé could have been regarded as the last influential leader in the security sector.

46. Reuters, December 12, 2001.

47. Nicolas Tiangaye, chairman of the LCDH, became the CNT president.

48. Inter alia between Dacko and Goumba. Dacko died only a few weeks later.

49. For more details on developments in 2003, see the U.N. Security Council report "The Situation in the Central African Republic and the Activities of the United Nations Peace-building Support Office in the Central African Republic: Report of the Secretary-General," June 20, 2003 (S/2003/661) and December 29, 2003 (S/2003/1209).

50. The compatibility of democracy and neopatrimonialism is sometimes disputed. Chabal and Daloz (1999, 162) assume that the lack of means to sustain neopatrimonial rule would lead to either war or crime as two forms of "disorder."

7 | The Fate of Madagascar's Democracy

Following the Rules while Eroding the Substance

Richard R. Marcus

By the mid-1990s, Madagascar had joined the ranks of those African countries deemed "democratic" by the international community because, as the U.S. Department of State said, it "completed its transition from 16 years of authoritarian Socialist rule with the free and fair election of Albert Zafy as president in 1993" (1997, 1). This view was held up until December 2001, when the country held its third multiparty presidential elections of the democratic era. Such assessments were predicated largely on the fact that key institutions associated with democracy—political rights for the citizenry, a constitution, and regular electoral contests—would continue to operate and shape the basic contours and evolution of national political life. In these respects, "democracy" had flourished in Madagascar. Not only had there been regular elections, but people protested in the streets, practiced the religion of their choice, and published newspaper articles lambasting not only the system but also specific politicians.Nonetheless, democracy in Madagascar is, to borrow from de Tocqueville's description of nineteenth-century France, without anything to lessen its vices and bring out its advantages. What is meant by this "democracy" is lost to a decade of debate that steers an uneasy course past an intellectual common ground. Madagascar, rife with predatory political agents that obfuscate, amend, and subvert political institutions, is a "success" by way of following electoral procedures.

As it turns out, Madagascar offers lessons not primarily about processes of democratic consolidation in Africa, but about the notion of consolidation itself and the limitations of perspectives that prioritize institutions over other processes. In such views, the establishment and operation of electoral processes is the first step toward the expansion of democratic freedoms and generation of democratic outcomes. The expectation is that elections can serve as the procedural means to usher in the more substantive exercise of democracy. Madagascar belies such visions. The installation of democratic "rules of the game," and, particularly, the successful conducting of elections, has failed to generate the two outcomes that one would most clearly expect from a democratic system: popular influence over government decisions and rule-governed behavior by key elites.

This issue is brought into sharp focus by the events surrounding Madagascar's third presidential elections of December 16, 2001. The electoral process itself went smoothly. There were no significant cases of ballot stuffing, no significant intimidation at the polls, and no significant cases of ballots washing up downriver. The rules of the election-day game were, for the most part, followed by all parties concerned. In this sense Madagascar's third presidential elections seemed to represent another step toward democratic consolidation.

There was a major and dramatic shortcoming to this "democratic consolidation," however: the elections did not produce a clear victor. Six months after the balloting, two candidates—the incumbent, Didier Ratsiraka, and the leading challenger, Marc Ravalomanana—were each still claiming victory, the island was balkanized, and military conflict loomed.[1] The repetition of elections under rules candidates have agreed upon is one definition of democratic consolidation. Yet, if this process cannot produce an institutionally sanctioned and accepted leader, then we are left asking if the electoral process—balloting—is serving its democratic function. The presidential elections of 2001 demonstrated that they are not. Marc Ravalomanana came into power months later by bringing his supporters to the streets and waging an armed conflict. "Democracy" may have prevailed, in a broader Jeffersonian sense, in that the candidate who was clearly preferred by the people took office. However, Ravalomanana accomplished this in spite of soft institutions that were incapable of staving off challenges from individual political agents, not because of the effective democratic institutions and the electoral procedures in place. Justified or not, he had to subvert the constitutional process to win his victory (Marcus and Razafindrakoto 2003). What exactly is it, then, that Madagascar is consolidating?

In this chapter, I argue that the problem lies in definitions of democratic consolidation that emphasize the process while ignoring the broader capacity of democratic institutions to produce the substance of democracy. Madagascar has begun the process of democratic consolidation in a narrow sense. However, the sort of democracy it is consolidating is one where fundamental democratic institutions of constitutions and elections fail to cultivate rule-governed behavior and meaningful participation by the people. Elites in Madagascar have maintained but also manipulated democratic institutions in ways that have allowed them to preserve the structures of democracy while precluding much of the substance. The first two elected presidents of the Third Republic, Zafy Albert and Didier Ratsiraka, both manipulated democratic institutions to suit their own ends—changing the rules via elections (specifically, referenda) that offered unclear choices to citizens. The third presidential elections appear to have added Marc Ravalomanana to this list of leaders willing to conflate the power of the office with personal power.

In this sense, Madagascar clearly exemplifies the problem described by Joshua Forrest in chapter 11 of this volume, hybridity—elements of democracy and liberal politics operating in contexts where neopatrimonial and authoritarian tendencies remain. Building from Herbst, moreover, there is no reason to expect that this hybridity cannot be a long-term equilibrium outcome (Herbst 2001, 359). While some scholars might argue that the elections themselves are a significant indicator of ongoing progress toward a democratic end (Dahl 1971; Huntington 1991; O'Donnell 1994), Madagascar's imperfect democratic transition may well persist as a more enduring situation than these views would suggest. Indeed, while the institutions of democracy have survived even the major crisis following the 2001 elections, these institutions have yet to produce the substance of a democratic system.

What Is Democracy Supposed to Provide?

We can build upon the classic work of Robert Dahl (1971) to think of democracy's attributes on a continuum. Dahl referred to one end of the continuum as a "limited democracy" and the other as a "full democracy."[2] A limited democracy is one that closely resembles Schumpeter's famed description: "that institutional arrangement for arriving at political decisions in which individuals acquire the power to decide by means of a competitive struggle for the people's vote" (Schumpeter 1950, 250). This sort of institutional process creates a competition primarily among elites. A full democracy, Dahl asserts, is one that allows for greater expectations, notably the individual freedoms associated with a classical definition of democracy.

A major argument for defining democracy in this limited fashion is that this seems to many to be a prerequisite to the emergence of a "full" democracy, replete with expansive political freedoms and perhaps even mechanisms for economic equality. Indeed, Dahl (1971) clearly accepts this view when he argues that the "normal" process is for countries to establish competition before inclusiveness. Here, he distinguished between political contestation ("the extent to which institutional conditions are openly available, publicly employed, and fully guaranteed to at least some members of the political system" [1971, 4]) and political inclusiveness ("the proportion of the population entitled to participate on a more or less equal plane in controlling and contesting the conduct of government" [1971, 4]). In order for participation to expand, the competition must already be in place. Further, in order for there to be a greater consolidation of institutions, certain preconditions must be met—a market economy, civic education, organized political parties, etc. (Dahl 1998). Electoral competition provides the opportunity for these preconditions to root. It is assumed that, over time, the further consolidation of institutions will lead to the expansion of personal freedoms, which will in turn lead to opportunities for participation (O'Donnell 1994).

In his later work (e.g., 1998), Dahl focuses on the necessary substance of equality for democracy. A full democracy is defined as a system that provides opportunity, effective participation, inclusion of adults, and the possibility of obtaining enlightened understanding the issues on the political agenda. Political contestation must be inclusive enough to ensure a degree of equality between citizens in determining political outcomes. Most fundamentally, without this level of inclusiveness it is difficult to consider the state to be democratic.

As the cases in this volume suggest, the institutional structure provided by a democratic constitution is crucial for the survival of a democratic system. We must also recognize, however, that such institutions are necessary but insufficient for the development of a full democracy. The Madagascar case offers testimony to this. In the description that follows, I highlight the interactions between elites and institutions over the course of Madagascar's recent democratic history. There are two central themes that I seek to establish.

First, as already indicated, despite the fact that fundamental democratic institutions have been established and operational since the early 1990s, the critical behavioral and substantive processes associated with democracy have not flourished. This is evident with respect to elections. Although competitive elections have been a regular feature of Malagasy political life for over a decade, the manner in which they have been conducted has precluded the effective translation of popular preferences into political outcomes. Further, the outcomes of elections have not always been respected by the key players in Madagascar politics. Who holds office has been determined as much by pure power politics (street-level social movements) and extra-electoral machinations (i.e., impeachment processes) as it has by polling contests. Indeed, as in the case of Guinea-Bissau, described by Joshua Forrest in chapter 11 of this volume, we have yet to see, during Madagascar's "democratic" period, an elected president leave office as a result of losing at the ballot box or the regularized means that one expects of leadership turnover in a democracy. On the other hand, the frailty of democratic institutions is evident in the status of the constitutional frameworks structuring political life. Although macro-level institutions have been in place to govern the behavior of political leaders, the more definitive pattern in recent history has been one of elites reshaping institutions to suit their own ends. Constitutions have functioned less as a constraint on the behavior of elites than as the object of elite manipulation. In short then, institutions have neither served their intended purpose, nor provided the means toward the end of democratic consolidation.

Yet there is a second, equally important, theme that deserves highlighting. Although institutions have been weak, manipulated, and only marginally effective in generating substantive outcomes, this does not mean that they have not mattered. To the contrary, an overview of Madagascar's first decade suggests that institutions have influenced political life. This is certainly one reason why elites—especially incumbents—have invested so much in manipulating them. Power-holders have not ignored the rules of the game, but rather they have changed those rules to serve their interests. Further, even would-be autocrats, such as Didier Ratsiraka, have been constrained by their need to maintain the guise of institutional legitimacy as opposed to acting unilaterally or autocratically. Were it otherwise, he, rather than Marc Ravalomanana, would likely still be in power. In some sense this recalls the statements by VonDoepp and Villalón in their introduction to this volume. As they rightly point out, while the consolidation of democracy has been problematic, there is little doubt that things have changed in Africa. The institutional framework of democracy has changed Malagasy political life in important ways.

From Founding Elections to Second Elections

In 1989 President Ratsiraka, then an undisputed autocratic leader for fourteen years, had a problem. His economy was in tatters, he had a debt crisis stemming from a donor bailout of his experiment in state-owned enterprise, and his most significant partner, the Soviet Union, was on the brink of collapse. For the first time his opponents were publicly challenging his legitimacy, and his authority was waning.

Ratsiraka had become tremendously weak by 1991. Yet, the institutional mechanisms for challenging his authority were underdeveloped. Opposition leader Zafy Albert thus took advantage of the political moment by leading an 80,000–strong civil servants' strike in the capital, Antananarivo. Malagasy economic life came to a crashing halt as banking, trading, and governance sectors ceased to function. The government was unable to stem the crisis. Rather than take over the ministries, which could have led to heightened conflict, Zafy Albert set up a shadow government proclaiming himself the prime minister and declaring as the National Assembly the *Haute Authorité*—sixteen parties in the opposition coalition, the *Hery Velona* (Living Forces). The surprisingly rapid challenge of this parallel legislature forced President Ratsiraka to the bargaining table. On October 31, 1991, he signed the Panorama Convention for a government transition. The terms of the convention left Ratsiraka as president, but removed the majority of his powers, and the *Haute Authorité* effectively became the legislature, pending the organization of elections. Multiparty elections were held on February 10, 1993. In the presidential elections, Zafy Albert won a resounding victory with 66.7 percent of the vote to Ratsiraka's 33.3 percent. He was sworn in on March 27, 1993, inaugurating Madagascar's Third Republic. The *Hery Velona* parties won a clear majority in the June 16, 1993, legislative elections. Madagascar was thus proclaimed a "democracy," earning it inclusion in the set of Africa's third wave "successes" explored in this book.

The Zafy presidency brought to the surface tendencies that came to characterize the Malagasy experiment with democracy. Although institutional structures and processes were in place, they nonetheless proved very weak and did not generate the substantive outcomes they were purportedly designed to create. Rather than live by the rules of the game, key elites (in this case Zafy) changed those rules to suit their purpose. Their means to do so was the electoral process. Yet while elections were free and fair in the minimal sense of the term, those contests proved hollow when measuring the degree to which they effectively translated popular preferences into political outcomes. Yet ironically, institutions still mattered enough to shape the evolution of national political life. Partially as a result of institutional processes, leaders failed to realize the political control that allowed them longevity.

Institutionally, Madagascar's Third Republic began as a variant of a French-style semi-presidential system, with provisions for significant powers for the National Assembly. The prime minister was elected by the National Assembly and was responsible for most executive duties in domestic affairs. The president maintained control of foreign relations, but had a limited domestic purview. Under Article 44 of the Constitution, "The president is responsible for the regular functioning of public powers; he shall be responsible for national independence and territorial integrity and shall assure protection of, and respect for, national sovereignty within national territory and abroad; he shall be the symbol of national unity."

One of the first efforts by Zafy Albert was to manipulate the governing institutions in an attempt to shift this constitutional division of authority and lend greater power to the executive office. Zafy sought to centralize authority in the hands of the president and to create a unitary government secured in his Antananarivo power base. His efforts to work through the legislature to accomplish these ends came up short, owing partially to the constitutional division of authority. Most notable were his regular tussles with then–prime minister Francisque Ravony. A more experienced political operator and member of a different political party, Ravony skillfully obtained parliamentary votes at Zafy's expense on the extension of judicial powers, revenue-counting methods, and, ultimately, even the makeup of the cabinet. Moreover, when Zafy tried to spurn the International Monetary Fund by engineering "parallel financing" schemes that set up bogus private-sector loans to benefit a select few, Ravony and the majority of the National Assembly resisted. When the opposition in the National Assembly fomented an impeachment movement against Zafy in July 1995, Ravony supported it.

On September 15, 1995, realizing he was unable to skirt the prime minister's power in the National Assembly, Zafy held a constitutional referendum on changes that would shift the nexus of power back to the president. Significantly, rather than focusing on the issues of constitutional import, Zafy ran a populist campaign emphasizing the goals of development growth and rooting out corruption. Parallel financing as a means to development was a central focus of Zafy's campaigning. In reality, the referendum was to increase presidential powers with which Zafy could circumvent the National Assembly in order to pursue parallel financing schemes (or nearly any other strategy). The cardinal shift introduced by the successful referendum was in Articles 53 and 90 of the Constitution, which now allowed the president to appoint the prime minister without the National Assembly's approval. Zafy won with a paltry voter turnout, below 40 percent. As Zafy's success undermined the powers of the prime minister, Ravony resigned a month later. Madagascar's democracy thus became one in which the president exerted a great deal of power not only over executive matters, but also over legislative matters.

Despite Zafy's successes in changing the rules of the game in his favor, his presidency was plagued by problems and, ultimately, cut short. He was accused of corruption and impeached by the National Assembly in July 1996. This may well have been a political act, but the ratification of the impeachment by the High Constitutional Court (HCC) on September 5, 1996, was a rare sign of institutional efficacy. The court proved capable of carrying out one of its most challenging functions. Norbert Ratsirahonana, then prime minister and former president of the HCC, became acting president until elections could be held in December of the same year. Zafy Albert was permitted to run and in a second round of elections he once again faced the former president, Ratsiraka, who ultimately emerged as the winner.

Various factors explain Ratsiraka's victory, but popularity was not among them. First, he was not Zafy. Not only was Zafy tainted by corruption scandals, but he had presided over an economic downturn in the country. Second, it was a propitious moment. The only four viable candidates for president in the political sphere were Ratsiraka, acting president Norbert Ratsirahonana, former industrial-promotion minister Herizo Razafimahaleo, and Zafy himself. Neither Ratsirahonana (and his party, *Asa Vita no Zfompitsorana* [AVI, "Judged By Your Work"]) nor Razafimahaleo (as head of the Leader-Fanilo party) had the stature or name recognition to gain the necessary electoral support outside of the capital or the regional capital of Fianarantsoa. Furthermore, ethnopolitics played a role in their downfall. Norbert Ratsirahonana is from the Merina highlands of Antananarivo, and Herizo Razafimahaleo is Betsileo from Fianarantsoa. Their highest votes were in their home provinces, which afforded them 10.1 percent and 15.1 percent of the vote, respectively. For his part, Zafy Albert, though from the northern province of Antsiranana, had long derived his base of support from the capital, and his ouster from power, which played so well in the capital, undermined his electability. In the end Ratsiraka won the first round with a less than convincing 36.6 percent. This was skewed heavily by the vote in his home province of Toamasina, where he captured 59.6 percent of the vote. Zafy Albert thus lost the election more than Ratsiraka won it. Whereas in 1992 Zafy secured 46 percent of the vote in Antananarivo province, in 1996 he secured less than 10 percent, indicating that his base of support was squandered. As one respondent in Antananarivo put it (in September 2001):

> If the people rise up and fly into a rage it is because politicians are not concerned about the people. People lose confidence because of the improper behavior [of politicians]. At the time [1993], people chased the president out of power. But then came Zafy Albert; he showed a flagrant inability to lead the country. So, he was kicked out through impeachment.[3]

Beyond the Second Presidential Elections

Madagascar's second round of elections met an acceptable procedural threshold. Vote-rigging was not a topic that raised a loud cry. The elections did not, however, bring in a leader that represented popular desires. Didier Ratsiraka was not well loved. He was the least of the evils. This was evident in the extent of voter apathy (Roubaud 2000). It was also evident in the first round of elections, where Ratsiraka won only 36.6 percent of the vote. Zafy Albert won 23.4 percent, and the remainder of the vote was spread over thirteen other candidates who lacked national stature. Even in the second round Ratsiraka won only 50.7 percent of the vote to Zafy's 49.3 percent—despite Zafy's conviction by the high court, national disgrace, and impeachment. The political recruitment process had been stymied during the 1993–97 interregnum, as both primary political agents thwarted the opportunity for a new political class to emerge. By the time the Malagasy people got to the polls, they were faced with electing either the corrupt populist or the former dictator. The functional elections were but a shadow of a process intended to translate popular preferences into governance practices.

Zafy's defeat did not signal the end of institutional manipulation by elites. Following his presidential victory in 1997, President Ratsiraka held his own constitutional referendum in March 1998. The referendum passed by a narrow margin (51 percent "yes," 49 percent "no"). Broadly viewed as an extension of the 1996–97 presidential elections, this was a significant victory for President Ratsiraka. The constitutional revisions brought a return to much of the state structure, if not the flavor, of the Second Republic. Perhaps most notably, under the new constitutional provisions, the national government hypothetically devolved both greater autonomy and fiscal power to regional governments. However, the institutional vacuum left in Antananarivo also allowed President Ratsiraka to expand the reach of his control. As regional governments remained subservient to the national government under Ratsiraka's form of decentralization, and since there were few constitutional guarantees to protect regional governments from encroachment from the center, regional governors had little power to challenge the president's newly expanded authority. As one more alert resident of the capital noted after the referendum:

> There is a big dilemma about the misunderstanding of people in general about the new system. They did not understand about the provinces during the referendum and what [the referendum's] goal was; as the new institutions have become effective as a part of the decentralization process, it has become more and more dark for people which helped put them in place. The conclusion is that those institutions are useless and budget consuming. Ratsiraka won by giving large favors to friends and old members of his court. He used nepotism and misinformation. (Interview with author, Antananarivo, September 2001)

As discussed below, the fact that many of the provincial governors were so close to Ratsiraka effectively centralized his power at the expense of the legislature and the president's potential challengers.

Events leading to the referendum undermined the prospect of real debate on the central questions of the referendum. As under Zafy, the constitutional issues were downplayed as Ratsiraka promoted the idea that a "yes" vote on the referendum meant development and security. There were efforts by civil society groups to overcome this knowledge gap and promote a wider discussion, but these failed. The *Hery Velona* (Living Forces) and other opposition protests coincided with student protests at the universities over fee increases and grant decreases. The two protests merged in the streets of the often-tumultuous *Place 13 Mai* and in the

Analakely quarter of Antananarivo. The first day of protests, March 13, was uneventful, but protesters were met with government warnings that no right to assemble had been granted. The government position was taken as a challenge by students and more than 10,000 filled the quarter the following day. A confused set of speeches had opposition leaders and student political groups challenging constitutional reform, while another set of speeches addressed students' economic shortfalls. In an event reminiscent of the Second Republic, gendarmes, police, and the military joined forces in great numbers to disperse the protesters with tear gas and batons.

Two months after the actual referendum, second legislative elections took place. Held on May 17, 1998, these elections were widely viewed to be "free and fair" in that challenges to the results were limited to a small number of districts. Yet here too the electoral mechanism proved to be a vapid tool for translating popular preferences into political outcomes. One of the problems was the nature of the electoral system itself. President Ratsiraka's AREMA party won 64 of the National Assembly's 150 seats, leaving him short of an absolute majority.[4] As independents (who tend to follow the president) took a record 31 seats and the Leader-Fanilo party (which commonly votes with AREMA) won 17 seats, President Ratsiraka in fact enjoyed great legislative support for his programs. In and of itself this would not seem problematic. Yet, while AREMA won 42 percent of the seats in the legislature, it only won some 23 percent of the popular vote nationwide, suggesting a considerable disjuncture between popular support for the party and its actual representation in the legislature.

The reasons for this discrepancy were based in Madagascar's electoral system. In 1998, the country used a mixed system of 116 constituencies to fill the 150 seats.[5] In 82 of the constituencies only one seat was at stake, and a simple majority within the constituency was all that was necessary to secure victory. In 34 constituencies two seats were at stake and the strongest party lists were allocated winners on a proportional basis; voters cast ballots for a list of candidates nominated by the political party of their choice rather than for individual candidates. The fact that AREMA won 23 percent of the popular vote nationwide but obtained 42 percent of the seats reflects the fact that the population lines on which constituencies are partitioned greatly favored President Ratsirikana's AREMA party.

Beyond the dynamics of the electoral system, Ratsiraka's success in the legislative contests can be attributed in part to low voter turnout. Rural voter turnout in Madagascar for the 1993 elections was remarkably high, but it dropped precipitously for all subsequent elections until 2001. Sociologist François Roubaud attributes this drop in voter turnout to apathy and abstentionism. Observing the 1996 presidential elections in which voter turnout nationwide was 41.6 percent in the first round and 50.3 percent in the second, Roubaud argues (2000, 62–65) that abstentionism is not particular to any one group. While there is variance, it includes rich and poor, women and men, all age groups, and various regions and ethnicities.

Such abstention, Roubaud convincingly points out, is particularly dangerous in

Madagascar, where civil society is still embryonic. Voting presents one of the few opportunities to participate in politics. With limited alternative areas of participation, meager voter turnout creates a crisis of legitimacy. It can also be argued that it opens the opportunity for alternative, more volatile forms of participation, such as the urban social movement supporting Ravalomanana in the months that followed the December 2001 elections.

The reasons for abstention are multiple. Apathy, what Roubaud (2000) calls "passive abstention," plays a large role since people feel that voting does not mean anything. However, Roubaud argues, "critical abstention"—the conscious choice to not vote because no candidate represents the voter's aspirations—plays an even larger role. Roubaud's analysis would seem to be most relevant to voters in the capital. It is likely that in the countryside critical abstention plays a much less significant role, because voters are less well informed not only about the candidates but also regarding the political process. In this case, apathy remains an important feature in voter turnout, but there are at least two more likely factors at work. Attention to these factors brings further light to the hollow nature of Madagascar's electoral process.

First, prior to the 1998 elections there was a large campaign to increase the percentage of the population with National Identity Cards; eligible individuals for these cards were estimated to be around 60 percent of the adult rural population. Once an individual obtained a National Identity Card, he or she could then receive an electoral card—a secondary document required to actually cast a vote. However, largely as a result of inaction on the part of local officials, the effects of the national campaign on voter turnout were often muted or skewed. Indeed, in research conducted by the author, the most common reason given for not voting (44 percent) was lack of an identity or electoral card.[6] A common complaint by would-be voters was that they submitted their National Identity Card to the local official as instructed, but the local official only actually handed out a small number of electoral cards. When questioned, local officials complained of the burden of writing so many cards by hand. Other would-be voters had even more grievous complaints. National Identity Cards were supposed to cost 150 FMG (FMG = Malagasy franc) ($0.02), and the electoral cards were supposed to be free. However, both were commonly sold by local officials, presumably for their personal gain. The price demanded, up to 10,000 FMG ($1.45), was generally too dear for the local citizen.

Second, until 1989 voting was viewed as compulsory (if meaningless) in Madagascar. The 1992–93 elections were the first national elections where voting was an option. With interest running high, however, the second round of the 1992 founding elections had a 79 percent turnout. By the 1997 presidential runoff, voter turnout dropped to 49.7 percent. It is likely that this can be explained at least in part by increased information about the process. By the 1996–97 elections, people in the countryside began to realize that they would not suffer repercussions by refusing to participate.

It was not only the electoral process but also the manipulation of outcomes that undermined the integrity of elections. In particular, this resulted from the actions of the judiciary with respect to contests. Judicial independence was enshrined in the 1992 Constitution (Articles 97–102) and made gains throughout the 1990s, passing the substantial test of upholding the impeachment of Zafy Albert in 1996. Since that time, however, questions have emerged about the integrity of the institution, in particular its willingness to exert power on behalf of the sitting government and at the expense of the popular will as expressed through elections. This was especially evident with the court's interventions and actions concerning the local elections of November 1999. Notably, by the time these local elections were held in 1999, Ratsiraka had used the opportunity to shape the composition of the court in his favor.

Arguably, one of the most important differences between these local elections and those that preceded them was the staggering success of independent candidates. Added to this, in the actual contests, the winnings of the governing party were weak.[7] Court decisions helped to reverse the fortunes of the party, however. For example, in Mahasoa Ouest, Toliara Province, a coalition of small parties called *Tranobe* (Big House) won the local elections. However, the results were contested by the second place Leader-Fanilo Party and the third place Rally for Socialism and Democracy Party (RSPD). Curiously, the HCC ruled that the mayor's post must go to President Ratsiraka's AREMA Party—this despite the fact that it did not place in the polls. Court actions in Betroka District were even more striking. Four men had been candidates for mayor, but, after court challenges regarding the results, the HCC ruled that the post be filled by a woman of the president's party who had not even been a candidate.

While judicial improprieties in the late 1990s were blatant, elections met basically acceptable standards. The legislative elections, presidential elections, and referendums were free from ballot stuffing, voter intimidation, and other direct criminality; yet there were sufficient problems in the process to raise questions about the quality of democracy being practiced. Ratsiraka, Zafy, and other state-level politicians regularly used the country's lack of communication infrastructure to manipulate voters, either to protect their positions or further their agenda. While it is unclear how strong the relationship was between local administrative irregularities and the actions of state level leaders, these irregularities were wide enough to raise questions about the quality of the electoral process and, by extension, of the democratic system itself.

The Institutional Context of Third Elections

The constitutional changes under Ratsiraka in 1998 set the context under which the elections of 2000–2001 would be contested. Indeed, in some respects, they represented an effort to lay the groundwork for the re-election campaign of President Ratsiraka. To understand the dynamics of the third presidential contest, it is important to first explain the nature of the changes that took place.

The significance of the change to the Constitution lies in the manner in which it expanded the power of the president within the political system relative to other locations of authority. For example, Constitutional Law 98–001 increased the authority of the president over regional governments. The constitutional change was hypothetically intended to shift significant governing authority from the state level to newly "autonomous" provinces. As implemented by Organic Law No. 2000–016 of August 29, 2000, Articles 42–50, the autonomous provinces were imbued with the authority to manage their own budgets and, importantly, levy taxes. Yet, even with this imbued power, the new authorities are guided by their responsibilities to fill state coffers and adhere to the will of the *Délégué Général,* the state's "advisor" to the provincial authorities. All of the decisions undertaken by the new provincial leadership occur under the oversight of the Ministry of Decentralization. As President Ratsiraka's support was in the provinces, not the capital, the shift to autonomous provinces in fact strengthened his position as it allowed the provincial councils to put in place provincial leaders that supported the president. With this action, President Ratsiraka was able to effectively remove many of the budgetary concerns from the eyes of political challengers in the capital, and even from the hands of the legislature, a possible source of challenges to his power. At the same time, he empowered the Minister of Decentralization, answerable directly to him, with oversight over provincial authorities.

Beyond this, 98–001 ended the last vestiges of parliamentary autonomy. Under Articles 58 and 95 of the revised Constitution, the president holds the right to dissolve the National Assembly. While presumably this would lead immediately to new elections, there are no specific provisions for this event. Related to this, Article 96 of the revised Constitution gives the National Assembly the right, by simple majority, to delegate its powers to the president. Given the close linkages between the president and the ruling party, which historically controls the majority vote in the National Assembly, this is a tremendous power.[8] The authority of parliament was also eroded because the president could henceforth appoint the Council of Ministers without the approval of the assembly, as well as appoint a prime minister from any party (including a minority party or an independent). Finally, the president can also claim absolute authority through the invocation of martial law (as Ratsiraka did on February 28, 2002).

These changes also touched directly on the electoral process. Under Article 6 of the Constitution, every citizen who possesses civil and political rights has the right to become an elector—a specific office that, as I describe below, plays a critical role in choosing the members of the Senate. However, whether or not an individual possesses civil and political rights can be determined by the judiciary. The extension of this is that the courts can remove electoral status. Given that the judiciary holds these (and other powers), the composition of the courts is a matter of great importance. Under Constitutional Law 98–001 (culminating in Article 119 of the revised Constitution), the president has significant influence in this composition. The HCC is comprised of nine members appointed for seven years. Three of the justices are named by the president of Madagascar, two are named by the National Assembly, two are named by the Senate, and two are elected by the Superior Judicial Council.

The head of the HCC is appointed by the president of the country, who also reserves the right to designate other justices by executive decree at the expense of the other appointments. Indeed, that is precisely the power that Ratsiraka exercised in November 2001, appointing a total of six of the court's nine justices.

Perhaps the most critical institutional issue for the political future of Didier Ratsiraka was the means of electing the Senate. While the 1992 Constitution specified a bicameral legislature, a Senate was only created in March 2001. Yet the importance of controlling this institution was readily apparent to Ratsiraka well before it actually came into existence. The president of the Senate is first in the line of succession should something happen to the state president. In addition, as mentioned, the Senate plays a critical role with respect to the composition of the judiciary. Moreover, with the 1998 constitutional changes, the Senate plays a crucial role in amending the Constitution. Two-thirds of both legislative houses are required to amend the Constitution. The 1992 Constitution specified that a referendum process could also be used, but the 1998 constitution removed that provision.

Of the ninety members of the Senate, thirty are appointed (by the president) and sixty are elected by an electoral college constituted of the provincial leadership (the "electors" described above). In all, an electoral college of 1,720 electors composed of mayors, councilors, and governors cast a ballot. Since the majority of the Senate is elected by the provincial electoral college, the means for selecting governors is critical to the composition of the Senate. Constitutional Law 98–001, Article 131, mandates that each provincial governor is elected by the provincial council for a period of five years (renewable). The governor is the chief executive of his "autonomous province" and names the general commissioners of the province. The provincial council is elected by universal suffrage within the province on a date consistent across the country.

However, Constitutional Law 98–001 provided the president with an important protection from the exercise of democracy at the provincial level. Article 129.2 gives the president the right to dissolve a provincial council for causes he determines, even though the provincial council is elected. Furthermore, if the president deems that any organ of an autonomous province has acted in contradiction to the Constitution, the president can "take all necessary measures to redress the situation." While this may mean that it will become a matter for the HCC, the president can also choose to remove any relevant official himself. If he should decide to pass an issue on to the HCC and he is unhappy with the ruling, then the president again has recourse against the court's judgment. Article 121 gives the president the power to determine if a judgment by the HCC is unconstitutional. If he determines that it is unconstitutional, then the ruling is vacated and the deliberation is given, at his discretion, either to the parliament or to his own cabinet. Finally, in Article 126 of the law, the delimitation of each local collectivity for the election of the provincial council can be modified by decree by the Council of Ministers (the governor and his appointed general ministers). Thus, if there appears to be some question about whether the governor will be reappointed by the provincial council, he has the power to alter electoral districts at will without oversight.

In short, the new constitutional changes greatly expanded the powers of the president to manipulate the electoral and political process to suit his interests. In the period leading into the December 2001 elections, President Ratsiraka attempted to invoke these new powers. His first target was the judiciary, which, as I have noted, had considerable potential to shape electoral status. At the end of November 2001, he appointed Georges T. Indrianjafy, a cabinet member and close advocate since 1976, to head the HCC following the appointment of other supporters to the court. As the *Indian Ocean Newsletter* noted at the time (December 1, 2001): "Intervening as it does right before the campaign for the presidential election of December 16 begins, the nomination of a former Ratsiraka minister to the head of the HCC illustrates the incumbent's determination to keep a sharp eye on the institution that will be in charge of validating the electoral results and of verifying cases of electoral fraud, should any arise." As it turned out, the HCC was in fact to rule on the elections, and their unsurprising decision was to validate the electoral results declared by Ratsiraka's government, without scrutiny of the documentation. This, as discussed below, had a profound effect on the reputation of the judiciary as an institution and also on the events that transpired in the months that followed.

This intervention of the judiciary was not the first time President Ratsiraka benefited from the 1998 constitutional changes. Madagascar held its first provincial elections a year earlier in December 2000. Overall, Ratsiraka's AREMA party won approximately 95 percent of the popular vote for provincial councilors. As a result, when gubernatorial elections were held on June 10, 2001, AREMA won five of the six provinces. At least part of the AREMA victory can be explained by voter turnout. While this was a general election, voter turnout was estimated to have been only 10 percent of registered voters (who themselves only include an estimated 60 percent of eligible voters). With Ratsiraka dominating the political life of the country, and without a provincial election, most Malagasy did not see this as an important election. At a minimum, they did not see this as an important enough election to warrant the costs associated with travel expenses and the time away from the fields necessary to vote. Such low voter turnout, even if it was relatively free of exogenous influence, put the incumbent party at a great advantage. This significantly impacted the composition of the Senate.

When the senatorial elections came on March 18, 2001, Ratsiraka had already exercised his one-third mandate over the composition of the Senate; only sixty remained to be chosen. Since those sixty seats are voted on by the provincial electors, and since the provincial leadership was dominated by AREMA party faithful, it was clear that Ratsiraka would win a great victory. In an outcome that grievously distorted popular support for AREMA, it won forty-nine of the sixty seats. The Leader-Fanilo party, which won five seats, joined with other opposition parties in immediately noting the discrepancy between popular support and electoral results. Although it had been presumed that the president would have significant influence over the senatorial agenda, his degree of influence after the elections appeared staggering. With the president's existing influence in the National Assembly, his legislative agenda was assured even if he chose not to use the diverse powers of executive decree granted him by Constitutional Law 98–001. As is evident, by creating an electoral code for the Senate that mandated indirect, rather than direct, elections, the provincial leadership became empowered to significantly affect the makeup of the upper chamber of the legislature. Given the significant exogenous influences on provincial leadership, popular will is not manifest in legislative representation at the national level. Prior to the creation of the autonomous provinces there was no Senate. The legislature was comprised solely of the popularly elected National Assembly. The indirectly elected Senate thus further distanced the population from the rule-making bodies at the national level.

For the whole of his political career Ratsiraka had fought to establish a federal system in Madagascar. The autonomous provinces manifest in 98–001 were the most recent attempt to create this federal system in his favor. While he often argued that decentralization brings government closer to the people, this was also a transparently strategic political position. His power base was in the coastal provinces. In a manifestation of Madagascar's largest political divide, Ratsiraka is a *côtier* (coastal person) fighting against the centralized power of the long-dominant *Merina* ethnic group of the Antananarivo region. Federalism, Ratsiraka found, gave him an acceptable structural guise for the realignment of political power in his favor. Taking these reforms together, as Malagasy scholar Jean-Eric Rakotoarisoa (2001) has argued, "Didier Ratsiraka bolted together a system for assuring his re-election. AREMA has obtained a relative majority in the National Assembly and an absolute majority in the Senate. It totally dominates the provincial councils and controls the six governors of the autonomous provinces. Public audio-visual is completely under the control of the Head of State."[9]

Third Elections and the Breakdown of Political Order

Yet the system that Ratsiraka developed was not without political costs. In September 2000 the leading organization of Malagasy federalists came out strongly against the president's plans for provincial autonomy. The Catholic Church and the Association of Parliamentarians for the Development of the South (APDS) followed suit. They joined a chorus of criticism of the president's plan by every leading opposition party, including the National Union for Democracy and Development (UNDD), the Movement for the Progress of Madagascar (MPM), and AVI. While these opposition parties have historically been proponents of a unitary government with firm support in the capital, the federalists and APDS are *côtiers* and had long been supporters of the president. With an additional challenge from two retired generals who backed Patrick Rajaonary, a once-faithful member of AREMA, as an opposition *Groupe d'Antanarivo* candidate, and a lack of support from the powerful Council of Christian Churches (FFKM), it seemed unlikely that President Ratsiraka could count on his traditional support in Madagascar's third presidential elections.

With this base of support in question by mid-2001, Ratsiraka needed to find a new way to secure electoral victory in December 2001. The presence of international observers and internationally funded civil-society organizations meant that vote rigging was out of the question. It also seemed unnecessary; using his new, constitutionally guaranteed right to manipulate the institutions and processes of the political system and his ability to exploit cleavages within the opposition, Ratsiraka hoped to control the process.

With a significant delay in the announcement of the date of the election, many thought that the president might try to postpone it for an extended period of time. This didn't materialize; instead he announced, on September 3, 2001, that the election would be held on December 16. While he won international praise by going out of his way to state that he would respect the Constitution, domestically he was accused of "poor governance" and manipulating institutions to influence the electoral outcome when he simultaneously announced decrees to guide the electoral process. First, the period between the announcement and the elections was scarcely more than three months; this did not give a lot of time for outsiders to build a name. Second, candidates had to declare their candidacy before an October 27 deadline. Justified in light of the limited time before the electoral contest, this was accompanied by a significant, and unexpected, increase in the required candidate-registration fee. Many independents and candidates of smaller parties were not able to raise the money that rapidly. Third, and more critical, candidates were only allowed to campaign between November 25 and December 15, thereby significantly limiting the exposure of lesser-known rivals outside the capital. Fourth, the only news sources allowed to directly cover the electoral process were comprised of journalists chosen by the president. And finally, no posters were allowed to be affixed to public buildings or structures and no political advertisements could be associated with purchasable goods. This last edict was directly aimed at the candidacy of Marc Ravalomanana, who ultimately replaced Ratsiraka in 2002. This former mayor of Antananarivo is the founder of Tiko, the country's largest dairy products company; his greatest potential to increase recognition outside the capital was to employ the supply lines established by his company.

Ratsiraka violated his own rule by giving an address to support his platform on election day. As *Agence France Presse* reported at the time, in a not-so-veiled threat, Ratsiraka proudly stated that he did not need to rig elections because "[I]f one of the other candidates won, there would be instability for two or three years, because none of them have a majority in the National Assembly, in the Senate or in the provincial councils, and he would have to break up all these levels, maybe even the constitution, and name a transition government."[10]

For his part, Ravalomanana proved to be an equally skilled political agent. He cleverly skirted Ratsiraka's edict against conflating business and politics. His campaign slogan, and ultimately the name of his new party, was *Tiako i Madagasikara* (I Love Madagascar). His company is called "Tiko." He emblazoned his yogurt and milk containers with a new corporate slogan, "Tia Tiko, Madagasikara" (Love Tiko, Madagascar) in an effort to create a linguistic link between his corporate identity and his political campaign. Ravalomanana then flooded the country with Tiko hats and T-shirts with the logo, "*Tiako i Madagasikara*" (featuring a photograph of Rava-lomanana). The quality of the merchandise was superior and the distribution into the countryside was broad, leading even supporters of other candidates to welcome the opportunity to own such a valuable commodity as a Ravalomanana T-shirt. While he carefully adhered to the letter of Ratsiraka's electoral edict, the play on language was not lost on the Malagasy population.

Ravalomanana may have needed to employ such strategies to win a foothold in the countryside, but in the capital his victory was already assured. He was seen as having improved the capital city in his brief stint as mayor. He had won the sup-port of the powerful FFKM (the United Group of Churches). Surprisingly, he had also won the backing of much of the *Forces Vives,* the coalition of opposition par-ties led by Zafy Albert in the founding elections of 1992–93. The coalescence of opposition forces around Marc Ravalomanana pushed Ratsiraka further into a cor-ner. With his "Tiko" campaign, Ravalomanana had undertaken the uphill battle of winning recognition in the countryside despite the restrictions placed on the elec-tions by presidential decree. He also was faced with overcoming ethnic cleavages. The *Merina–côtier* divide has long characterized the Malagasy polity, and the con-stitutional changes in 1998 further aggravated this divide. Announcing his candi-dacy from his home village of Imerikasinina only furthered Ravalomanana's *Merina* identity. This should not be overstated, however; as noted by Roubaud (2000), the ethnic divide in Madagascar had already been fading. The population in both ru-ral and urban areas has grown increasingly disillusioned with the leadership, which they see as only driven by desires to fill their bellies, and any leader who appeared to be beyond corruption could stand a chance of gaining a great deal of popular support across ethnic lines not only in the capital but also in the countryside.

In the end, Ravalomanana was largely successful in overcoming these difficul-ties. By any count, he won more votes than any other candidate, including Ratsir-aka, in the December 2001 elections. The rub was not in the polling process, but rather in the credibility of the institutions doing the counting of the first-round votes. The official count by the National Electoral Commission (CNE, overseen by Ratsiraka's government) saw Ratsiraka win 40 percent and Ravalomanana 46 per-cent. The independent *Consortium des observateurs des élections* (CNOE), comprised of civil society groups, had Ratsiraka winning 37.7 percent and Ravalomanana win-ning 50.5 percent of the vote. Ravalomanana's own support committee, the KMMR (Committee to Elect Marc Ravalomanana), claimed that he had won 52.2 percent. The critical point here is that with 50 percent or greater Ravalomanana could avoid a runoff. Judging from the votes for other candidates, it appears that such a runoff, if held immediately and free from election tampering, would have yielded an in-crease in approximately 4 percent of the vote for Ratsiraka and the remaining per-centage for Ravalomanana. Thus, Ravalomanana's victory in a runoff should have been assured.

Ravalomanana, however, claimed that the institutions in place, though consti-tutional, lacked the strength and capacity to guarantee a valid electoral result. The National Electoral Commission had announced a result without a transparent bal-

Table 7.1. Comparison of Vote Totals: CNE, CNOE, and KMMR (in percentages)

	CNE	CNOE	KMMR
Didier Ratsiraka	40.4	37.7	35.7
Marc Ravalomanana	46.6	50.5	52.2

lot count, he argued, and the High Constitutional Court (HCC) (filled with Ratsiraka supporters) upheld the National Electoral Commission's right to an opaque vote-counting process. Ravalomanana thus took the *un*-constitutional position that he would refuse to accept the High Court's ruling as the last word. In effect, he argued that democracy, measured in terms of the influence of popular preferences on government representation, was better served by subverting the institutions that governed electoral processes. He would only follow the electoral results if he was shown to have won less than 50 percent of the vote in a transparent counting of the first round, and only if international observers would monitor a transparent counting of the second round. Only then would he be willing to stand for the second round.

This did not happen. By the end of January 2002 hundreds of thousands of Ravalomanana supporters took to the streets in support of their candidate's position. Ratsiraka claimed in turn that since Ravalomanana refused to stand in a second round he could not be declared the winner. Ravalomanana countered that since Ratsiraka used the Constitution to subvert a transparent democratic process and intentionally miscount the votes, he had in fact already won, and he declared himself president. This touched off a maelstrom leading to a country with two presidents, high conflict, and a high potential for violence.

There were two significant attempts by the Organization of African Unity to mediate an accord. Both of these ended in failure because the power of the two political agents, Ravalomanana and Ratsiraka, outstripped the power of the institutions that could guide a compromise. An initiative in Dakar undertaken by Senegalese president Wade led to the signing of a transitional agreement on April 18, 2002. Back in Madagascar two other important events happened concurrently. General Raymond Andrianaivo, a close ally of President Ratsiraka, was shot and killed in Fianarantsoa, marking the escalation of violence, and the Malagasy Supreme Court annulled the presidential election results from December. This is an important distinction: while the HCC has jurisdiction over the elections, the Supreme Court has jurisdiction over criminal manipulation of the HCC. The Supreme Court ruled that the changes in composition Ratsiraka had made in the HCC shortly before the December elections were illegal. It therefore reinstated the HCC as it was composed prior to the change in November 2002. Nascent as it might have been, a critical government institution creaked into action at a pivotal time.

Yet, the institutional efforts didn't produce the sought ends. As a result of judicial actions, even as the planes of the two presidents touched back down in Madagascar, accusations of violations were flying. Ratsiraka's guards, loyalists in the military, and youth groups were further mobilized just as the military defectors, popular supporters, and youth groups were mobilized by Ravalomanana. By April 21, Ravalomanana's troops took a second province, Fianarantsoa. On April 29, the reconstituted HCC reversed the ruling of the previous HCC and declared Ravalomanana the winner of the December balloting with 51.46 percent to Ratsiraka's 35.90 percent. Ratsiraka immediately declared the declaration a result of an illegal institutional shift in the court and thus said the results themselves were illegal. On the surface this appeared to be a great victory for judicial independence. However, left unanswered in this explanation is why the Supreme Court did not act before the elections when the initial change in the HCC was enacted, or after the elections in the months of extreme judicial marginalization. The most probable answer is not an institutional one. Rather, with the writing on the wall, the justices likely saw Ravalomanana through Cassandra's eyes. By the end of April they could see that Ratsiraka would ultimately not have the necessary support to hold on to the provinces. The leadership of the four remaining provinces not under Ravalomanana's control showed their loyalty to Ratsiraka by proclaiming their independence from Ravalomanana's Madagascar. With poor connections to Ratsiraka's military, and little military of their own, all but Ratsiraka's Toamasina fell to Ravalomanana with relatively little bloodshed within the month. In the heat of crisis, both Ravalomanana and Ratsiraka agreed to meet for a second round of talks in Dakar on June 8. However, the time was, to borrow I. William Zartman's (1989) term, hardly "ripe." There was very little to talk about at this point as Ravalomanana's victory had already taken place in the courts, and it was clearly going to take place at the hands of his generals in the provinces. On July 7, 2002, Ravalomanana's military took Ratsiraka's stronghold of Toamasina; Ratsiraka fled for France. This struggle was a victory over what had become a virtual constitutional dictatorship. However, it came at a high cost to the strength of the Constitution and the legitimacy of the fledgling institutions needed to serve Madagascar's democratization process.

▼▼▼▼

Madagascar's 1992 Constitution was a flawed but viable starting place for the birth of a new, institutionally stable democracy. However, the constitutional change of 1995 that shifted power back to the president undermined the efforts to establish and maintain an institutional balance of powers. More critically, it has become clear that when he re-secured his office in 1997, President Ratsiraka actively tried to reverse whatever gains had been made during Madagascar's democratization process. Rather than using second elections as an opportunity to demonstrate that electoral competition and the development of democratic institutions were viable alternatives for the country, Ratsiraka used his victory to limit the inclusiveness of political competition and further sink in roots of political patronage. He successfully moved the country significantly back toward the autocracy of the Second Republic, using numerous ploys to enhance his own self-interest. Through the promulgation of misinformation he successfully manipulated the Constitution to move the nexus of power to the countryside, where he has long held to his roots against the onslaught of *Merina* competitors from Antananarivo province. Critically, he continually raised the specter of ethnopolitics while customizing electoral law and political institutions to his personal advantage.

The irony is of course that institutional manipulation, however destabilizing, failed. Ratsiraka did not win back office. This failure of institutional manipulation transcends the 2001 election to demonstrate a theme in Malagasy politics. Zafy Albert tried and failed at institutional manipulation before Ratsiraka himself tried and failed to gain office through this mechanism.

The Malagasy political elite that emerged from the democratization process has by and large not been committed to seeking the consolidation of an inclusive democracy. The AREMA party members who are most likely to succeed Ratsiraka as party leader do not come with untarnished democratic credentials. The old guard of opposition leaders, Albert Zafy and Norbert Ratsirahonana, both used their time in office to feed their packs rather than reach out to the masses. The legislature has demonstrated that it prefers to marginalize the rural masses rather than educate or serve them. The judiciary has proven that it is willing to intervene in the most egregious of ways if it stands to benefit from it. Ravalomanana, while a political neophyte, has shown a remarkable ability to direct his popular sources of power toward the erosion of the very institutions that could legitimate him.

With a political sphere comprised of elites willing to exploit the lack of institutional consolidation in an attempt to perpetuate their hold on power, there is no one in the capital to champion the inclusion of the rural majority into the political system. The 80 percent of the people who live outside of the cities are left out in the effort to broaden and deepen the democratic process by moving beyond institutional form to substantive content. Yet the rural population is ill-prepared for this job. In Madagascar, there is no viable rural middle class to energize such a movement. Voting exercises have been devoid of meaning for most citizens, associational life is weak, civic associations are nascent at best, and even revolutionary fervor is muted. Indeed, in few countries in the world could a conflict over the highest political office be maintained for an extended period of time with so little social upheaval countrywide.

Following the third presidential elections in Madagascar's Third Republic, the potential for meaningful democracy to become consolidated appeared beyond the pale. Madagascar offered its people the illusion of democracy by offering them the ballot box, but on the front of the ballot slips were the faces of men they did not know or did not care about and, worse, who they believed did not care about them. Moreover, the institutional flaws highlighted by the electoral process appear to have only made it more clear that Madagascar is unable to move beyond an entrenched hybridity of its political system.

With the garrisons of 2002 dismantled and the reservists decommissioned, there appears to be a silver lining in the clouds of Balkanization and despair. Popular action is not a sufficient replacement for democratic participation via the ballot box. Yet it may prove a harbinger for a larger, quieter, more visceral social movement that raises Malagasy political consciousness and mandates greater political transparency. In an environment where institutions fail to produce meaningful participation, the urban social movement following the December 2001 elections may in fact have the effect of producing more valuable institutions. If a social movement can succeed where elections failed to bring about the leadership that the majority of the population wants, then the process succeeded *despite* institutions, not because of them. The role of institutions thus needs to be reassessed, and they may paradoxically have been strengthened by their very failure. At a minimum, in such a broadly public and politicized environment, it will be difficult for any Malagasy leader to act as elites have done in previous elections, building on lines of patronage. At a minimum, leaders should begin recognizing that institutional manipulation has not been a successful means of garnering power in Madagascar. Short of revolution, the failure of the electoral process may have given Madagascar its most promising opportunity to build and consolidate the state institutions necessary for a deeper democracy.

NOTES

1. At this point the nature of the military threat was a bit unclear. The military leadership was split between the two self-proclaimed presidents, but it showed a remarkable lack of desire to get involved in the political tussle. A united military would have ultimately resulted in a coup d'état by reluctant military leaders seeking to avoid catastrophic social unrest. A divided military, it seemed, would ultimately lead to civil war. In either instance the militias of the two leaders remained a threat to stability.

2. A recent, more nuanced discussion of qualifications for the term "democracy" has been offered by David Collier and Steve Levitsky (1997).

3. This quote is from a response to a question posed in a survey conducted by the author and Paul Razafindrakoto in Antananarivo in September 2001.

4. AREMA originally stood for *Antoky ny Revolisiona Malagasy* ("Vanguard of the Malagasy Revolution"). In 1997 it was renamed *Andry sy Riana Enti-Manavotra an'i Madagasicora* ("Pillar and Structure for the Salvation of Madagascar").

5. The electoral code revision of October 11, 2002, changed the number of constituencies to 160, each with one seat in the National Assembly. The system is therefore now based solely on "winner-take-all," single-member districts, not proportional representation.

6. Unless otherwise stated, all statistics are drawn from surveys conducted by the author in three rural regions of Madagascar in 1997–98. The survey was based on 1,358 individual responses taken by random sample of the adult populations of the twenty-six participating villages. The respondent quotes from outside of Antananarivo are drawn from the fifty focus groups or associated individual interviews conducted by the author in the same villages. Respondent quotes from Antananarivo were conducted by

the author's research assistant in Antananarivo between July and September 2001. For a broader discussion, see Marcus (2000).

7. In point of fact, it was in this election that a political unknown, Marc Ravalomanana, hitherto merely a contributor to AVI party campaigns, beat both the AREMA candidate, General Rakotosoa, and the opposition candidate, Ny Hasina Andriamanjato, for the post of mayor of Antananarivo.

8. For a broader discussion on the relationship between political parties and their leaders, see Marcus and Ratsimbaharison (forthcoming).

9. Yet despite Ratsiraka's invigoration of cultural cleavages with the 1998 referendum, this consequence was not clear to the majority of the population until quite some time later. One resident of Antananarivo who had voted for the referendum in 1998 thus argued, in September 2001, that the autonomous provinces that had been created "means that every province has its own leader; but when it is led by a bad person there is ethnic conflict. We don't need autonomous provinces for this reason." Response to a question posed in a survey conducted by the author and Paul Razafindrakoto in September 2001.

10. *Agence France Presse,* "Ratsiraka Confident as Madagascar Votes Calmly in Presidential Poll," December 16, 2001.

8 | Institutions, Resources, and Elite Strategies
Making Sense of Malawi's Democratic Trajectory

Peter VonDoepp

In his 1998 discussion of democratic consolidation, Andreas Schedler argues that the demise of nascent democratic regimes can result from two distinct processes. The first is described as "quick death," meaning the rapid breakdown of democratic institutions via collapses of civil peace and/or sudden returns to authoritarian rule. The second is a more subtle process of "slow death," whereby elected officials progressively weaken integral elements of democratic rule. By undermining electoral contestation, eroding checks on executive authority and placing constraints on political participation, elected leaders are able to entrench power at the level of the state. The resulting political context is one where the basic skeleton of democracy remains, but principles of accountability, limited government, and fair contestation fail to operate.

This chapter examines how Malawi has negotiated both of these threats to its recently inaugurated democratic system. In the early 1990s, Malawi underwent a transition to multiparty politics after thirty years of authoritarian rule under "President for Life" Kamuzu Banda. Since the election in 1994 of Bakili Muluzi, leader of the United Democratic Front (UDF), Malawi has stood out as somewhat of a success story within the larger African experience. Basic institutions of democracy have continued to operate and there have been no dramatic breakdowns of order suggesting the imminent demise of the regime. Yet threats of both quick death and slow death have haunted democratic Malawi. Understanding the country's experience with democracy requires consideration of how these threats have manifested themselves and affected the character of the system that emerged in 1994.

The chapter begins from the premise that elite behavior represents the central variable shaping Malawi's democratic experience. That is, both quick death and slow death are understood as ultimately authored by political elites who, operating in the context of other factors, have the power to shape the survival and character of Malawi's democracy. With this in mind, the chapter examines two distinct periods of Malawi's democratic history, asking questions about elite choices and actions with respect to democracy.

The first period under study is that running from 1994 to May 2000. During this initial period of democratic rule, a central political issue facing Malawi concerned whether key elites would effectively leave the democratic system intact, or if they would undertake actions to derail or delegitimize it. As I detail below, democratic institutions posed real risks for governing elites who might be displaced or undermined through their operation. Moreover, with the passage of time, it became evident that democratic institutions yielded few benefits to opposition players—and even appeared manifestly biased against their interests. Still, Malawi's elites, both governing and opposition, avoided strategies or tactics that might have caused the rapid demise of democratic institutions. The key analytical issues here concern how to account for the elite choices that allowed for democratic survival and relative stability during this period.

The second time period extends from May 2000 to the present. With the final resolution of Malawi's second national elections in May of 2000, the political context changed considerably—as did the central issues facing the new democracy. From that point, threats of slow death emerged as government insiders sought to maintain and extend their hold on power beyond the scheduled 2004 elections. As I detail, in pursuit of these objectives, these elites embraced strategies that held the potential to undermine prospects for accountability and good governance. Focused on these issues, the analysis examines the strategies and actions of these key players, and the subsequent impact on Malawi's democratic trajectory.

The examination of elite actions during both of these periods illuminates three important issues, all of which carry relevance for the larger investigation of the fates of new African democracies. First, economic factors have affected Malawi's experience with democracy. Specifically, owing to relatively limited resource bases, Malawi's elites have been somewhat constrained in terms of strategic options. Working with and within the democratic system has been the most reasonable strategy in light of their limited capacities.

Second, institutional dynamics have also played an important role in Malawian politics. During the initial period of democratic rule, Malawi's institutions provided incentives for potentially unruly opposition players to continue to play by the rules. Of special importance in this respect is how judicial institutions provided an arena where opposition leaders felt they might effectively pursue and protect their interests. In the more recent era, the distribution of power within Malawi's parties and legislative institutions has presented a potential check against ruling elites who have attempted to aggrandize political power by changing the rules of the political game. As a result, efforts to alter the institutional framework of democracy in a manner that does violence to principles of checks and balances and fair contestation have not always been successful.

Finally, while institutions have played an important role in Malawi, recent trends also highlight how "extra-institutional" politics are shaping the country's democracy. Specifically, in efforts to consolidate and extend power, ruling elites demonstrated a propensity to engage in classic political tactics such as thuggery and intimidation to advance their objectives. Thus, democratic institutions persist, but they do so in a climate of violence and tension that raises questions about the quality of democratic governance emerging in Malawi.

Elite Choices and the Survival of Democracy in Malawi: 1994–2000

With multiparty elections in 1994, Malawi concluded a tumultuous period of political liberalization and embarked on an uncertain experiment with democratic rule. As is the case in many new democracies, one of the primary issues facing the new regime concerned the question of whether key elites would accept democratic institutions or attempt to derail them and create political arrangements more conducive to their interests. The fate of democracy in this sense lay in the hands of a few players who had the power to undermine the system. Understanding the choices of these elites helps to illuminate why Malawi's democracy survived and did so in a context where threats of breakdown or instability were minimal.

As indicated in the introductory chapter, the literature offers different perspectives on how to explain elite behavior in new democracies. Some suggest that elite conformity to democracy reflects a normative consensus among the key players. Extended learning processes and repeated bargaining possibilities can give elites an attitudinal commitment to the rules of the game. This allows for the survival and stability of democratic systems (Levine 1978; Field and Higley 1985; Burton, Gunther, and Higley 1992). While this approach may help to account for democratic stability in other contexts, it comes up short in accounting for elite actions in Malawi. There is no reason to assume normative commitments to democracy among elites, many of whom only a few years earlier were part and parcel of the authoritarian system. Moreover, the processes that might have led to such consensus over the rules of the game have been absent in Malawi.

A different view, adopted here, argues that elite choices with respect to democratic systems need to be understood in terms of the strategic considerations that elites bring to the political arena. In this respect, elites are viewed as rational actors seeking to preserve and maximize their interests. Democracy endures when the expectations and calculations of the key players direct them to work within, or comply with, the system, rather than subvert it. The clearest statement of this perspective emerges in the choice-theoretic work of Przeworski. As he argues, the survival of democracy reflects an equilibrium "of the decentralized strategies of all the relevant political forces" (1991, 26). Making sense of elite choices with respect to democracy thus requires consideration of the larger conditions that have shaped their capabilities and expectations.

Drawing further on the work of Przeworski, I maintain that elite choices during Malawi's initial interregnum with democracy can be understood with reference to two issues. The first concerns economic influences on elite behavior. As several other studies have aptly demonstrated, the economic interests of key elites can exert a powerful influence on the kinds of choices they make with respect to political arrangements (see esp. Boone 1998). When considering elite choices about whether to accept or subvert democratic institutions, the role of economic factors stands out for two reasons. First, attention to such factors helps us to understand what Przeworski (1991, 24) calls the "power resources" of the primary players in the political game. The extent of these resources affects the range of strategic alternatives that are available to elites. For example, if opposition elites have access to income streams that allow them to garner disruptive resources (such as weapons or clients), they can use those resources to undertake extralegal efforts to advance their political objectives. Moreover, to the extent that governing elites control trade for resources valuable on the international market, they obtain limited power to ignore international donors who condition aid disbursement on respect for democracy and human rights. In short, access to resources enables the use of antidemocratic strategies by the key players in the game. Second, economic factors may also give elites an interest in maintaining domestic stability. Where elites are invested in enterprises that hinge on the effective functioning of a domestic market, the likelihood is diminished that they will disrupt that market for political objectives.

The second issue concerns the institutional environment in which elites operate. As the works of Przeworski (1991), DiPalma (1990), and Rustow (1970) argue, in the context of new democracies, institutions affect actors' perceptions of their ability to pursue and protect their interests. To the extent that such institutions offer key players some hope of surviving or eventually prevailing in the political process, the prospects increase for their choosing to work within the democratic system. The presence and perception of fair and efficacious institutions, for example, allows the losers of electoral contests to discount current losses and envision future gains by working through the democratic system (Przeworski 1991). Moreover, if institutions offer some sort of "*garantismo*"—specific guarantees of representation or interest preservation—to potential regime opponents, their willingness to accept the potential setbacks of democratic contestation increases (DiPalma 1990).[1]

Focusing on these two issues offers important insight into why the key players in Malawian politics opted to essentially leave the democratic game intact. Attention to the economic dimension highlights the constraints on the choices available to the key players—both governing and opposition. In turn, attention to the institutional environment helps to reveal why elite strategies took the particular direction that they did during the first six years of democratic rule. Of special importance in this regard is how institutions shaped the strategies of the opposition. The sections that follow illuminate these issues in greater detail. The first focuses on the activities of the governing elite, examining the kinds of strategies they employed during the first six years of Malawi's democracy (1994–2000). This sets the context for the more fundamental examination of opposition choices during this same period.

Government Strategies: Making Democracy Work

Malawi's basic political structure follows the design of most of the former British colonies in East and Southern Africa. A directly elected executive shares power with a unicameral legislature, creating a situation where primary governing authority is divided between two branches.[2] The seats for parliament (or the National Assembly) are based on single-member districts. Authority over legislation lies in the hands of the National Assembly, which passes laws by a simple majority. After such passage, the legislation goes to the president for his assent. Should the latter be withheld, the legislation is returned to the National Assembly, which can then reconsider it. The president names the cabinet, and is granted the authority to "exercise all powers necessary and incidental to the functions of his or her office in accordance with this Constitution."[3] The constitution also established a judiciary, with a High and a Supreme Court, with the authority to review any action or decisions of government for conformity with the constitution. Other notable bodies created in the constitution include an Ombudsman and a Human Rights Commission.

At the time of Malawi's founding multiparty elections of 1994, three major regional parties dominated political life in the country. The primary players in the political game were those who occupied positions of leadership in these parties. The ruling Malawi Congress Party (MCP) retained a large base of support in the center of the country and was headed by incumbent President Kamuzu Banda. In an effort to expand the appeal of the party, Banda chose as his running mate Gwanda Chakuamba, a former political detainee who came from the deep south of the country. Based in the north was the Alliance for Democracy (AFORD), headed by Chakufwa Chihana, who had gained considerable prominence in previous years as one of the first pro-democracy activists to challenge Banda's authoritarian rule. The United Democratic Front (UDF), headed by Bakili Muluzi, garnered support largely, but by no means exclusively, in the highly populous south of the country.

From the outset, it was relatively clear that the regional nature of Malawi's politics would affect the character of political life in the country by dividing support among the key political players. The results of the first elections brought victory to Bakili Muluzi and the UDF. Yet neither the parliamentary nor the presidential elections yielded a majority for the new government, as the vote was split between the three major parties, largely on regional lines.[4] The ensuing lack of a parliamentary majority for the UDF placed initial limitations on their ability to govern,[5] and, indeed, an early alliance between the MCP and AFORD left an oppositional bloc in control of the National Assembly. Moreover, the electoral results raised questions about the ability of the UDF to stay in office beyond their first term. The message conveyed by the first elections was that Muluzi and the UDF could be vulnerable in subsequent electoral contests. The system of institutionalized competition clearly imposed risks for these initial winners in the democratic game.

Yet in the effort to exercise and retain power, Muluzi and other leaders of the UDF essentially opted to work with the democratic institutions that encumbered and potentially left them vulnerable. Understanding government strategies in this context requires consideration first of the basic political economy of Malawi's democracy. Economic factors surely foreclosed certain strategic options that might have been available to Muluzi and the ruling clique in the UDF. For one, Malawi remains heavily dependent on aid, and openly flouting democratic norms ran the risk of upsetting donors. Grants alone provide 25 percent of government finances (Economist Intelligence Unit 2001). Moreover, many of the business interests and income sources of key government elites were themselves tied to the operation of the domestic economy. These included transport, construction, and building-supply companies that benefited from government contracts, distribution operations involved in the trade of important commodities such as sugar or agricultural inputs, and rental properties.[6] In this respect the income of state elites depended on continued inflows of aid money and a functioning domestic economy. Violating the democratic expectations of international donors could have cut resources for the regime and had damaging impacts on the enterprises of governing elites. The risks of sanctions from external players were thus greater than those posed by the system of institutionalized competition within.

In this context, governing elites were able to devise effective strategies to retain and exercise power without altering the basic institutional framework of democracy. In particular, specific tactics allowed them to successfully negotiate the challenges and risks imposed by divided government and electoral contestation. One of the initial challenges confronted by the UDF government lay in the division of parliamentary seats resulting from the 1994 elections. Although AFORD, more specifically Chihana, and the UDF had worked together during the campaign to unseat Banda, this did not facilitate easy cooperation in the multiparty era. Indeed, as mentioned above, shortly after the founding elections in May of 1994, AFORD entered into an unlikely alliance with the former-ruling MCP, a move that stymied the UDF's ability to govern. By December of the same year, AFORD and Chihana effectively pulled out of the opposition alliance, joining forces with the UDF. Chihana received the post of second vice-president. However, within a year the coalition entered a rocky period as Chihana blasted the UDF for alleged corruption and monopolization of economic opportunities. Months later, in July 1996, Chihana officially pulled out of the coalition—a move partially directed toward maintaining support among AFORD backbenchers and party cadres opposed to the alliance with the UDF (Kaunda 1998, 435).

Yet the collapse of the coalition did not undermine the ability of the UDF to govern, despite the fact that the MCP and AFORD formally held a three-seat edge over the UDF in parliament. By manipulating divisions within AFORD, and more generally encouraging defections among opposition members, the UDF was able to retain a majority of votes in parliament. As Chihana withdrew from the coalition, the government maintained its willingness to work with the opposition (Kaunda 1998, 436). In turn, several AFORD cabinet ministers broke with Chihana and refused to resign their cabinet posts. Other AFORD members continued to back the UDF, allegedly enticed by patronage from the ruling party. Subsequently, both AFORD and the MCP walked out of parliament, leaving the UDF and AFORD "rebels" sitting in parliament (passing legislation) without a quorum. Both the presence of these rebels and the continued sitting of parliament in the absence of a quorum were challenged by the opposition in court. Both rulings went in favor of the government however.[7]

Electoral contests represented another, and perhaps more important, challenge, and the ruling party developed tactics for managing and manipulating them to serve its interests. Here the basic strategy was twofold. The first was to use state power to financially enfeeble the opposition, thus limiting its capacity to effectively compete in the electoral arena. The primary targets of this were elites in the Malawi Congress Party, the primary electoral threat to the UDF. Perhaps the clearest instance was legislation in 1995 that stripped the MCP leadership of a giant economic conglomerate, the Press Trust.[8] The Trust was essentially a holding company for a number of enterprises owned by Banda and the MCP, allegedly accounting for 40 percent of the economy (Economist Intelligence Unit 1996). In addition, after Banda's death in 1997, government-sponsored court cases challenged, and suspended distribution of, the contents of Banda's will, which specified that key MCP insiders should obtain the bulk of his assets.[9] The resulting economic difficulties experienced by the party were quite severe. Press reports indicated that the party experienced problems holding national conventions, making rent payments, and paying party workers.[10]

Coupled with the fact that state power allowed the UDF to aggrandize significant opportunities for accumulating wealth,[11] the ruling elite clearly obtained a resource advantage that translated into a political advantage. Offers of patronage allegedly induced several MPs of the MCP to defect to the ruling party. This in turn required their parliamentary seats to be declared vacant, generating the need for new parliamentary by-elections.[12] In actual by-election contests, caused by such defections and (more frequently) by the deaths of MPs,[13] the UDF capitalized on the resource disparity. In some cases this entailed using offers of cash or material goods to induce opposition candidates to rescind their candidacies shortly before election dates.[14] More generally, the resources at the disposal of the UDF allowed them to present an image of beneficence to local communities. During campaigns, UDF functionaries and candidates bought coffins for funerals, provided donations to churches, gave food to hospital patients, and promised the construction of new schools and health clinics.[15]

The second strategy vis-à-vis elections involved manipulating the electoral process itself, in effect tilting the playing field in the UDF's favor so as to increase chances of success. To be sure, such tactics tainted the electoral process considerably, garnering criticism from domestic and international observers. In addition, the actions of the ruling elite in this regard served as one of the primary sources of political tension in the country during this period. Yet the strategy nonetheless allowed the government to keep the basic trappings of contestation in place, while minimizing the threat of losing at the polls.

Such tactics were especially evident during the more critical electoral contests during the period under review. Englund (2002), for example, describes the measures undertaken by the government during the campaign for the Blantyre City Central Constituency by-election of 1997. Occasioned by the death of a UDF MP in July 1996, the elections presented the opposition MCP and AFORD with very real prospects for taking the seat, thereby chipping away at the slim UDF advantage in the legislature. Part of the reason for this lay in the basic demographics of the constituency—a poor urban township populated by individuals from all areas of the country. Yet, the actions of the UDF during the campaign helped to foreclose any hopes for an opposition victory. For example, knife-wielding youths were sent by UDF leaders to break up opposition rallies. Even more remarkably, UDF leaders threatened the MCP candidate with termination from employment should he continue to stand for the seat. When that failed to convince the candidate, he was allegedly abducted and held at the house of a prominent UDF member. This in turn led to his resignation from the MCP days before the originally scheduled election date in November 1996. Complaints to the Electoral Commission, and later to the High Court, led to the postponing of the polls to April 1997. By that time both the MCP and AFORD had opted to boycott the elections.

The actions of the government in the runup to the 1999 presidential and parliamentary elections similarly illuminate the government's strategy of manipulating the electoral process to minimize the risks of losing. In the lead-up to the polls, the MCP undertook an alliance with AFORD, placing Gwanda Chakuamba as the presidential candidate with Chakufwa Chihana as the running mate.[16] This presented a very real threat to Bakili Muluzi and the UDF. In the 1994 polls, the presidential candidates of the two parties had claimed a combined 52 percent of the electorate, suggesting real possibilities for displacing Muluzi.

Yet the opposition encountered an uneven playing field throughout the campaign. Some of their most significant problems emerged from the government-appointed Electoral Commission. Suspicions about the impartiality of the commission heightened in August 1998, when President Muluzi replaced the board of the commission with a new set of members—only eight months before the polls were to be conducted. Subsequent actions by the leadership of the commission confirmed these fears. Shortly after the MCP-AFORD alliance was announced, the head of the commission claimed that joint tickets were illegal and would not be recognized. Though subsequently overturned by the courts, the decision frustrated the initial efforts of the opposition alliance to mount an effective campaign. Beyond this, the commission mismanaged the registration process before the polls. Only weeks before the polling date, over one hundred voter registration centers reported that they lacked materials necessary to carry out the registration process. Opposition parties and civic groups accused the commission of failing to conduct its operations transparently and pointed to biases in the distribution of registration materials. Subsequent pressure by these actors as well as international donors forced the Electoral Commission to extend the registration period by three weeks. Despite the extension, when registration centers were closed more than 100,000 eligible voters allegedly had not yet registered.[17] In a later report on the elections, the Institute for Electoral Systems (an American NGO) claimed, "the Commission's credibility was eroded because its members adopted clear political positions" (*The Nation,* September 29, 1999).

Access to the broadcast media represented another area where the opposition encountered problems. Statutorily, the Malawi Broadcast Company is supposed to provide each party with a series of broadcast time-slots of equal number, duration, and time-placements (Patel 2000, 36). Yet the campaign period witnessed disproportionate media attention going to the UDF and President Muluzi. Efforts by the opposition to rectify the situation met with delay tactics, leaving the radio essentially a mouthpiece of the ruling party (Article 19, 1999).

The results of the polls brought victory again to Muluzi and the UDF, yet at the cost of generating new levels of political tension in the country. The opposition immediately pointed to irregularities and intimidation during the polling process. In the north, protesters took to the streets, calling for army intervention and ransacking a number of mosques—which reflected hostility toward the religion of President Muluzi. Clashes between partisan supporters brought violence to the region, and a number of families identified as UDF supporters reportedly fled Mzuzu, the capital of the northern region.[18] While the grassroots outbursts dissipated with modest state intervention, political tension nonetheless remained high. As the opposition challenged the UDF victory in court, bellicose rhetoric came to typify the political discourse. Echoing allegations made during the campaign, the government claimed that AFORD and the MCP were preparing to "go to the bush," to prepare for armed conflict, while opposition figures stated that Muluzi had retained Libyan assassins to eliminate his opponents.

While it is important to recognize the political tension that ensued in the wake of the polls, the more fundamental point concerns the relative success of ruling-elite tactics for managing democracy. Although these elections were tainted by accusations of foul play, the basic framework of contestation remained intact. While the opposition questioned Muluzi's legitimacy, international players, and indeed much of Malawian civil society, did not.[19] In this sense, the UDF and Muluzi were able to successfully negotiate the risks posed by institutionalized competition. Despite its encumbrances and risks, then, democracy proved to be a manageable arrangement for the ruling elite.

Opposition Strategies: Constrained Choices and Institutional Opportunities

The more critical question that emerges from this description concerns the behavior of the primary losers in the democratic game. As chapters in this volume on Congo-Brazzaville and the CAR indicate, it is frequently these players who engage in the kind of disruptive tactics that destabilize democracy and even lead to its quick death.

The choices of key elites in the MCP represent one of the more important issues in this respect. Many (though not all) of the leading figures in the MCP during this time were former Banda loyalists and clients—most of whom benefited considerably while he was in power. Yet these individuals certainly did not fare well with the transition to democracy. Indeed, they had limited reason to support "democracy" as it operated in the Malawian context. For one, MCP elites suffered significant setbacks and hardships at the hands of President Muluzi and the ruling UDF. Starting with the first year of the Muluzi government, for instance, key leaders in the party were charged with various offenses. While virtually none of the leaders were prosecuted, the charges presented threats to these individuals and highlighted their potential insecurity. Moreover, as detailed above, many of the MCP elite were stripped of economic resources. This not only hurt them individually but also undermined their capacity to challenge the ruling party in the electoral arena. Beyond this, Malawi's electoral and representative institutions garnered little confidence among the opposition. As described, despite the fact that Muluzi and the UDF did not hold a parliamentary majority, they were nonetheless able to control the legislature. Electoral contests were tainted by the manipulative tactics of the government.

Despite these setbacks and problems, however, the MCP never attempted to derail the democratic game. Harassed and weakened by the state, and confronted by an uneven playing field in the electoral arena, they neither resorted to political destabilization nor undertook efforts to delegitimize the democratic machinery. In the wake of the Blantyre City by-election described above, for example, the opposition response was fairly subdued. As Englund describes it, "no violence or peaceful protest followed the by-election. MCP and AFORD had advised their activists not to organize protests and calmly await the 1999 general elections" (2002, 182). The response to the 1999 elections is also instructive. While grassroots supporters made calls for military intervention, such suggestions were never put forward by opposition leaders. Militant rhetoric emerged, with some opposition figures predicting violence should the outcomes in court cases go against them. But such rhetoric was sporadic, paralleled by a discourse that decidedly downplayed the consideration of such strategies.

Understanding opposition behavior in this context returns us to several themes raised in the discussion above. In particular, opposition decisions to leave the democratic game intact need to be understood in terms of how economic factors and the institutional environment shaped their choices. Owing to limited resources, the strategic options available to opposition players have been relatively constrained. In turn, the institutional context of democratic Malawi enabled and encouraged the use of specific strategies that kept the opposition operating within the democratic framework.

As described above, the MCP became the victim of financial enfeeblement at the hands of the UDF—most evident in the wresting of the Press Trust from the MCP elite. One result was that few of these elites retained access to income streams, which could have been used to challenge the status quo political situation through extralegal tactics. Interestingly, rumors indicate that such tactics were contemplated by MCP elites in the early days of the multiparty era. Allegedly, several groups of the Malawi Young Pioneers—the former armed wing of the party—went to Mozambique waiting for eventual conflict.[20] But as resources dwindled, the capacity to sustain an armed following diminished, and many Pioneers apparently defected from MCP patrons. Moreover, several important assets held by the MCP elites—filling stations, rental properties, hotels, and agricultural estates—hinged on the operation of the domestic economy (*Malawi News Online* 1998; Nhane 1997). Political disruption could undermine such enterprises.

The prospects for disruption from the other opposition elites in the country, particularly AFORD leader Chakufwa Chihana, were also quite limited. Although Chihana and his lieutenants on occasion alluded to the possibility of armed conflict and even secession, their resource base afforded few means to put such threats into action. Chihana's primary economic assets were allegedly motels and distribution operations[21]—certainly not the kinds of enterprises that offer the sustained income that a "warlord" strategy might require (see Reno 1999). As such, his primary efforts went to creating (and maintaining) a cohesive political organization and working through established political channels.

The institutional environment of Malawi's democracy also shaped the choices of the opposition. Two issues stand out. In the first place, the distribution of power in Malawi, as manifested in electoral returns and symbolized in the allocation of parliamentary seats, gave opposition players incentives to play the electoral game. As the UDF advantage in parliament was quite slim from 1995 to 1999, by-elections mattered a great deal, offering the limited prospect of actually chipping away at UDF control of parliament. Early by-elections in 1995 indicated that the MCP could effectively contest and even prevail in these contests. One of the first by-elections was actually rerun by the Electoral Commission after the MCP voiced complaints about the polling process.[22] In a later contest in December 1995, the party actually stole a seat from AFORD—which at that time was aligned with the government. These kinds of successes would be much less frequent with the passage of time. But the initial victories at least demonstrated that working through democratic institutions was a viable option. Moreover, when looking toward the bigger prize of winning national elections, the numbers appeared to work in favor of the opposition. As mentioned, in the 1994 elections the MCP and AFORD had won a majority of the electorate. As such, victory in the 1999 contests was not inconceivable.

In the second place, one needs to consider the important, and in some sense complementary, role that judicial institutions played during Malawi's first six years of democracy. Whereas other state institutions came to be perceived as manifestly biased against the opposition, the judiciary was viewed as an arena where they might effectively protect and advance their personal and political interests. Especially during the first six years of democratic rule, the judicial system offered the opposition a modicum of faith in the possibility of prevailing through established channels. As they pursued a strategy of "judicializing" key political challenges, their propensity to engage in more disruptive tactics decreased.

Two reasons help to account for MCP's faith in and use of Malawi's judicial institutions. The first concerns the historical experience of the courts. To some extent, both the character of the judiciary in the multiparty era, as well as opposition perceptions of the institution, have been rooted in its experience under the Banda regime.[23] In some respects, Banda was unique in how he reworked the judiciary to suit his objectives. In the late 1960s it became apparent that the court system inherited from the British could effectively interfere with the prerogatives and objectives of his government—especially insofar as European judges who sat on the courts rendered decisions contrary to these objectives. To deal with this problem, Banda developed a system of "traditional courts" that could be used to deal with criminal (and political) cases. In turn, the common law courts were relegated the task of simply handling civil and lesser criminal cases (Brietzke 1974; Williams 1977, 254).

The subsequent character of the judiciary under Banda reflected this development. In one respect, the common law courts were clearly the subjects of a highly repressive order, and sometimes acted as accomplices as well. Fearing for their safety, judges remained wholly subservient to Banda, and judicial decisions avoided any line of reasoning that might upset the "Life-President." As one justice put it, "there was no one in that system who felt they could apply the principles of the law to the limit . . . we realigned our legal thinking with the dictates from on high."[24] Moreover, magistrates appointed to serve with chiefs on traditional courts were compelled to write judgments in cases against Banda's political opponents. At the same time, however, the formal courts were never used as primary instruments of repression. Their scope of authority was specifically limited to a narrow set of legal issues—contracts, debts, lesser criminal cases, and so on. In this respect, their work experienced little interference from the government. One court justice maintained, "Banda was careful not to try to influence the formal system" because he "always wanted to do things in a legalistic kind of way."[25] In this context, the judiciary was able to maintain an important degree of professionalism and propriety in its operation. Some even suggest that a specific legal culture emerged, wherein highly formalistic approaches to legal reasoning predominated. In their marginalized role, judges adopted strict methods of interpretation guided by training in common law techniques, but also consistent with survival strategies necessary during the Banda regime (Ngongola 2003).[26]

The close of the one-party era catapulted the courts to a much more visible and active role in Malawian politics. During the period of transition from 1992 to 1994, the courts emerged as important players in the more fundamental struggle between the one-party regime and pro-democracy groups. And although justices backed efforts to silence and imprison pro-democracy advocates, they also handed down numerous decisions that effectively supported the cause of multipartyism (Nzunda 1998). With the actual move to democracy, moreover, the courts received a much broader mandate. The new constitution enacted in 1995 empowered the High Court and Supreme Court of Appeal with the authority to "review any law, and any action or decision of the Government, for conformity with the Constitution." It is in this context that the role of the courts in political life increased, propelled in no small part by the opposition's use of the judiciary to advance and protect political interests.

Understanding the courts' historical evolution helps to account for why certain members of the opposition had faith in the judiciary during Malawi's first few years under the multiparty system. Despite its new constitutional role, the institution of the judiciary in and of itself had not changed dramatically in the democratic era. Many of the same personnel who had been appointed under Banda remained on the bench. Although several new appointments took place under President Bakili Muluzi, his capacity to manifestly politicize judicial appointments was limited. Until recently, the talent pool of personnel has been quite small in Malawi, limiting the range of individuals available for judicial appointment.

Thus, the lines of continuity with the Banda era were clear. Importantly, for opposition players in the MCP, this did not imply that the justices were biased in their favor. As mentioned, several important cases had gone against the MCP during their final days of power. Instead, the perception was that the judiciary would operate with some level of fairness and propriety. One leading figure recounted considerations during the Mwanza trial of 1995, when Kamuzu Banda and several other ranking MCP elites were charged with the murders of four government officials killed in the early 80s. Rather than fearing potential political biases of the court, this individual believed the justices would simply "do their job."

> We saw the justices as a group of people that look at things objectively; they just did their work. Even during the transition we saw them this way. . . . Our past president [Banda] believed in principles and propriety. We saw them practicing these ideals.[27]

Initial and periodic successes in court represent the second reason for the opposition's perceptions and ongoing use of judicial institutions. During the period under review, court decisions both checked state actions detrimental to opposition interests and even supported their efforts to advance goals through the legal system. The Mwanza case, mentioned above, was one of the first examples. During the trial, important court rulings on evidence and testimony went in favor of the accused, enhancing their prospects for acquittal—the ultimate outcome of the case (van Donge 1998). Later appeals to the Supreme Court by the prosecution were rejected. Subsequent state attempts to press opposition elites on criminal charges met with limited success, as did efforts to prosecute MCP leaders for embezzlement of state funds while in office.

The courts also presented challenges to the government's efforts to financially undermine the MCP. The Press Trust Act of 1995, which removed the largest economic conglomerate in the country from the MCP elite, was first overturned by the High Court. After an appeal of that decision to the Supreme Court, however, the High Court was overruled and the legislation survived. While the courts halted the dispersal of Kamuzu Banda's assets to MCP elites, they also stopped government efforts to appoint new directors to the Banda companies with contested ownership. The Supreme Court also upheld a High Court decision that overturned government legislation suspending the distribution of party funds and parliamentary salaries to the opposition.[28]

Finally, court decisions enhanced the prospects of the opposition succeeding in the political process. During the first term, the High Court granted several injunctions to delay the conducting of parliamentary by-elections, this after the opposition challenged the fairness of registration processes. In the runup to the 1999 elections, moreover, the High Court overturned the Electoral Commission decision to disallow the joint MCP-AFORD candidacy for the executive. When the registration process was extended, the High Court forbade the commission from holding polls on the originally set date, effectively requiring an extension of the campaign period.

To be sure, the courts also undertook actions and rendered decisions very contrary to the MCP's interests, leading to accusations of bias and political favoritism. Nonetheless, especially in the context of Malawi's first six years of democracy, the judiciary was an arena in which the opposition could at least envision prevailing in political contests. This helps to explain why one of their primary strategies was to operate through the judicial system in efforts to preserve and advance their interests. Opposition leaders turned to the courts for injunctions to halt government actions antithetical to their interests. Of equal importance, they used the courts to challenge the results of electoral contests that they felt were either rigged or inappropriately conducted. Suggesting the extent of the opposition's faith in the institution, one MCP official commented in response to his party's disputing the results of three by-elections: "the Electoral Commission has failed. . . . We believe that the Commission is not independent. Therefore we will go to court *where we are assured of judicial independence*" (*Malawi News Online* 1997b, emphasis mine).

One of the clearest examples of this strategy is seen in the opposition response to their loss in the May 1999 elections. Rather than destabilize the political situation, MCP party leaders turned to the courts to challenge the outcome, investing time, money (to the point of hiring British attorneys), and public relations efforts in the judicial process. Moreover, when the government accused the MCP and AFORD of planning violence, the opposition issued statements that not only denied such claims, but highlighted their acceptance of judicial mediation in politics.[29]

Of course, the avoidance of disruptive strategies and investment in the judicial process reflected the reality that the MCP elite had few strategic alternatives given their resource base and power relative to the government. In this sense, the efforts to work through the courts might have simply been "the only option" available. Yet even with this consideration in mind, it is quite difficult to suggest that the judiciary did not play a stabilizing role in Malawi's democracy. For one, the political climate might have been much more volatile if the judicial route was not available to the opposition. Consider the challenge to the electoral results of 1999. Shortly after the results were announced, the base of the opposition appeared ready to engage in extended civil disruption, yet the leadership chose the route of judicial mediation. As was demonstrated in the American experience in 2000, working through the courts can prolong the resolution of a disputed electoral contest. In this process, initially volatile reactions dissipate and losers may even accept the eventuality of defeat. Moreover, even if MCP elites lacked the capacity to engage in efforts to disrupt the democratic regime in Malawi, a scorched-earth strategy was not outside the realm of the possible. The protection and possibilities presented by the judicial route made this strategy less necessary however. Without their minimal successes in the courts, Malawi's opposition elites could very well have been backed into a corner by the Muluzi regime. In such a context, acts of desperation—appeals to the military or anti-systemic behavior—would in all likelihood emerge as the "the only option."

Following the resolution of the elections case in May of 2000 (affirming the electoral victory of Muluzi), opposition perceptions of the "judicial option" changed considerably as these elites increasingly questioned the willingness of the judiciary to take antigovernment positions in key cases. One of the primary reasons is that certain opposition victories in the High Court were subsequently reversed by Supreme Court decisions. Moreover, even where they had registered "victories" in court, these had not been over major issues. However, the change in opposition perceptions of the judiciary did not imply the onset of more disruptive strategies. With the resolution of the elections case, the political context changed considerably. This provided the leading faction of the MCP the opportunity of advancing their interest through an informal alliance with the ruling party—an option they pursued.

Elites, Institutions, and the Character of Malawian Democracy: Beyond 2000

May 2000 represents a watershed for Malawi's democracy. Politics up to that point had largely been characterized by interactions among the three major parties as they vied for political advantage. By the second year of President Muluzi's second term, the tripartite structure of Malawian politics had vanished—if only temporarily. Reflecting lingering rifts between the titular leadership and central power-holders, the MCP split into two factions, each claiming rightful title to the party name.[30] The stronger of these factions—and notably the one headed by individuals who had come to doubt the judicial strategy—entered into an informal alliance with the ruling UDF. Months later, the ruling UDF witnessed its own fractionalization when three leading ministers were charged with corruption. Ousted from power, one of these individuals and his allies split from the UDF to form a new pressure group, the National Democratic Alliance (NDA). Of significance, with the breaking away of the NDA, the UDF lost its parliamentary majority gained during the 1999 elections, making the alliance with the MCP all the more important to their interests. The NDA, in turn, launched a political campaign ostensibly to challenge efforts within the ruling party to amend the constitution to clear the way for President Muluzi's running for a third presidential term.

It was within this fluid context that the central dynamic in the political system changed as well. From 2000 to 2003, the primary political issues in the country revolved around the efforts of a small clique within the ruling party seeking to increase and extend its hold on power. In pursuit of this end, key political insiders openly sought to extend the rule of President Muluzi beyond his constitutionally limited second term. In addition to seeking to change the constitutional provision regarding term limits, their program entailed more general efforts to increase the power of the executive and minimize the ability of political opponents to challenge the governing regime. One of the primary strategies they took toward these goals was to alter the basic rules of the game in Malawian politics.[31]

In the 2000–2003 era, the key analytical question thus no longer concerned whether or not key elites would leave democracy intact, but how the actions of governing insiders would shape the character of the emergent regime. The fate of democracy in Malawi in this sense was tied to the ruling elite's efforts to maintain and maximize power. Understanding the unfolding political trajectory demands attention to their strategies toward these ends, as well as the circumstances that affected the nature and success of these strategies. In this respect two central issues stand out.

First, the institutional environment in which the ruling clique operated presented impediments to their efforts to rewrite the rules of the game in their favor. Most clearly, dynamics within the ruling party and among the key parties in parliament affected the prospects for successfully changing political institutions. In addition, the judiciary remained an important player that complicated the efforts of government insiders seeking to extend their hold on power.

This said, overly sanguine assessments about the role of institutions in this respect should be avoided. This brings us to our second point. In addition to trying to rewrite the rules, regime insiders also demonstrated a willingness to work outside of the rules to advance political objectives. Especially as resistance to their project emerged in the state, political society, and civil society, they engaged in more classic power-political strategies of thuggery and intimidation against suspected opponents. The resulting context was one in which democratic forms coexisted with a climate of violence authored largely by ruling elites. This reminds us that "extra-institutional" political machinations will shape the fate of Malawi's democratic experiment into the foreseeable future.

Institutional Obstacles to Rewriting the Rules

The strategy of rewriting the rules of the game became especially evident in the period after the May 2000 resolution of the elections case. The clearest example of this strategy was the effort from within the ruling United Democratic Front to amend the constitution to allow President Muluzi to stand for a third term. Yet beyond this, there were other, less dramatic examples of such a strategy at work. For instance, drawing on recommendations of an impartial Constitutional Review Commission, parliament in July 2001 amended the constitution in a manner that limited the ability of MPs to defect from their parties. With the amendment, the speaker of the parliament obtained the authority to declare vacant the seats of individual MPs who abandoned the party with which they affiliated at the time of election. Yet another of the commission's recommendations was to decrease the quorum in the legislature. The goal of this was to minimize the impact of parliamentary boycotts, an exercise that the opposition used to hamper the operation of the government during the first term. While the commission proposed a quorum of two-fifths of all MPs, the ruling party sought to decrease the quorum to one-third.[32] Other examples include proposed legislation that would have allowed the president to select certain municipal and local government authorities, and an effort to curtail the powers of the Ombudsman.[33] The latter had been an ongoing source of irritation to the ruling regime—especially in his challenges to efforts by the ruling party to remove opposition sympathizers from the civil service.

These proposed changes carried potentially critical implications for the character of Malawi's democracy. If successful, they might have represented the first steps in a process of slow democratic death aptly described by Schedler (1998). Centralizing executive authority over semi-autonomous institutions like local government or the bureaucracy, or enhancing presidential and party control over parliament, betray basic principles of limited government that underpin democratic rule. Moreover, these kinds of measures would have opened the way to enacting more fundamental changes in the rules: curtailing checks and balances, restricting civil freedoms, or simply expanding UDF power in a way that limited the possibilities for other parties to effectively compete in electoral contests.

However, ruling insiders faced significant obstacles in their efforts to change Malawi's institutions. And while challenges from donors and civil society groups were important, of equal if not greater significance was the resistance that emerged from within Malawi's institutions of governance. This resistance came from three institutional locations in particular: the ruling party itself, the parliament, and the judiciary.

As the chapter by Manning effectively elucidates (see chapter 10, this volume), internal party dynamics represent one of the central variables affecting the political experience of new African democracies. In the case of Malawi, internal divisions and struggles within the UDF shaped the course of democratic development as the country headed toward third elections in 2004. Like other parties in new African democracies, the coherence and mobilizational capacities of the ruling UDF in Malawi has hinged on the presence and skill of specific personalities. The party was formed in late 1991 from a small nucleus of discontented elites eager to topple the Banda regime. Key players included former ranking MCP elites, successful businessmen, and, to a lesser extent, disaffected intellectuals (Lwanda 1996; Meinhardt 1997). In 1992, Bakili Muluzi, a wealthy businessman and former secretary general of the MCP, emerged as the first leader of the party. From that time to 2000, both his towering persona and pure political expediency provided the glue that held the party together. With his scheduled departure, however, cracks within the UDF became more apparent.

The primary issue dividing the party was whether or not Muluzi should stand for a third term. The initial fissures became apparent in November 2000 when President Muluzi targeted apparently disloyal ministers and MPs, purging them from government positions and charging several with corruption. Significantly, the two most prominent ministers targeted were viewed as potential candidates for the presidency in 2004; these were individuals who had the most to lose if the constitution were amended to allow Muluzi to stand again. In turn, one of these ministers and several of his parliamentary backers went on to form the NDA, which then effectively became part of the political opposition in parliament. This increased the number of antigovernment MPs by five. This minor shift in the balance of legislative power later carried important consequences for the government's effort to amend the constitution to allow Muluzi to stand for a third term.

Given the initial purge, as well as the clear messages from the ruling clique that disloyalty would be weeded out and punished, it is not very surprising that many prominent UDF members remained silent about the third term over most of the next two years. Even as party insiders began to openly promote the idea of a third term for Muluzi and organized a bill in parliament to amend the constitution, open debate on the issue within the UDF was nonexistent. This silence was all the more striking given the degree to which civil society groups and the political opposition had mobilized against the program. The silence, however, did not imply unanimity in support for the third term. As I detail below, after forces favoring a third term failed in their initial effort to amend the constitution, several prominent UDF members joined the growing movement to oppose the program to allow Muluzi to stand again.

Dynamics within parliament presented a second point of resistance. Most fundamentally, the fragmentation and increasing fluidity of the party system in the post-2000 period limited the capacity of the ruling party to have its way with both simple legislation and efforts to amend the constitution. Indeed, with the emergence of the NDA, the ruling party temporarily lost its majority in parliament. This forced the government to obtain the cooperation of other parties in parliament to pass simple legislation (requiring a majority) or constitutional amendments (requiring two-thirds of the legislature).[34] And while the UDF majority was later recaptured through by-election victories and defections, the dynamics of interparty interactions continued to complicate government efforts to change the rules of the game in a way that suited the power-maximizing and power-extending objectives of key insiders.

Finally, the judiciary remained an important player on the political scene—this despite the fact that public statements by the opposition indicated that faith in the judicial route had diminished. Especially at the High Court, the government's ability to monitor and control justices remained limited.[35] What this meant in practice was that High Court justices could render decisions that contradicted government interests. As the battle to amend the constitution was being waged, several High Court decisions supported the efforts of those opposed to the third term.

The importance of resistance from these three institutional locations becomes especially evident when we consider several instances where the government sought, but then failed, to change the rules of the game in its favor. One example is seen in the UDF's efforts to amend the Local Government Act in parliament. As described above, this bill would have given the executive greater control over local government. One initial bill seeking to modify the act was withdrawn after donors and civil society protested a section that would have given the president the power to appoint and remove local government officers (Africa News Service 2000). A second bill removed that section, but included a provision that district officials ("Chief Executives") could be transferred by the Minister of Local Government. The provision concerned the MCP (the UDF's apparent parliamentary ally), given the important role of such officials in elections. As one prominent MCP MP put it in parliament:

> I have great difficulty in understanding that provision and would ask Government to reconsider it. . . . Can the Minister reconsider this because it is dangerous particularly when it comes to the power of Chief Executives with respect to matters of an electoral nature. We have seen transfers in levels of staff of that caliber close to election or by-election periods, and the impression being created is that they want to be positioned, so they can do game plans with respect to electoral matters.[36]

Owing to the MCP's open opposition to this provision in parliament, the bill was subsequently revised, giving the minister transfer power only in consultation with a semi-autonomous local government commission. Similarly, owing to resistance from the MCP, the government came up short in revising the constitution to change the specifications regarding a quorum. Originally the government sought to change the constitutional provision from a two-thirds requirement to one-third. The MCP, however, only agreed to reduce quorum to 50 percent plus one.[37]

To be sure, eliciting cooperation from other parties in efforts to increase the power of the government was not always problematic. For example, the constitutional amendment that curtailed MP autonomy was enabled by the working alliance with the dominant faction of the MCP in parliament—whose leaders also benefited directly from the amendment. Moreover, the same faction supported government efforts to impeach three High Court justices who had rendered decisions contrary to the interests of the UDF. And at later points, several AFORD MPs were persuaded to back government's efforts to amend the constitution for a third term. Given the resources at the disposal of the government, the ability to entice erstwhile opponents to support its agenda was not surprising. One ranking member of the MCP described how the cooperative strategy had generated important benefits for him, as his constituency had finally received government boreholes. No such help was forthcoming while the MCP represented the formal opposition.

Yet even at that, overcoming potential parliamentary opposition to rewriting the rules represented only one hurdle. The judiciary represented another, and in several instances they stood to challenge the government's program. One of the clearest instances was a High Court decision in November 2001 that challenged the efforts of the pro-government faction in parliament to remove from the legislature (among others) those members who had defected from the UDF and formed the pressure group the NDA. Using the constitutional amendment regarding party defections, the speaker of the parliament declared that the seats of all NDA MPs (and several others) were vacant—a move that decreased the strength of antigovernment forces in the legislature by seven votes. However, a subsequent court ruling granted an injunction against the speaker (leaving the previously expelled MPs in parliament), and called for judicial review of the Speaker's actions. Nine months later, when pro-government MPs sought to amend the constitution to allow Muluzi to stand for a third term, the issue remained unresolved. The continued seating of the seven MPs in parliament at this time proved to be critical, as the proposed constitutional amendment failed by three votes.[38]

On this note, the problems the ruling elite encountered in seeking to amend the constitution to allow for Muluzi's standing for a third term clearly bespeak the importance of these institutional locations of resistance to their project. The effort came to an initial apex in July 2002 when a private members bill was introduced in the National Assembly, calling for the elimination of the term limits clause from the constitution. Despite the setback from the November 2001 court decision leaving seven antigovernment MPs in parliament, by June 2002 the ruling elite felt it had mustered enough backing for the so-called Open Terms Bill. This was the case despite the fact that rumors indicated that several prominent UDF government ministers were opposed to the bill, and despite the fact that the extent of MCP and AFORD support for the bill was not clear. The support of some of these parties' MPs was critical if the bill was to pass.

To the surprise of the government, however, several MCP MPs from the pro-government faction either voted against the bill or abstained altogether (in contrast to the leadership of the faction). The failure of the bill by three votes clearly demonstrated that apparent parliamentary allies could not be trusted.

Although some felt that this would nail the coffin on Muluzi's third term, months later, in the face of opposition from well-organized civil society groups, and in the context of a highly polarized and fluid political environment, the government made public its plans to submit yet another bill to parliament. At this point, however, two UDF MPs publicly announced that they did not support the measure. Notably, efforts by the UDF leadership to have their seats declared vacant—for allegedly crossing the floor when they met with a group opposed to the bill—failed when the High Court issued an injunction against the speaker of parliament, restraining him from declaring the seats vacant. With support in the party uncertain, questions arising about partisan allies, and civil society emboldened, the president asked that the bill be withdrawn. A final effort in January 2003 also failed in the face of dramatic civil society opposition and dissent within the ruling party. Two months later, Muluzi announced that he would not seek a third term and named his successor.[39]

Thuggery: Tactic or Modus Operandi

While it is important to recognize how institutions have shaped the fate of Malawi's democracy, it also important to not overstate their role in defining the content of the political drama. For the recent political history clearly reveals that institutions are not the only channels through which "politics" is conducted. While machinations within institutional arenas have affected Malawi's political future, so have the dynamics of extra-institutional politics. Especially as resistance to the power-maximizing project of regime insiders emerged within political and civil society, those insiders increasingly relied on extra-institutional strategies to advance political aims. To be sure, the use of the classic "neopatrimonial" technique of clientelism has coexisted with the formal operation of democratic institutions since the early days of multiparty rule in Malawi. What is especially striking about the recent struggle over institutional change is the extent to which thuggery and intimidation surfaced as parallel strategies. Violence became one of the primary means used by regime insiders to keep political threats or challengers at bay. Extra-institutional politics haunted the political climate and raised questions about the quality of democratic governance emerging in Malawi.

The targets of intimidation represented a broad array of potential threats to those within the regime seeking to extend and maximize power. For example, suspected disloyal members of the ruling UDF were victims of intimidation. As the NDA splintered from the UDF in 2000, two UDF MPs were assaulted by party insiders who questioned their loyalty to the ruling party. Moreover, partisan opponents of the UDF—especially the NDA—witnessed considerable hostility. Ruling party thugs assaulted NDA officials, destroyed property, and broke up opposition rallies. Perhaps even more disturbing were assaults on various elements of civil society. Two religious leaders who voiced critical sentiments about the government were targeted for attack, one of whom was left in critical condition after being assaulted. "Young Democrats," the youth wing of the UDF, even broke up a fundraising march by the Blantyre Justice and Peace Commission of the Catholic Church (*Malawi Update* 2001). News reporters were also harassed and targeted. In one particular instance, a reporter was assaulted and thrown into a waiting vehicle in front of the international press corps at the 2001 SADC meetings held in the city of Blantyre. None were prosecuted for violence, suggesting that police were hesitant to pursue the perpetrators.[40]

From an analytical standpoint, the emergence of violence in Malawian politics needs to be understood as part of elite strategies within the democratic framework. As indicated, governing elites have been constrained with respect to their options about whether or not to leave the basic institutions of democracy intact. In this context, the use of thuggery and intimidation presented a potentially viable strategy for keeping power—quieting political foes and keeping potentially disloyal elements in line. To be sure, there were risks with this strategy—especially if it generated condemnation from civil society and the donor community. Indeed, human rights concerns were cited by the Danish government when it pulled its aid and diplomatic mission out of Malawi in 2002. Yet to the extent that the authors of thuggery remain concealed, the risks posed by such extra-institutional strategies were low, while the payoffs high. This represents one of the primary challenges for Malawi's democracy into the foreseeable future.

▼▼▼▼

The persistence of democratic institutions in Malawi represents an important accomplishment for the country, especially when juxtaposed against the experiences of certain other countries discussed in this volume. To be sure, such institutions have operated very imperfectly. But assuming that Mexico and/or Senegal offer a model, the endurance of democratic institutions in Malawi may open the door to the deepening of democracy in the future.

This said, the section above reminds us to some degree that the primary challenges in Africa's new democracies extend far beyond the question of whether or not institutions survive. As Manning argues in this volume, African leaders have proven quite adept at retaining the paraphernalia of democracy to achieve a minimum of presentability to international observers. Yet the presence of democratic institutions should not blind us to the fact that extra-institutional tactics play a central role in political life. In this sense, the climate of violence should not be considered inconsistent with the persistence of democratic institutions. Indeed, thuggery and democratic politics may coexist in tension, representing a potentially stable equilibrium.

The (re)emergence of thuggery politics as a primary tactic represents a particularly disturbing development for those concerned with the political future of the country. To the extent that extra-institutional strategies are the primary focus of elite action, it suggests that some of the primary players have ceased to invest in democratic politics as a system of governance. Habituation to democratic norms is highly unlikely in this context. More fundamentally, these tendencies suggest that force—as opposed to resources, popular wishes, and laws—may emerge as one of the key arbiters of central political questions in the country: who will rule, for how long, and in what manner. As such, Malawi's democratic institutions may come to represent mere window dressing—kept intact to appease international donors, but devoid of any real role in determining the fundamental political issues in the country. Here lies one of the primary threats to Malawi's democracy in the foreseeable future. The challenge at this point may be less one of retaining institutional edifices of democracy, but rather insuring that those institutions actually inform the conduct of political life in the country.

NOTES

1. I am indebted to Carrie Manning, whose presentation, "The State of Democratic Transition in Mozambique" (University of Florida, Center for African Studies, November 6, 1998), encouraged adoption of this framework.

2. The 1995 Constitution actually specified a bicameral legislature. The provision for a Senate was later scrapped via a constitutional amendment in 2001.

3. Constitution of the Republic of Malawi, 48.

4. In the presidential contest, Muluzi of the UDF obtained 47.2 percent of the vote, while Banda of the MCP and Chihana of AFORD obtained 33.5 and 18.9 percent, respectively. Parliamentary elections left the UDF with 48 percent of the legislative seats, while the MCP and AFORD obtained 31.6 and 20.3 percent, respectively (Meinhardt 1999, 559).

5. The division of powers described above necessitates executive-legislature co-operation to pass legislation.

6. This information is gleaned from Consumer Association of Malawi (1997), Chimgwede and Kulapani (2000), Kulapani (2001), and *The Daily Times,* May 15, 2000, and February 7, 2000.

7. Part of this account is derived from biweekly reports issued by the offices of the National Democratic Institute in Malawi, particularly those issued February 12, 1996, and July 10, 1996. The author gratefully acknowledges the access to these reports.

8. Court cases delayed the actual execution of the act until 1997.

9. The BBC claimed that Banda's estate was valued at $319 million. See *BBC News Online,* "Mystery of Banda's Millions," May 17, 2000. Available at: http://news.bbc.co.uk/1/hi/world/africa/752462.stm. Accessed October 14, 2004.

10. See *Mail and Guardian,* "Malawi Opposition Too Broke to Elect New Leader," April 14, 1997; *The Nation,* February 16, 2000, and November 3, 2000.

11. This is described in more detail in VonDoepp 2001.

12. On defections, see *The Nation,* "Why the Steady Defections," June 17, 1996, and *The Saturday Nation,* "Principles in Question," December 16–22, 1995.

13. Englund (2002) indicates that twenty MPs died during the first three years of Malawi's new democracy.

14. Reported in the *Malawi News Online* (1997a).

15. Such stories are reported in *The Daily Times,* January 21, 1999, and April 16, 1999; and *The Nation,* March 25, 1999. The importance of such displays is highlighted by Englund (2002).

16. Chakuamba obtained titular leadership of the MCP in the wake of Banda's death in 1997.

17. For a useful review of these problems, see Patel (2000). Specific information is derived from ANB-BIA News Supplements for June 17, 1999.

18. The violence is described in various international and Malawian press reports. For specific information, see ANB-BIA News Supplements for June 24, 1999.

19. For example, the eight Catholic bishops in the country called on the key players to "win with dignity and lose with grace"—effectively calling for acceptance of the polls. Quoted in Kanjaye (1999).

20. As late as 1998 a Malawian army commander claimed that Young Pioneers had organized in the "forests" of Mozambique (*Sabanews Weekend Edition,* August 1, 1998). Such rumors circulated considerably during Malawi's first few years of democratic rule. See Tukula (1996). Later claims indicated that the MYP had resurfaced as a criminal element in Malawi, partially because the MCP leaders could not support them. See Economist Intelligence Unit (1998).

21. Chihana's role in the lucrative sugar trade is described in *The Nation,* "Bitter Truth about Sugar: Nothing Changes," April 10, 1996.

22. Reference is made here to the Nkhotakota by-elections of 1995.

23. Widner (2001, 85) singles out Malawi for its difference with other African countries in this regard.

24. Interview with author, August 7, 2001.

25. Interview with author, August 15, 2001.

26. I am indebted to Clement Ngongola for several of the points raised in the paragraph above; as provided in a personal communication in March 2001.

27. Interview with author, August 14, 2001.

28. Reference is made here to the case *Attorney General versus Masauli,* Miscellaneous Civil Appeal No. 28 of 1998.

29. In *The Daily Times,* September 3, 1999, an editorial by a leading opposition figure called on the government to "let the courts do their work."

30. The party label is of critical importance for two reasons. First, in Malawi's highly regionalized party system, most voters in the country follow party labels when choosing candidates. Second, the party is named as the beneficiary of several of Kamuzu Banda's enterprises held in trust.

31. Of importance, this strategy is consistent with their earlier approach of manipulating electoral institutions to their advantage—in some sense a means of retaining power without openly flouting democratic norms upheld by international donors.

32. *The Chronicle,* "Editorial: Changing the Parliamentary Quorum—A Sure Way of Creating 'Single-Party,' Multi-Party Rule," June 12, 2001.

33. See Semu (2000) (on the proposed amendment to the Local Government Act) and *The Nation,* June 7, 2001 (on the Ombudsman).

34. A referendum can also be used to amend the constitution.

35. The reasons for this are described in VonDoepp (2002b).

36. Malawi: National Assembly Debates (Hansard), Sixth Meeting—Thirty-Fourth Session, Second Day, Friday, January 12, 2001, 4.

37. *Daily Times,* "Government Bows to Opposition Demands," November 6, 2001.

38. Also significant was a High Court decision in October 2002 that declared unconstitutional a presidential ban on demonstrations regarding the third term.

39. Certain parts of this discussion are covered in VonDoepp (2003b).

40. The increase of violence is of course a major cause of concern. The Human Rights Commission, a statutory body, indicated that the number of human rights abuses had doubled between 1999 and 2000. Several donors and international observers view this trend as one of the primary threats to political stability in the country.

9 | Democracy Unrealized
Zambia's Third Republic under Frederick Chiluba

David J. Simon

When Frederick Chiluba defeated Kenneth Kaunda in a competitive, multiparty presidential election in Zambia in 1991, hopes for democracy in Africa were high (e.g., van Donge 1995; Joseph 1992). Kaunda and his United National Independence Party (UNIP) had been in power for twenty-seven years, much of that time as the sole legal political party in Zambia. Chiluba's Movement for Multiparty Democracy (MMD) suggested—by its name alone, as well as by its slogan—that the hour had indeed come for democracy in Africa. Over the course of Chiluba's ten years in office, however, Zambian democracy struggled to live up to its early promise. A decade later, following two declared states of emergency, two sets of flawed and controversial elections, and sporadic political violence, many had begun to feel that Chiluba and the MMD resembled their predecessors in political style. For example, Richard Joseph (1998, 6), one of Zambian democracy's early and most prominent boosters, declared the Zambian experience to be "the archetypical example of . . . political closure," accusing Chiluba of having "taken Zambia back to the worst period of . . . [the] relatively mild authoritarian governance under Kaunda" (see also Chabal and Daloz 1999, 35; Mphaisha 1996, 65; Nyambe 1999).

Following elections in 1996, Zambia's Freedom House rating reverted back to 4.5 ("partly free"), after having surged from 5.5 ("not free") to 2.5 ("free") in 1991.[1] The general elections in December 2001 brought an end to the Chiluba era, but revealed additional weaknesses in Zambia's democracy: no presidential candidate (including the winner, the MMD's Levy Mwanawasa) earned as much as 30 percent of the vote, while international observers decried the lack of transparency in the counting and tabulating of the votes (e.g., Carter Center 2002). The opposition initially challenged the outcome in court and pursued strategies of noncooperation with the government.

By the end of Chiluba's two terms, the promise of the 1991 transition remained mostly unrealized. The fundamental institutional changes of 1991 made regular elections possible,[2] made opposition parties legal, and gave increased protection to the press. Yet, though these changes are necessary elements of democratization, they have not proved sufficient. In this chapter, I examine the shortcomings of the Zambian democratic experience using the Dahlian lenses of competition and participation that Bratton and van de Walle (1997) employ in the work that stands as a backdrop for this volume. After surveying political patterns and events along those dimensions, I address the extent to which deficiencies in institutional design can account for the shortcomings of Zambian democracy. In Zambia, institutions have failed to constrain political behavior (of elites and the masses alike)—which may indeed be the hallmark of an unconsolidated democracy. Accordingly, I also address the extra-institutional influences on political behavior in Zambia, including historically informed norms, the economic context, and the role of international actors.

Democracy in the Third Republic

According to Robert Dahl (1971), the essential components of democracy are participation and competition. While the prescriptive value of Dahl's work is a matter of some dispute, one may assess and compare levels of democracy across polities using these dimensions. One means of acquiring a handle on the disputed concept of democratic consolidation (O'Donnell 1996; Schedler 1998) is to consider the extent to which participation and contestation have become (or have yet to become) permanent and nonviolent features of politics in a country—such as Zambia—that has undergone a transition.

Participation

Participation is a fundamental element of democracy. It is essential both to have opportunities to make political choices, and to take advantage of those opportunities, in order to constrain the incumbent from pursuing goals that are antithetical to the public interest. Ideally, vibrant political participation forces politicians to subordinate their own interests to those of the public—or at least to some majoritarian subset thereof.

Zambian politics appeared to live up to this ideal in 1991, when protests, rallies, and election-day voting forced out a regime that had presided over mostly deteriorating economic and social conditions for the previous twenty-seven years. Without the thousands of people who turned out to rallies and the nearly one million Zambians who turned out to vote for the MMD, the transition period would have involved a protracted power struggle between elites. Even if the elites who led the call for multipartyism had been fundamentally self-interested, they astutely recognized that mass participation in a competitive political process could both legitimize their desires (to hold high office themselves) and provide a widely supported means of getting there.

The vibrant and inspiring levels of political participation in the transition from authoritarian rule have not been sustained. In local government elections held in 1992 and 1998, as well as in numerous parliamentary by-elections held during the MMD's first five years, turnout averaged below 20 percent of registered voters. At a low, a mere 6 percent of registered voters turned out for an October 1995 by-election in the Copperbelt constituency of Lufwanyama. Eight other by-elections featured single-digit turnout rates during the MMD's first term.

The nature of national electoral contests is also telling. The 1996 electoral season saw few of the massive demonstrations—either for or against the ruling party—that characterized 1990–91. Although voter turnout, expressed as a percentage of registered voters, increased by 12 percentage points over 1991, turnout declined by 3 percent according to the more telling baseline of eligible citizens (Simon 2002). In late 1995 and early 1996, a disastrous voter registration exercise had resulted in the registration of barely half of the estimated eligible population—despite three extensions of the exercise's deadline that added two-and-a-half months to its original duration. Opposition political parties were quite suspicious of the contract awarded to the Israeli company Nikuv to compile the voters' rolls. Perhaps most damaging to the exercise, however, was that few politicians, parties, or civil society organizations took it upon themselves to mobilize would-be registrants.[3]

The registration exercise prior to the 2001 election also drew scant participation. Once again, barely half of the estimated eligible population became eligible to vote through the exercise.[4] With the presidential race and many parliamentary races so close as to defy any prediction, election-day turnout was relatively high: 1.7 million voted in the presidential contest, representing almost 70 percent of those registered, and 35 percent of eligible citizens.

Contestation

Dahl's second dimension of democracy concerns the extent to which political alternatives compete for support. At the ideal level of contestation, a polity must feature the space and opportunity for challenges to political incumbents to arise. Viable, popular alternatives to incumbents would constrain the latter from purely self-benefiting policies and actions.

Meaningful competition in these terms was mostly absent from politics during the first decade of Zambia's Third Republic. No opposition party seriously challenged the MMD until late 2001, while the strongest opposition party in 1991—UNIP, the former ruling party—gradually but steadily withered away over the ten-year period.[5] Besides UNIP and the MMD, no other party galvanized much support in 1996 (although as many as thirty-five had emerged over the course of the preceding five years). Even in 2001, the United Party for National Development (UPND) ran a close second to the MMD in the presidential and parliamentary races, but still earned barely a quarter of the vote in its own right.

A major reason for the lack of credible opposition is that the MMD took several steps to minimize the prospect of the emergence of a rival political threat. In February 1993, less than a year-and-a-half after the transitional election, the government-controlled press reported an alleged plan by UNIP to retake power by desta-bilizing the MMD regime (Ihonvbere 1996, 224–45). The government responded by declaring a state of emergency, which permitted, among other practices, arrests without bringing charges (as otherwise required under the constitution). The state of emergency lasted several months, leading to criticism from within the regime and from its former allies within civil society. Ironically, the state of emergency it-self harmed the ruling party's unity: in protest, four cabinet members and four other members of parliament left the MMD and formed the National Party.

Efforts to revise the constitution provide another glimpse at the ruling party's distaste for political competition. A central promise of the MMD's campaign in 1991 had been to create a new, democratic constitution upon assuming office.[6] In 1993, the MMD created a commission to collect input from around the country, suggesting what a new constitution should contain. Individuals, civil society organizations, and political parties were all solicited to contribute to the commission, with the MMD duly submitting a list of proposals of its own. When the commission's rec-ommendations did not conform to the ruling party's suggestions, the MMD lead-ership decided to push through parliament a Constitutional Amendment Bill that essentially replicated its original submission. In doing so, the MMD not only aban-doned its promise to forge an entirely new document but also ignored the recom-mendations of the committee it had created and demonstrated an unwillingness to recognize the standing of others in the political discourse.

The ruling party's intolerance of competition was evident not just in the con-stitutional revision process, but in the substance of the MMD's constitutional revi-sions, as well. The proposals drawing the most ire from MMD's foes were those re-garding the eligibility requirements to stand for president: candidates were required to have been born in Zambia to parents who were Zambian citizens by birth (ef-fectively eliminating Kenneth Kaunda, whom the MMD perceived to be the most formidable threat to Chiluba), and candidates could not be traditional leaders (i.e., tribal chiefs—effectively eliminating UNIP's second-in-command).

The MMD responded to criticism over constitutional revision with means rem-iniscent of heavy-handed, UNIP-era street politics. In October 1995, the police broke up a small protest by civil society groups, declaring that the protest was illegal in the absence of a permit. (The protesters had applied for a permit but their appli-cation was refused.) Later, after the Supreme Court mandated that permits be granted more liberally and the same groups organized a larger protest outside par-liament, buses full of young MMD partisans menacingly jeered the protesters. The MMD party chairman for Lusaka Province, Richard Sakala, specifically threatened violence against one the protest's organizers.[7]

Political tensions escalated as the 1996 election approached. By-election cam-paigns became increasingly violent (Human Rights Watch 1997, 42–45). While the tension itself may have represented nascent—but growing—political competition, the MMD found various means of exploiting that tension to subvert its actual competition. Early in the run-up to the general elections that year, police discovered several unexploded bombs; each was accompanied by a mysterious anti-government note bearing a signature, "the Black Mamba." The MMD soon arrested eight of its opponents, all of whom were affiliated with opposition parties. After a lengthy trial that occupied opposition leaders' time, energy, and resources for several months, each of the accused was exonerated, shortly before the election. The judge on the case harshly reprimanded the state prosecutors for bringing cases insufficiently supported by evidence.[8] Their members exonerated, the opposition forces nonetheless found themselves unprepared to contest the election.

The 1996 elections themselves further highlighted the weakness of political competition. Although most observers found no evidence of outright rigging, such manipulation was rendered unnecessary by political tricks made earlier in the electoral cycle—such as reworking the rules of the constitution in the MMD's favor, or exploiting the government-run press while cracking down on the independent press. The MMD earned slightly less of the presidential and parliamentary vote than it had received in 1991, but the party increased its share of seats in the National Assembly. With UNIP boycotting the election, the most successful opposition group consisted of ten victorious independent candidates. All had been MMD members who either had either fallen out with the national party apparatus or had been overlooked by the apparatus when it selected the candidates for each constituency.

Despite the weakness of the opposition faced by the MMD in the 1996 election, events in the years that followed suggest that the party remained wary of any challenge to its power. In August 1997, Kaunda was shot and wounded by provincial police officers at a political rally in Central Province. A fellow speaker, MMD founder-turned-opponent Rodger Chongwe, was injured more seriously. Although speculation regarding responsibility for the incident has centered on provincial security officials rather than national-level party officials, the incident suggests that the ruling party had failed to cultivate a culture of political tolerance.[9] Indeed, the ruling party made little effort to condemn the shooting or to prosecute its perpetrators.

Later in 1997, an abortive coup attempt gave the MMD pretense to circumscribe political contestation yet again. A small group of disgruntled army officers managed to take control of the national broadcasting headquarters long enough to declare—falsely, it turned out—that they had executed a coup.[10] Although the military remained supportive of the government and regained control of the station a few hours later, the shaken ruling party once again declared a state of emergency. The police arrested Kaunda, detaining him under house arrest for several months. Other politicians, including Dean Mung'omba, the runner-up to Chiluba in the 1996 presidential race, were also detained and, allegedly, tortured.[11]

The run-up to the 2001 election featured further evidence of the MMD's hard line against dissent, in the form of violent incidents involving the ruling party's opponents. In July 2001, for example, MMD cadres allegedly ransacked houses belonging to leaders of a new opposition party, the Forum for Democracy and Development (FDD).[12] That same night, the former MMD party vice-chair and new member of the FDD, Paul Tembo, was killed in his home. Opposition leaders called the killing a political assassination, noting that Tembo was due to testify shortly at a corruption trial of three MMD ministers.[13]

Harassment of the media also demonstrates the Chiluba administration's intolerance of dissenting views.[14] The highest-profile incident—the arrest and imprisonment of Masautso Phiri, an editor for the *Post*—drew notice and condemnation from Amnesty International.[15] Later, in 2001, the government prosecuted an editor and opposition politicians for defaming the president in an article that appeared in the *Post*.[16] Intolerance of dissent from (or via) the media reached street-level politics as well. Seven weeks prior to the election, MMD youths on the Copperbelt stormed an independent radio station that was broadcasting an interview with an opposition politician.[17]

While often boxed in by MMD tactics, the opposition did little to advance democracy. Stepan's (1990) instruction that an opposition must pose a viable alternative to the ruling party is no less true after a transitional moment than it is beforehand. To give life to the Dahlian contestation element of democracy in Zambia, the opposition would have had to appear to have a reasonable chance of defeating the MMD via institutionally available means. To do so, it would have had to be strong enough to convert the ruling party's misdeeds into electoral opposition. Yet, as Peter Burnell notes, the political opposition "has failed Zambia by its inattention to the most basic functions like researching and formulating credible policy alternatives and mobilizing grass-roots support" (2001, 259). In essence, it failed to force the MMD to be more democratic.

The opposition's behavior around the time of the 1996 voter registration exercise illustrates Burnell's condemnation: most parties concentrated their rhetoric and resources on fighting the contract to prepare the rolls, vying to have the exercise itself terminated and restarted—a strategy, given the cost and timing of the exercise, that was unlikely to succeed. The Electoral Commission simply did not have the resources to stop and start all over again. Meanwhile, opposition parties devoted little energy to encouraging potential supporters to register. If the final voters' rolls were packed with MMD supporters, as some opposition politicians alleged, it was largely due to the failure of other parties to make sure their own supporters were on the rolls as well.

An inability to act collectively also undermined the opposition's viability. As Duverger (1964) tells us, a first-past-the-post, single-member-district presidential system such as Zambia's should tend toward a system featuring two major parties to maximize competitiveness within the system. With the MMD assuming the position of one of those parties simply by virtue of its incumbency, it falls upon the opposition to coalesce, so as to serves as a single, credible alternative. In 1996, the MMD won twenty-seven parliamentary seats in races in which it garnered less than 50 percent of the vote. The MMD's dominance of parliament would have been significantly reduced if the opposition had been able to consolidate the vote in those constituencies. The UNIP-led boycott further undermined the prospects for an effective showing by the opposition, as the Zambia Democratic Congress (ZDC) perceived the boycott as an opportunity to absorb would-be UNIP votes. In the end, ZDC's participation undermined UNIP's boycott, while UNIP's boycott diluted the potential anti-MMD vote.

The problems with collective action also undermined the opposition in the aftermath of Chiluba's failed effort to amend the constitutions to allow himself to stand for a third presidential term—this despite the very favorable circumstances for displacing the MMD. Beginning in 1999, the question of succession dominated Zambian politics. The 1991 constitution, even as amended in 1996, limited Chiluba to two terms in office. In early 2001, however, Chiluba's backers within the party began to call for a constitutional amendment to allow the president to stand again. The tumultuous months that followed witnessed heightened political debate and tension as parts of civil society, the political opposition, and even some elements of the MMD arose to challenge the effort. Several (indeed, the majority of) provincial-level party committees voiced support for Chiluba's third term. Events culminated in April 2001. Just before the MMD held a national party convention in order to endorse Chiluba's bid for a third term, a large number of MMD politicians voiced their opposition to Chiluba. With these individuals boycotting, Chiluba and his supporters proceeded to hold the convention, during which it was decided both to amend the party constitution, allowing Chiluba to stand again, and to expel from the party several members who were opposed to Chiluba. The latter followed the established pattern of curtailing political competition by excluding potential opponents from critical contests. Yet a High Court decision invalidated the actions of the party convention with respect to its dissident members. Several of these then initiated impeachment proceedings against Chiluba, backed by more than a third of all MPs. With much of parliament arrayed against him, Chiluba announced his intention to not seek a third term.

In 2001, despite its success in derailing the third term, the opposition remained highly fractured. Four of the five major parties as of 1996 that were led by national figures (UNIP, ZDC, the National Party, and the Agenda for Zambia Party) were still on the scene, but they were struggling in 2001.[18] New parties included former vice-president Godfrey Miyanda's Heritage Party, media-savvy pastor Nevers Mumba's National Citizen's Coalition (NCC), former Defense Minister Ben Mwila's Republican Party, former Anglo-American Mining Company executive Anderson Mazoka's United Party for National Development (UPND), Michael Sata's Patriotic Front, and the Front for Democracy and Development (FDD), which featured several recent MMD cabinet members who had left the party in a dispute over the third-term issue. These parties reflect what Burnell calls the "Zambian phenomenon whereby many politicians . . . conceive of themselves as president of a political party and envisage being the next republican president" (2001, 245). The proliferation of opposition parties led by ex-MMD politicians served the ruling party so well that it might as well have been orchestrated by the MMD itself. Moreover, following the logic of party-centered, neopatrimonial politics, the erstwhile defectors were often likely to return to the party, just as one-time defectors

Derrick Chitala, Enoch Kavindele, Emmanuel Kasonde, Baldwin Nkumbula, and Ludwig Sondashi had done at various points throughout the MMD's first two terms.

Cooperation and unity among these groups remained low in 2001. When NCC and ZDC leaders formed the Zambian Alliance Party, the UPND and UNIP—the other two major parties at the time of the merger—declined to participate, with considerations of who would lead the party constituting a major sticking point. Some non-MMD members of parliament were apparently dissuaded from joining the alliance, despite sympathy with its objectives, because of the possibility that they would lose their party status and that the speaker of parliament would declare their seats vacant. At an intra-opposition party meeting in July 2001, participants could only agree to campaign fairly, while rejecting the prospect of fielding single parliamentary or presidential candidates or of creating a unified governance structure.[19] Eleven different parties ultimately put forth presidential candidates.

The MMD's Levy Mwanawasa won the 2001 presidential election by a narrow margin, even though over 70 percent of voters opposed the ruling party on their ballots. Indeed, Mwanawasa's 29.2 percent of the vote is surely one of the smallest fractions ever to produce a victor in a popular presidential election anywhere. The UPND's Anderson Mazoka finished two percentage points behind, while the major ex-MMD candidates (the FDD's Tembo, the ZRP's Mwila, and the PF's Sata) received a combined 21.5 percent of the vote. The opposition's collective rejection of the results (perhaps the first unified stance it took during the entire 2001 election season) had some basis, in that the winning candidate received so little support. Yet apparently lost in their outrage was any recognition of the fact that no single other candidate proved any more capable of garnering nationwide support.

Although the ruling party failed to win a majority in parliament in 2001, it still won a plurality with 69 of the 150 seats. The MMD candidates received an outright majority of the votes in only nine constituencies. In one Ndola constituency, the MMD candidate emerged victorious despite having received only 22 percent of the vote.

In sum, over the course of its first two terms in power, the MMD has appeared to be more interested in consolidating its hold on power than in consolidating democracy. The ruling party frequently dealt with challenges to its hold on power by changing the rules of the game. The presidential qualifications clauses of the constitution allowed it to avoid—rather than confront on the ballot—its immediate competition. The arrest of Kaunda successfully undermined UNIP's viability as an opposition party; today, contending factions claim to lead and represent it. The possibility of attempted political assassination in Kabwe suggests even cruder, less democratic strategies of holding on to power. Meanwhile, divisions within the opposition rendered it nonthreatening throughout the first decade of the Third Republic. The first decade of the Third Republic witnessed low levels of participation, and the weak nature of political competition made the triumphs over authoritarianism and the one-party state seem both remote and endangered on the eve of the 2001 election.

Explanations for the Zambian Democratic Experience

The events and trends in the preceding section paint a picture of re-emergent and persistent undemocratic behavior. The current government was unable to win the electoral support of even one-sixth of the eligible voting population, and opposition parties have yet to acknowledge their own strategic shortcomings in the contest, showing that both sides have quite a distance to travel before elections can become a truly effective mechanism of transmitting popular preferences, or before accountable democratic governance is the norm *between* elections. How can we account for nondemocratic patterns in the wake of Zambia's democratic transition?

Per Bratton and van de Walle, to have made a successful "democratic transition" (as of 1994) is to have undergone major institutional change.[20] It is reasonable, therefore, that evaluations of whether these countries have maintained, deepened, or consolidated the gains made in democratic transitions, on the one hand—or reversed or undermined them, on the other—hinge first on questions of institutions. Specifically, one must ask if, in new democracies, institutions have successfully constrained elites from reverting to the undemocratic politics of old, or whether, to employ Dahl's framework, institutions bear some responsibility for the noncompetitive and/or nonparticipatory patterns observed in Zambia during the 1991–2001 period.

In the first part of this section, I examine aspects of the formal institutional setting in Zambia that help to account for the unevenness of Zambian democracy under Chiluba. Noting that the failure of new institutions to constrain various actors was a fundamental feature of post-transition politics in Zambia, I then consider extra-institutional explanations for the Zambian experience with democracy.

Institutional Factors

Despite the changes that took place in 1991, the Zambian legal and constitutional framework—in short, formal institutions—provided ample opportunities for undemocratic political behavior. Three aspects of the institutional framework have been critical in their capacity to undermine the potential for meaningful participation and competition within the new democracy. First, some institutional legacies from the previous era have provided resources to the MMD elite and accordingly allowed them to thwart the opposition. Second, the separation of powers and the independence of the nonexecutive branches of government have often been weak. Third, the laws and procedures governing the electoral process undermined both participation and contestation in Zambian politics.

1. *Institutionalized Resource Advantage for Incumbents.* The essence of the transition from single-party rule to democracy in the early 1990s was the end of an institutionalized political monopoly. However, the transition failed to do away with many of the resources available to an incumbent regime that could be used in the course of competition with its challengers.[21] Principal among these is control over the media. Aside from the European and South African cable channels that few can af-

ford, the only available television station is run by the government. The government controls the two oldest and largest newspapers (the *Times of Zambia* and the *Zambia Daily Mail*) and—until 1996—the only licensed radio station in the country. Just as Kaunda tried to use its media monopoly to its advantage in 1991, the MMD did so as well, once it had gained power. The ruling party pressured journalists in the state-controlled media to hew to the party line (Phiri 1999, 59). During the 1996 and 2001 election campaigns, newspaper and television coverage heavily favored the ruling party.[22]

Publicly owned segments of the Zambian economy constituted another political resource that the party in government could use to maintain a competitive imbalance in its favor. The government of Zambia controls a wide range of assets, from national banks to copper mines. As Rakner (1998) describes, the MMD delayed privatization reforms through the Chiluba administration. The result—most likely by intent—was the maintenance of state-owned resources that could serve political patronage and lead to an electoral advantage (van de Walle 2001, 82–83, 164).

2. *Executive Dominance.* A key institutional pattern that characterized postcolonial, pre-transition African politics was the strong executive—indeed it hardly makes sense to talk about authoritarianism without one. Bratton and van de Walle (1994, 66) note that in pre-transition Africa, "[p]ower [was not] not constrained by legal niceties or systems of checks and balances" and that "neo-patrimonial rulers were deeply suspicious of any form of institutional pluralism." Thus, on the eve of Africa's transition period, Diamond decried "the tendency for presidential authority to run rampant over legislatures and judiciaries" and noted that "[i]nstitutional means . . . for checking and balancing executive power [via] more power and autonomy for each of the other branches of government" would be fundamental to the prospects for democracy in Africa (1988, 28).

Throughout Africa, constitutional engineers advocated stronger checks and balances on executive power. Visions of more democratic post-transition politics thereby included stronger and more independent judiciaries and legislatures. As one observer commented, "multipartyism will make it possible for genuine parliamentary opposition to emerge; in time, it will no longer be possible to write off African parliaments as rubber stamps for the executive" (Gyimah-Boadi 1998, 25–26).

As in other African countries, the executive branch in Zambia historically dominated the other branches (Tordoff and Molteno 1974; Gertzel 1984). Democracy has indeed brought about some changes. In the Third Republic, the judiciary at times demonstrated laudable independence. Many life-term judges and justices were Kaunda appointees, leaving them less beholden to the new government than they might have been otherwise. Although it did not accede to the opposition's most radical request—that the MMD government be declared illegitimate—the judiciary has not consistently hewed to the MMD line. For example, the Supreme Court threw out an overly restrictive version of the Public Order Act in early 1996. In this sense, Zambia's experience has been similar to that of Malawi and Benin, as described in this volume.

Contrary to the hopes and expectations of constitutional engineers, however, and the willingness of donors to provide technical and material assistance, the presidency has remained dominant over the legislative branch. In van de Walle's words, "executive dominance [has] eaten away at Zambian democracy" (2002, 74). Philip Alderfer (1997) notes little change in either the quality or quantity of parliamentary activity after 1991: "for every step forward on the path of legislative development, there were two steps backward" (135).

For example, although on paper the legislature has acquired a more significant role in crafting and implementing the country's budget, in practice the power remains with the executive. The president presents the budget in a speech to parliament, offering no additional documentation regarding its content. Actual ministerial expenditures generally vary significantly from the budget as presented; as one observer noted, "current management practices give the executive almost unbridled discretion during budget implementation" (Wehner 2001, 1). Furthermore, the existence of a discretionary and essentially unmonitored "Presidential Fund" gives the executive additional capacity to finance political or personal endeavors without sanction (Burnell 2001, 251). Although less than one percent of the total budget is allocated to the fund, the president has no requirement to divulge its recipients, the total amount of resources disbursed through the fund, or even if disbursements stayed within the fund's budgeted limits (Mwanawina et al. 2002).

Not surprisingly, Chiluba appears to have been keenly aware of the advantages of executive dominance, and intent on maintaining an imbalance that favored the executive. Thomas Carothers reports that the speaker of the Zambian National Assembly rejected a USAID-sponsored capacity-building program on the grounds that the program would be "hostile to the interests of his country or at least to his party" (1999, 185).

For these reasons, and also because MMD had a commanding majority in the National Assembly throughout his administration, Chiluba seldom felt inter-branch pressure on his policy choices. Whether involving the budget (through his finance minister), constitutional amendments, or the divestiture of state assets such as the copper mines and publicly owned houses, Chiluba could count on parliament to assent to his plans without meaningful criticism—constructive or otherwise.

3. *The Electoral Process.* The laws governing the electoral process have also stifled Zambian democracy by undermining the prospects of expanded political participation (Bratton 1999a). The failure to maintain a continuously updated voter's roll—which would require a legislative act—necessitates the costly task of registering and re-registering voters every five years. That the registration exercise takes place at a time when the date of the elections themselves is unknown also lowers participation. Registration for the sake of keeping open the possibility of voting in a yet-to-be-announced election is something of an abstract proposition, for which many Zambians clearly did not feel compelled to take time away from their everyday activities. Without a preset election date, the ruling party has the ability to call elections at a time that could be either conducive or not conducive to mass participation (depending on whether it perceived any advantage one way or another).

Meanwhile, the first-past-the-post nature of electoral contests undermines the prospects for greater contestation in Zambian democracy, allowing the MMD to retain power with less than a majority of votes. Opposition parties, who would have gained greater representation in parliament under a proportional representation system, lose out. In 1996, non-MMD candidates won just 13 percent of the seats in the National Assembly despite having earned 42 percent of the total parliamentary vote. In 2001, Mwanawasa won the presidential race with a mere 29 percent of the presidential vote. A system requiring runoffs would have encouraged coalition-making in the second round, and could even have deprived the MMD of its plurality in parliament.

A 1993 interpretation of the law regarding party affiliation and by-elections further raised the cost (and decreased the supply) of opposition to the MMD. After eight MMD members resigned from the MMD during the 1993 state of emergency, the Supreme Court ruled that in doing so they relinquished their seats in parliament. They would have to stand in a by-election if they wished to win them back. As a number of those who had resigned lost to MMD candidates in the subsequent by-elections, this undoubtedly deterred others from leaving the party.

Beyond Formal Institutions

The preceding section implies that there may be certain institutional strategies—for example, constitutional reforms that lead to proportional representation or runoff voting, or legal reforms that lighten the requirements for voter registration—that might strengthen the prospects of democratic consolidation in Zambia. However, as Bratton and van de Walle generalize, institutional changes "did not necessarily break the mold of African politics or prevent the endurance of deeply ingrained habits of rule" (1994, 121). To suggest that the weaknesses of Zambian democracy from 1991 through 2001 are the consequence of insufficient institutional engineering is to understate the challenges facing democratization in Zambia and elsewhere in Africa. Non-institutional factors, such as patterns of behavior from earlier eras, the economic context of the Third Republic, and the role of international actors necessarily complement the institutional story.

1. *Norms and Patterns of Behavior.* Many of the political attitudes and behavior in the Third Republic have antecedents from the UNIP era, when—as a classic neopatrimonial polity—the dearth of remunerative avenues outside of the government made public office a relatively lucrative position. Politicians endeavored to confer upon themselves a monopoly on political office. They would go to great lengths to maintain this monopoly, raising the costs of entry for would-be political competitors. Thus, after 1973, UNIP banned opposition parties outright, and it made opposition to the sole legal party tantamount to treason and accordingly subject to severe reprisals.

By virtue of the circumstances that brought it to power, the MMD could do nothing so overt. Yet it has, at times, adhered to the same basic principles. The manipulation of the constitutional revision process in 1996 illustrates the MMD's desire to consolidate power before it consolidated democracy. The party, through the 1996

Constitutional Amendment Bill, essentially wrote its major rivals out of competitive politics. Another provision would have granted the president the power to remove judges at will, but it was dropped in an effort to appease donors.

Meanwhile, the party resorted to the thuggery of its local "youth wings"—often unemployed or underemployed young men—to intimidate opponents and to enforce viewpoint homogeneity, illustrating the extent to which the extra-institutional dimension of neopatrimonialism survived into the Third Republic as well.[23] The expectation of loyalty still prevailed over that of pluralism in the runup to the 2001 elections. A presidential directive prohibited campaigning for (or by) any putative presidential candidates, lest disunity undermine Chiluba's authority as the republican and party president. At least one ward-level MMD youth secretary warned that youths would "'sort out' those that did not comply."[24]

The UNIP's attempt at hegemonic rule leads to two historicist explanations for the lack of competitiveness of Zambian democracy under Chiluba. First, the party was seen as the means of channeling patronage, as well as a way of defining who deserved access to patronage resources. Under UNIP, the party was superior to the offices of government, as its oft-used phrase "the Party and its State" indicated. Given that many of the major players in the MMD—particularly those holding prominent party positions, including Michael Sata, Vernon Mwaanga, and Sikota Wina—were veterans of the UNIP regime, it is not surprising that some continued to define party–state relations according to the Second Republic paradigm. Thus, the MMD has at times been willing to employ state resources in the service of party objectives during political campaigns.

Second, over the course of time, the Kaunda regime made enemies of a broad range of actors. When it came together to challenge UNIP, the MMD was basically a collection of individuals (some of whom represented larger groups) with few shared interests beyond the removal of then-president Kaunda from power. Businessmen, agricultural interests, labor leaders, and church groups—each with divergent agendas regarding economic policy—cooperated for a year-and-a-half of lobbying and campaigning against the UNIP regime. Among the party leadership, labor leaders (e.g., Chiluba and Newstead Zimba) coexisted with businessmen (e.g., Ben Mwila and Dipak Patel) and career politicians (e.g., Michael Sata and Vernon Mwaanga). The consequence was that with little ideological glue to keep the party together, the new ruling party clearly felt it had to resort to restrictive measures to preserve its newfound political monopoly.

The ruling party's desire to protect the private gains of office has limited the avenues that theoretically independent government agencies and nongovernmental organizations (NGOs) might use to hold the administration accountable. Along with the Human Rights Commission and the Electoral Commission, a newly created Anti-Corruption Commission generally lacked funds and institutional support.[25] The legal code governing NGOs required them to remain nonpartisan. The MMD interpreted the requirement to mean that NGOs should refrain from criticizing the government.[26]

The first-past-the-post rules, along with the requirement that party-switchers face a by-election, dovetailed nicely with the MMD's zero-sum approach to partisan politics. These measures effectively limited the emergence of a strong opposition (outside of the runup to the next election), as would-be opposition politicians were unwilling to forsake their own ambition in order to attain the goal of unseating the ruling party. Until the succession issue became dominant in 2001, it was only in cases when either the party had passed over individual candidates to represent the MMD in parliamentary elections, or when politicians (generally mistakenly) believed they could create a viable alternative political force, that politicians were generally willing to leave the ruling party.

Meanwhile, with its own rise in mind, the MMD was well aware of the threat that mass mobilization presented to political monopolies. As Nelson Kasfir (1976) has noted, for the neopatrimonialist politician, the antidote to such threats is to limit the avenues for meaningful participation in politics. Leaders seek to protect their offices and the advantages they bring by discouraging (and often outlawing) potential means of challenging them. Thus, while the low level of participation in the 1995–96 voter registration exercise was a matter of some embarrassment to the government, the ruling party invested little in taking to the countryside to mobilize more registrants. Meanwhile, whether or not it was the result of an intentional strategy on the part of the MMD, the Black Mamba incident and constitutional revision escapade led the opposition to focus on Lusaka-based court cases throughout 1996 and to forsake the task of voter mobilization as the election approached. Finally, many viewed in a similar light Chiluba's call to hold the 2001 election on December 27—shortly after Christmas, when many urban residents were likely to be visiting family in rural areas (and thus unable to make it to their appointed polling stations), and during the rainy season, when many rural Zambians were likely to face difficult travel conditions (see Dole 2001).

The ruling party is not alone in adhering to pre-democratic norms of behavior. The opposition's initial refusal to accept the results of both the 1996 and 2001 elections reflects a tendency—typical of neopatrimonial politics—for procedures to remain subservient to outcomes. When the opposition failed to unseat an increasingly unpopular incumbent party despite a large *collective* numerical advantage, the opposition's immediate reaction was to vow disobedience, and even war.[27] Ironically, in doing so they gave the new president, Levy Mwanawasa, an immediate opportunity to appear as cool-headed, responsible, and— to most outsiders— a deserving choice: "Zambia will always be a government of laws, not of men," proclaimed Mwanawasa in his inauguration speech.

2. *The Economic Context.* The Zambian economy was, on average, stagnant in the first decade following the advent of multiparty politics. It grew an average of only 0.2 percent per annum between 1990 and 1999 (World Bank 2001). Factoring in population growth, per capita incomes have therefore been declining. Within the first year of the MMD era, Zambia suffered from Southern Africa's worst drought in over a hundred years. Although the MMD government responded to the drought effectively,[28] the small-holder agricultural sector struggled thereafter. As crops failed, the state withdrew from agricultural financing and marketing. Fledgling private

agricultural credit enterprises collapsed, while private marketers found it profitable to ignore smaller-scale farms. Farmers had little access to inputs such as fertilizer, and they struggled to grow on land stressed by decades of monocropping and growing population (Rakner, van de Walle, and Mulaisho 2001, 560–61; Pletcher 2000).

Economic crisis influenced mass and elite political behavior in several ways. When Zambians sought change in 1991, most assumed that economic improvement would accompany new political faces. Yet continued poverty in the constituencies potentially has undermined voters' faith in electoral change and the efficacy of political action. The result was to deter political participation, in turn making electoral strategies like vote-buying feasible.[29]

Near-permanent economic crisis has also meant that few career alternatives have emerged to rival holding political office as a means by which to accumulate wealth. In many of the ways described by van de Walle (2001), the Zambian state has responded to the economic crisis with variations on the familiar neo-patrimonial theme. For example, MMD politicians have individually benefited from the privatization of formerly state-owned enterprises.[30] Meanwhile, tight financial constraints make it easier to defend the underfunding of agencies of restraint such as the Electoral Commission, the Revenue Authority, or the judiciary.

Economic issues are certainly only part of the story. After all, in 1990, economic crisis undermined the capacity of the one-party UNIP regime to run a neopatrimonial regime (Bratton and van de Walle 1997). Discontent with the economy heavily influenced politics in 1990–91, when democracy made its biggest gains. Yet grievances over the economy did not yield electoral punishment for the ruling party in 1996 (Posner and Simon 2002). Moreover, economic difficulties are somewhat correlated with retreat from electoral participation, but hardly to the exclusion of other factors (Simon 2002). At a minimum, however, it is fair to say that persistent poverty and deteriorating prospects for many in the middle class are less than ideally conducive for the regularization of democratic behavior.

3. *External Influences.* A third set of factors influencing political behavior—especially that of elites—during the MMD era concerns the actions of the international community. Multilateral and bilateral donors both played an important role in the transition period. The World Bank had insisted upon the reduction in the subsidization of mealie meal that triggered the street protests of June 1990—which, in turn, catalyzed the mass pro-democracy movement. In the months prior to the 1991 election, the World Bank refused to release a tranche of an adjustment loan to Zambia—citing a failure to comply with conditions, including the failure to lower food subsidies sufficiently. The UNIP was thus deprived of resources it might have used to woo voters. Meanwhile, American aid financed election monitors and civil society groups in 1991. Pressure from the Carter Center and others helped convince Kaunda to stick to his pledge to abide by the election results.

There is no doubt that international actors retained an influential role on the Zambian political scene after 1991. Upon assuming office, the MMD almost immediately recommitted Zambia to structural adjustment. It took advantage of a honeymoon period to reduce subsidies and liberalize the kwacha, thereby ending shortages that had plagued the country and creating better terms for exporters. The MMD also responded to pressure from donors on matters that were less strictly economic. On the eve of the Consultative Group meetings—at which donors and the government were to agree on future programs, principles of policy and governance, and aid levels—the donors pressed for the resignation of cabinet officials believed to be corrupt (in 1993) and the liquidation of Zambia Airlines (in 1994). In these cases and in others, the government reluctantly complied (Rakner, van de Walle, and Mulaisho 2001). Meanwhile, Zambia became one of sub-Saharan Africa's leading recipients of aid. Over the course of the 1990s, among African countries with populations above two million, only Mauritania averaged more aid received per capita than Zambia (World Bank 2001, table 12–15).

Via this role, donors became major players in the politics of democratization in Zambia. Yet, on balance, their actions actually undermined consolidation processes. This is true despite the fact many of their efforts were expressly geared to help to democratization. Bilateral donors annually gave Zambia about $9 million for the purpose of promoting democracy and governance between 1992 and 2000.[31] Spending activities in this vein included improving the technical capacities of the judiciary and the legislature, and funding NGOs that promoted democratic behavior and institutions. Given their intentions, it is certainly a bit counterintuitive to suggest that their efforts had deleterious effects on Zambia's nascent democracy.

The ill effects of donor involvement can be seen in a number of different respects. For example, consider the effect of donor criticism regarding the constitutional reform process and the 1996 elections. Several prominent politicians called for donors to impose sanctions on the country (Burnell 2001, 254). Indeed, Zambia's aid receipts during 1996–98 fell by almost 50 percent compared to 1991–95, from $1.175 billion per year to $546 million per year.[32] The MMD turned calls for donor withdrawal into the claim that the opposition was fundamentally treasonous.[33] As such, the opposition played into the hand of the incumbent regime's efforts to define its opponents as non-Zambian—a strategy also pursued through the presidential eligibility clause in the constitutional revision, and the labeling of individual politicians, including Kaunda, as non-citizens.

Civic education NGOs reflect the curious dynamic of donor–elite relations in Zambia. Nongovernmental organizations such as the Foundation for Democratic Progress (FODEP), the NGO Coordinating Council (NGOCC), and the Committee for a Clean Campaign (CCC) were established to promote democracy. They took on tasks that were the substance of democratic consolidation, such as educating citizens about their democratic rights, tutoring politicians about their responsibilities and opportunities to serve their constituencies, and supporting greater participation in politics by women.

In doing so, these NGOs became the targets of the ruling party, who accused them of links to outside forces. In the runup to the 1996 election, provincial MMD leaders called for the banning of the three major election-oriented NGOs: FODEP, ZIMT, and the CCC. Groups that were outspokenly critical of the MMD were labeled pawns of foreign governments. In the wake of the 1996 election, Chiluba decried local nongovernmental organizations as "conveyor belts of outside NGOs" that resembled "mercenary operations." Later, the MMD tried to clamp down on the NGO sector by forcing additional registration and conduct requirements.[34]

Yet while such attacks reveal the MMD's intolerance of opposition and indicate the general strategy of linking opposition to outsiders, they also speak to the thin nature of many such NGOs. Indeed, many *were* financed by non-Zambian sources, as the domestic resources were too scarce to provide for their independent function. Nongovernmental organizations—particularly those involved with civic governance and education—became something of a cottage industry in Lusaka. Few made much effort to establish a presence in other parts of the country, while the energy of politically knowledgeable and committed Zambians often seemed to be devoted toward winning more grants and funds, rather than toward spreading political ideas and establishing democratic norms throughout the country. Even the most dedicated—of whom there are many—must devote a significant amount of time and energy to the solicitation of funds. To the extent that a proliferation of NGOs creates more competition for an ultimately limited pool of funds, the bad thus has a tendency to drive out the good. By funneling money through grants to NGOs, donors carelessly fostered a more rootless civil society than might have developed organically (Ottaway and Chung 1999, 106–108).

The 2001 election further illustrates the impact of international actors. Observers from the European Union concluded that the "consistently unleveled playing field" had "undermine[d] the concept of a free and fair election," thereby emboldening losing candidates to reject the results of the election outright.[35] The international press also reported projections from pre-election polling and exit polls that the UPND's Mazoka would win. Yet the margins of error on the polls—which certainly would have to be far greater than the projected margin of victory—remained unreported. These polls fed both domestic and international expectations of a leadership turnover, further hardening opposition-party resolve to reject the actual results.

▼▼▼▼

The 2001 election serves as a reminder that that the change in formal institutions of a decade earlier has indeed altered the bounds on politics. The very fact of electoral competition put into the hands of Zambian citizens a power, however bounded, that they did not have prior to 1991. The fact that an election was held and that multiple political parties were able to compete represent how politics had changed from the earlier period. Consequently, while the new regime may have reminded some of its pre-democratic predecessor, the institutional form of multiparty elections nonetheless forced that regime to undertake a new breed of political survival strategies. Some of those entailed manipulating government rules or institutions (including the elections themselves), but others involved appeals to the electorate that would have been unlikely in an earlier era. The sale of council houses—domiciles previously owned by local governments—in 1996 is a clear example of this trend. Opposition complaints that the sales represented an election-year gimmick missed the point. In selling the houses, the MMD was in fact divesting itself of a resource that local politicians could otherwise have used as a source of political favors (albeit for a potential political windfall in the short term). In doing so, the government gave Zambian citizens—voters—the opportunity to increase their personal equity in a way that had been rarely available before.

There were also encouraging signs in the months following the 2001 election that, with the succession of Chiluba by Mwanawasa, laws and institutions would attain greater meaning relative to neopatrimonial-style political imperatives. Mwanawasa gave greater presidential support to the Anti-Corruption Commission than his predecessor ever did. With Mwanawasa's blessing, the National Assembly revoked what was to have been the perpetual presidential immunity of ex-president Chiluba. Meanwhile, in the wake of the 2001 election, judicial avenues of protest quickly supplanted extralegal options—another encouraging development. After initially engaging in inflammatory rhetoric, several losing candidates chose to protest by filing court petitions (as opposed to, say, taking up arms). Doubly encouraging was that the new president indicated that he would abide by the Supreme Court's rulings on these matters.

Still, for all the changes in political substance that institutional changes have wrought, it is clear that institutions are only part of the democratization story. While the democratic institutions of the Third Republic constrain politicians in ways that the one-party system of the Second Republic did not, institutions do not define the constraints on (or the possibilities of) elite political behavior by themselves. Rather, historically informed informal institutions (including the norms that some might call "political culture"), the economic context, and interaction with international actors each provide alternative influences on political behavior that can be entirely independent of institutions.

If the promise of democracy in Zambia remains unrealized, what can improve upon its chances? One lesson is that Zambian economic conditions continue to pose barriers to democratic consolidation. Some policy interventions—such as reducing the requirements for voting (like preregistering) or providing logistical support for independent agencies—may help in specific ways, but what remains is the broader overlay of incentives that structure political behavior. Economic development will not automatically produce greater democracy, but it will create conditions more conducive both to functional formal democratic institutions and to more democratic patterns of political behavior.

Another lesson is that international actions in support of democracy should not discount the value of development assistance more generally. Inasmuch as many answers remain elusive with respect to that realm as well, it is meaningful to add that donors should be more aware of the unintended political consequences of their interventions. Often, their interventions in Zambia have served to distract political elites from the important task of defining the parameters of meaningful political contestation.

Critics are right to point out that the consolidation of democracy in a country having undergone a democratic transition is not inevitable, and perhaps not even likely. However, it remains true that if democratic consolidation is to occur—in terms of more meaningful participation and contestation—it will take time. First, democratic institutions stand a greater chance to succeed when a cohort that began political engagement in the new era replaces the political elite that was raised in an era of nondemocratic institutions. Furthermore, democratic institutions will only succeed when the benefits of having one's rivals subordinate their respective ambitions exceed the cost of subordinating one's own ambitions. For this to happen, there must be a measure of political experimentation on the part of elites so that possibility can emerge—which might accurately describe Mwanawasa's actions in at least the half-year following his election.

While the fate of democratic transitions is contingent upon historical factors, it is not strictly path-dependent. Undeniably, there is a role for human agency in stories of African transitions, particularly given the relatively small size of the circle of political elites in many countries. In Zambia, the decisions of a Kaunda or a Chiluba reflect more than merely the incentives and constraints each has faced. They are also a function of their respective tastes and values. It is instructive that in neighboring Zimbabwe, quite similar pressures only hardened Robert Mugabe's resolve to remain in power, and that in Madagascar an equally tight election produced a tinderbox situation with two unrelenting claimants to power. These glimpses of paths not taken in Zambia highlight the elusiveness of democratization and of a model that might account for it. Moreover, they serve as reminder that, for all of its shortcomings, the Zambian experience remains a model for Africa, albeit in realistic rather than idealistic terms.

NOTES

1. Freedom House ratings run from 1 (most democratic) to 7 (least democratic) on two vectors: one vector for political rights and one vector for civil liberties. The aggregate rating is the average of the two components. Zambia's component scores were as follows: in 1990–91, 5 in civil liberties, 6 in political rights; in 1991–92, 3 in civil liberties, 2 in political rights; in 1996–97, 4 in civil liberties, 5 in political rights. An alternative system, the Polity IV index, which ranges from -10 (least democratic) to 10 (most democratic), records a similar trajectory: from -9 for 1990, to 6 for 1991, to 1 for 1996.

2. Local elections have not been held regularly. The first set of local elections of the Third Republic was held in April 1992. Although the term of office of the local councils was to have expired by 1996, subsequent elections did not take place until December 1998. A third set was held at the same time as the presidential and parliamentary elections in December 2001.

3. For the importance of mobilizing agents, see Rosenstone and Hansen (1993).

4. See "2.5m Register for Polls," *Zambia Daily Mail,* August 1, 2001; and "Voters' Registration Ends Amid Apathy," *Times of Zambia,* August 1, 2001. The government

presented a more optimistic face, claiming that close to two-thirds of the estimated eligible population had registered—but only after revising the estimate of those eligible downward by approximately one million.

5. A resurgence of UNIP is not impossible, given that no other party except the MMD has the name recognition of the former ruling party, and that not even the MMD can match UNIP's ground-level organization. However, at the top, the party was in complete disarray in 2002, with no sign of a visionary leader to rescue the party.

6. The 1991 election had taken place under what was understood to be a provisional constitution that had been hammered out over a very short period of time at a "summit" between MMD and UNIP leaders in July 1991.

7. See "Sakala Warns Morse," *Post of Zambia*, January 24, 1996. For other examples of partisan violence, including some initiated by UNIP cadres, see "MMD Cadres Invade Patel's Business," *Post of Zambia*, August 23, 2001; "MMD Youths, Bus Drivers Showdown Looming," *Zambia Daily Mail*, April 5, 1999; "UNIP Youths Hurt in Punch Up," *Times of Zambia*, July 30, 1998; "UNIP Cadres Assault Man over MMD T-shirt," *Post of Zambia*, August 13, 1996.

8. See "Treason Trial Transcript, Parts 1–5," *Post of Zambia*, November 4–8, 1996.

9. See "Police Chief Axed," *Times of Zambia*, August 28, 1997; and "Top Cops Linked to KK's Shooting," *Post of Zambia*, September 29, 1997. Human Rights Watch reports that the government inquiry into the shooting was shelved on account of insufficient funds (1998).

10. The incident eerily echoed one of the primary precipitants of the movement for democratization in 1990: a "radio coup" that followed a week of urban rioting over food prices. The difference between 1990 and 1998 was that in the first instance, Lusakans reportedly danced in the streets in celebration—emboldening the elites who supported multipartyism to believe that they would have widespread support for their cause—while in 1998 the city reacted with anxiety and fear.

11. For details on the allegation of torture, see "Mung'omba Tortured," *Post of Zambia*, November 5, 1997; and Human Rights Watch (1998, 84). Human Rights Watch also cites sources from Zambia's military hospital that another detainee, Corp. Robert Chiulo, died from "injuries resulting from torture" (1998, 84).

12. See "MMD Cadres Destroy FDD Officials' Houses in Kanyama," *Post of Zambia*, July 6, 2001.

13. See "Key Zambia Politician 'Shot Dead,'" *BBC News Online*, July 6, 2001. Available at: http://news.bbc.co.uk/1/world/africa/1425508.stm. Accessed September 15, 2004. Tembo's was the latest in a long history of politically suspicious deaths. In 1998, former finance minister Ronald Penza was murdered in his home. In 1994, Baldwin Nkumbula was killed in the company of President Chiluba's son. See Human Rights Watch (1997, 30–31), which also lists four other "deaths in disputed circumstances."

14. Human Rights Watch details more than two dozen instances of press harassment in late 1996 and early 1997 (1997, 12–23); see also Phiri (1999, 61).

15. See "Zambian Journalists Rapid Response Action Network: Action 7," February 4, 1997; cited in Human Rights Watch (1997, 19).

16. Specifically, the offense was to have called Chiluba a "thief" in the course of a story questioning the alleged diversion of $4 million worth of food aid. See "Three Charged with Defaming Chiluba," *BBC News Online*, August 22, 2001. Available at: http://news.bbc.co.uk/1/hi/world/africa/1500926.stm. Accessed September 15, 2004.

17. Foundation for the Democratic Process, 2002.

18. The fifth, the agriculturally based Lima Party, was not a political force in 2001.

19. Newspaper articles from mid-1999 offer more information on the ZAP merger and the difficulties surrounding it. See, for example, "Parties Submit Merger Papers," *Times of Zambia,* May 4, 1999; "ZAP Riles UPND," *Zambia Daily Mail,* June 21, 1999; "Parties Rule Out Merger," *Times of Zambia,* July 25, 2001; "ZAP Leaders Told Off," *Times of Zambia,* August 5, 1999; and "ZAP Leadership Row Rages," *Zambia Daily Mail,* August 30, 1999. Similar issues plagued cooperation efforts even as the 2001 election approached: see "Opposition Parties Differ over National Unity Government Calls," *Zambia Daily Mail,* September 17, 2001.

20. In their words, to overhaul completely the "formal architecture of political regimes" (1994, 121).

21. It is worth noting here that the discussion that follows varies from Bratton and van de Walle's discussion of "state resources" as an informal institution used by neopatrimonial leaders to maintain their office (1997, 66). I am referring specifically to those resources that, by virtue of the country's laws, remain at the disposal of the regime in power and can be used for political (rather than administrative) ends without effective counter-check.

22. See Banda 1997 (cited in Phiri [1999, 59]) and Burnell (2001, 252) for discussions of media bias in 1996. My own review of the headlining stories on the online editions of the two papers over the course of the last full week before the 2001 election (December 17–21) shows an imbalance in favor of the ruling party. During this period, the *Times* featured five headlined stories lauding the incumbent administration and its political candidates, no headlined stories that could be read as critical of the MMD, none lauding opposition politicians, and eight stories that were critical of the opposition. The *Daily Mail* was slightly more balanced, but still favored the incumbents as it featured two headlined stories favoring the MMD, one each criticizing the incumbents and lauding the opposition, and six criticizing the opposition.

23. For examples of UNIP-era "street" politics, see Bates (1976, 248–49); and Molteno and Scott (1974, 181–82).

24. See "2001 Race: No Secret Campaign Meetings, Warn MMD Youths," *Zambia Daily Mail,* January 11, 2000.

25. For examples, see Human Rights Watch (1998) on the government's relationship with the Human Rights and the Anti-Corruption Commissions. See "Opposition Seeks Change of Electoral Commission," *Post of Zambia,* January 22, 1999; "FODEP Challenges Integrity of Electoral Commission," *Post of Zambia,* March 5, 1997; and "Polls Body Seeks Cash," *Times of Zambia,* March 30, 1999 (on the Electoral Commission). The October 9, 2001, edition of the *Post of Zambia* reports two instances of government obstacles to opposition-party activities: "Mpongwe Police Block ZAP Meeting" and "ZIS Denies B.Y. PA System."

26. For an example, see "MMD Youths Challenge LAZ," *Times of Zambia,* March 30, 1999.

27. See the following three articles in the January 2, 2002, edition of the *Post of Zambia:* "We'll Use All Means at Our Disposal—Mazoka"; "War Has Just Started, Declares Sata"; and "FDD Will Not Accept a Government Arising from Dec. 27 Polls." For similar statements following the 1996 general election, see "It'll Be Ungovernable: I Mean It, Warns KK," *Post of Zambia,* November 18, 1996.

28. It was oft repeated that not a single Zambian died of famine.

29. For example, see "MMD's Campaign Methods Criticized," *Post of Zambia*, November 26, 1999. See also FODEP by-election reports.

30. See "18 Political Leaders Buy Firms—ZPA," *Zambia Daily Mail*, May 2, 1998.

31. Source: OECD-CRS database. The largest source—by far—of democracy and governance funds for Zambia was the World Bank, which gave Zambia over $200 million in both 1991 and 2000.

32. Both figures in 1995 dollars. Source: World Bank 2001, table 12–5. The link between the aid cut and criticism over the run-up to the 1996 election is direct: in July, USAID announced an initial 10 percent cut in bilateral aid—including the cessation of a number of democracy-promotion projects, citing concerns about the government's "commitment to the open, multi-party democratic political system" ("US Government Cuts Aid to Zambia," *Post of Zambia*, July 17, 1996).

33. E.g., "Stop It, Mwanajiti Warned," *Times of Zambia*, October 11, 2001; "Stop Playing Double Standards, Chiluba Tells Donors," *Times of Zambia*, April 6, 2000; and "Chiluba Tells Off Political Donors," *Times of Zambia*, September 27, 2001. Katele Kalumba made a related accusation in 1998, singling out for blame NGOs who had advocated more stringent political conditionality for the high level of poverty in Zambia ("Kalumba Blames NGOs for Donors Aid Squeeze," *Post of Zambia*, December 23, 1998); for an example of the NGO–political conditionality issue, see "Mwanajiti Criticizes Donors of Funding Rights Abusers," *Post of Zambia*, May 13, 1998.

34. See "MMD Accuses NGOs," *Zambia Daily Mail*, October 6, 1996; "Monitors' Chicanery Unmasked," *Zambia Today*, November 24, 1996; "FTJ Warns of Mercenaries," *Post of Zambia*, December 20, 1996; "NGOs Must Be Controlled—Minister," *Zambia Daily Mail*, January 30, 1997; "Let's Work Together, NGOs Told," *Times of Zambia*, March 13, 1997.

35. See "EU Acknowledges Polls Irregularities," *Post of Zambia*, January 2, 2002. A series of Carter Center reports (summarized in Carter Center [2002]) drew similar conclusions.

10 | Assessing Adaptation to Democratic Politics in Mozambique

The Case of Frelimo

Carrie Manning

This chapter examines Mozambique's postwar democratization process from 1992 to 2003, with a focus on the dynamics within the country's dominant party, Frelimo, and the party system more generally. Analyses of recent democratic breakthroughs in longtime, single-party-dominant regimes elsewhere suggest that changes *within* dominant parties can help to generate important transformations that enrich processes of inter-party competition. These changes may be occurring for a substantial period before they affect inter-party competition. With this in mind, the chapter views Frelimo first from the perspective of a dependent variable, investigating how institutional changes associated with the liberalization and democratization of politics have affected internal party dynamics. I then consider these changes within the larger context of multiparty competition, examining the nature of inter-party relations between Frelimo and its only real rival, the former rebel group Renamo.

The evidence suggests that the installation and operation of democratic processes and institutions have had an impact on the ruling party that could well be considered positive for democracy. Among the more significant changes have been the emergence of greater internal pluralism and the development of a stake in democratic institutions for some groups within the party. However, attention to the nature of inter-party relations suggests that the changes observed within Frelimo are far from sufficient to ensure the stability and survival of democracy. Changes within Frelimo—and the generally accommodative behavior of Frelimo through 1999—have themselves been contingent upon the ruling party staying in power. Party responses to the prospect of electoral turnover reveal the tenuous and limited commitment to the democratization process in Mozambique.

"Qualified" Democracy:
Assessing Democratic Disappointments

The third wave of democratization has been characterized in Africa more than elsewhere by the establishment of "qualified democracies"—pseudo-democracies, illiberal and quasi-democracies, even virtual democracies (Zakaria 1997; Joseph 1997; Schmitter 1995; Karl 1985). As Richard Joseph has noted with respect to Africa's "virtual democracies," "what distinguishes this type of regime is the illusory nature of its democratic institutions and practices, and the fact that they are deliberately contrived to satisfy prevailing international norms of 'presentability'" (Joseph 1998). Joseph counsels scholars of Africa to "actively analyze and criticize configurations of power that involve the adoption and distortion of democratic institutions [by rulers], rather than simply recommend policy adjustments based on their acceptance" (Joseph 1998, 9).

There is no contesting the fact that many rulers in Africa have mastered the art of democratic forgery, instituting just enough change to keep themselves in the good graces of donors while keeping the political playing field tilted firmly in their own favor. In most African countries, the third wave of democratization ushered in a new source of legitimation (elections) for old parties. Former ruling parties enjoy legislative majorities in most sub-Saharan African countries that have made a peaceful transition to multiparty politics. In twenty-five out of forty-six countries that held multiparty elections between 1990 and 1998, the majority party in the legislature won more than two-thirds of the vote. In twenty-one of those countries, the figure is 75 percent (Nohlen, Krennerich, and Thibaut 1999).

These tendencies remind us that, in much of the developing world, "democracy" makes an unsatisfying dependent variable. Indeed, if consolidated democracy is the outcome to be studied, students of African politics may well have a long and frustrating wait. However, the study of democratization processes is a different story, particularly if we are permitted to use the term "democratization" without presuming that the final result will in fact be consolidated liberal democracy. I argue here that democratization can be fruitfully studied as a series of processes that occur within different arenas of a political system: civil society, the party system, the local level, and so on. The processes sometimes collide and sometimes converge; collectively, they define a country's political trajectory. In assessing a country's democratic transition, it is important to be attentive to the different pace, character, and implications of changes in each of these arenas, as well as to the ways in which these discreet processes of change affect one another. From this perspective, analyses of recent electoral victories of opposition parties in longtime, one-party-dominant regimes, such as Mexico, Taiwan, Senegal, South Korea, and Ghana, provide at least a limited basis for challenging unmitigated pessimism when it comes to the establishment of workable democratic regimes. Two important lessons surface from a close reading of events in these countries.

First, in these cases "the lengthy process of unraveling of single-party dominance" was a product, rather than a precondition, of a long, nonlinear process of establishing workable formal democratic institutions in those countries (Solinger 2001). The factors that finally allowed opposition parties successfully to challenge long-time incumbents were the accumulated product of years of practicing competitive politics in an imperfect environment. The interaction of political parties with the democratic institutional framework and with one another, through both formal and informal channels, produced adjustments in parties' expectations, in the institutional framework itself, in the social bases of various parties, in state–society relations, and in the nature of civil society. As Solinger and others have pointed out, not all of these changes were in a positive direction, either in the short term or from the point of view of democratic consolidation. But together they changed the calculus of politics in a way that ultimately cleared a path for more meaningful political competition (Solinger 2001; Rigger 1999; Dickson 1996; Galvan 2001; Schedler 2000; Horcasitas 1996; Camp 1999; Kim 1999).

Changes within the ruling party as a result of this process were especially important in this regard. Solinger argues that the rise of successful opposition politics was "given a critical boost by the perhaps necessary result of those [limited] elections, a split in the ruling party" (Solinger 2001, 30). Indeed, there are sound reasons to expect that elections are likely to put pressure on a party's preexisting internal fault lines. Democratization has also tended to provide the means through which internal differentiation within ruling parties could find practical expression. These include, most importantly, limited territorial decentralization and the establishment of multiparty national legislatures. The proliferation of political arenas, which enjoyed some degree of autonomy (if only by virtue of their different responsibilities, resources, and recruitment methods), helped to harden internal cleavages within ruling parties, and facilitated mobilization of or alliances with different social groups.

This dynamic points to a second, broader lesson from these cases: in some respects, late democratizers stand conventional wisdom about democratization on its head. Rather than representing the culmination of a set of political, socioeconomic, or cultural preconditions that make a country "ripe" for successful democratization, the establishment of formal democracy can increasingly be a means to some other end. The establishment of formal democratic institutions, then, can be the beginning of a democratization process. Such a process might easily stumble or collapse at any number of points along the way. But over time and within the context of periodic setbacks, it might also generate the development of more vibrant and substantively operational democracies. Mexico, Senegal, Ghana, Taiwan, and other cases suggest that this inverted process is indeed an available, if rare, alternate path by which countries may reach reasonable levels of democratic functioning. At any given moment during the decades in which these regimes practiced a problematic form of pluralism, it could justifiably have been said that these were not genuine democracies, with the implication that they never would be. Although democratic consolidation is far from a foregone conclusion in these countries, the fact that each has had at least one peaceful turnover of power in the context of free and fair elections makes them stand out among third wave democracies in the developing world.

While the second lesson reminds us that there is some cause for guarded optimism with respect to Mozambique's democracy, it is the insights from the first lesson that I incorporate more directly into this analysis. The chapter explores developments within Mozambique's ruling Frelimo party, and within the party system more generally, with an eye to evaluating how these developments are shaping the country's democratic trajectory. In the first place, I examine the ways in which participation in democratic politics has affected the internal dynamics, and particularly the balance of power among rival subgroups, within the dominant party. Second, and related to this, I assess the behavior of the dominant political actors (parties) as they seek either to adapt themselves to the new political system or to manipulate the system to suit their own needs.

To accommodate these two lines of inquiry, the chapter's empirical discussion is divided into two sections. The first treats Mozambique's ruling party, Frelimo, as the dependent variable, examining the impact of various aspects of democratization on party dynamics. Here, I argue that democratization has encouraged internal differentiation within the party and furthered the process of separating party and state. In parliament, party leaders have found a platform from which to flex their muscles vis-à-vis their colleagues and government while at the same time building a stronger postwar identity for the party. Elections, at central and municipal levels, have both brought a broadening of the party tent and produced the first serious, albeit limited, political challenge to the party from its own dissident ranks.

The second section treats Frelimo as an independent variable, a political actor trying to define the boundaries, rules, and outcomes of democratic processes. Examining the party's role in the political system as a whole, the picture of Mozambique democracy is less encouraging. Both Frelimo and Renamo have shown a reluctance to surrender to the combination of predetermined procedures and uncertain outcomes that are the hallmarks of democracy (Przeworski 1986, 58). Mozambique's de facto two-party system operates on the basis of contrasting notions of democracy and system legitimacy held by the two dominant parties. Both parties have become habituated to a pattern in which the processes and outcomes of formal politics are routinely subject to informal elite bargaining, in which one or both parties seeks to modify the process, the outcome, or both. Whether this can provide the basis for sustained, genuine, inter-party competition is an open question.

The Case of Mozambique

Mozambique's formal democratization process weaves together a threefold transformation: from war to peace, from centrally controlled to market economy, and from single-party state to multiparty electoral democracy. As in cases elsewhere in Africa, the simultaneity of these three processes affects the particular strategies that elites will follow in order to survive, benefit from, evade, or alter democratic processes that have been partially imposed from the outside.

Democratization in Mozambique signified political accommodation, as the ruling Frelimo party (Mozambican Liberation Front) opened the political arena to political competitors, and most importantly, to its longtime military enemy, the Renamo rebel group (Mozambican National Resistance), and also an increase in the intensity and scope of political conflict and debate, even as competition was redirected from military to relatively peaceful political channels. For both Frelimo and Renamo, these processes implied major adjustments.

In the short term, Mozambique has enjoyed startling success in the postwar period. Long ranking as one of the poorest countries in the world, Mozambique emerged from a protracted armed liberation struggle from Portuguese rule in 1975 only to be plunged, almost immediately, into conflict with an externally sponsored guerrilla organization that, over time, built on a variety of grievances within Mozambique to turn the conflict into a full-blown civil war lasting for nearly two decades. In 1992, the government signed an internationally mediated peace accord with Renamo. The implementation of the peace agreement, which centered around the establishment of a competitive democratic system, was overseen by a United Nations observer mission, ONUMOZ, and the coordinated efforts of the country's major international donors. The first general elections, held in 1994, went peacefully and led to the seating of a multiparty parliament and a legitimately elected government.

Mozambique's history of civil war has had lasting implications for its political system. Because the political arena is polarized after many years of civil conflict during which each side demonized the other, defections from one party to another are rare. The existence of one party helps keep the other party together; wartime alienation maintains a stable two-party system. Would-be defectors from Frelimo or Renamo are loath to associate themselves directly with the other side, as each represents a former military as well as political enemy. At the same time, they are reluctant to break off and form their own parties because they calculate that doing so might well put the opposing party over the top.

The party system is also influenced by the residual effects of the ruling party's longtime control of the economy. While the 1990s have seen substantial movement toward the privatization of banking and industry and the growth of a broader and more robust private economic sector, access to the state remains an important source of socioeconomic advancement.

Mozambique is a semi-presidential system in which a directly elected president appoints a prime minister and full cabinet. The prime minister serves essentially as "head minister" in this system, and is responsible to the president rather than to parliament. Parliament is elected according to a system of proportional representation, under closed party lists. The country is divided into eleven electoral circles, corresponding to the ten provinces plus the capital city of Maputo. A party must win at least 5 percent of total ballots cast for parliament nationwide in order to be awarded representation in the legislature.

While more than a dozen parties have competed in both general elections (1994 and 1999), in practice Mozambique is a two-party system, dominated by Frelimo and Renamo. In the 1999 elections, however, Renamo formed an electoral coalition with ten other parties, known as the Electoral Union (known by its Portuguese acronym, UE). Of Renamo-UE's 117 parliamentary seats, 18 belong to UE coalition party members and the rest to Renamo. Parliamentary elections are held simultaneously with presidential elections, which in practice ensures that the top leader of the party in opposition will not be a member of parliament.

While most leading opposition figures were at one time or another associated with Frelimo in some capacity, their parties are not in any sense Trojan horses for the ruling party. Most are fierce critics of the government and longtime opponents of Frelimo policy and/or ideology. While there is a normal amount of alliance-shifting within these "third parties" prior to elections, the rivalry between Renamo and Frelimo has brooked no defections from one party to another. A few figures have quietly left active party life within Frelimo, and Renamo's top peace negotiator in Rome and former chief of staff of its guerrilla army, Raul Domingos, was expelled from the party in 2000, allegedly for using his position as head of the parliamentary bench to try to extract emoluments from Frelimo. But Domingos did not defect to Frelimo, nor have there been any aisle crossings between the two parties at all. As noted above, this is a function of Mozambique's recent history.

Frelimo faced surprisingly stiff challenges from Renamo in the first two general elections, and the 1998 municipal elections saw the emergence of a flurry of independent citizens' groups which ran as "non-parties," interested in the nuts and bolts of governance rather than in politics per se. Many leading members of these non-parties had been high level officials with the Frelimo party. Their ranks included former ministers and deputy ministers, provincial governors, and business people who had been close to the ruling party.

The results of the 1999 general elections, and the near-total boycott of the 1998 municipal elections by major opposition parties, were widely seen as rebukes of the Frelimo party. In 1994, Renamo's unexpectedly strong results (Frelimo had a seventeen-seat margin in parliament and a 19 percent spread in the presidential race) were seen as reflecting a "vote for peace," meaning that people voted for Renamo out of fear that if it lost, Renamo would go back to war. The debacle of the 1998 municipal elections, in which turnout averaged around 15 percent and fell to 6 percent in some areas, was laid largely at the feet of poor electoral administration and apathy toward Frelimo, rather than attributing it to support for the near-total opposition boycott of the poll.[1]

The 1999 elections proved even more disturbing for the longtime ruling party, however. After presiding over a very respectable postwar economic recovery, in which average annual GDP (Gross Domestic Product) growth hovered between 8 and 10 percent for much of the period and foreign investment reached historic highs, Frelimo's presidential candidate, Joaquim Chissano, defeated Renamo's Afonso Dhlakama by just over 200,000 votes, roughly 4 percent of the national vote. Dhlakama's vote share increased by 13 percent over the 1994 elections, while Chissano's held the line at around 53 percent for both races. In the parliamentary race, Frelimo and the Renamo-UE coalition shut out all other parties in 1999, with the two major parties splitting the seats held in the first legislature by the Democratic Union coalition for a roughly even gain over their respective 1994 seat shares. Thus after the 1999 elections Frelimo held just over 53 percent of the seats, while Renamo controlled nearly 47 percent. Nevertheless, Frelimo retained exclusive control of the executive at all levels as well as a comfortable majority in parliament. In 2002, the party entered its twenty-seventh continuous year in power, Chissano his sixteenth year as president.

All three postwar general elections, in 1994, 1999, and 2004 appear to reflect little change. Support for Frelimo and Renamo in each election mirrors their respective wartime patterns of support, with Renamo finding its strongest social base in the country's five central provinces and in rural areas. Frelimo's base in the south and extreme north, as well as in the larger cities, follows a long-established pattern. In each election, Frelimo has won a comfortable, though not overwhelming, majority in parliament. Presidential contests between Frelimo's Joaquim Chissano and Renamo's leader Afonso Dhlakama have been somewhat closer. These electoral results place Mozambique with the majority of sub-Saharan countries in which elections have brought little change in the underlying configuration of inter-party politics.

Nevertheless, participation in the democratization process has had visible effects on internal dynamics in both major parties, and this may well influence party-system development over the long term. The rest of the chapter examines in some detail the impact of this process on the Frelimo party and explores some of the possible implications for the durability and quality of democracy in Mozambique. In the next section, we explore how Frelimo has been shaped by participation in the democratic process. While certain developments within the party appear to bode well for democratic development, the implications of these changes for the long-term fate of democracy are still uncertain. Most important is the question of whether the system could withstand electoral turnover. Are the processes of internal differentiation within the party contingent upon a belief that the party is secure in power? In the following section, then, I examine inter-party dynamics. Here the analysis focuses on the ways in which Frelimo's leaders, while responding to the organizational challenges presented by Mozambique's manifold transition, have sought to shape that process in ways consistent with the organization's own comparative advantages and objectives.

Impact of Democratization: Frelimo as Dependent Variable

As the investigations of democratization in party-dominant systems indicate, the establishment and operation of democratic institutions can generate important changes within ruling parties. Consistent with this insight, examination of the evolution of Frelimo reveals that democratization has encouraged internal differentiation and adaptation within the party. This is especially evident in how the party has been reshaped by the following factors: the institutionalization of elections at various levels, the separation of party and state, the party's participation in parliament, and the decentralization of the structures of political authority. Taken as a whole these changes have enriched the level of pluralism in the Mozambican polity and helped to balance the power of the executive.

Electoral Politics

The advent of multiparty politics brought adjustments for Frelimo both in terms of appeals to its base and its relations among the party elite. Most importantly, elections have led to a dilution of Frelimo's ideological identity and a broadening of the party tent to include increasingly important social sectors, including private business and religious leaders. Following the revision of the constitution in 1990, Frelimo was no longer a Marxist-Leninist party with a transformative mandate born of armed struggle, but a party competing for popular support like everyone else.

Efforts to broaden the party's base began even before the constitutional changes that introduced multipartyism. At the Fifth Party Congress in 1989, Frelimo invited businesspeople, religious leaders, and others who had previously been excluded from party membership to join the party. Efforts were also made to bring younger party members into leadership positions, and to seek regional balance in top leadership positions. In part, the changes made at the Fifth Party Congress can be seen as an attempt to heal the rift created when Frelimo declared itself a Marxist-Leninist party in 1977. The change from a broad front to a vanguard Leninist party had alienated a considerable number of party members and put greater distance between the party leadership and those upon whom it sought to work its transformation. At the Sixth Party Congress two years later, the Central Committee publicly repented of earlier excesses in a bid to reunite the party and to build a broad social base in preparation for eventual electoral competition (Frelimo 1991).

One interesting indication of these shifts can be found in the language of the Central Committee reports for party congresses over the years. In the Third Congress, at which Frelimo declared itself a Marxist-Leninist vanguard party (1977), the phrase *O Povo* (the people) was a unit, a proper noun, a collectivity. "*O Povo* was an abstract entity, an ideal projection of the object of the finished model. Lost was the dimension of the individual, of the small community. . . . Whoever was not *O Povo* would be educated" (Cabaço 1995, 87). By the Fifth Congress in 1989, when party membership was expressly opened to all the Mozambican people, *O Povo* had become *o povo*. The shift from proper to ordinary noun suggests an implied plurality among the people. More marked however is the change from the Fifth to Sixth Congress. While at the Fifth Congress Frelimo was declared open to all the Mozambican people, and Fifth Congress documents are still full of references to revolutionary struggle, the Sixth Congress issues an appeal to all who had been excluded in the past, including those who disagreed with party ideology. "The

Frelimo party is open to all Mozambican citizens who share its national project, regardless of gender, ethnicity, race, social condition, wealth, religion, or *philosophical convictions* [emphasis mine]" (Frelimo 1991, 3). Moreover, there is explicit reference to respect for cultural and ethnic diversity and the free expression of this diversity. This is a radical change for an organization that once proclaimed this very diversity to be a threat to the party's entire project.

A second major impact of elections has been that they have brought into open debate within the party issues that had previously been treated as taboo. Chief among these is the question of ethnic dominance and discrimination within the party and government. Both the Fifth and Sixth Party congresses sought to address charges of ethnic discrimination and southern dominance within the party. Electoral competition brought the issue further into the open, as party activists in several provinces charged that the central party hierarchy sought to foment ethnic division. In one instance, a group of fifty-eight party members, representing Macuas from Nampula province, sent an open letter to President Chissano to voice their grievances. The letter, which ran in the weekly newspaper *Savana,* claimed that party leaders had withdrawn from the Nampula parliamentary list Macua intellectuals from Nampula who were residing in Maputo. The party justified the decision by saying they sought to weight the list in favor of people residing in the province, but the letter's authors saw it differently. They charged that Frelimo "wants to keep our people in ignorance and continue to say that we are capable of nothing . . . it is a superiority complex of the South over the North" (*Savana,* March 3, 1995). The letter went on to complain that Nampula continued to be neglected by the state in terms of economic and social development.

In another example, the government's ambassador to the United Nations circulated a letter, which was published in the Mozambican press, calling for greater representation of his own ethnic group, the Massena, in positions of power. This kind of public debate about ethnic balance within the party was unheard of prior to the first elections.

Following the 1994 elections, the government did make an effort to broaden ethnic representation within the government. A Massena was appointed governor of Sofala province, home to the largest concentration of that ethnic group. In Nampula, the government appointed its first Macua governor, the former secretary-general of a fairly new but influential provincial voluntary association, the Friends of Nampula Association.

Separating Party and State

A logical priority for the multiparty elections was the need to separate party and state, and to reconstitute Frelimo as a competitive, democratic party. This process began in 1990 with the revision of the constitution and the legalization of multiparty politics. On the surface, it appeared that competitive advantages were provided by the extensive organizational structures that Frelimo had sought to develop as a vanguard party. In practice, however, the separation of party and state contributed to a weakening of Frelimo's internal party structures, particularly at sub-national levels.

As a self-declared Marxist-Leninist party that was supposed to be in the vanguard of social and economic transformation, Frelimo had sought to establish an organizational infrastructure that reached down to the grassroots and into virtually all aspects of social and productive activity. Mass-based organizations for youth, women, and labor, for example, were all established as wings of the party. Party cells, at least in some nominal form, could be found in the most remote rural areas and in every enterprise.

When the role of the Frelimo party changed with the stroke of a pen under the new constitution (1990), little concerted effort was made to communicate to the grassroots and to mass-based organizations what the change meant for them. No formal plan was made to reform the party organization in conformance with changes in its role. As the party's secretary-general has put it,

> suddenly we said—multipartyism! But we didn't have the capacity to say look, the party cells now have to carry out new functions. And our cells were abandoned. If we had gone to the cells at the time they were still functioning, with clear instructions, they could have easily made the transition to new roles. But instead there was paralysis. And now what are people doing? They say, we are awaiting instructions.[2]

The leaders of local party structures were left adrift by the changes of the early 1990s, and while party leaders struggled to comprehend and address the implications, Frelimo began to feel the centrifugal force of political and economic liberalism. It was manifested first in the departure of the mass organizations, which were not consistent with the new role of the party. Marxist-Leninist vanguard parties mobilize key social sectors through mass-based organizations that by definition include all workers, all youth, all women. Modern democratic parties do not. In a liberal democratic state, interest aggregation and mobilization is done by competing parties, not by organized wings of the ruling party. Civil society arises organically in response to long-term socioeconomic changes.

Accordingly, the Organization of Mozambican Women (OMM) and the Organization of Mozambican Youth (OJM), for example, declared themselves to be autonomous nongovernmental organizations that had severed ties with the ruling party.[3] This made them eligible for funds from donors who wanted to support civil society, and particularly organizations without ties to the ruling party. In this the mass organizations joined company with a host of individuals and groups who rushed to fill the space created by political change, to plug the hole where donors expected civil society to be.

Intermediate party structures were also thrown into disarray. Provincial governors were no longer provincial first secretaries, as they had been in the party-state era. Without the direct linkage to the state, without playing the official role of projecting state power and enjoying the full benefit of state resources, party structures already languishing in the hinterlands began to dissolve.

Finally, the party leadership outside of government began to feel distanced from the state. "Those [party representatives] who went to the state, even militants, arrived there and said now I am part of the state, I don't want to know about Frelimo, period."[4] The party leadership found itself at a loss to define its role and to assert its identity and authority in the new context. As I discuss below, however, the establishment of parliament substantially aided in the creation of a platform from which the Frelimo party could begin to address these issues. Parliament acted as the repository for a more ideological, "historical" wing of the Frelimo leadership, who, together with the new party leadership charged with renovating the party, effectively began to forge an identity for the party separate from the state, to build a practical understanding of the role of the party in the multiparty context.

The same difficulties the party encountered in the early 1990s were still evident in the 1994 electoral period. Four months after the first multiparty elections, Frelimo's campaign staff met to analyze the party's performance. According to the director of Frelimo's elections office, Mariano Matsinhe, in future the party would have to work to improve communication between the leadership and the base, and he urged all party leaders to make greater efforts to interact with the grassroots.

In the aftermath of the 1994 elections, dramatic changes were made within the party hierarchy. In July 1995, the Central Committee met and elected an entirely new party secretariat, halfway through the term of the incumbent secretariat. This, according to some observers, was a compromise move designed to placate the reformist wing of the party without engaging in the more sweeping internal reforms advocated by that group. Still, there was clear evidence that some in the party leadership recognized the need for change.

A five-member committee was appointed to recommend structural reforms to the party. Chief among these were to be the injection of new, younger members into the leadership structure, and the further separation of party and governance functions. The newly elected secretary-general, Manuel Tome, was the first person to hold the post who was not a veteran of the armed liberation struggle of the 1960s and 70s. In addition, the leadership stressed the need for local party organs to play a more dynamic mobilizing and organizing role in preparation for elections. According to Tome, "since we did not adapt the structure of the party to the realities of '91–92, today we have to undertake the changes that should have been made in 1992 plus those that should have been done after 1992."[5]

Despite these efforts, the same difficulties were still evident by the Seventh Party Congress, held in 1997. The Central Committee's report to the Congress noted that communication problems between different party organs continued, and cited the party's "weak capacity to integrate militants and cadres into the work of the party, and the lack of permanent organized contacts with the population" (Frelimo 1997). Though the establishment of parliament ended up strengthening the party hierarchy at the national level, it did little to shore up Frelimo's intermediate party structures.

The implications of this for democratic politics in Mozambique are unclear. In the run-up to the 1999 elections, for example, provincial party officials in several instances took it upon themselves to use both the police and the party faithful to systematically obstruct Renamo rallies. In a number of cases there were violent clashes, in which provincial party secretaries were reported to have been leading the charge.[6] In several provinces, notably in the center and north of the country whence Renamo draws much of its electoral support, provincial government officials clashed with Renamo party delegates, who complained that they were prevented from observing the vote-counting process (The Carter Center 2000). There were also consistent complaints of provincial party officials or government officials violating electoral regulations by, for example, declaring school and business holidays during Frelimo rallies, or using government resources to campaign (The Carter Center 2000; Hanlon 2000b; *Savana,* October 29, 1999). One year later, provincial authorities clashed with Renamo protestors in several provinces in the center and north, in the worst violence the country has seen since the end of the war. Dozens were killed and more than a hundred wounded during the confrontations. More than eighty prisoners, arrested in the wake of these protests, later suffocated in an overcrowded jail cell in Cabo Delgado.

In each of these cases, Frelimo officials at the national level either denied wrongdoing by provincial authorities or suggested that they were acting on their own initiative. It is difficult to say whether provincial authorities acted on their own in these cases or on instructions from party superiors. But neither possibility bodes well, and the exploitation of uncertainty about who is in charge in these situations could easily work to the advantage of those seeking to disrupt consolidation of the postwar political settlement.

Parliament

In new democracies, parliament often constitutes the only place where the opposition participates in governance.[7] As such it is the only regular, institutional point of interaction for political parties between elections, and acts as the focal point of party activity between elections. This tends to raise the stakes of participation in parliament for opposition parties, who see it as both an important way to keep themselves in the public view and their only opportunity to influence governance.

Parliaments also present organizational challenges to new parties. As Duverger notes, power struggles between the party hierarchy outside parliament and the party's parliamentary bench have long been a central feature of party life in most systems (Duverger 1964). Members of the party's parliamentary delegation enjoy regular salaries, publicity, and sometimes celebrity, as well as a potential base from which to challenge the party hierarchy. Particularly where parties are neither staffed by paid professionals nor endowed with strong intermediate structures (local or regional branches), the parliamentary bench has the potential to exercise significant amounts of power within the party.

As with elections, the particular challenges that participation in parliament poses to parties as organizations depends to some extent on institutional design. For example, Mozambique's semi-presidential system means that the degree of overlap between party hierarchy and parliamentary bench becomes an important question. Where party hierarchy and bench leadership overlap, parliament can promote both the formation of party identity and the boosting of party capacity (as it would in parliamentary systems), while also improving the effectiveness of parliament itself (because the party hierarchy is not obsessed with trying to weaken the party bench). In Mozambique, we can see this effect by contrasting the impact of parliament on Renamo and Frelimo.

Particularly under presidential or semi-presidential systems, parliament can provide a basis for internal differentiation within parties, as has happened within Frelimo. The Frelimo party hierarchy has used parliament as a platform on which to forge its own identity and niche in the political system (vis-à-vis the party-in-government). This in turn has facilitated the process of separating party and state.

Though Frelimo came to power in 1975 with a plan for the socioeconomic transformation of Mozambique, this vision soon ran into economic and political barriers. By the end of the 1980s, the party had embarked on economic and political liberalization. In 1989–90, as early talks began with the Renamo rebels, the country's constitution was rewritten, removing Frelimo from its role as the vanguard and sole legal party and opening the way to multiparty competition. Economic liberalization in the 1980s jettisoned many of the party's ideals of socialist transformation, and official separation of party and state formalized a process that was already underway. This separation reinforced a division that had already taken shape within Frelimo: between the technocratic and liberal economic vision of party leaders who occupied key government posts and the ideals of those who hewed to the party's traditional line, not only with respect to economic policy, but more importantly with respect to the idea that the party should remain subordinate to the state.

As noted above, the greatest challenge to the Frelimo party was the struggle first to define its relationship to the state in a satisfactory way, and second to assert effective authority over the state. Parliament offered a way to accomplish both tasks. The establishment of the new parliament offered opportunities for those in the party hierarchy to increase their power relative to the party-in-government. While Frelimo has always emphasized its own ability to be self-critical and to accommodate internal dissidents, the party's participation in parliament has posed important challenges to its self-image and internal cohesion. These changes had roots in the broadening of the party base at the 1989 Fifth Party Congress, even before the formal introduction of multiparty politics in the 1990 constitution. The Sixth Party Congress in 1991 sought to consolidate the party's wider appeal in preparation for the 1994 elections. The challenges to party coherence wrought by this expansion of the fold were made considerably more acute by the creation of a semi-autonomous political arena, in the form of the new parliament. This created the possibility that existing divisions within the party could be reinforced by the different responsibilities and incentive structures faced by members of parliament and members of government.

As it happened, from Frelimo's perspective as the party-in-government, parliament presented an ideal repository for the party's "historic generation." These more ideologically inclined party militants led the party through the liberation struggle and the early years of independence, but they were also increasingly out of step with the technocratic and liberal economic vision of many party leaders in the government. While the party has placed younger, more technocratic figures in high-profile leadership positions within the bench and the parliamentary committees, the most forceful and outspoken members of the bench have been members of this "old guard."

It is not possible to draw a straight, clear line between Frelimo deputies and their party colleagues in government. Beginning with the first multiparty legislature, seated in 1994, the Frelimo bench has been quite mixed in terms of ideological, political, and professional backgrounds. It comprises a mixture of former top-level party and government officials, including ministers, governors, and heads of government boards and ministerial departments, alongside teachers, clerks, independent professionals, and businesspeople. To be sure, there is a broad spectrum in terms of ideology as well as professional background. On the one hand is the leader of the Frelimo bench during the first and second legislatures, Armando Guebuza. He is a longtime, top-ranking government and party official, who led the government delegation in peace talks with Renamo, and became a prominent private businessman in the wake of economic liberalization.[8] On the other hand is the bench's rapporteur in the first and second legislatures, Sergio Vieira, one of the most outspoken of Frelimo deputies, who plays a major role in all important debates and committees. He is one of the "historic generation" of leftist intellectual ideologues, having served in top posts at the university and in the security establishment during the war. Vieira led the charge within the Assembleia da Republica against some of the government's more important economic-liberalization measures.

Despite diversity within the Frelimo bench, this "historic generation" has played a dominant role both in plenary sessions of the assembly and in committee leadership roles. While the group holds mixed views on substantive issues like economic policy, its members tend to share strong beliefs about the relationship between party and state. A prominent figure from this group, Mariano Matsinha, Frelimo deputy and member of the party's Political Commission, maintained that one of the key challenges for the party now was to "combat *tecnicismo* in government. Government officials have to have some partisan spirit. We have to ensure that everything is not done just on a technical basis."[9] This echoes comments made by party leaders regarding the process of separating party and state more generally (Manning 1997).

The interests of the "historic generation" in maintaining a hand in government policy fit nicely with those of the party hierarchy, most of whom were also members of parliament. In 1995, the party secretariat was replaced midway through its term by the younger generation. For the first time, the secretary-general was someone who had not fought in the liberation struggle. This new leadership was charged with "renovating" and modernizing the party, of overseeing changes in mentality as well as structural changes in the party, all without the resources of the state, to which it had become accustomed. As Tome, the new secretary-general, said in 1996, "the party, which was after all the one that was in the vanguard of promoting these changes, ended up progressing more slowly, particularly from the point of view of changing its structures, but also in the work of changing mentalities."[10]

> We had some cases in which we accepted the change but we continued with the methods of monopartyism. There were comrades who said for example, we have to reduce the expenses of the party. Others said what! We are in power! Let us give orders to the government to give us money.[11]

Thus at the time the Assembly of the Republic was first seated at the end of 1994, and with the next general elections five years away, Frelimo party officials were engaged in a struggle to keep the party relevant vis-à-vis the state, in order to obtain some measure of control over state policies and orientations. Parliament presented a way for the party to obtain control, by offering a venue in which the party had a prominent and clear cut role to play vis-à-vis the state. The party bureaucracy, outside of the executive, found in parliament a forum for expressing and consolidating a party identity and program that at times publicly challenged positions of those in government. One important example of policy divergence between the Frelimo bench and the government is the battle over the privatization of the cashew industry. A group of Frelimo members of parliament successfully collaborated with the local cashew-producing interests to push legislation that reintroduced a surtax on raw cashew exports. This was an effort to revive Mozambique's cashew industry, which had been all but eliminated following the gradual liberalization of cashew exports at the insistence of the World Bank. Previously, the government itself had declined to reverse the policy after the World Bank acknowledged that it may have erred in pushing the liberalization of cashew exports.[12]

This effect derived in part from the fact that most of the party's top leaders outside of government are prominent members of parliament.[13] (Deputies may not simultaneously hold posts in government.) This includes some members of the "historic generation" who had previously been retired from top party posts but were subsequently brought back in.[14] At the party's Seventh Congress, held in May 1997, for example, the party brought back Sergio Vieira, who had been dropped from the Central Committee in 1991. One observer commented that "doubtless his performance as one of Frelimo's most prominent parliamentarians contributed to this comeback" (AIM 1997). The party also brought some of its younger parliamentary bench members into the Central Committee.

Even more striking is the dominance by members of parliament of the Political Commission, the top decision-making body of the party. Of fifteen Political Commission members, all but five were members of parliament, and four of the five who were not deputies held positions that are incompatible with being a deputy. With the exception of Mozambique's president and prime minister, then, the leadership of Frelimo's party bench since 1994 has been comprised of the party's own internal leadership.[15] In 2003, Armando Emilio Guebuza, head of Frelimo's parliamentary bench, was elected as the new secretary-general of the party and would be the party's presidential candidate in 2004.

Decentralization

As noted above, the 1998 municipal elections were disastrous in terms of voter turnout. Most parties abstained from the competition, including Renamo. Frelimo ran unopposed in all but eight races, and won control of all of the municipal assemblies and all mayoral positions. Municipal elections were held again in November 2003. This time voter turnout was roughly 25 percent, and Renamo contested races in all thirty-three municipalities. Frelimo won absolute majorities in twenty-nine municipal assemblies and took twenty-eight mayoral races. Renamo won mayoral positions in five municipalities, all in Nampula and Sofala provinces. In the town of Marromeu, in northern Sofala, Frelimo controls the municipal assembly, sharing power with a mayor from Renamo.

Despite serious flaws in the first elections and persistent problems with transparency in vote tabulation in the second poll, the creation of autonomous municipalities has created additional political arenas that provide potential venues in which differentiation within the party might be operationalized. Municipal elections created an opportunity for longtime Frelimo dissenters to venture out of the world of civil society, where they challenged government policies as a loyal, nonthreatening, and nonpolitical "opposition," and into the world of opposition politics, albeit without calling it by that name. Indeed, in 1998 these groups were extraordinarily careful to make clear that they were not interested in politics, but in becoming involved in the everyday issues of local governance in those municipalities where they contested elections. Nevertheless, at least some of these groups were deeply divided about whether or not to venture openly into the political arena for the general elections the following year. However, the electoral law prohibited "independents" from running for parliament, and strict laws on registering as a presidential candidate discouraged independents from running for that office. In the municipal elections, independent citizens' groups, which included prominent former members and officials of Frelimo, made significant gains in Maputo and Beira, the capital and second-largest city respectively. Citizens' groups also won considerable shares of seats in a handful of other cities throughout the country.

Thus, on the surface, the results of the two rounds of municipal elections appeared merely to reinforce ruling-party dominance and to demonstrate the weakness of competitive politics in Mozambique. Nevertheless they provided evidence of longstanding lines of dissent within the country's political elite, those currently and formerly identified prominently with the Frelimo party.

It is worth examining these independent citizens' groups briefly. By far the most influential of these groups, the Maputo-based *Juntos pela Cidade* (United for the City or JPC), is comprised of a large number of former leading members of Frelimo. Some had served in government or been university lecturers, some were businesspeople and professionals. Most of those who had been active party members left the party quietly at the beginning of the 1990s, feeling that there was no room for dissent within the party, yet unwilling to challenge the party openly or to give Renamo any advantage. Many formed nongovernmental organizations concerned with social issues, such as urban development, housing, health care, or education.

According to one leading member, JPC members were as disillusioned with politics in the multiparty era as they had been in the "monoparty" period. And, this member noted, serving in parliament now required a national political base. Municipal politics seemed a natural fit for those who looked back to the days of the 1970s, when, in the words of this individual, ideologically committed members of the party worked for progress and development. The JPC party has been an outspoken, trenchant, and constructive critic of government policy within the Maputo municipal assembly.[16]

Thus the prospect and reality of electoral competition contributed to structural change within the party hierarchy as well as to changes in the party's program and ideology. These changes were facilitated by Frelimo's tradition of allowing internal dissent within parameters that are well understood by its leading members. Relatively strong, institutionalized, and organizational decision-making routines allowed for the orderly processing of internal tensions that gave rise to democratic politics, a relatively low-risk channel through which longtime internal party dissidents could confront the party in open electoral competition, namely, municipal elections. Combined with the stimulus for action, which was provided by a real threat of being unseated by Renamo, these factors contributed to fairly orderly and considerable internal reforms within the Frelimo party.

Interparty Dynamics: Frelimo as Independent Variable

The influences of the process on Frelimo as a party must be considered in the context of Frelimo's attempts to define the underlying principles and defining rules of the postwar political settlement. Taking Frelimo as a whole as the unit of analysis (though not necessarily a unitary actor), as an actor engaged in a competitive struggle to shape both the terms and the outcomes of the political system, we gain a rather different perspective on democratization in Mozambique. If a close analysis of Frelimo's internal party dynamics suggests a process of differentiation and adaptation that may bode well for the future, the dynamics of interaction between the two dominant parties as they struggle to shape the definitive political settlement offer indications of the limits of democratization in Mozambique under current conditions.

Interpreting the Political Settlement: Theory and Practice

At the opening session of Mozambique's first multiparty legislature, President Joaquim Chissano laid out the fundamental tension faced by the Assembly of the Republic.

> You have received from the country a mandate to preserve peace and to make war only a bitter memory, to make national reconciliation a daily reality. . . . The dialogue between deputies cannot be limited to a mere relation of majority and minority. Throughout the history of a country, majorities and minorities are transitory, but national interest is permanent. *The search for consensus is more important than simple voting, although voting is indispensable to make the decisions that will transform ideas into laws.* (emphasis added)[17]

Even before the signing of the Rome peace accord in 1992, it was clear that each of the two major parties would champion a different side of the democracy-as-consensus versus majority-rule debate. Each party has insisted upon its own understanding of the source of the postwar political system's legitimacy and operating principles. At least until the 1999 elections, the system functioned on the basis of a tacitly agreed "creative ambiguity" regarding the postwar political settlement. As we discuss below, however, the 1999 general elections raised important questions about the limits of this arrangement.

The parties' positions reflected their own strengths and drew support from different but equally plausible sources. For Renamo, the General Peace Accord (GPA) signed in Rome in 1992, and the mechanisms created to implement it, are definitive and its underlying principles remain in force. The GPA created politically balanced commissions, usually with representation of the international community. These commissions were essentially an extension of the Rome negotiating process, and decisions were based on discussion and consensus, rather than on majority vote.

The GPA put the two former military adversaries on a roughly equal footing, and enshrined negotiation, "political balance," and consensual decision-making procedures as the basis of interaction. Renamo, in opposition from the beginning, sought to minimize the winner-take-all logic of Mozambique's majoritarian brand of democracy and to restore the parties to the rough parity of the battlefield and negotiation table by insisting on consensus (unanimity) as the basis of decision-making for all important issues.

For Frelimo, on the other hand, it is the 1990 Constitution, passed before the legalization of Renamo as a political actor, which provides both the letter and the spirit of the law in postwar Mozambique. The GPA, for Frelimo, created mechanisms and principles with a limited lifespan—the period between its signing and the seating of the first new government. After that, the 1990 Constitution supersedes anything in the GPA. As Manuel Tome, secretary-general of Frelimo, said,

> the peace accord was a means to an end, and not an end in itself. It was an exceptional regime for a predetermined length of time, after which we return to the full norms of the constitution . . . the lifetime of the norms and mechanisms established in the peace accord has clearly run out.[18]

The ruling party routinely takes refuge in strict interpretations of the rules of the game, in which numerical majorities prevail and all decisions that matter are taken by vote. As the government news agency AIM put it, consensus is "a very different concept [from democracy]. Laws are drafted and elections are held precisely because there are differences which cannot be resolved by talking about them. In these circumstances, the democratic option is to take a vote, and accept the will of the majority" (AIM 1998).

The parties' contrasting attitudes have reflected their relative positions as majority and minority and matched their very different levels of political and organizational capacity. From the beginning, there have been clear imbalances in the degree to which Frelimo and Renamo have been able to use formal democratic processes to advance their interests. First, compared with Frelimo, Renamo has been far less well prepared to compete in the political arena. The party has suffered from a lack of well-prepared and trusted cadres and has consistently had difficulty filling its allotment of political slots. Significant tensions exist between the wartime leadership of the party and new members recruited to bolster the party's political capacity. Power within the party is highly centralized and personalized around its wartime leader, Afonso Dhlakama, who has no experience in government and is not part of the party's delegation to parliament.

With these organizational handicaps, combined with the party's minority position in parliament and exclusion from the executive, Renamo has been unable to use the political system effectively to advance its goals. Instead, it has sought to avoid the use of formal institutions whenever the stakes are high, using its participation in democratic processes as a bargaining chip to change the terms of its inclusion in the system. More often than not, Renamo has forced the most important decisions out of parliament and into informal bargaining processes between top elites. This has mitigated Frelimo's comparative advantage (in terms of numerical superiority and greater ability to achieve its own goals within the formal institutional framework), and it has also allowed Dhlakama to exert maximum control over his own party's actions.[19]

Frelimo, for its part, has used narrow legalistic interpretations of its obligations toward the opposition in part as a way to deal with internal tensions of its own. The legalistic line helps answer criticism by those who believe the party has made too many concessions to the opposition. At the same time, it makes it more difficult for the international community to fault the ruling party. While Frelimo may violate the spirit of national reconciliation, it does not openly flaunt the letter of accepted democratic practice.

The two parties' contrasting views of system legitimacy have given rise to two contradictory tracks for the management of political conflict. One such track consists of the formal processes and institutions of majoritarian democracy. The second comprises informal negotiating processes involving the top leadership of the two major parties. This two-track process is evident both in parliament and in the country's three postwar electoral processes.

Each of Mozambique's elections has been marred by the opposition's accusations of fraud or mismanagement, and each has been subject to an opposition boycott of some kind. And in each case, formal electoral processes have been accompanied or followed by parallel, informal processes of elite negotiation, which provide a safety valve for political dissatisfaction. These side negotiations have helped to lower the stakes of formal politics and reassure those on the losing side that politics need not be zero-sum. In 1994, for example, Renamo first sought to boycott the elections when it feared for its ability to win under prevailing conditions; then Renamo boycotted parliament when it immediately became clear that Frelimo meant to make full use of its majority seat share. Renamo went on to boycott the 1998 municipal elections, citing fraud and bias in the arrangements for electoral administration. In each case, Renamo appealed directly to the international donor community in Mozambique, playing both upon donor concerns about political stability and upon the government's desire to avoid falling into disfavor with a donor community that contributed the lion's share of the country's annual budget. Certain parallels in this sense operate between the behavior of Mozambique's opposition and the activities of the opposition in the Central African Republic as described by Mehler in this volume (see chapter 6).

While Renamo's boycotts and subsequent appeals to the international community and the Frelimo leadership did not succeed in changing the outcomes of the elections, they marked a significant and not wholly unsuccessful attempt to revise, in practice, the principles on which political power would be distributed in postwar Mozambique. Thus while nominally agreeing to the postwar political settlement, Renamo sought to use its participation in the formal institutions as leverage to challenge the terms of that settlement. Renamo managed to keep alive the notion that negotiation and consensus could not be wholly replaced by the institutions of majoritarian democracy. By treating the international community as a kind of political third force, Renamo has in several instances kept Frelimo from enjoying fully the power granted to the ruling party under the constitution.

Frelimo's consistent response has been to try to pull decision-making back into parliament, where it can rely on parliamentary procedure and its numerical majority to override the opposition. Interestingly, this strengthens Frelimo's stake in the institutions of formal democracy. Only by insisting on the sovereignty of credible formal governing institutions can Frelimo hope to weaken Renamo's ability to continually renegotiate the distribution of political power through boycotts and appeals to donors. Thus the more powerful party, whose long-standing dominance of the state apparatus and disproportionate resource base give it the power to derail democracy entirely, has had self-interested reasons for strengthening the formal institutions in order to weaken Renamo's gadfly role.

The Limits of Creative Ambiguity

Up until the second general elections, it seemed as though democracy in Mozambique might muddle through on the basis of the two parties' tacit acceptance of creative ambiguity as to the underlying principles of the system, with the consequences for institutional consistency and efficiency which that implied. The 1999 general elections and their aftermath may demonstrate the limits of the two parties' ability both to compete and coexist under the existing terms of play.

Following a very close presidential election in December 1999, serious doubts were raised by opposition parties, international observers, and the independent media regarding the probity of the counting process. However, recourse to the usual methods of closed-door negotiations between the top leaderships of the two parties proved ineffective. Instead, it provoked the first postwar split in Renamo's leadership. The subsequent breakdown of elite-level negotiations over election results contributed to the outbreak of the worst politically linked violence in Mozambique since the end of the war.

As results from the 1999 general elections trickled in from the provinces, for the first time the possibility of a Renamo government seemed real. Renamo's coalition with the ten most significant small parties (none of which won more than about 2 percent of the vote in the 1994 elections) swept up all the slack of the Chissano-Dhlakama race of 1994, with Dhlakama increasing his vote share by 13 percent or roughly the share taken by the "unarmed" parties in those first elections.[20]

With more than 300,000 votes still to be counted, mostly from areas of the country where Dhlakama was expected to do very well, the National Electoral Commission (CNE) suddenly called a halt to the retabulation of votes at the central level and decided to accept the tallies sent in by the provinces.[21] Renamo's representatives on the CNE boycotted this decision, and later Renamo refused to accept the results. Chissano's margin of victory was 204,000 votes. Officially, tally sheets representing more than 377,000 ballots had been ruled uncountable and were not included in the final count. Renamo then lodged a poorly documented challenge with the Supreme Court.[22] The court rejected all of Renamo's claims as groundless after conducting its own inquiry, without however addressing the central issues of transparency and credibility. The CNE has never published a polling-station-by-polling-station list of official electoral results.

While international donors, who had once again helped finance these elections, formally accepted that the case was closed after the Supreme Court ruling, Renamo continued to insist that it did not accept the results. The party first boycotted parliament and insisted on a recount, then demanded a share in executive power (namely governorships in the provinces where it had won a majority of the votes), declaring that it would establish shadow governments in those provinces. At least in public, all of these maneuvers were roundly ignored by the ruling party. Chissano did delay the appointment of governors, fueling rumors of secret negotiations between Renamo and the government, but a few months after the elections he named governors to all ten provinces without consulting Renamo, as was his prerogative.

Meanwhile, persistent reports of secret negotiations suggested that at least some within the ruling party hoped to buy Renamo's acquiescence through positions on boards of public companies and other enticements. When, however, Dhlakama publicly declared that there really were such secret negotiations, the government denied this and alleged that members of the government had in fact met only with one of Dhlakama's top deputies, Raul Domingos, at his own request, to discuss helping him out of personal financial difficulties. This tactic, which struck at one of Renamo's vulnerable spots (division over the contrasting lifestyles of national party leaders and provincial leaders and militants, and mistrust over the loyalty of its parliamentary representatives), temporarily succeeded in disarming Renamo's challenge to the electoral process. Domingos was expelled from the party, in the first high-level departure since the peace.

Months later, however, President Chissano invited Dhlakama to engage in a series of dialogues with him about the challenges facing the nation. This initiative was carefully couched in terms of initiating a dialogue to debate the country's economic future, rather than to discuss the disputed elections. However, the underlying purpose was to allay fears among both the Mozambican public and international investors and donors about renewed political instability as a result of problems with the 1999 elections.

Those fears appeared to be realized when, in November 2000, with the electoral dispute still dragging on, Renamo organized a series of initially peaceful demonstrations that resulted in violent confrontations with police in several provinces. As noted above, more than forty people were killed in the most serious violence since the end of the war. In several instances, police fired into crowds and attacked demonstrators. In at least one case, protesters attacked a police station in an apparent attempt to take weapons. Several weeks later, eighty-three prisoners, arrested during one such confrontation, died of suffocation in a tiny jail cell while awaiting trial.[23]

One month later, Chissano and Dhlakama again met face-to-face to discuss Renamo's complaints regarding the elections and other grievances, including the behavior of the police. These talks eventually produced an agreement to form bipartisan working commissions, which produced no significant results.

While Frelimo and Renamo have developed over the years a fairly flexible but predictable pattern in which formal democratic processes are supplemented by informal elite bargaining, the events of 1999 and 2000 suggest the possible limits of this particular adaptive behavior. Most importantly, the success of this strategy depends on the individual choices made by leaders on both sides, who are in turn constrained by the strength of their own positions within their respective parties.

How, then, do we evaluate Mozambique's experiment with democracy? In this chapter I have tried to suggest that in order to answer this question, we need to approach democratization not as a single, macro-level process, but rather as a series of micro-level processes that have important and fairly unpredictable effects on one another. Democratization can be usefully viewed as a series of processes that sometimes collide and sometimes converge, and which together define a country's political trajectory. In the case of Mozambique, we can see two analytically separate tendencies at work, each of which affects the ruling party in different ways. A tendency toward greater openness *within* the party coexists with a reluctance to surrender to the uncertainties of democratic competition *between* parties. As elsewhere in Africa, state domination of a weak economy and a legacy of political violence make it a tall order to build trust in other parties and in nominally impartial institutions. Even where the competitive pressures of democratic politics may contribute to increased pluralism within parties, we should expect that same dynamic to lag behind when it comes to inter-party competition.

At the level of intra-party dynamics, it seems clear that elections at the central and municipal levels, and the establishment of parliament, have led to greater internal pluralism within Frelimo and have created distinct political arenas within which party actors can voice and act upon competing views. The establishment of parliament in particular has helped further the separation of party and state and has given some within the party leadership a vested interest in parliament as a means for balancing the power of the party-in-government. However, while this chapter has stressed the more positive effects of elite differentiation within the party as a result of the proliferation of political arenas, one should also bear in mind that political actors, newly empowered by their positions in municipal government or the assembly, might very well adopt positions inimical to the survival or consolidation of democracy. It is reasonable to assume, for example, that local-level officials whose party is voted out of office (whether in local or general elections) may feel they have fewer economic survival strategies, or face greater physical security risks, than their central-level counterparts and hence feel more threatened by the potential loss of political power.

Finally, the nature of the relationship between Frelimo and its major rival, Renamo, raises serious questions about both the depth and the meaning of the changes within Frelimo discussed here. The 1999 elections and their aftermath clearly highlight the current limits of democratization in Mozambique. The most serious question is whether, given the country's past, Frelimo would find it possible under any circumstances to yield control of the government to Renamo. Could the current state of democratic development in Mozambique support an electoral turnover? The events of 1999 and 2000 suggest that the answer is no. They point instead to the possibility that the flexibility and adaptive behavior of the Frelimo party is contingent on the assumption that Frelimo will not in fact lose power. When control of the state is at stake, democratic pretenses may be rapidly abandoned. This, of course, puts to the test claims about the impact of democratization on parties as organizations. The 2004 elections, in which Frelimo won with a more comfortable margin, shed little light on the issue.

And here we return to the dilemma described at the outset. We know democratization is a contingent process. The question is, how contingent? If the transition falls apart at a given point, does that mean it was unsustainable to begin with and has simply met its inevitable demise? Or might fragile progress made on various fronts have survived had it not been tested at particular points in time? Perhaps the most that can be said now is that the survival of the postwar political settlement in Mozambique will depend upon the ways in which the two dominant parties adapt themselves to that settlement. The study of that process thus becomes an essential point of leverage for understanding the prospects and limits of post-conflict democratization.

NOTES

1. Municipal elections were conducted in all of Mozambique's provincial capitals and twenty-three other towns and districts. Renamo and other opposition parties boycotted over alleged irregularities in electoral administration in the run-up to elections, but most parties had been unable to meet the onerous requirements for registration anyway. The elections were marred by widespread accusations of fraud and intimidation on the part of the ruling party.

2. Author interview, Manuel Tome, secretary-general of the Frelimo party, Maputo, October 22, 1995.

3. By 1995, OMM had re-affiliated itself with Frelimo.

4. Author interview, member of Frelimo secretariat, Maputo, October 5, 1995.

5. Author interview, Manuel Tome, secretary-general of the Frelimo party, Maputo, October 22, 1995.

6. Even the state-aligned daily *Noticias* noted that in one instance, when Frelimo militants clogged the street to block the passage of Renamo presidential candidate Afonso Dhlakama and one member of his security detail was run down by a van bedecked with Frelimo posters, "the forces of law and order witnessed this sad spectacle without taking action, which in turn aroused public fury." See *Noticias,* October 27, 1999. For additional accounts of this period, see *Savana,* October 29, 1999.

7. This section draws on Manning (2002a).

8. Guebuza became Frelimo's presidential candidate for the 2004 elections.

9. Author interview, Mariano Matsinha, Maputo, May 9, 2000.

10. Author interview, Manuel Tome, secretary-general of the Frelimo party, October 22, 1995.

11. Author interview, Manuel Tome, secretary-general of the Frelimo party, October 22, 1995.

12. For a detailed discussion of the cashew issue, see Hanlon (2000a). For more on parliament and internal party dynamics in both Renamo and Frelimo, see Manning (2002a).

13. Under Mozambique's presidential system, an executive post and a seat in the legislature may not be held simultaneously.

14. It is worth noting, however, that in Frelimo as in Renamo, some deputies put their interests as parliamentarians above their party identity, by working on legislative initiatives with the rival party and by espousing issues that were not priorities for their parties, and subsequently they lost their seats in the second general elections. Two prominent examples are Abdul Carimo (F) and Jafar Gulamo Jafar (R).

15. The five exceptions included the president of the Republic and the prime minister, another government minister, the governor of Manica province, and one party functionary. Political Commission members who are deputies include the party's secretary-general and his predecessor, the leader of the Frelimo bench, the future vice president of the AR, and several members of the assembly's Permanent Commission. Political Commission members named at the Seventh Congress (1997) were: President Chissano, Prime Minister Mocumbi, Feliciano Gundana (former secretary-general), Manuel Tome (current secretary-general), Armando Guebuza (bench leader), Veronica Macamo (MP), Margarida Talapa (MP), Chipande (MP), Mariano Matsinha (MP), Rafael Maguni (MP), Alcido Nguenha (first vice president of AR), Eneas Comiche (minister in the Presidency for Economic and Social Affairs), and Artur Canana (governor of Manica province).

16. Author interview, Maria dos Anjos, Maputo, May 1999.

17. Transcript of assembly proceedings, December 8, 1994, 8–9.

18. Manuel Tome speaking in plenary session of the Assembly of the Republic on April 1, 1996. Cited in AIM, *Mozambiquefile,* May 1996, 11.

19. This section draws upon Manning (2002b).

20. In the 1999 presidential race, Chissano and Dhlakama were the only two candidates.

21. This was consistent with the electoral law, according to which provincial results were the legal final results. However, due to Renamo's lack of confidence in some of the provincial tabulation efforts, a retabulation was underway in Maputo. It was this latter process that was called off.

22. The Supreme Court was acting in this instance in the capacity of Constitutional Court. The Constitutional Court, which according to electoral law should hear election-related disputes, has not yet been established. All members of the Supreme Court were appointed by President Joaquim Chissano, prior to the advent of multiparty politics.

23. Also in November, the well-known journalist Carlos Cardoso was gunned down in broad daylight in a Maputo street. Cardoso was in the midst of investigating a $14–million-dollar embezzlement scandal involving a recently privatized commercial bank. He had long been openly critical of corruption in government and political circles more generally. His murder was widely interpreted as a warning to those who would seek to lift the lid on the corruption issue in any serious way. Since then, a number of other officials and journalists have been murdered or died in suspicious circumstances. The alleged triggermen behind Cardoso's killing were eventually apprehended after a lethargic investigation. But despite widespread and open speculation about who might be responsible (certain businessmen with links to the ruling party), no one with any profile has been arrested.

11 | Democratization in a Divided Urban Political Culture
Guinea-Bissau

Joshua B. Forrest

The West African coastal nation of Guinea-Bissau, a proud lusophone mini-state wedged defiantly in between Francophone Senegal and the Republic of Guinea, shares with Mozambique and Angola the distinction within Africa of having fought a bloody nationalist war (1962–74) to wrest free from the colonial grip of Portugal's dying Salazarist empire. But Guinea-Bissau's postcolonial prelude to democratic transition would prove unique in comparison with its more southerly lusophone cousins in that the country was politically stable for the first two decades after independence, while Angola and Mozambique became entrenched in civil war. To some extent, this relative political stability helped to provide a context that would eventually give rise to political institutions, which would seek to encourage political pluralism and democratization. By 1994, the inauguration of a new institutional framework—marked by competitive presidential elections, opposition political parties, and a multiparty parliament—appeared to outside observers to harbor considerable democratic promise. Bratton and Van de Walle, in fact, declared in 1997 that Guinea-Bissau had achieved a successful transition to electoral democratic status (Bratton and de Walle 1997, 120).

However, closer analysis reveals a more complex, mixed scenario than can be depicted by a simple declaration of transitional success. To be sure, the inauguration of a multiparty system and electoral institutions represented an important change from the first two decades of independence, 1974 through 1994, when authoritarian regimes were in place. In the mid-1990s, a window of political mobilization and political expression had been created by pro-democracy activists—including the influential, educated urban elite—and was reflected in the creation of new political associations and the organization of political parties. Yet Guinea-Bissau's contemporary political order also reflects an older, entrenched set of divisions within the urban political milieu—the arena of operations for urban civil society (already-established or newly activated social organizations) as well as government agencies and leaders. Within this arena, actors have historically approached politics with a determination to win at all costs and to promote one's own personal or factional interests without being overly hindered by formal institutional rules.

In VonDoepp and Villalón's introduction to this book (see chapter 1), it is emphasized that elite members of civil society can play vital roles in the process of democratization. This is particularly the case when political party leaders, political activists, and government leaders form an "elite pact" oriented around consensus and rule-abidance (Harbeson, Rothchild, and Chazan 1994). However, in Guinea-Bissau's urban political milieu, the course of democratization reflected a struggle between authoritarian and liberal values more than the formation of a viable elite pact. Some urban elites—government leaders and city-based activists—sought to lobby for greater openness and pluralism, but others behaved in a way that did not promote the spirit of constitutional rule abidance. A dualistic urban political culture has characterized Guinea-Bissau's experience—reflected in elites' tendency to shift between zero-sum politics and liberal pluralism, between a culture predicated on constraint and bargaining and a culture oriented toward the type of individualized opportunism that trumps institutional boundary-adherence.

This dualism between civic/democratic impulses, on the one hand, and zero-sum political intolerance, on the other, is manifested in Guinea-Bissau by what Ekeh, writing more generally about Africa, refers to as the "two publics" (Ekeh 1975). In the case of Guinea-Bissau, one "public" is represented by a diverse set of urban activists struggling for a constitutional and pluralistic political order; the other "public" reflects the older, inherited tendency toward unilateral politics that deprioritizes rule-oriented political behavior. As utilized in this chapter, the notion of the two publics calls attention to *both* institutional developments in urban areas and the historical, economic, and cultural setting in which political processes operate. Urban civil-society activists have struggled with a degree of success to establish a political structure within which voting, party mobilization, and parliamentary representation become institutionalized features of the political system. In turn, the institutions that have been established have played an important role in political life. Most evidently, political institutions and the formal structures and processes of democracy—electoral turnover, a national legislature, an elected president—have provided a degree of progress toward postwar reconciliation and reconstruction. At the same time, the colonial experience and history of fractionalized, combative behavior have conditioned the extent to which contemporary political institutions have been able to strengthen and consolidate Guinea-Bissau's democratic opening. Thus, democratic institutions today operate in an urban political environment that is unstable and divisive, one in which political elites have tentatively, haltingly embraced pluralistic, rules-abiding values.

Guinea-Bissau may today be considered more than what Bratton would term a "survivalistic" democracy (Bratton 1999b, 31), but substantially less than what Linz and Stepan would consider a transitional democratic framework that is in the process of consolidation (Linz and Stepan 1996). Guinea-Bissau may therefore be

best analyzed as what Levitsky and Way (2002) refer to as a "hybrid" political order, one that is characterized by the persistence of authoritarian values combined
with the partially stabilizing impact of democratic institutions. The dynamic, back-
and-forth entendre between political elites and democratic institutions in Guinea-
Bissau has produced a frequently changing political order characterized both by
persistent efforts at electoral legitimization and equally powerful retractive forces
that rely more heavily on force than on democratic procedures.

While Guinea-Bissau's syncretistic, hybrid political character suggests that the
current transition is unlikely to produce a steady consolidation of institutional pluralism, it should also be recognized that some elites nonetheless pursue democratic
pact-making and the regularized holding of free and fair elections.[1] The second set
of elections and the alternation of ruling party and president that occurred in 1999
and that were planned for March 2004 represent progress toward a generalized elite
embrace of a formalistic democratic framework. Diamond and Bratton argue com-
pellingly that the sheer act of holding elections—even if they occur without the
generation of a more deeply entrenched and genuinely pluralistic, rules-respecting
political culture—can prove significant by providing a measure of democratic space,
especially if an electoral *alternance* of power-holders occurs (Diamond 1999b, xi;
Bratton 1999b, 32). The cases of Nigeria (1999) and Senegal (2000), where relatively free and fair elections produced a change of presidential and ruling-party national leaderships, are promising in this respect. Guinea-Bissau's 1999 second elections proved similarly significant, both because they bucked the continental trend
toward a decline in the quality of second elections (Bratton 1999b, 26–28), and
because they provided what Gyimah-Boadi refers to as a structural foundation for
the continuity of multiparty democratization (Gyimah-Boadi 1999a, 43–44).

At the same time, however, considering that Guinea-Bissau's founding and second elections took place within a deeply divided urban political culture, it is important not to exaggerate the implications of the repeated use of the balloting process.
Despite the power alternation, the country in the post–second election period (2000–
2004) still lacked the transparency, accountability, presidential restraint, interest-
group maturation, and overall political stability requisite for democratic consolidation. This was more than a "virtual democracy" (Joseph 1999; Monga 1999), for
political institutions help to account for the progress the country has made toward
at least a partial reconciliation following the 1998–99 civil war. However, the relative fragility that characterized those institutions, along with the hybrid character
of the "two publics" more generally, limited the extent to which this progress would
result in a deepening of the process of democratic consolidation.

A necessary starting point in understanding these limitations is the historical
evolution of urban political activism. As VonDoepp and Villalón suggest in the introduction to this volume (see chapter 1), attention to the historical-cultural context of the dynamic relationship between elites and institutions is necessary to fully
appreciate the extent of—and limitations to—democratic transition. The origins
of the cultural dualism within urban Guinea-Bissau lie in the colonial period, when
the town-centered segments of the petty bourgeoisie were politically groomed in

a political environment defined by the politics of autocracy and harsh economic policies.

Background to Democracy and Urban Activism

To a large extent, the historical roots of Guinea-Bissau's urban political life lie in the proto-nationalist political formation of *mestiço* (*crioulo* or creole) elite groupings in Bissau and Bolama in the 1910s–1920s (Havik 1995–99). These groupings were part of a long history of interethnic and interracial trading ties that hark back to the formation of commercial *entrepôts* (trading posts) in the towns of Portuguese Guinea (Havik 1995–99, 118; Galli and Jones 1987, 21, 28).[2] The initial political articulation of grievances by the *mestiço* community took place in 1911 with the formation of the *Liga Guineense* (Guinean League), which sought to assure a more democratic expansion of political rights as well as a more effective, national-scale implantation of the colonial bureaucracy (Havik 1995–99, 120–22). An additional, important inspiration for the activism of this *Liga* was to reduce the level of taxes and commercial tariffs imposed by the Portuguese state (Havik 1995–99, 121)—a crucial point, because the commercial interests of the proto-nationalist Guinea-Bissauan petty bourgeoisie would inspire similar bouts of political activism not only at various points during the remainder of the colonial period but also during the 1990s.

However, in the early 1910s, the *Liga Guineense*'s effectiveness and impact were diminished as a consequence of the extent of internal policy disagreements and factionalism that emerged within it (Havik 1995–99, 122–24). It also came to be viewed as a growing political threat by the Portuguese authorities, who abolished the *Liga* in 1915. The *mestiço* community reemerged during the late 1920s–1950s as assertive political activists opposed to the strict control over trade (especially regarding rice and peanuts) and authoritarian politics imposed by the Portuguese "New State" during these decades (Havik 1995–99, 123). Private farmer-traders— the so-called *ponteiros,* named because their trading-farms often occupied a point of land jutting out (like "points") into a river—formed loose alliances with *mestiço* employees within the public bureaucracy to promote free trade and upward mobility for *crioulo* speakers (Havik 1995–99, 124). Sports clubs facilitated the ability of young urban *mestiços* to provide a meeting-ground for political discussion; the 1948 creation of a short-lived Socialist Party of Guinea proved the forerunner of a flurry of small proto-nationalist political parties that emerged in the 1950s (Havik 1995–99, 130–31; Dhada 1993).

In addition to these sports clubs, it is important to take cognizance of the formation of "work clubs" (*clubos de trabalho*), such as Club Vélia and Club Palmeiro, which were created in the central towns, including Bissau, Bafatá, Farim, and Bolama (Cunha 1959, 38). These clubs, in addition to serving as social and cultural organizations, brought together young workers who were seeking ways to begin thinking about organizing politically so as to promote their long-term professional and political interests as would-be urban elites. These were not dominated by *mestiços*, but rather by a broad variety of individuals from indigenous ethnic groups who had gravitated into the tiny *crioulo*-speaking urban centers of Portuguese Guinea and were considered "detribalized" by colonial authorities (Cunha 1959, 42). These "work clubs" did not outright reject the legitimacy of the colonial system, but they often functioned as mutual aid societies to pay for colonial taxes, work tools, business license fees, or motor cars (in the case of professional chauffeurs). They often worked within the colonial economy, sought ways of organizing to improve their social conditions, and collected money to pay their own social expenses such as funeral costs, house construction, or health care (Cunha 1959, 39–40).

At the same time, they sought to assure that colonial laws were applied fairly to them. In doing so, however, they began the process of mobilizing for sectarian purposes: although broadly proto-nationalist, they did not work together but rather as social factions that competed with one another for greater rights and material benefits. Thus, an important aspect of early proto-nationalist political activity was the multiplicity of divisions based on language, educational level, and religion. Divisions were also (ominously) based on a broad split between indigenous Guinea-Bissauans from a variety of backgrounds, on the one hand, and the descendants of immigrants from Cape Verde and *mestiços,* on the other (Havik 1995–99, 131–32; Galli and Jones 1987, 23). This large division further weakened the nascent, urban-based, anticolonial activists through the 1950s–early 1960s, not only pitting those from a Cape Verdean (and *mestiço*) background against those from indigenous black African heritage but also compartmentalizing emergent political parties into ethnically and regionally defined categories (Dhada 1993).

Eventually, a political party created by highly educated intellectuals, the *Partido Africano da Independência da Guiné e Cabo Verde* (PAIGC), which operated largely in the rural areas, forged alliances with a broad spectrum of peasant actors by building on a tradition of inter-ethnic activism in the countryside (Forrest 2003, 181–201). The PAIGC would also succeed in incorporating into their mobilization efforts the aforementioned *ponteiros*—the commercial core of the *mestiço* community—and *mestiços* who worked at the lower administrative levels of the colonial administration (Forrest 2002).

The PAIGC acceded to national power in 1974 after a lengthy nationalist war. After independence, the PAIGC opted to pursue an economic policy favoring state control over markets, despite the pro-PAIGC support that had been provided by the *ponteiro* private traders (Forrest 2002). The 1974–85 period of PAIGC-led, government-controlled trade produced severe economic stagnation, in turn generating enormous popular discontent. Desperate to reverse the economic slide (the country was ranked by the United Nations in the bottom ten of the world's poorest nations), and under strong IMF and World Bank pressure to join sub-Saharan Africa's collective shift toward privatized economies, the government of President Nino Vieira agreed to legalize private trading-farm concessions in 1985. This made possible the reintroduction of the *ponteiros,* not only into the formal Guinea-Bissauan economy but also, informally, more directly into the country's political life. As in the early episodes of *mestiço* activism, here again the *ponteiros'* reconsolidation of political ties in Bolama, Bissau, Cacheu, and other towns was manifested by the formation of strongly divided, multiple networks of commercial-politico actors (Havik 1995–99, 139).

Moreover, the IMF/World Bank structural adjustment program was implemented in Guinea-Bissau (as of 1987) in a way that assured that the credit-distribution program would be headed by state elites, who favored personal contacts among the cashew- and rice-producing *ponteiros*. This, in turn, exacerbated the extent of socioeconomically driven divisiveness and inequality, which now became directly linked to the problem of *political* factionalism (Havik 1995–99, 144). One reason for this was that competition ensued among state bureaucrats for access to the structural adjustment disbursements, reflecting the "privatization of the state" such that political power differentials were reinforced according to those who were able to provide credits to *ponteiros* (Havik 1995–99, 144–45). As this occurred, structural adjustment bore a decidedly negative outcome on the overall quality of economic life in the countryside, with peasants suffering the ill effects of consumer price increases (Havik 1995–99, 146).

It is within this context that disquiet mounted among urban civil-societal elites, who sought political change in a pluralistic direction as a way of broadening access to economic decision-making. When this social pressure was combined with strong international pressure to follow up the privatizing reforms with liberalization in the political realm, the president and his associates within the ruling PAIGC initiated the process of democratic transition. At the second "Extraordinary Congress" of the PAIGC in 1991, the party leadership moved forward with the legalization of new political parties, a new guarantee of free and fair elections, as well as with an internal democratization of the PAIGC itself (Havik 1995–99, 152–55). This latter process was important because it suggested the extent to which a segment of the urban political elite—members of the PAIGC—recognized, and struggled to address and revise, the general anti-participatory character of the PAIGC (Dhada 2001, 86–87). This process gave rise to a "backbencher" constellation of young party cadres, calling themselves the "Group of 121," who demanded internal party reform. This intra-party opposition represented a greater threat to President Vieira and to party leaders than did the process of creating a multiparty opening (Dhada 2002; Havik 1995–99).

The move toward internal PAIGC democratization had taken place precisely to rebroaden the popular base of the party—according to party leaders, through the inclusion of lower-ranking party cadres in decision-making and party voting and by trying to revivify various regional-level party organs. However, the process of internal party democratization had, in fact, failed to achieve the goal of seriously opening up procedures to give younger cadres a meaningful stake in party decision-making. As a result, even before the 1994 elections took place, the Group of 121 backbenchers, realizing the limited impact of their internal reform efforts, abandoned the PAIGC altogether and created a new opposition party (one of many, as indicated below). This guaranteed that the Vieira-led PAIGC would emerge as an elite-oriented political party. Indeed, by the time of the party's 1999 National Conference, the percentage of peasant attendees had declined to a mere 10 percent; by contrast, an overwhelming 73 percent of those attending were directly affiliated with the urban-based central state (Cardoso 2001).

Guinea-Bissau's Democratic Opening and Founding Elections

As the pace of reform mounted, Guinea-Bissau's democratic opening was continually marked by the struggle between the aforementioned "two publics," and by tension between authoritarian and democratic tendencies. Momentum toward democratization was sustained by elements of urban civil society (workers, educated youth, businesspeople) attracted by the potential opportunities of a rules-abiding constitutional framework. Important institutional developments exemplified the liberalizing trend, including the creation and mobilization of new opposition political parties; founding multiparty presidential and parliamentary elections (1994) and second elections (1999); and the introduction of debates within parliament, through which opposition members seriously challenged ruling party decision-making. The newly inaugurated institutional framework generated growing expectations by urban factions regarding their ability to engage in critical debate and to compete electorally for political power. In this regard, pluralistic values were promoted by Guinea-Bissau's democratic institutions. Here, it is also important to note that certain segments of the armed forces would act as a further institutional source of stability for Guinea-Bissau's fledgling democracy.

Nonetheless, members of the urban political milieu, including both the very highest political leaders and key players in the opposition, could not cleanly disentangle themselves from more fractious and autocratic inheritances. Prior to democratization in the 1990s, the culture of intolerance was reflected by the formation of single-party regimes characterized by personalist autocracy. These included the government of President Luiz Cabral (1974–80), followed by the harsh rulership of President João "Nino" Vieira, who had unseated Cabral in a 1980 coup d'état.

With the liberalization of politics, the inherited zero-sum cultural tendencies were especially evident in the activities of the new political opposition that emerged to challenge the Vieira regime.

The 1991–94 period of political-party pluralism, which preceded and helped to make possible the country's first multiparty elections, witnessed an extraordinary outpouring of pluralistic expression; however, that early, initial democratic opening proved highly unstable. In 1991, stipulations were enacted that were intended to lessen the potential for the new political parties to multiply in a way that might lead to disorder. Thus, the minimal rules for legal approval of a political party necessitated obtaining a minimum of 1,000 signatures—60 in each of the country's regions—as well as the forbidding of tribally based parties. It was decided that once new opposition parties were established and given time to campaign, national parliamentary elections would be held. A total of 102 delegates would be elected to the unicameral national legislature. The electoral system divided the country into twenty-nine multimember districts, with legislative seats allocated on the basis of proportional representation within those districts. A direct popular presidential election was to be held separately (Dhada 2001, 88).

A number of opposition parties officially registered by the end of 1991, most of which critiqued the PAIGC for failing to manage the economic readjustment program in a way that improved living standards. These parties also attacked the ruling party for its culture of secrecy and rulership through clientelism. Opposition-party leaders such as Rafael Barbosa, Vitor Saude Maria, Vitor Mandinga, and Aristides Menezes were intimately familiar with the PAIGC, as they had played key roles in the party leadership or the state bureaucracy at earlier stages of their own political careers or during the country's independence struggle (Havik 1995–99, 154). This, in turn, represented a relative weakness of the new opposition parties formed by such elites, such as the Democratic Front (FD), the Social Democratic Front (FDS), and the Party of Social Democracy (PUSD). It was not clear whether and to what extent they would be able to generate political support outside the urban areas in which they had established their political contacts, that is, Bissau and Bafatá (Havik 1995–99, 155).

A second wave of political-party creation in 1992 resulted in the formation of new parties formerly associated with the ruling party or representing breakaway factions of the first wave of parties. This second wave of parties appeared to hold a greater potential to wield a significant influence on multiparty expansion because their respective leaders had followings within Guinea-Bissau's towns and in pockets of the countryside. As such, they represented a more legitimate electoral threat than did the initial spate of parties created as breakaways from the PAIGC. This second wave of opposition leaders and parties included João da Costa, head of the Party of Renovation and Development (PRD); Filinto Vaz Martins, leader of the Movement for Unity and Democracy (MUD); and Kumba Yala, head of the Party of Social Renovation (PRS) (Havik 1995–99, 155). Most of the members of the PRD formed part of the Group of 121, the aforementioned PAIGC dissidents who had abandoned the ruling party. Kumba Yala of the PRS was a highly popular politician respected for his image of integrity and intelligence, who managed to win support from a broad variety of ethnic groups. Portending the new organizational and mobilizational opportunities for these parties was the legalization of opposition newspapers in 1992 and the access of opposition parties to radio and television outlets.

However, despite the flourishing of political activity in this environment, opposition parties and political leaders repeatedly demonstrated impatience, mutual suspicion, and political immaturity by creating factional blocks that often shifted in membership or allegiance (Havik 1995–99, 156). Helping to ensure a sense of growing distrust among opposition leaders was a broad suspicion of former PAIGC cadres (apart from the Group of 121) who were now playing the role of opposition party activists. One important example was that of Rafael Barbosa, a founding member of the PAIGC, who had previously abandoned his erstwhile party and became a key figure within the FDS. Other opposition figures suspected Barbosa of retaining close links with the PAIGC, and planning to win forthcoming elections simply to ensure the appearance of ruling party *alternance*. This suspicion helped raise support for parties led by younger activists respected for their relative independence and forthrightness. This included Kumba Yala of the PRS and Domingos Fernandes Gomes of the *Resistência da Guiné-Bissau Movimento-Bafatá* (RGB-MB) (Dhada 2001, 86–87). Smaller parties such as the *Partido Unido Social Democrático* led by Vitor Saúde Maria, a well-liked former prime minister, essentially demonstrated the extent to which the opposition had become divided into an overabundance of political tendencies and leader-specific groupings. Maria attracted a corps of support but could not adequately broaden his appeal; the problem was that the diversity of the political-party playing field and the difficulty of cross-party alliance-building helped to assure a splintering of the opposition.

Disputes among the members of political opposition parties ensued over the very process of democratization, including disagreements over exactly how long parties needed to prepare for national elections. When President Nino Vieira, in May 1994, announced that those elections would be held in July 1994, and that there would be only a three-week campaign period (beginning June 11, 1994), opposition party leaders predictably complained loudly, even while continuing to bicker amongst themselves over what recourse they should pursue (Havik 1995–99, 157). There were also inter-party disputes over whether the military should be allowed a role in the new political system, and there were generational splits between young activists and older independence war veterans (Dhada 2001, 86–87).

An effort by a handful of opposition leaders to overcome this infighting and create an alliance finally did produce a partial coalition, *União para a Mudança* (UM), including the Barbosa-led FDS, the da Costa–led PRD, and several other smaller parties (including the Ecology Party) (Dhada 2001, 87). This UM coalition ran as a single party in the 1994 elections, and ended up receiving the fourth-highest vote total. However, it did not manage to attract a broad enough span of popular support outside the urban areas to out-compete the RGMB, the PRS, or the ruling PAIGC. Ultimately it was the latter, incumbent party—exploiting its dominance of the media, the state administrative structure, and a general lack of familiarity in the countryside with most opposition party figures—that obtained a majority of parliamentary seats. The PAIGC retained control of the national parliament by winning 62 seats in the 1994 legislative elections, in contrast to the 19 seats won by the Social Renovation Movement-Bafatá (RGMB), 12 seats by the PRS, 6 seats by the Union for Change (UM), and 1 seat for FLING (other parties obtained too few votes to obtain parliamentary seats) (Forrest 2002).[3] In the presidential balloting, President Vieira won the first round with 46 percent of the vote, as opposition party candidates' votes were divided mainly between Kumba Yala (21 percent) of the PRS and Domingos Fernandes Gomes (17 percent) of the RGMB. All candidates inundated the political discourse with harsh charges and counter-charges of corruption, flouting of the law, Mobutism, and rules violations (Dhada 2001, 88–89). In the end, Vieira was able to pull in a concordance of votes not only from the urban zones, where he had built strong bases of support, but also from the eastern regions, which are dominated by Islamic peoples who had strongly opposed the PAIGC at the start of the post-independence period (in the mid- to late 1970s) (Havik 1995–99, 159). This change in part reflected the fact that Muslim ethnic groups such as the Mandinga and Fulbe did not have strong ties to the opposition parties, but it also reflected their appreciation of Vieira's approval (in the late 1980s) of the restoration of traditional chiefships, and might have reflected an expectation that Vieira would win the presidency and that it would be strategically wise to demonstrate support for the incumbent. In the presidential runoff, Vieira obtained 52 percent of the votes, mostly from the urban areas and the eastern regions, with Yala demonstrating significant support in the north and in the south—based largely on his charisma and his reputation for integrity, trustworthiness, and competence—and gaining a national total of 47 percent of the vote (Havik 1995–99, 159; Dhada 2001, 88; Forrest 2002).

Guinea-Bissau's founding elections of 1994 suggest the emergence of a sophisticated electorate interested in selecting out from the opposition smorgasbord those leaders and parties devoted to development and reflecting capable and competent leadership abilities. Voters' strong interest in candidate quality, economic issues, and the cross-ethnic character of the balloting process may be regarded as important progress toward democratization. However, the highly factionalized character of the political opposition tempered such progress. The roots of this factionalism lie less in institutional dynamics than in historical, economic and cultural tendencies. Although the proportional representation system may have encouraged a high degree of oppositional pluralism, the difficulty of political factions to work together must primarily be ascribed to deeply entrenched habits of political factionalism and unilateral political behavior in urban Guinea-Bissau. In this respect, the patterns and sources of political behavior in Guinea-Bissau resemble those characterizing key players in Zambia's new democracy, as depicted by David Simon in this volume.

The 1998 Civil War and Second Elections

The limitations of Guinea-Bissau's democratic opening and its founding multiparty elections of 1994 were also visible regarding presidential behavior and the continuation of economic decline in the aftermath of those elections. The initial electoral experience did not help to restrain the autocratic character of the Vieira personalist regime, nor did it lead to a halt in the country's economic deterioration. These two factors contributed substantially to the subsequent rebellion of the country's armed forces in 1998, which quickly expanded into a popularly supported war against President Vieira. In the end, the rebel sector of the army successfully ousted President Vieira and his loyalists. From this perspective, the 1994 transition may be considered more flawed than successful. Divisions within the Guinea-Bissauan polity proved too wide, and the initial democratization process could not mend the breach.

President Vieira's own authoritarian presidential behavior in the 1995–98 period made clear that the 1994 founding democratic election had not generated the type of rules-respecting leadership required to further strengthen (much less consolidate) the process of democratic transition. Indeed, after the 1994 founding elections, President Vieira grew increasingly "bonapartistic"—flagrantly intervening in other government and civil society institutions, removing perceived opponents from the government, and proving intolerant of criticism. In these respects, Vieira pursued the path previously tread by such "electoral autocrats" as Mobutu, Moi, and Mugabe, making a mockery of the concept of electoral legitimization by relying on the national police to harass or imprison opposition party activists and nongovernmental media personnel.

Vieira's growing political detachment from the rural sector (the majority of the country), his alienation from his own army, and his overall abuse of the 1994 electoral mandate culminated, in 1998, with the outbreak of civil war in Guinea-Bissau. That war was precipitated by President Vieira's decision to remove from office his army chief-of-staff, Ansumane Mané, and to rely increasingly on a hardened core of pro-Vieira loyalists while isolating himself from the majority of his own officer corps (Forrest 2002, 255–59). Mané was highly popular among the general soldiery, and Vieira may have resented Mané, especially in the wake of the president's own declining popularity (Dhada 2002, 92). It is important to emphasize that the broader political context was one in which President's Vieira's long-term economic misrule and autocratic repression had generated intensive and widening enmity toward the president, both within society at large and within the armed forces (Forrest 2003, 230). The majority of the country's soldiers increasingly gathered around pro-Mané officers after Mané's dismissal, separating themselves from pro-Vieira loyalist soldiers. President Vieira's regime had become so fully delegitimized that many soldiers sensed a broad (if unarticulated) political mandate to challenge the president's right to rule; Vieira's perceived mistreatment of Mané served as adequate motivation and catalyzed the rebels' mobilization. Ensuing battles between pro-Mané rebels and loyalist factions took place in Bissau, but soon spread to key barracks located in various rural regions (Forrest 2002, 255–59; Dhada 2002, 92). Most soldiers decided to attach themselves to rebel columns; in response, President Vieira requested—and received—the support of Senegalese army sharpshooters, who were sent to Guinea-Bissau on the legal justification of a mutual defense pact that had been signed by the two countries in previous years (Ndiaye 2000).

Guinea-Bissau's rebel forces shocked the Francophone *tirailleurs* (sharpshooters) with their savvy fighting ability, both in the eastern regions, where several Senegalese troop battalions had been sent, and in Bissau, where rebel street fighters outgunned both the Senegalese and the remaining Guinea-Bissauan loyalist troops

(Forrest 2002, 259–60). When the last of the Senegalese had been killed or forced to flee by the Guinea-Bissauan rebel soldiery, loyalist army factions could no longer turn back the tide of the anti-Vieira rebellion, and the president's bonapartist dream collapsed. Vieira fled to Lisbon, and a transitional regime was pieced together in the first months of 1999 by the victorious military junta—generals and army commanders who had led the uprising and who now appointed a number of civilian administrators and politicians to manage the political system. Most of the appointees were either unaffiliated with the Vieira regime or were presumed trustworthy by the rebel (now ruling) generals.

After several months of junta rulership, to the surprise of many observers, the junta decided to restore the democratic process and to hold national elections as soon as they could be arranged. It was widely assumed that a strong motive behind this decision was the country's desperate need to obtain financial credit and humanitarian aid after suffering massive economic devastation during the 1998 civil war, and the presumption that the holding of a new national vote would hurry this process along. Moreover, it appeared likely that the junta would somehow seek to remain strongly involved in the political process, either shaping the electoral outcome in their favor or entering their own presidential candidate—presumably Ansumane Mané, head of the junta—in the upcoming elections.

However, after wavering for a number of months, Mané decided not to enter the presidential campaign himself but rather to support the presidential candidacy of the interim president Malam Bacai Sanha, who had been appointed by the junta and who had its full backing. The junta then proceeded to allow a broad array of already-formed political parties—those who had participated in the founding election five years earlier—to contest separate parliamentary and presidential ballots in November and December 1999. In the November 1999 parliamentary balloting, the PRS won a plurality, and the right to form a new government, with 38 of parliament's 102 seats; the RG-MB obtained 28 seats, becoming the second leading party in the national assembly; and the PAIGC was reduced to the third legislative party, with 24 seats (*Africa Research Bulletin* 2000b). A sprinkling of additional opposition parties also obtained representation, including the Democratic Alliance (4 seats), the Union for Change (3 seats), the Social Democratic Party (3 seats), and the National Union for Democracy and Progress (1 seat). Here it deserves noting that although the majority party was designated to form the government, the powers of the dominant parliamentary party were in practice quite weak; real power lay in the hands of the president, which meant that the outcome of the presidential elections would prove more politically significant than the parliamentary ballot.

The first round of presidential voting was held in December 1999; a plurality of candidates emerged, with the top two vote-getters, interim president Malam Bacai Sanha and Kumba Yala of the PRS, then competing in a runoff in January 2000. That contest was won handily by Yala, who captured 72 percent of the votes cast (*Africa Research Bulletin* 2000a). To his credit, Sanha immediately accepted the outcome, and to the credit of the junta, there was no hint of military dissatisfaction or intervention despite the fact that Sanha had been their preferred candidate. Yala was allowed to take control of the presidency exactly according to the electoral timetable (the following month, February 2000). Moreover, all three balloting events (parliamentary, first-round, and second-round presidential votes) were declared free, fair, and transparent by international observers (*Africa Research Bulletin* 2000a).

It is important to observe that it was the military rebel junta, consisting of the leaders of the uprising, who assumed power after the defeat of the Vieira regime following the 1998–99 war and led the country to its second set of free and fair democratic elections. Even more significantly, the ruling junta then allowed the newly elected presidential candidate, who had *not* been the preferred candidate of the military junta, to assume the presidency as scheduled in February 2000. It should also be underlined that the former ruling party, the PAIGC, appeared to accept its new role as opposition party.

The army's behavior in overseeing this transition suggests its key institutional role as democratic guide and referee. The formal re-installment of a multiparty parliament and a parliamentary political order is impressive in itself, and is suggestive of the extent to which a strong cadre of influential elites within and outside of the national government have been committed to struggling for a rules-based polity grounded in electoral legitimacy rather than violent contestation. The joining of the erstwhile ruling PAIGC to the new parliament suggested progress toward elite pact formation in terms of a broad acceptance of the democratic rules of the political process.

At the same time, however, the depth of this democratic commitment and pact-making ought not to be exaggerated. The ruling army commanders who so impressively managed the transition to democracy in late 1999–early 2000 were exactly the same people who, a year-and-a-half earlier, had instigated the civil war. Indeed, the democratic institutions that were erected in 1994 were not able to serve as channels of popular protest, and did not prove capable of providing discontented elites (much less the majority of the people) with an effective mechanism of regime displacement or even of popular protest. Nor did Guinea-Bissau's democratic institutions in the 1990s serve to constrain the bonapartist, autocratic, and repressive tendencies of President Vieira. On the contrary, he had managed to abuse those institutions to such a degree that, in a real sense, popular discontent could only have been mobilized through a violent uprising rather than through more democratic practices such as opposition party organizing. In this respect, the experience of Guinea-Bissau resembles that of Madagascar in the aftermath of third presidential elections (see the chapter by Marcus in this volume).

Here again, the notion of the "two publics" and a divided political culture helps to make sense of the range of political behavior engaged in by Guinea-Bissau's political elites, referring especially to the choice to engage in open rebellion in 1998 and the choice to return to a democratic order in 1999–2000. The turn toward war in 1998 meant that military and political elites were not accepting of the permanent legitimacy of democratic institutions and of democratic rules for their own sake, particularly in a context in which those institutions were used by political leaders (even if elected) to reinforce their own power and to exclude urban civil society and rural civil society from de facto, meaningful access to the political process. Nondemocratic options remained under consideration, and the subsequent embrace of democratic politics must be viewed as partial and conditional. Still, assuming that democratic institutions appeared to function in a way that opens the door to meaningful political participation, elites in Guinea-Bissau have been positively disposed to embrace those institutions. This was reflected in the late 1999–early 2000 restoration of electoral legitimization as the primary process through which the national leadership accedes to power. Notably, the military junta itself not only successfully managed the post–civil war transition back to multiparty democracy by holding a second set of national elections but also insisted on the practice of democratic values by assuring that only civilian (and not military) candidates compete for the votes of the citizenry. A positive disposition toward democratic institutions was clearly at play here, as was elite participation in democratic pact-making by embracing the return to democratic rule-playing. In this respect, as we noted earlier, even a partial and conditional embrace of electoral institutions can have pro-democratic consequences.

Among those consequences in Guinea-Bissau was the installment of a newly elected government. In early 2000, the ruling PRS created a cabinet that included members of RG-MB and other opposition parties that had supported Kumba Yala in the second round (*Africa Research Bulletin* 2000c). President-elect Yala began office as an immensely popular politician, reflecting his prior role as opposition mobilizer; now as the post-second election began, the question was whether Yala's rulership would further strengthen a commitment to democratic institutions, or whether his presidency would reflect the historically entrenched autocratic-cum-liberal syncretism of Guinea-Bissau's hybrid political culture.

Presidential Bonapartism
and a Divided Political Culture

President Yala's first six months in office (the first half of 2000) were marked by the emergence of serious tensions between Yala and General Ansumane Mané, reflecting the fact that Mané sought to retain some political influence while Yala was anxious to consolidate his presidential powers. This closely paralleled the tensions that undid the presidency of Nino Vieira in the 1990s. Here again, in the early 2000s, bonapartism, zero-sum politics, and authoritarian behavior reemerged, even as the institutional framework of a new democracy had now been established. The mixture of institutional democratization with a dysfunctional intensification of internal disputation characterized the second democratic interregnum.

The armed forces once again became characterized by the formation of politically charged factions, with a number of soldiers backing Mané, while others supported Yala, wanting to see their generals recede from the political process (Dias 2000). The complexity of this division should be understood as more than a simple tug of war between military and democratic power; Mané was at least in part determined to assure that the civil war and the country's second elections had not been fought in vain, that is, that they had not simply produced another autocratic head of state. Mané's concerns would eventually prove prescient, but not before tensions between the erstwhile junta leader and the president reached a violent conclusion.

In November 2000, tensions between President Kumba Yala and Mané heightened over Mané's rejection of Yala's army officer appointees. Interestingly, it was this same issue—presidential intervention in internal army appointments—that had (among other incentives) provoked Nino Vieira to stage a coup d'état and to assume the presidency of Guinea-Bissau in 1980 (Forrest 1987). Twenty years later, President Yala, perhaps in reflection of this prior event, overreacted and sought the arrest of General Mané to undercut a potential coup effort. Troops loyal to President Yala tracked and found the general, and then proceeded to brutally murder him. Although this ended what Yala assumed was a potential threat to his presidency, intra-military factionalism remained acute due to the loyalty of Mané's supporters, their horror at what had been done to Mané, as well as their more general determination that the armed forces be allowed to play a background role as an institutional check on presidential overreach (Dias 2000).

Religious complexities also became inserted into the cauldron of tensions that increasingly pervaded Guinea-Bissau's polity. From 1995 until 2001, a small Islamic group known as Ahmadiyya with strong Pakistani roots and membership sought to expand its influence within Guinea-Bissau. The group was distinguished by its unorthodox religious beliefs, including a rejection of the necessity to make a pilgrimage to Mecca and a claim that its founder (Ahmady) is a prophet.[4] In August 2001, President Yala suddenly decided to expel the entire group from Guinea-Bissau. The president explained in a meeting with 500 Muslim clerics that not only were the beliefs of Ahmadiyya rejected by most Muslims in the country but also that Ahmadiyya's adherents were interfering in Guinea-Bissau's political life (Integrated Regional Information Network 2001b). It is not clear what the president meant by this, but Yala's pedantic lecturing to Muslim clerics is unlikely to have been well received. The controversial nature of the expulsion was reflected in the resignation of the president's religious advisor, Sory Djalo (a Muslim), claiming that he was not consulted.

President Kumba Yala's strong-handed presidential style became increasingly manifested in a number of policy areas and issue disputes, calling into question his ability to resist reproducing the autocratic tendencies of his predecessors. As noted by the Guinea-Bissauan political analyst Carlos Cardoso, with his election to the presidency, Kumba Yala demonstrated a type of presidential bonapartism duplicative of the autocratic leadership of Nino Vieira against which Yala had strenuously railed (Cardoso 2001). Under Yala's leadership, the national government jailed journalists accused of favoring opposition political parties, and detained and questioned suspected anti-PRS activists (Mendes 2001). A progression of government-provoked violent incidents and illegal detentions led Amnesty International to call for a thoroughgoing investigation of human rights violations in Guinea-Bissau in September 2001.[5] Government-inspired acts of violence helped to provoke a political atmosphere characterized by fear and instability. This was made especially clear by President Yala's firing of the country's director of state security, Baciro Dabo, on suspicion of coup-plotting (Mendes 2001). Such actions support the interpretation of Yala as pursuing the path of presidential bonapartism originally carved out by Nino Vieira, who had commonly invented pretexts on the basis of which he proceeded to purge his real or imagined enemies. Under Yala's rule, the murder of Mané, the ouster of an Islamic group, and the persistent abuse of human rights through unwarranted jailing and harassment of opposition activists all made clear that political elites in Guinea-Bissau would deviate substantially from a rules-based democratic culture if it was in their interest to do so.

In regard to ethnic policy, President Yala, despite enjoying extensive political support from communities reflecting a broad diversity of ethnic backgrounds, packed the key organs of the state with members of his own Balanta group. These included the prime minister, the vice prime minister, military officials, dozens of mid-level public administrators, and thirty-five sector presidents (sectors are local government units)—all appointed in the first weeks of Yala's rulership (Mendes 2001; Dias 2000). This Balanta ethnic favoritism is to some extent replicative of the narrow, cliquey style of rulership established by Yala's presidential predecessor; however, important caveats are in order. First, the Balanta are Guinea-Bissau's most numerous ethnic group, representing approximately a third of the overall population. Second, the Balanta were historically exploited by the Portuguese and were targeted for repression—including execution of Balanta leaders on trumped-up charges—during Vieira's regime. They were also alienated from all political institutions throughout the postcolonial period until Yala's election (Forrest 1992, 59–62). Thus, the appointment of Balanta to a large percentage of high-level positions can be considered to have represented an effort to implement de facto affirmative action. Considering their long history of exclusion, most Balanta would have probably been outraged had Yala failed to promote Balanta within the government, because they would have regarded him as continuing the ethnic discrimination of the past. In this sense, Balanta affirmative action applied within the country's public sector may actually have helped to forestall ethnically inspired unrest.

The issue of Yala's promotion of Balanta interests illuminates the considerable ambiguity that surrounds the question of whether Yala was acting as an electoral autocrat or a democratic statesman. The same can be said of his efforts to promote the security of his government from potential internal threats. For example, during most of 2000, Prime Minister Caetano N'Tchama and selected units of the armed forces (particularly the police and marine sharpshooters) consolidated ties behind the scenes. At the same time, Minister of the Interior Artur Sanha appeared to pose a threat to the president's control over the state administration through his (Sanha's) command over the well-armed and specially trained (by France) Rapid Intervention Forces of the Police and State Security (Mendes 2001). Moreover, Prime Minister N'Tchama and Minister Sanha each headed mini-factions within the armed forces that represented potential sources of political instability for the Yala regime. In this highly unsettled context, it may well be interpreted as a mark of presidential leadership—not simply bonapartism, but also self-protection and a defense of electoral democracy itself in a highly unstable context—that Yala removed the head of state security. The highly combustible political context in post–civil war Guinea-Bissau enables us to interpret some of Yala's strong-headed measures as contributing to stability and to the continuity of at least the formalistic trappings of democracy, even if this occurred at the expense of the broader popular political legitimacy of his government.

Ultimately, Yala's rulership reflected the dual set of values that have operated in Guinea-Bissau. This entails the germination of proto-democratic priorities within the political opposition (of which Yala had been a part) during the democratic opening, as well as the inheritance of authoritarian values that continued to shape the behavior of the Guinea-Bissauan president and the ruling party (the PRS) after their ascension to power via the ballot box in a second election. With respect to the latter, Yala's presidency offers a refractive, mirrored glare from the post-1994 period of Vieira's rulership. In both cases, elected presidents relied on formal democratic legitimization to further consolidate personalistic regimes through strong-handed, even militaristic actions that at times meant the setting aside of basic rules requisite to democratic pluralism. This is what Cardoso means by presidential bonapartism, or, we might say, electorally legitimated personal autocracy. In effect, the trappings of democratic institutions shielded these presidents (both Vieira and Yala) and provided them with sufficient international and domestic approval so that when opponents were removed from office on unspecified charges or when opposition activists were harassed or jailed, the president was nonetheless able to carry on as before, waving the banner of electoral confirmation.

The similarities extend to their respective departures from political power as well. Just as democratically elected Vieira was effectively chased from power by a majoritarian faction of the military, so too was Yala. By 2001, in the wake of the tendencies described above, relations between Yala and representatives of other government branches had begun to deteriorate considerably. Late in the year he dismissed and later arrested three Supreme Court justices on charges of corruption—a move that brought condemnation not only from domestic political forces, but also from the United Nations and Amnesty International.[6] The following year, as the government failed for five months to pay civil servants, he came into an open dispute with the prime minister, Alamara Nhasse (his former interior minister), whom he accused of incompetence with respect to tax collection. In response, in November 2002, Yala dissolved parliament, calling for legislative elections.[7] Although elections were required by law to be held in three months time, the government delayed the conducting of the polls four times. The final rescheduling, announced on September 13, was clearly indicative of Yala's disinterest in the reinstatement of parliament and led to army intervention and a bloodless coup the following day,

September 14, 2003. As described below, the army chief of staff who had led the coup, General Verissimo Correia Seabra, then became head of a transitional government, which was designated to leave power as soon as elections were held.

This political hybridity was similarly manifest in urban civil society, including elites who were associated with the government and those who were not. Some elements within the political opposition appeared to genuinely favor a continuity of free and fair elections and embraced the diversity of political parties. Growing numbers of students, the intelligentsia, journalists, businesspeople, and party activists (including some current and former PAIGC members) insisted on the need to abide by formal rules that promoted behavioral pluralism. However, the splintered character of urban political activism and the zero-sum attitudes embraced by some activists must also be considered a significant factor in the limited ability of the political opposition to struggle for a fuller expansion of democratic rights, despite the second elections. Thus, the struggle between authoritarian and liberal values takes place within the heart of the state leadership as well as within and among political parties active in town-based political life.

These dualistic tendencies are also evident within Guinea-Bissau's armed forces. Despite having suffered an all-out civil war, involving massive relocations and thousands of deaths, the country's military leadership managed to guide the country to free and fair second elections in 1999–2000 and allowed the popularly chosen presidential candidate (Yala) to assume office. This occurred even though the junta had made clear their preference for the second-place vote-getter, and suggests the emergence in the heart of the military leadership of proto-democratic values, including respect for constitutional rules, neutrality, a commitment to electoral procedures, and political tolerance. It further highlights the fact that, despite the civil war of 1998, the military in Guinea-Bissau served as a "republican" barrier to democratic breakdown.

The armed forces again played this role in September 2003, when General Verissimo Correia Seabra and other military commanders successfully carried out a bloodless coup d'état—removing the increasingly autocratic President Yala from power without any loss of life—and established a transitional National Council headed by General Seabra. This military-dominated council proposed a six-month timeline for national parliamentary elections and appointed an interim president, Henrique Pereira Rosa. The army kept fast to this timeline, quickly recreating a pluralistic political climate in which a dozen opposition political parties and three multiparty alliances became mobilized and campaigned in earnest for parliamentary elections to be held in March 2004. By the end of February 2004, 740,457 voters had been registered for those elections—representing a major increase from 1999, when 523,507 were registered; this increase was suggestive both of technical improvements in the registration process and of the extent of popular enthusiasm for this 2004 voting opportunity (*Publico* 2004; *Angola Press* 2004). At the time of this writing, balloting for those elections was in process; it was clear that the 102 parliamentary seats would be divided among a heterogeneous set of political parties and alliances. New presidential elections were scheduled for March 2005.

The important point here is the fact that, both in 2000 and in 2004, it was the army that assured Guinea-Bissau's return to democracy and that restored the primacy of the country's electoral institutions. This verifies the insight made by Von-Doepp and Villalón in this volume's introduction that, in recent years, the military in Africa has often acted as a decisively pro-democratic political institution (see chapter 1, this volume). Here we may add that, in some cases, the military may in fact be considered part of the institutional framework of democracy that has importantly influenced the behavior of political elites in a way that encourages consensual norms and conformity to fair rule-playing. That said, however, it should be added that in Guinea-Bissau, the political values that are predominant within the armed forces are more broadly reflective of the syncretistic hybridity that is characteristic of the political culture of urban civil society. For the soldiery as for political elites more generally, violence remains an option and may be perceived to be justifiable by leaders if political institutions (the presidency in particular) fail to allow for the articulation of alternative views and give rise to autocratic or repressive policymaking. This was made clear both by the army-instigated rebellion of 1998–99 and by the military intervention of September 2003. Thus, the commitment to rule-abiding behavior is somewhat conditional. Nonetheless, the pro-democratic side of that conditionality, with the armed forces in both cases moving to assure the country's transition back to a reliance on electoral institutions, is suggestive of the extent to which consensus-oriented values can prevail in a favorable political environment.

▼▼▼▼

This discussion has focused on the urban core in which electoral democracy has been introduced to Guinea-Bissau. Urban political participation continues to be characterized by a "two publics" division and a simultaneous struggle between liberal and authoritarian values. Still, the fact that a substantial portion of this struggle between 1994 and 2004 took place among electorally competitive elites represents a noteworthy change from the univision single-party framework of the 1970s and 1980s. One of the central strands of the flourishing of economic, social, and political life in precolonial Guinea-Bissau was the interethnic heterogeneity of human relations; by no means is it clear that this social diversity can be shifted to the political plane of pluralist democracy, but the effort of *some* political elites to do so could point the country's political future in a more tolerant direction. The fact is that a number of elites within and outside of the government have pressed hard to assure a continuing commitment to democratic institutions and respect for the electoral process, and this has helped to provide some actors with a degree of political restraint.

Furthermore, the second election represented a significant institutional factor in making possible a greater degree of political party inclusion than was formerly the case. The multiparty National Assembly was in early 2002 engaged in serious deliberation of key policy agenda items, including economic development programs, a restructuring of the legal system, and organizing local-level elections (United Nations Security Council 2002)). Potentially, this may serve to help set the stage for further policy activism by the national parliament following the March 2004 elections.

Overall, Guinea-Bissau's hybrid political order suggests the importance of democratic institutions for promoting political pluralism and counterchecking (or at least modestly restraining) autocratic elite tendencies, but also makes clear the extent to which elite political behavior is reflective of a syncretistic inheritance of values that promote both rules-abiding political behavior and zero-sum factionalism. When thinking about the importance of elite political culture that was emphasized in this volume's introduction, and in reflecting on the "meaning of second elections" as raised by Michael Bratton (1999b), we may suggest that while Guinea-Bissau's second elections have played an important role in furthering the potential for political reconciliation, intolerant political attitudes also persist. Elite fragmentation and a hybrid political culture is reflected in the embrace of a pluralistic political order by a portion of urban political actors, while other urban elites opt for more autocratically oriented or violence-prone political behavior. In regard to the country's president during the post–second election period, President Yala did not display the same degree of repression as his counterpart, Nino Vieira, did during the post–first election period (1994–99), but Yala's intolerance of the political opposition and his ignorance of institutional rules grew more dramatically evident each year of his presidency. The army's bloodless intervention in September 2003 and the subsequent redirection back toward a democratic electoral path, along with the remobilization of urban civil society and the open political campaigning by parties in early 2004, are strongly suggestive of the pro-democracy tendencies that have struggled to establish a more institutionalized democratic order. More generally, the holding of the 1999–2000 second elections, the 2004 transition back to a pluralistic political framework, the overall protective republican role played by the armed forces, and the range of critical opposition voices within the multiparty parliament represent important pro-democratic institutional influences and suggest movement toward more a consensual embrace of common rules, despite the fractious and non-consensual behavioral patterns that are also manifested within Guinea-Bissau's hybrid urban political milieu.

NOTES

1. On contingent factors in the process of democratic transition, see Bratton and de Walle (1997, 184–86).

2. On the inter-ethnic character of politics in Guinea-Bissau, see Forrest (2003).

3. The disjuncture between the actual percentage of votes obtained by the UM, on

the one hand, and its share of legislative seats, on the other, reflected the nature of the electoral system—a proportional representation system with twenty-nine multimember districts.

4. Integrated Regional Information Network, "Government Expels Ahmadiyya Islamic Group," August 21, 2001. Available at: http://allafrica.com/stories/200108220376.html. Accessed October 14, 2004.

5. Integrated Regional Information Network, "Amnesty International Calls For Investigations," September 8, 2001. Available at: http://allafrica.com/stories/200109080002.html. Accessed October 14, 2004.

6. *BBC News Online*, "Guinea-Bissau Arrests Top Judges," November 15, 2001. Available at: http://news.bbc.co.uk/1/hi/world/africa/1657577.stm. Accessed May 2, 2004.

7. *BBC News Online*, "Bissau to Hold Early Elections," November 15, 2002. Available at: http://news.bbc.co.uk/1/hi/world/africa/2479929.stm. Accessed May 2, 2004.

12 | Democratic Governance in Africa at the Start of the Twenty-first Century

Lessons of Experience

Michael Chege

Evaluating Democracy in Africa under "The Third Wave"

There has been a long debate on whether the standards of democratic governance ought to be based on procedural criteria (such as the quality of competitive elections, openness of access to public office, voter turnout, etc.) or on the achievements of substantive political goals (like personal liberty and the rule of law [Zakaria 2003]). Inside the democratizing states, progress on both fronts is often unequal; movements in one end up frequently exerting pressure on the other. Since democracy by definition is an endogenous, citizen-driven process, and people have different priorities, any broad assessment of the fate of democratic experiments in any region—whether Africa or elsewhere—is bound to reflect the national variation resulting from that. Democratic experience in sub-Saharan Africa in the past fifteen years reflects unequal gains by country, and uneven progress in attainment of the procedural and substantive goals of democracy. In a number of significant states, however, democratic innovations aborted early, yielding to chronic violence and instability that has received much international publicity. The main intellectual challenge, therefore, is to explain these uneven achievements, rather than to provide a single theory that accounts for the political woes that supposedly afflict Africa as a whole. For in all fairness, the death of democratic government in Africa has been vastly exaggerated.

This book opened with a justification for assessing the fate of democratic experiments in Africa after the Cold War. In one of the first efforts to explain the contemporary upsurge of democratic governments worldwide, Samuel Huntington remarked that of the three distinct historic outbreaks of democratic governments since the American Revolution of 1776, the latest ("the third wave") began with the anti-fascist Portuguese coup d'etat of April 1974, and the free elections that followed it ushering in Mario Soares's Socialist Party administration in 1975 (Huntington 1991). If so, then sub-Saharan Africa's entry into the "third wave" began with the release of Nelson Mandela from prison after twenty-seven years of incarceration by South Africa's apartheid regime; the popular uprising that toppled the Mathieu Kérékou dictatorship in Benin; and the landmark all-Africa conference in Kampala, Uganda, on "Security, Stability, Development and Cooperation" in Africa. All of them took place in rapid succession between early 1990 and mid-1991. This was the high point of the most widespread pro-democracy protests in African states since independence in the 1960s.

By caving in to popular pressure, the collapse of the tottering authoritarian regimes in Benin and apartheid South Africa demonstrated that it was possible to initiate a transition to democracy through nonviolent means, particularly now that Africa had ceased to be a pawn in the Cold War struggles between East and West, under which all opponents to pro-Western dictatorships—not least South Africa— were tainted as pro-Communist by powerful conservative forces in the West. With the Cold War over, Western strategic interests in the region waned, an event best evidenced by America's abandonment of Liberia, once a key American intelligence-gathering post, and its vile dictator Samuel K Doe, who was executed by a brutal rebel leader (Prince Y. Johnson) in 1991. Gathering in Uganda, as another U.S.-supported dictator in next-door Zaire, Mobutu Sese Seko, was facing open rebellion in the streets for the first time, the Kampala forum was the point of departure toward the current, homegrown, pan-African initiatives to take charge of African regional security in the post–Cold War era. Under those new approaches, democratization and economic cooperation in Africa are considered vital correlates to African security. These efforts culminated in the inauguration of the African Union and the New Partnership for African Development (NEPAD) in 2002, under which democratic governance is the overarching principle.

The Kampala conference brought together over five hundred participants from a wide range of African countries—heads of government, leading intellectuals, journalists, community development activists, charity groups, and religious leaders. It laid unprecedented emphasis on governments' accountability to the governed, as a foundation of national security. Its final product, "the Kampala Document," whose principal goals—after many detours—are now enshrined in the charter of the African Union (formerly the Organization of African Unity, OAU), and the New Partnership for African Development, stated that democracy was the key solution for the continent's chronic problems of violence, political instability, and underdevelopment.[1] In a memorable *ex tempore* speech, widely covered in the African press, the late ex-president Julius Nyerere of Tanzania admitted the mistake made at the founding of the OAU in 1963, when African heads of state pledged noninterference in each other's internal affairs. This, he said, had allowed despotic regimes to escape censure by their peers, thus leading to a situation where "the deficit of democracy, and oppression are perhaps our main deficit" (Nyerere 1992, 255). As always, Nyerere was not beyond admitting his own mistakes and culpability in that process. Not surprisingly, the Kampala Document declared democracy "a necessity" while candidly pointing out that many African leaders had preached democracy and practiced authoritarianism, leading to widespread popular "agitation for the revival of democracy" (Obasanjo and Mosha 1992, 356).

Yet even as the pro-democracy protesters took to the streets, often risking their lives in the process, not everyone was as sanguine about the prospects for democracy in Africa. Writing from within the continent some five years after the transition had begun, a group of distinguished African scholars warned against the potential of resistance against political liberalization by African dictators, and about the grave risks posed by a patronizing intervention by intellectuals and powerful governments from the West, whose previous commitment to democracy and human rights in Africa was highly questionable.[2] On the opposite end of the spectrum, some American scholars and political observers came to the same conclusion but for the opposite reason: they pointed to the domestic—as opposed to externally driven—characteristics of African political systems. Thus Henry Bienen and Jeffrey Herbst provided an early warning that, due to their structural foundations, the staying power of long-established African dictatorships should not be underestimated, no matter how forceful the winds of political liberalization might have been. They expected African dictatorships to prove more resistant to liberalizing political trends than their counterparts "elsewhere in the world" (Bratton and van de Walle 1997, 8). For his part, Keith Richburg, the *Washington Post* correspondent for Africa during the tumultuous 1990s, was even less optimistic. In his view, "[W]estern policymakers must recognize that in Africa the holding of elections does not necessarily mean true democracy—in many cases, the exact opposite holds true" (Richburg 1997). Put differently, experimentation with democracy in Africa might lead to more tyranny and fewer democratic rights, the opposite of what was intended.

In the most detailed and balanced account of Africa's "democratic experiments" up to the middle of the 90s, however, Bratton and van de Walle provided a more complex picture. Their mid-decade evaluation, which constitutes the benchmark for this volume, provided statistical illustration of the widespread popular demonstrations and riots starting in 1989, peaking in 1991, and then tailing off thereafter, which resulted in an unprecedented rise in the political liberties enjoyed by African citizens. This trend reached its zenith in 1992 before declining slightly in 1994 (Bratton and van de Walle 1997). Bratton and van de Walle concluded that by 1994, a substantive political transformation had taken place in key sub-Saharan African states, but they also stressed that the initial wave of political liberalization in Africa appeared to be tapering off. In their estimation, while some African states could make the critical "transition" to democracy, most were constrained by structural factors, notably "patrimonial leadership," weak public institutions, a fledgling civil society, and a resurgence of ethnic rivalry. Considering the stereotypical and inaccurate generalizations about African politics in the press and in the social sciences, this was a prescient distinction.

Picking up from where Bratton and van de Walle left off, this volume set off with the intention of evaluating the fate of democratic transitions in Africa, one decade after the historic events of 1991. There are, however, significant method-ological differences between the Bratton and van de Walle study and this volume. Whereas the former used aggregated statistical data to track progress of democracy in Africa after 1989, this book uses fairly representative case studies toward the same end. Secondly, the contributions to this book are informed by the overriding theme of how political action among elites shapes the institutional structures of national governance on which democratic rule is founded. Like Bratton and van de Walle, however, the editors and the authors of this book sought to determine what the African experience with transition to democracy could contribute to the general theoretical "transition" literature on the change from authoritarian gov-ernment to a pluralistic democracy, especially under the "third wave." Thirdly, Brat-ton and van de Walle did not pay specific attention to the set of states that would implode violently in the course of aborted transitions—Democratic Republic of the Congo, Central African Republic, Burundi, Congo-Brazzaville, and Rwanda. Attention to that issue has fortuitously found its way into this volume. For, in the meantime, state failure and the role of democracy in counteracting the deleterious consequences of state collapse, and terrorism in particular, has stimulated a roar-ing public and academic interest since the bombings of September 11, 2001, in New York and Washington.[3] Two chapters in this volume deal with the fate of democracy and civic order in two failed African states—Congo-Brazzaville and the Central African Republic.

The contributors to this volume therefore provide us with a rich variety of African case studies and interpretations on the decade-long national attempts to make the transition from one-party rule to democracy. After a brief survey of the status of democratic governance in Africa over the past decade, this concluding chapter at-tempts to account for the nature of the diversity in national experiences presented here. In the course of doing so, it also seeks to pull together the findings provided by the contributors with the intention of weaving a composite picture of the com-mon themes that have emerged independently from individual case studies, as well as the major differences observed. In the process, it also attempts to relate these common themes to the lessons contained in the canonical literature on transition in "third wave" democracies. That sets the stage for some concluding remarks on the outstanding issues worth further academic attention that arise from the em-pirical findings in the chapters on individual countries, and from the book's cen-tral argument that elite political behavior underpins the evolution and function-ing of democratic political institutions in Africa's emerging democracies.

A Decade of Experimentation with Democracy in Africa: Some Overall Evidence

Departing from the gloomy and pessimistic images of Africa as a homogenous and volatile place, which had become so common in the press and sections of academia over the last decade, the *Financial Times* of London published a full-page article on democracy in Africa as of early 2003, stating that the number of democracies on the continent had risen from 4 in 1989 to "as many as 17" at the time. It based its conclusions on the UNDP Polity Index, a composite figure that combines data on state respect for rights, accountability, and the extent to which citizens enjoy individual and civil liberties (White 2003).

The *Financial Times* was not alone in its conclusion. According to Freedom House, there were only eleven African states with any semblance of political freedom in 1972. Of these, only two were classified as "free," and nine as "partly free." Roughly speaking therefore, only one out of four African states had the potential to consolidate or advance to democratic governance. But by 2003, however, the number of African "free" or "partly free" states had risen to thirty-two, out of a total of forty-eight states in Africa south of the Sahara; that is, seven out of ten countries were classified as either free (eleven) or partially free (twenty-one). Over the thirty years from 1972, therefore, the proportion of African states showing potential to achieve "consolidated" democratic status had grown from one out of four to seven out of ten. Without attempting to minimize the political disasters evident in one set of African states, this is no mean achievement.

Critics will point out immediately that small African states tend to dominate the democracy league compared to the large instability-prone ones like Sudan, Nigeria, Democratic Republic of the Congo, and Ethiopia. But that hypothesis is only partly true. African democratic trends tend to be geographic-size neutral.[4] The best index in enumerating the spread of democracy as a public good, however, is the total national population that has access to individual liberties, rather than the commonly used one of the number of democratic states per se, irrespective of their size. This is because the fundamental element of democracy is a government based, to quote Locke, "on the consent of the governed," with the principle goal of preservation of individual liberty and property to the highest extent consistent with the respect of the rights of others. The number of Africa's residents who now enjoy the substantive freedoms—of speech, religion, movement, press, and the right to vote— would therefore be a better index on the fate of democratic government in Africa, rather than the total figure of democratic states, since their population sizes vary enormously. Democratization in South Africa, Ghana, and Kenya, with a combined total population of 94 million people in 2002, for example, has a vastly different impact on the lives of the *people* of Africa as compared to that of Seychelles, Botswana, and Gambia with a total population of 4 million people during the same year.

By adding the total population recorded in each country, it can be demonstrated that the number of African citizens in what Freedom House classifies as "free" African states, enjoying substantive freedoms and the protection of those freedoms by an elected government, rose from 3 million (from Botswana, Mauritius, and Gambia) in 1989, before widespread political reforms began, to 100.8 million in 2003 (from Benin, Botswana, Ghana, Lesotho, Mali, Mauritius, Senegal, São Tomé, South Africa, and Cape Verde), the set of "free" African states that year. Concrete evidence of this expansion in civil liberties can be observed today in the proliferation of independent newspapers, FM radio talk shows in local languages, the right to vote, and open political debate everywhere, with the exception of a handful of states—Eritrea, Equatorial Guinea, Sudan, Gabon, and Zimbabwe. Overall, the main story here is that the number of African democratic states has risen fourfold while the population of African peoples classified as "free" has grown thirty-fold! Significantly, the bulk of African countries (and peoples) can now be placed in the "partly free," middle-range category. As Adrian Karatnycky of Freedom House commented in 2003, "the general trend for freedom in sub-Saharan Africa has been positive over the last thirty years" (Karatnycky 2003).

And yet there are chronically serious problems of violence in failed or failing states, and bad governance under cruel dictatorships in the so-called "neopatrimonial" states of Africa—the kind of state that has hogged newspaper headlines and generated much academic pessimism about Africa as a whole in the past decade. There should be nothing wrong with such horrifying publicity as long as it is counterbalanced by what has gone right, in order to generate a more objective picture—one that reflects the enormous diversity we alluded to earlier. As we have seen, however, quintessential "Afro-pessimists" in the West deride advances toward democracy in Africa, or pronounce them trivial and ephemeral.[5] Objectively speaking, however, there is no choice to make between political progress and regress in Africa. Both are fundamental parts of the story, and the only worthwhile analytical challenge is to delineate the factors that make for the difference and to prove empirically that such variables are indeed responsible for the material political variations observed.

Some of the most violently egregious setbacks, in fact, resulted from aborted democratic experimentation gone haywire under the command of high-handed autocrats: Liberia under Charles Taylor (1997–2003), Congo-Brazzaville before and after the Pascal Lissouba government, Sudan under Omar Bashir since 1989, and the Central African Republic under Ange Félix Patassé. In yet another category, political liberalization has in fact had the opposite result, namely the buttressing of authoritarianism: Kenya under Moi (1991–2002), Nigeria under Sani Abacha (1993–98), Cameroon under Biya, Togo under Eyadema, and Guinea-Conakry under Lansana Conté. Yet even within this disappointing category, authoritarian recalcitrance is not the whole story. Insofar as one is concerned about the fate of democratic forces, there have been examples of formidable determination by opposition groups to reverse the baleful political trend. Zairian, Nigerien, Kenyan, and Cameroonian opposition parties and civil societies remained on the forefront of struggles for good governance in their countries even as autocrats dug in to resist pressures for democratic change by the use of force, manipulation of the vote, and buying off pliable opposition groups. The test of wills between autocrats and pro-democracy forces is an essential part of the story of democracy in Africa too. And an account of the balance of forces is just as important to comprehend as the celebrated staying power of African authoritarian regimes and the culture of tyranny that sustains them.

Table 12.1. Spread of Democratic Freedoms in Africa by Country and Population: 1989–2003

	No. of countries surveyed		Total population (millions)	
	1989	2003	1989	2003
Free	3	11	3.3	100.8
Partly Free	11	21	226	404.7
Not Free	30	16	264.8	210.8
Total	44	48	494	716.3

Sources: Freedom in the World (Annual), New York: Freedom House; UN World Statistics Division, World Population (Annual) (Angola, Eritrea, Djibouti, and Namibia were not included in the 1989 survey).

To sum up, as we can see from table 12.1, the majority of African states moved from a "not free" status in 1989 to either "free" or "partly free" status, according to Freedom House classifications in 2003. Over one-half (54 percent) of Africa's inhabitants, representing 264 million people, lived under "unfree," highly oppressive political conditions in 1989, while only 3.3 million enjoyed democratic freedom at the time. By 2003, however, the population under oppressive rule had declined in proportionate and absolute terms to 29 percent of the total, an estimated 210 million people, respectively. Over half (56 percent) of the population in 2003 now lived in "partly free" states, representing the statistical mode. Nevertheless, among the oppressive sixteen states were to be found a set of chronically violent and unstable states, whose conditions had perverse, spillover political and economic effects on their reformist neighbors. One may debate the precision of the Freedom House rankings and the UN population data used here, but the broad trend toward freer states and peoples is clearly unmistakable. To the extent that any study seeks to provide an objective survey of African democratic experiments between 1989 and 2003, it must account for the causes behind success, mixed results, and political tragedy as represented here.

Success and Checkered Results
of Democratic Governance in Africa

If there is one truly commendable quality in the set of case studies presented in this book, it is that they reflect the diversity in experiences that we see in the wider "population" of African states discussed above. In the sub-discipline of comparative politics, under which this book falls, knowledge is best accumulated by comparison of political behavior in countries, or societies, that (ideally) bear similar social and economic characteristics, but whose achievements over a period of time diverge significantly—the closest political science comes to the principle of double-blind experimentation in medicine (Sartori 1991).[6] Such comparison makes it easier for us to isolate the putative causal factor, observed in one case but absent in the other, which might account for the difference observed between the two cases. Although the countries examined in the cases studies here do not share an identical history, nor similar internal conditions, the diversity they present provides us with an opportunity to tease out some lessons of experience, particularly when countries in roughly similar social and political circumstances, in or out of this set, arrive at divergent political ends. Identifying such factors should, of course, not be an end in itself. Rather it should provide an explanation on which further empirical tests can be conducted to confirm or refute whether the cause-effect relationship proffered is indeed valid. Comparative politics thus explains most when it generates a new agenda in the form of fresh, testable hypotheses that derogate from old norms. For, in the words of Max Weber, "every scientific fulfillment raises new questions; it asks to be surpassed and outdated" (Weber 1958, 138).

In that context, lessons from comparisons often arise from the most unlikely sources. Compare Benin's democratic experience to that of her coup-prone peers of the 1970s, which share a similar heritage of French colonial rule and sharp internal ethnic cleavages, notably the Central African Republic and Congo-Brazzaville. In the first fifteen years of independence from France in 1960, Benin (then known as Dahomey) held "the unenviable record of having the largest number of military coups—six of them in just nine years (1963–72)" (Decalo 1976, 39). It acquired a stability of sorts under the self-styled Marxist military dictatorship of General Mathieu Kérékou between 1972 and 1990 when—bankrupt and unloved—he was forced out of office by strikes and pro-democracy demonstrators. With a per capita income of U.S. \$360 (in 1990), a weak economic base, and a history of interethnic political struggles, Benin, as Magnusson remarks in this volume (see chapter 4), violated all the preconditions to a transition in democracy offered by broad theories in comparative politics. After popular demonstrations had brought the state to paralysis, the first multiparty election took place in 1991, throwing Kérékou and his government out of office. By 1996, Benin, moving a step further, made a successful switch of power from government to the opposition through the ballot box, a valued marker in the "transition to democracy" literature.

If Benin, as Magnusson rightfully says, is "an anomaly," then we should be grateful for this case study because, as Thomas Kuhn insists in *The Structure of Scientific Revolutions,* observation of anomalies by scientific investigators is the critical first step toward growing intellectual dissent in advance of a paradigmatic revolution (Kuhn 1970).[7] For Kuhn, accumulation of anomalies eventually challenges the theoretical hegemony of a paradigm whose eclipse only comes when a successor takes its place. Quite apart from that, Benin's party leaders learned the benefit of inclusiveness (at national and local levels), in the manner recommended by advocates of "consociational democracy," such as Arendt Lijphart, for conflict-prone, ethnically pluralistic societies. Here Magnusson assigns critical significance to the political learning process of Beninese elites. From the past history of the country they had learned the dangers of zero-sum politics and the benefits of consensus. This paid off. Under better economic management, income per head grew at a faster rate (1.6 percent) in the 1990s than it had in the previous decade. This small West African country is not out of the political woods yet, as there are serious economic and governance problems to deal with, including corruption, and wayward economic reforms have generated huge social problems, in particular unemployment and inequality. But Benin is a very different and better place in 2004 compared to what it was in 1991.

Whether Benin's glass is half-full or half-empty is a matter of debate. And yet there are lessons of political theory and practice to be gained from the country's experience with democratic rule over the past decade that may be valuable to the rest of Africa. Magnusson's tongue-in-cheek comment that "Benin is generally ignored by the international press, perhaps one of the better indicators of success" reveals more than he intends. For as the old saying goes, "no news is good news." This is probably why we read less about the eleven states classified as "free" by Freedom House in 2002 than we do about their problem-ridden neighbors, in both the academic and popular literature.[8] Of the tentative democratic "successes" in Africa today, Benin's recent experience with democratic governance has this in common with South Africa in 1994, and Kenya in the 2002 elections: power-sharing and a determination to reach consensus across a wide spectrum of political parties, some of which bear a history of rivalry. Zimbabwe's 1980 constitution and Namibia's 1990 constitution were based on compromise and minority safeguards between African liberation movements and entrenched white minorities who had fought the policy of nonracial majority rule. A broad pro-democracy coalition of unlikely partners was the defining characteristic of the 1991 Movement for Multiparty Democracy in Zambia, which put an end to eighteen years of one-party rule under Kenneth Kaunda's United National Independence Party. It was also the trademark of the 1998 multiregional alliance of forces that brought Olusegun Obasanjo to power in Nigeria, and it was the bedrock of the popular Sudanese movements that overthrew the General Abboud regime in 1964 and the Jaffer Nimeiri dictatorship in 1985. The thread of consensus and coalition-building thus runs through major breakthroughs from autocratic rule to democracy in Africa, but that is not to say it is a cure-all. A lot of what followed the triumph of grand alliances depended on what the consensus and coalition-building consisted of.

In the current, mainstream, transition-to-democracy literature, the critical role that could be played by broad coalitions of democratic forces, in alliance with disaffected "progressive" forces of the vanishing *ancien regime,* has received endorsement in Samuel Huntington's *The Third Wave* (1993), which recommends a "forgive but do not forget" approach to the culpable members of the old order. A variant of this process, called "pact making," has been observed and recommended by O'Donnell and Schmitter (1986) with specific reference to the southern cone of Latin America. But as radically different results from the African cases presented here have demonstrated—contrast Benin's success with Zambia's failure, for one—the technical aspects of consensus building and pact-making counts less than substantive goals and aims underlying a broad coalition, pact, or alliance.

We owe to Barrington Moore the observation that what happened to national democratic politics after the violent ouster of pre-capitalist authoritarian regimes in Europe and Asia depended hugely on *which* alliance of forces—among a strong monarchy, landlords, and peasants—supported, opposed, or was vanquished by a rising democratic capitalist class as it pursued the path of modernization through commercialization of agriculture and industrialization (Moore 1966). In a modified form, this proposition may be of relevance to Africa too. The historical case studies of England, France, the United States, Japan, China, and India are vastly different from those of contemporary Africa discussed in this volume and elsewhere. But a comparative analysis of the principal political actors and their goals, and of the alliances they strike in moving from authoritarianism to democracy in Africa, might help clarify why some of them succeed, why others regress to violence, and why others stagnate for extended periods. A more focused national case-study in that context is bound to be more useful than generalized searches on the political behavior of African states as a whole.

A promising beginning toward that end has been made by yet another set of case studies in this volume—that representing the collection of cases where progress toward democratic rule is checkered, characterized by fits and starts, presenting us with the dilemma of what a "partially free" state really means. Such states, as we saw in the general survey of democratic trends in the continent, dominate the statistical mode. It is impossible to state in advance whether the set of countries in this category are destined to succeed or regress. Again, much depends on the balance of forces at play, and on the substantive political goals motivating the actors, regarding which a clearer role may be gleamed from successes as much as from disasters.

Consider the case of Guinea-Bissau in West Africa. In his chapter, Forrest considers Guinea-Bissau's experiment with democratic rule as symptomatic of two contesting urban political forces, both composed of civil servants *and* civic groups. This is an unusual observation because contemporary independent civic organizations are often seen as a vigorous counterbalance to governmental institutions, and also as a public watchdog against the abuse of power. In Guinea-Bissau, however, we are informed that one alliance of these forces stands for a more progressive, open political system and the rule of law, while its opponents reflect the conservative, crusty, authoritarian streak inherited from Portuguese colonialism and the heyday of single-party rule, which valued order and stability above civil rights. In the balance resulting from this two-way competition, Forrest concludes that it is the position of the armed forces that is likely to tip the balance, to determine the fate of democracy in Guinea-Bissau. Much therefore depends on what side the military chooses to support. Considering the principle that armed forces in a democracy are wholly subject to civilian control, that conclusion must give pause to the pro-democracy movement in Guinea-Bissau and its supporters abroad. And yet the chapter does not rule out the prospects of progressive consolidation of gains made by democratic rule in Guinea-Bissau, assuming a way could be found to neutralize the army and make it professional.

Likewise, in Mozambique, Manning describes the studied intransigence of Frelimo—the party that liberated the country from a long and brutal period of Portuguese colonial rule in 1974—against accommodating full-scale multiparty competition and open dissent. Ironically, she states, political liberalization has had the unintended result of accelerating open debate *inside* this dominant ruling party, as various party factions debate ways of reconfiguring the dominant political establishment in order to accommodate the dramatic global and national changes that have taken place in the last decade. As in Guinea-Bissau, political liberalization has developed fastest inside the ranks of the government rather than outside it—yet another case of checkered progress toward political liberalization. Not surprisingly, Freedom House rated Mozambique as "partly free" in 2003. Between 1994 and 2004, Mozambique achieved some of the fastest annual rates of economic growth in the developing world, based on infusions of external aid, privatization of public assets, and direct foreign investments.

This is remarkable progress, compared with the years before 1991 when Frelimo, the only party in the country, was dedicated to a monolithic Marxist-Leninist program that included compulsory collectivization of agriculture and banishment of private property (including urban family housing). Not until 1992 did the Frelimo party congress endorse changes toward economic and political liberalization, primarily for two reasons. Firstly, the country experienced consistently negative economic growth rates in the 1980s due to counterproductive macroeconomic policies and diminishing external assistance, as friendly communist-bloc allies ran into severe problems of their own in the waning years of international communism. This forced Mozambique to turn to the International Monetary Fund and the World Bank for development assistance. Second, Mozambique's anti-apartheid foreign policy stance had provoked a series of brutal attacks from South Africa and white-ruled Rhodesia. Both South Africa and Rhodesia bankrolled the anti-Frelimo rebellion organized by the Renamo movement, itself a product of rural discontent spawned by an intrusive collectivization program and ethnic grievances from central Mozambique.

Something had to give. On the military front, victory against Renamo eluded the Frelimo government, which was forced to come to the negotiating table with Renamo in 1990 after mediation by Italy and Mozambique's neighbors. On the political front, Western donor pressure and increasing local agitation for reforms goaded Frelimo into allowing inter-party competition and wider space for individual liberties, even though, as Manning shows, only to the extent that the concessions did not threaten Frelimo's hold on power. Frelimo has therefore placed handicaps on Renamo, the main opposition party, and combined with the antipathy of local authorities, Renamo has been denied any substantial power-sharing. A new liberal trend (in civil society rather than in Renamo) now opposes the authoritarian tradition derived from Frelimo's past. To close ranks from within, Frelimo was compelled by the new developments, as noted above, to espouse a more tolerant and pluralistic posture *within* itself, rather than between it and its opponents. This is unlike the factional inclusiveness found in Benin and other more politically liberal African states. Because this cleavage reinforces the old north–south divide in Mozambique, it remains the principal obstacle to political liberalization in the country.

The situation VonDoepp reports on Malawi is also discouragingly mixed. Unlike in Mozambique and Guinea-Bissau, where pro-democracy movements in the early 1990s confronted entrenched Marxist-Leninist parties that sprang out of triumphant anticolonial national liberation movements, the Malawi Congress Party (which brought the country to independence in 1964) had been a loose organization of young nationalist elites who made a fatal error in inviting Hastings Kamuzu Banda, a Malawian medical doctor who had spent nearly all his adult life in exile, to come home and lead the party in the late 1950s. After independence, however, Banda swiftly dispensed with any perceived internal dissent, built a personality cult around himself, and then perfected ruthless dictatorship under his personal imprint. Whereas Frelimo and other national liberation movements disdained apartheid, the Malawi Congress Party under Banda became an ally of South Africa starting from 1966 onward. By 1993, however, Banda the aging autocrat was facing the same pro-democracy agitation as his left-wing peers in Mozambique, not to mention Congo-Brazzaville, Madagascar, and elsewhere. In 1994, as VonDoepp demonstrates, the party lost power to the United Democratic Front (UDF), a coalition of unionists, intellectuals, southern politicians, and disaffected ex–Banda allies like Bakili Muluzi, who became the new president that year.

Muluzi's first term (1994–99) was characterized by innovative pro-democracy reforms. His administration established an anticorruption agency, a law commission to weed out the Banda regime's draconian laws, and an Ombudsman. His second term (1999–2004), however, was marked by a turn toward an uncaring authoritarianism and tolerance of financial corruption. His government was profligate in spending public funds, even under conditions of famine. The World Bank and the IMF therefore withheld U.S. $100 million in development aid in 2000 citing poor economic stewardship and corruption, with good reason. But the UDF establishment was nonchalant. When in 2001 the Danish ambassador closed his aid mission after reproaching the Muluzi government for corruption and extravagance, the Malawi president demanded his recall, and celebrated his exit as good riddance. He added, "we would rather remain poor" than take Danish assistance. It is doubtful whether most Malawians, whose material circumstances largely deteriorated under Muluzi's tenure, shared that opinion. Under Muluzi's stewardship, famine struck Malawi and, after an initial rise, per capita GDP fell steadily from 1999 onward by a record 3.5 percent in 2001.

Yet, the prospects for national democratic governance in Malawi are not wholly bleak. When UDF sycophants sought to extend Muluzi's time in office through constitutional amendments abolishing term limits on the executive, popular opposition, protests from the clergy, and challenges from within state institutions and the ruling party undermined and brought their campaign to a halt. Still, unchecked self-interest and gross dereliction of national duty by Malawian political elites has curiously thrived alongside growing confidence in national democratic institutions, notably parliament and the judiciary. Despite the outer shell of democratic politics, VonDoepp remarks, struggles for personal (or factional) gain have become increasingly violent. Party thugs for hire, of the kind used by Banda's MCP, have made it to the political scene. Whereas MCP used its Young Pioneers as ruthless enforcers of party policy, UDF increasingly used its Young Democrats for the same purpose. However, this is not a vindication of the literature from Chabal and others on an ingrained violent political culture in black Africa. On the whole, Malawi politics has been characterized by less civil conflict than any of her neighbors, including South Africa.

As in Guinea-Bissau and Mozambique, the predominant handicap to democratic change in Malawi lies in the failure among political elites in that country to agree on, and to respect, the fundamentals of democratic governance in the long run. The opportunism displayed by leaders in Malawi's political opposition as they crossed over to government in return for high office after the 2004 election is the latest evidence of this. The long-run danger to democracy lies in self-seeking and divisive political strategies by Malawian political elites, rather than the inclusive ones of the kind characterizing democratic transitions in such states as South Africa, Ghana, Mauritius, and Kenya in 2002. However, according to VonDoepp (chapter 8), Malawian courts and some legislators have been a constant check on self-serving and authoritarian tendencies among political elites on both sides of the power divide—government and opposition party leaders. Before the 2004 elections, it was clear that the prospects of democracy in Malawi depended on the capacity of the badly split opposition parties in Malawi to unite, and on whether Muluzi's hand-picked successor, Mbingu wa Mutharika, would strike a more liberal pose than his mentor. But despite repeated exhortation to the split opposition to unite against the baleful UDF by church and civic groups, anti-UDF party leaders would not yield to each other and thus handed UDF a dubious electoral victory in May 2004.

The cases of Zambia and Madagascar are even less inspiring. In both countries, the exhilarating defeat of the all-powerful single-party government at the polls has unfortunately produced dysfunctional public institutions at the hands of would-be democratic victors, a deterioration made worse by economic regress. Again, as the contributors to this volume state, elite behavior explains a lot. This said, the liberties now enjoyed by citizens have grown into proportions unknown before the agitation for democratic governance began in the early 1990s, something corroborated by the Freedom House indices mentioned earlier. In 2003, Freedom House classified both countries as "partly free," in comparison to their unfree status in 1989.

Thus, with respect to Zambia, according to Simon (chapter 9), "the promise of the 1991 transition remained mostly unrealized." Frederick Chiluba's Movement for Multiparty Democracy (MMD) party, which defeated Kenneth Kaunda's United National Independence Party (UNIP) at widely hailed elections in 1991, turned out to be more arbitrary, autocratic, and corrupt than UNIP ever was. As in Malawi,

Simon acknowledges the expansion of individual freedoms all the same. There was guarded hope under the Levi Mwanawasa government, elected in the controversial general elections of 2001, which were held after a spirited rebuff by Zambian demonstrators of Chiluba's attempt to run for an unconstitutional third term. But by mid-2004 that hope was wearing thin. One especially positive development early in Mwanawasa's rule was that Chiluba was brought to justice for a long list of transgressions, principally on financial corruption. Two years after the charges were brought, however, the case was still held up in courts. This inspired neither Zambian pro-democracy fighters nor their international sympathizers. The Mwanawasa administration had in turn taken an unpopular streak of intolerance against its opponents, especially in the press. With an unusually high HIV infection rate, economic mismanagement, and food shortages, the Zambian democratic experiment in 2004 was hardly inspiring.

In a similar vein, Marcus writes that in contrast to the situation ten years ago (when one-party "socialist" rule under Didier Ratsiraka ended in Madagascar), democracy flourished in the sense that "not only had there been regular elections, but people protested in the streets, practiced the religion of their choice, and published newspaper articles lambasting not only the system but also specific politicians." Here again we encounter the theme of an expanded domain of civil liberties in Africa. The procedural aspects of democracy (competitive elections especially) function reasonably well in that country, give or take a tortured presidential transition. In 2002, the presidential succession problem was resolved by armed intervention after Ratsiraka (reelected in 1996 after an ineffectual term by his pro-democracy opponents) resisted handing over the reins of government to Marc Ravalomanana. As in Guinea-Bissau, the army became an arbiter in party electoral contests, which is disallowed by constitutional democratic procedure. The hard part, therefore, is one of constructing a national governance institutional framework to sustain "substantive" democratic norms the Madagascar public enjoys. On that there is no workable solution on the horizon, as Madagascar and a large number of former French colonies continue to experiment with a French Fifth Republic–style constitution in a party system and society that differ so much from France, in an African environment that calls for deep-seated constitutional innovation.

While more benign in waging electoral conflict than their Madagascar counterpart, political elites in Niger seem to be also handicapped by a French Fifth Republic–style constitution that has been aggravated by a perverse party competition that has harmed the state's institutions. This lesson is writ large in Niger's experience with democracy after 1989. The incapacity of Niger's French–style constitution to function in the country's ethnically conflicted political system should have been predicted by adherents of Arendt Lijphart's (1977) proposition that inclusive, "grand coalitions" work better than zero-sum electoral politics in culturally pluralistic systems. Even that would require a level of mutual trust greater than what Villalón and Idrissa describe as the dysfunctional "cohabitation" of two parties in Niger's Third Republic, proved to be the main handicap toward democratization in that country.

If there is one crosscutting lesson that could be distilled from the mixed outcomes in these case studies, it would be that despite the rising expanse of democratic freedoms in sub-Saharan Africa, considerable work remains to be done in crafting a functional governance institutional framework to moderate the effects of what Zakaria (2003) calls "illiberal democracy": bona fide legislatures that approve abuse of individual rights and private property by elected ruling parties, dodging the rule of law, undermining party loyalties by financial inducement, inadequately respecting separation of powers, and cultivating personality cults. In chapter 7, as we saw, Marcus contends that the state in Madagascar follows the formal electoral rules but undermines the substance of democracy. Such is the challenge that now faces ruling and opposition parties as well as non-state actors committed to sustaining a democratic culture in Africa.

According to the contributors, differentiated democratic experience in all these countries, from Benin to Madagascar, can be traced to elite political behavior and specifically, it would appear, to the extent of a civic tradition and inclusiveness that produces institutional capability to handle change. The more consensual and devoted to fundamental democratic values elites are, and the higher they place national interests above those of the faction, the better for democracy and the institutional framework it requires.

Lessons from Failed Democratic Experiments

In contrast to the success and the mixed results cases narrated above, aborted democracy and systemic violence can be traced to factional leadership that values self-interested raw power above community and national interest, even at the cost of breakdowns in law and order. The consequences for democratic governance in this cluster of luckless cases fits the popular apocalyptic scenario of African states mentioned earlier. Rather than democracy and expanded space for political liberties, however qualified that may be, state institutions imploded, making daily survival a hazard in such countries as Congo-Brazzaville and the Central African Republic. In a reputed international survey of the quality of life in cities of the world in 2003, Brazzaville and Bangui, the respective capitals of these two countries, ranked just above war-torn Baghdad as the most violent and inhospitable urban spaces on earth.[9] That alone ought to say a lot about the political conditions in those countries as of 2004.

In *Leviathan*, Thomas Hobbes advocates a supreme body with complete monopoly on the use of armed force in any peacefully governed country. He assumed that conflict among individuals, of the type found in places like Brazzaville and Bangui, is so deeply ingrained that the right to bear arms leads to a society so violent that life becomes "solitary, nasty, brutish and short" (1985,186). Hobbes was writing during a period of catastrophic civil wars: the English Civil War and the Thirty Years War in continental Europe. This is a period that resembled *some* countries of Africa in the 1990s onward. In addition to Congo-Brazzaville and the Central African Republic, these states include Somalia, Liberia, Sierra Leone, Southern Sudan, and the northeastern quadrant of the Democratic Republic of the Congo. Hobbes stressed the point that without political stability (as he understood it) there would be no individual security, industry, culture, international trade, "commodious buildings," arts, or science. In the turbulent 1960s, similarly, Samuel P. Huntington made the case for political stability in developing countries that, he claimed, suffered from an excess of participation in politics (by sundry new groups like trade unions, students, and political parties) in an environment of fragile governance institutions. Political stability could therefore only be achieved by reining in popular "participation" in politics until political institutions (and the economy) are sufficiently developed (Huntington 1968). This theme recurs in a more succinct variation in the work of Linz and Stepan (1996). As quoted by VonDoepp and Villalón in their introduction, these authors maintain that without a state that has capacities, there can be no democratic governance. Essentially, therefore, building firm institutions of the state, an issue central to the studies in this volume, is the foundation on which democratic politics is founded, and which democracy in turn nurtures, in a continuously virtuous cycle.

That, at any rate, appears to be the lesson gained from the case studies on the fate of democratic experiments in Congo-Brazzaville and the Central African Republic (CAR). For the outcome of failed political reform in the two states is an affront to the sanctity of human life, let alone democratic governance. If as Magnusson remarks, Benin's success is cause for little international publicity, Congo-Brazzaville and the CAR—like Sudan, DRC, and Liberia—have been in the world news precisely because of their mayhem and instability, thus reinforcing the stereotype of perpetual disorder in Africa. It is by no means clear, as Mehler and Clark indicate in their respective chapters, that the worst is over. Bangui was torn by yet another round of factional violence in April 2004. Recurrent, internal armed conflicts involving outsiders and resulting in civilian casualties have become a matter of life. Democracy and elections may indeed have featured prominently (as the two chapters reveal) in the national politics of these states in the early 1990s, but the central drama they report on features violent factional conflicts in which democratic governance and the rule of law were treated as ammunition in the struggle for an uncompromising defeat of political opponents.

As stated earlier, it is now commonplace to read learned academic treatises on disorder and violence as a characteristic African cultural affliction going centuries back toward the time of Hobbes, except when it was reined in by colonial rule. Looking at these two states (and to Liberia and Sierra Leone during earlier periods), attempts to democratize had the opposite effect, as Richburg (1997) and Chabal (2002) claim. But the violent contests that undermine efforts to democratize the CAR, Congo-Brazzaville, and a cluster of other African states (like Côte d'Ivoire between 1999 and 2004, Rwanda before 1994, and Nigeria between 1993 to 2000), is absent in some states like Ghana, Mali, and Tanzania, which are no less "African" in cultural content, assuming such a thing exists. The disorder reported in the two countries is also far beyond the violence reported in the chapters on Malawi, Zambia, and Mozambique in this book. That variation in degree defies the cascading, pessimistic, continental generalizations that defy any sense of proportion. And yet, as stated earlier, explaining the causal factors behind this variation is a more assured path toward understanding the origins of violent subversion of democratization, so that the problem can be dealt with.

In that connection, the political elites of the African states in dire straits, such as Congo-Brazzaville and the CAR, seem to suffer from the scarcity of civic virtue—the capacity to place the common good above self-interest—to an even greater degree than those that have fared much better under democratic governance, like Benin, Ghana, Senegal, and South Africa. That much is clear from what Mehler and Clark write. As Putnam states, civic virtue is a vital ingredient of social capital and it is one of the most vital social inputs toward "making democracy work" (1993, 87–88). Mutual trust and intense civic engagement in public affairs is the cement that binds civic virtue. Yet so endemic is the degree of mistrust among operators at the top of the political hierarchy and further below, that politics in these states involve scheming against the institutional integrity of the country, often with external support. Mehler in fact opens his chapter by highlighting the "high levels of inter-elite distrust" in the CAR that lay behind the introduction of inter-ethnic violence by rival elites in mortal political combat. And yet far from being culturally derived, ethnic identity in the CAR, we are informed, was not a factor in political and social life before the early 1980s. In Congo-Brazzaville, Clark informs us that fatalism, similar to that what Putnam describes in southern Italy, "has the unintended consequence of absolving contemporary actors for the misdeeds they commit for purely selfish purposes."

The truth is that when one looks at the Democratic Republic of the Congo, Burundi, Liberia, Côte d'Ivoire, Sudan, and Somalia in 2005, peace and security, law and order, and functional institutions are an obvious first priority in any advance toward democratic governance. So grave are the political conditions there.

But as we take a long-term view of politics in sub-Saharan Africa as a whole, we must remember that it has been possible to stop many civil wars by reversing that order: using a democratic constitution, universal adult suffrage, set-asides for minorities and aggrieved parties, local autonomy for oppressed groups, and so on. The Sudanese civil war that started in 1956 went into full remission after the Addis Ababa Accords of 1972, negotiated between the Jaffar Nimeiri government and southern Sudanese "Anyanya" rebel groups, gave southerners considerable political autonomy (including a regional judiciary, legislature, and public services), and a proportion of positions in the national government at Khartoum. Peace and economic progress ensued. When the south rose up in arms again in 1983, it was because Nimeiri, under pressure from the National Islamic Party and its allies, abrogated the 1972 constitution, unilaterally bringing "sharia" law to the Sudanese south and to the north. Negotiated constitutions with special guarantees for white minorities, in what was then Rhodesia (in 1980) and Namibia (in 1990), brought both countries to independence and political stability at least for a while—eighteen years in Zimbabwe, and up to the present in Namibia. South Africa's 1994 constitutional setup was a compromise intended to secure majority rule against the backdrop of "sunset clauses" that gave ample guarantees to the white minority (in business and the civil service) and thinly veiled concessions to some of the most egregious violators of human rights in the apartheid years. The same could be said of the Rome Accords and the new multiparty constitution in Mozambique in 1994, which helped wind down one of the most vicious and devastating civil wars in southern Africa. In fact, the Mandela government had recommended a government of national unity to Mozambique in 1994, a proposal that Frelimo firmly rebuffed.

To conclude this section, Hobbesian scenarios may call for stability and order (in countries like Congo-Brazzaville and the CAR) before democracy can make it to the national political agenda. But the reverse is also a distinct possibility that ingenuous statecraft should not ignore. Democratic rights and a widening space for political participation can on their own serve to usher in political stability. Those who claim that violence, rather than the art of compromise, is fundamental to African politics have provided a partial, self-serving picture of history. There is as much evidence of constitutionally negotiated resolution of political violence as there is of violent rupture of the democratic order. The truly vital intellectual challenge lies in why and when differences occur, and the import of lessons obtained thereof.

The Emerging Agenda

Ever since Richard Sklar (1987) made his unprecedented plea for a theory and practice of "developmental democracy" in Africa, we have witnessed a steady growth of knowledge concerning the principal factors at play in the checkered expansion of democratic space in the continent. Predictably, there is no consensus on the causal factors behind success or failure of democracy in Africa. Even more, as we saw in the beginning of this chapter, some reputed academic quarters consider Africa hostile territory for the long-term growth of democracy, either for structural domestic reasons or because the international (i.e., Western) political forces are bound to undermine it for their own reasons. To those familiar with the debate on the origins of economic underdevelopment in Africa in the 1960s and 1970s, this polemical intellectual divide ought to be familiar. Then as now, the result is a hardening of political positions under which expanding the frontiers of knowledge takes a secondary position.

In the meantime, something has gone terribly wrong in the attempt to obtain a more objective account of the trends in democratic governance in Africa. We now have a substantial literature that promotes wide generalizations about political liberalization in Africa that are at variance with the realities in African states as we know them. One significant contribution made by the studies in this volume is that they have collectively broken new ground toward a more realistic and variegated rendition of events, in contradiction to many received quasi-laws and generalizations on democratic political life in sub-Saharan Africa as a whole—minus South Africa, the so-called special case. In concluding this chapter we touch on the substantive and methodological weaknesses inherent in such mainstream African democratic studies that have been addressed to one extent or another in this volume, and whose resolution might constitute part of the agenda toward a more profound understanding of political liberalization in Africa in the future.

Firstly, it is necessary to rest the myth of a poor democratic performance in Africa compared to other developing regions. In its 2002 *Freedom in the World* report, Freedom House concluded that in North Africa and the Middle East "there has been virtually no significant progress toward democratization" since that organization began monitoring global democratic trends in 1972 (Freedom House 2002, 3). With regard to the states that once formed the USSR (outside of the Baltic states), in 2004 Freedom House (2004, 8) stated that "there were no free countries," and that the ratio of "*not* free" to "partly free" post-Soviet states was on the order of seven to five, the opposite of sub-Saharan Africa, which is reported "to have experienced a positive trend in the last thirty years." Yet to look at a substantive scholarly description and prognosis of problems encountered by the current wave of democratization in Africa south of the Sahara, that region appears to be the most politically deracinated region of the world, a position that reinforces the biases associated with ill-informed sections of the Western press.

Against the backdrop of Freedom House's global and regional indices, and those of the UNDP Polity Index, it is difficult to understand the basis of the conclusions alluded to earlier in this chapter, that democratization is bound to experience greater handicaps in Africa than in most other (unspecified) parts of the world. For the most part, Good (2002) presents the cavalier conclusion that contemporary democracy in most of Africa (and curiously also in the West) constitutes "legitimization of autocracy through the ballot." No assessment of political liberalization in Africa, however unconventional, should be dismissed offhand. Nevertheless, grand negative conclusions—whether of progress or regress made by democracy in Africa itself over the last decade, or comparing Africa with the rest of the world—that run counter to conventional data, ought to be subjected to searing doubt and eliminated if found wanting on empirical grounds. For science is essentially an enterprise in the elimination of error, rather than a repeat of conventional wisdoms.

Secondly, one must express reservations abut the increasingly popular and widespread methodological error, which excludes South Africa from any sample of trends in African democratization, primarily on account of its history and racial composition. We need a better explanation than the spurious variable of race to account for such exclusion to prevail on a scientific basis. In fundamental methodology instruction, leaving out an observation in a given population, in advance of experimentation on the basis of its exceptional qualities, would be unconscionable. By understanding what lies behind the features that distinguish the exception (like Putnam's observation of social and economic vitality of northern Italy), we understand better what ails the failing cases. It ought to be made clearer why South Africa is excluded from all-Africa comparative studies because ad hoc exclusion of contradictory evidence is impermissible under baseline research rules.

If a large white ethnic minority, geographic location, functional institutions, or level of economic development were to be cited as reasons for omitting South Africa, none of them would hold. Over the last thirty years, South Africa has had more inter-ethnic killings per capita than Ghana, Zambia, or Tanzania. The majority of her 22 million (black) population had a Human Development Index of 0.462 in 1998, about the same as that of 29 million Kenyans (0.498). And if a history of (white) ethnic minority domination is given as the reason, then Zanzibar, Liberia, Rwanda, and Burundi—all cases of prolonged ethnocracy—should be considered exceptions too, along with colonial Kenya and Rhodesia (now Zimbabwe). One does not have to buy into Mahmood Mamdani's idea that South Africa experienced a "generic" African colonialism, and that its exceptionalism is largely contrived (1996). South Africa has fundamental similarities with the other African states, but has also had some very dramatic differences too. But that is not even a novel observation. Chad resembles her African neighbors in many ways, but also differs from them in some fundamental ways—oil wealth, for example. The same in fact might be said of virtually every African (and non-African) state in relation to its neighbors. The real question is what comparative theoretical issues are at stake— inequalities in ethnic power, violence between ethnic groups and its resolution, politics of income distribution, or affirmative action and how results vary from one case to the next. It is the concrete issues that should drive empirical observation where other African states resemble South Africa. As we know, the collection of relevant facts depends on the conceptual tools employed by the investigator; theory comes prior to facts.

Thirdly, neither is our understanding of democracy in Africa likely to flourish if confined to one method or objective. In his eloquent defense of value pluralism, Isaiah Berlin (2002), perhaps the most distinguished theorist of liberalism in our times, made the case for toleration of a wide plurality of methodological paths toward expanding our knowledge in the social sciences and in history. He railed against the belief that studies in social behavior aim at generating laws of change, similar to those found in the natural sciences, a trend he considered dangerous for freedom as evidenced by the cruel application of the "laws of history" under Nazism and Soviet Communism through cast-iron deterministic programs by totalitarian governments. Freedom and value pluralism are underpinned by methodological diversity. In *Conjectures and Refutations,* Karl Popper (1968) arrives at a similar conclusion from a very different route. Science, he argues, proceeds by bold conjectures and their refutation through experimentation at multiple points. For Popper, policymaking under democratic pluralism approximates that process. Popper upbraids the idea of lasting universal theories, because the best scientific theories contained specific causal relationships that were always subject to falsification. All scientific propositions were therefore tentative. Monistic theories (such as cultural, geographical, economic, and race-determinism theories) were impossible to disprove and, like Berlin, Popper thought their espousal highly inimical to human freedom.

None of the chapters presented in this book come anywhere close to advocating a single theoretical approach toward our understanding of the experiences encountered in the efforts to introduce democratic rule in the states of sub-Saharan Africa. The eclectic methods of investigation applied are largely reflective of the contemporary trends in most of the best work on the politics of Africa and the rest of "area studies." What we must remain on guard against, however, is the tendency, increasingly common in studies of democracy in Africa, bemoaning the inability of Africanists to match the attention given to Latin America, Eastern Europe, the Iberian Peninsula, and Greece in applying the "regime transition to democracy" theories of O'Donnell, Schmitter (1986), Whitehead (1996), Horowitz (1991), Huntington (1991), Rustow (1970), DiPalma (1990), and Linz and Stepan (1996).

There is no reason why these theories cannot be tested in Africa, subject to observation of the comparison rules mentioned earlier. However, it would be a tragic mistake for political science and for African studies, especially, to espouse a unidirectional perspective that the most ideal political analysis of African regime transitions, to the extent that these exist, is to match the methods and the language at the frontier of *one* version of comparative political theories of democracy, made in the United States. This is inconsistent with the scientific method. In any case, there is vast disagreement among these theories. It provides little succor to those practically involved in promoting democracy in Africa to hear one of the leading social scientists in contemporary regime transition studies candidly proclaim that, although democratization studies were a "major growth industry within political science over the past decade, our chances of producing a strong predictive theory are slight" unless we tolerate a plurality of methods, and emphasize understanding over methodological formalism (Whitehead 1986, 353). These wise sentiments are almost identical to those expressed by Berlin. To the extent that Africanists involved in democratic studies wish to push our frontiers of knowledge on this subject they should heed this advice.

We opened this chapter with a survey of the growth and limits of democratic government in Africa since 1989, relying primarily on Freedom House (procedural) indicators of the spread of liberty and state respect of individual rights in the region. The impressive record that we observed has been tempered by uneven progress across states. It has also been characterized by adoption of formally legal democratic measures that violate the spirit of democracy, the rule of law, and individual liberties. Examples of the latter include electoral systems that penalize disunited majorities, the extension of presidential term limits in Namibia, a majority vote in Senegal that overrides minority grievances in Casamance, and procedurally correct legislation that discriminates against minorities like the ethnic Indians in Eastern Africa. Such aspects of "illiberal democracy" (Zakaria 2003) remain a problem even in the best-rated African democracies, while the majority of African states (and peoples) deal with a mixed record of political gains that is on balance better than that observed in 1989. Some would-be democracies like Congo-Brazzaville and the Central African Republic are now among the most inhospitable places in the world.

But rather than being an obstacle, the lopsided development of democracy in Africa also presents an opportunity. In the new African democracies, the prevalence of procedural-based rights represents a political base to campaign for an institutional framework associated with protection of substantive freedoms: an independent judiciary, separation of powers, and constitutional checks and balances. Likewise, uneven progress of democracy across African countries provides successful states with an opportunity to exert pressure on the laggards and the remaining dictatorships.[10] In addition, success in one country has a demonstration effect in the next. To the extent that it will succeed, democratization of politics in Africa will inevitably be a discontinuous, uneven, and disjointed process of the kind Sklar (1987) believes to characterize developmental democracy in general. That is the main lesson and the basis for hope that emerges from the chapter contributions to this volume.

NOTES

1. Obasanjo and Mosha (1992) contains the proceedings of the "Conference on Security, Stability, Development and Cooperation in Africa," Kampala, May 19–23, 1991. Inaugurated in 2001, the African Union (AU) is intended to promote economic integration in Africa, and to assume peacekeeping responsibilities. Under the AU, NEPAD, based in Johannesburg, South Africa, proposes to establish an African peer-review mechanism to encourage democratic governance, elections, and human rights and to promote regional integration. It now has G-8 support.

2. See especially the essays by Bathily, Lumumba-Kasongo, Buende, and Krichen, in Mamdani and Wamba-dia-Wamba (1995); those in Nzongola-Ntalaja and Lee (1997); and Ake (2000). For a dissenting African scholar's view, which traces the failure of democracy and development in Africa to perverse, everyday, subjective, popular norms, see Mbembe (2001) (this view is itself symptomatic of a growing tradition against the norm). It claims to show Africa is the source of its culturally grounded political problems.

3. For some illustrations of state failure and reconstructions, see Michael Chege, "Sierra Leone: The State That Came Back from the Dead," *The Washington Quarterly* 25, no. 2 (2002).

4. In 2003, four of the twelve conventionally defined democracies in Africa had populations in excess of 10 million (South Africa, Ghana, Kenya, Mali). Of the fourteen most chaotic and repressive governments, five (Cameroon, Sudan, Angola, Democratic Republic of the Congo, and Zimbabwe) had national populations in excess of 10 million. The rest were "small" states.

5. See, for instance, Chabal (2002) for the argument that democracy in Africa, outside of South Africa and Arab North Africa, has not experienced any internally driven progress but rather has suffered a monumental setback underwritten by a perverse, self-destructive "cultural matrix" that defines local politics in black Africa.

6. Sartori (1991) scathingly attacks what he calls "cat-dog" comparisons of states

that bear radically different initial conditions, and differing internal social and economic characteristics, which in our view is a tragically common phenomenon in African political studies.

7. Kuhn (1970) argues that paradigms are incommensurate, and hence our use of "hopefully."

8. The eleven states in 2003 were: South Africa, Ghana, Mali, Senegal, Cape Verde, Benin, Botswana, São Tomé, Namibia, Mauritius, and Lesotho.

9. Mercer International, "World-wide Quality of Life Survey; Personal Safety Rankings," March 3, 2003. Available at: http://www.mercerhr.com/pressrelease/details.jhtml/dynamic/idContepnt/1128760. Accessed September 24, 2004.

10. The inability of African democracies to rein in the Robert Mugabe dictatorship in Zimbabwe has been repeatedly cited as an example of African leaders' reluctance to counteract the authoritarian excesses of their peers. That criticism holds. However, it ignores cases in which African states have nudged their neighbors into domestic peace and elections, e.g., Mozambique in 1994.

REFERENCES

Abdourhamane, Boubacar Issa. 2001. "Madagascar: Situation Institutionnelle." CEAN, IEP-Université Montesquieu-Bordeaux IV. Available at: http://www.etat.sciencespobordeaux.fr/institutionnel/madagascar.html. Accessed October 14, 2004.

Abrahams, Ray. 1989. "Law and Order and the State in the Nyamwezi and Sukuma Area of Tanzania." *Africa* 59, no. 3: 356–70.

Achikbache, Bahjat, and Francis Anglade. 1988. "Les villes prises d'assaut: les migrations internes." *Politique Africaine* 31: 7–14.

Africa Confidential (London). 1992. Newsletter. March 6.

Africa Consulting. 1999. "Evaluation Sociale et Institutionnelle, Republique Centrafricaine, Rapport final." Unpublished report written on behalf of the World Bank, January 1999.

Africa News Service. 2000. "Malawi Withdraws Controversial Bill." November 2.

Africa Research Bulletin. 2000a. "Guinea-Bissau: Kumba Yala Wins." 37, no. 1 (January 1–31): 13828.

———. 2000b. Untitled. 37, no. 1 (January 1–31): 13829.

———. 2000c. "Guinea-Bissau: New Government Formed." 37, no. 2 (February 1–29): 12860–13861.

Africa South of the Sahara. 2004. London and New York: Europa Publishers.

Afrique Contemporaine (Paris). 1995. "La constitution de la république centrafricaine." 175: 61–79.

———. 1992. "La constitution de la république du Congo." 162: 35–59.

Afrique Express. Online news service. Available at: http://www.afrique-express.com. Dates as listed. Accessed October 14, 2004.

Agence France Presse. Online news service. Available at: www.afp.com. Dates as listed.

AIM (Mozambique News Agency). 1996. *Mozambiquefile.* May.

———. 1997. *Mozambiquefile.* June.

———. 1998. *Mozambiquefile.* August.

Ake, Claude. 1995. "The Democratization of Disempowerment in Africa." In *The Democra-*

tisation of Disempowerment: The Problem of Democracy in the Third World, ed. Jochen Hippler. London: Pluto Press, 70–89.

———. 2000. *The Feasibility of Democracy in Africa.* Dakar: CODESRIA.

Alderfer, Philip W. 1997. "Institutional Development in a New Democracy: The Zambian National Assembly, 1964 to 1996." Ph.D. dissertation, Michigan State University.

Allen, Chris. 1989. "Benin." In *Benin, The Congo, Burkina Faso: Politics, Economics and Society,* ed. Bogdan Szajkowski. New York: Pinter, 1–144.

Almond, Gabriel, and Sydney Verba. 1963. *The Civic Culture: Political Attitudes in Five Nations.* Princeton, N.J.: Princeton University Press.

ANB-BIA News Supplements. 1999a. No title. June 17. Available at: http://ospiti.peacelink.it/anb-bia.html. Accessed October 14, 2004.

———. 1999b. No title. June 24. Available at: http://ospiti.peacelink.it/anb-bia.html. Accessed October 14, 2004.

Angola Press. 2004. "Legislative Elections in Guinea-Bissau." Available at: http://www.angola press-angop.ao/noticia.asp?ID=240019. Accessed March 21, 2004.

Article 19. 1999. "At the Crossroads—Freedom of Expression in Malawi." Available at: http://www.article19.org/docimages/456.htm. Accessed October 14, 2004.

Association des Cours Constitutionnel. 1998. "Extraits de la Constitution du 18 septembre 1992 modifiée par la loi constitutionnelle no. 98–001 du 8 avril 1998; Dispositions constitutionnelles relatives à l'institution." Available at: http://www.accpuf.org/mad/. Accessed September 14, 2004.

Ayoob, Mohammed. 1995. *The Third World Security Predicament: State-Making, Regional Conflict, and the International System.* Boulder, Colo.: Lynne Rienner.

Banda, Fackson. 1997. *Elections and the Press in Zambia: The Case of the 1996 Polls.* Lusaka: Independent Media Association.

Baniafouna, Calixte. 1995. *Congo Démocratie: Les Déboires de L'Apparentissage.* Vol. 1. Paris: L'Harmattan.

Barkan, Joel. 1995. "Elections in Agrarian Societies." *Journal of Democracy* 6, no. 4: 106–16.

Basedau, Matthias. 1999. "Niger." In *Elections in Africa: A Data Handbook,* ed. Dieter Nohlen, Michael Krennerich, and Bernard Thibaut. Oxford: Oxford University Press, 677–96.

Bates, Robert H. 1976. *Markets and States in Tropical Africa.* Berkeley: University of California Press.

———. 1981. *Rural Responses to Industrialization: A Study of Village Zambia.* New Haven, Conn.: Yale University Press.

Bayart, Jean-François. 1993. *The State in Africa: The Politics of the Belly.* New York: Longman.

Bayart, Jean-François, Stephen Ellis, and Béatrice Hibou. 1997. *La criminalisation de l'Etat en Afrique.* Brussels: Ed. Complexe.

Bazenguissa-Ganga, Rémy. 1994. "Ninja, Cobra et la milice d'Aubeville: Sociologies des pratiques de la violence urbaine à Brazzaville." In *Urban Management and Urban Violence in Africa,* ed. Isaac O. Albert, J. Adisa, T. Agbola, and G. Hérrault. Ibadan: IFRA, 329–61.

———. 1997. *Les voies du politique au Congo: Essai de sociologie historique.* Paris: Karthala.

———. 1999. "The Spread of Political Violence in Congo-Brazzaville." *African Affairs* 98, no. 390: 37–54.

Bazoum, Mohamed. 1997. "L'Avenir de la Démocratie en Afrique se joue au Niger." Interview in *Démocraties Africaines* 9 (Jan./Feb./Mar.): 13.

BBC News Online. Dates as listed. Available at: http://news.bbc.co.uk/hi/english/world/africa/default.stm.

References

Berlin, Isaiah. 2002. "Historical Inevitability." In *Liberty,* ed. Henry Hardy. Oxford: Oxford University Press.

Bernault, Florence. 1996. *Démocraties Ambiguës: Congo-Brazzaville, Gabon, 1940–1965.* Paris: Karthala.

Bierschenk, Thomas, and Jean-Pierre Olivier de Sardan. 1997. "Local Powers and a Distant State in Rural Central African Republic." *Journal of Modern African Studies* 35, no. 3: 441–68.

Bigo, Didier. 1988. *Pouvoir et obéissance en Centrafrique.* Paris: Karthala.

Boone, Catherine. 1998. "Empirical Statehood and Reconfigurations of Political Order." In *The African State at a Critical Juncture: Between Disintegration and Reconfiguration,* ed. Leonardo Villalón and Philip Huxtable. Boulder, Colo.: Lynne Rienner, 129–42.

———. 2003a. "Decentralization as Political Strategy in West Africa." *Comparative Political Studies* 36, no. 4: 355–80.

———. 2003b. *Political Topographies of the African State: Territorial Authority and Institutional Choice.* Cambridge: Cambridge University Press.

Boulaga, F. Eboussi. 1993. *Les Conférences Nationales en Afrique Noire.* Paris: Karthala.

Bourdieu, Pierre. 1998. *Acts of Resistance: Against the Tyranny of the Market.* New York: New Press.

Bratton, Michael. 1980. *The Local Politics of Rural Development: Peasant and Party-State in Zambia.* Hanover, N.H.: New England Press.

———. 1998. "Second Elections in Africa." *Journal of Democracy* 9, no. 3: 51–66.

———. 1999a. "Political Participation in a New Democracy: Institutional Considerations from Zambia." *Comparative Political Studies* 32, no. 5: 549–88.

———. 1999b. "Second Elections in Africa." In *Democratization in Africa,* ed. Larry Diamond and Marc F. Plattner. Baltimore: Johns Hopkins University Press, 18–33.

Bratton, Michael, and Nicolas van de Walle. 1994. "Neopatrimonial Regimes and Political Transitions in Africa." *World Politics* 46, no. 4: 453–89.

———. 1997. *Democratic Experiments in Africa: Regime Transitions in Comparative Perspective.* Cambridge: Cambridge University Press.

Brietzke, Paul. 1974. "The Chilobwe Murders Trial." *African Studies Review* 17, no. 2: 361–79.

Bunce, Valerie. 2000. "Comparative Democratization: Big and Bounded Generalizations." *Comparative Political Studies* 33, nos. 6/7: 703–34.

Burch, Kurt. 2002. "Toward a Constructivist Comparative Politics." In *Constructivism and Comparative Politics,* ed. Daniel Green. Armonk, N.Y.: M. E. Sharpe, 60–87.

Burnell, Peter. 2001. "The Party System and Party Politics in Zambia: Continuities Past, Present, and Future." *African Affairs* 100, no. 399: 239–63.

Burton, Michael, Richard Gunther, and John Higley. 1992. "Introduction: Elite Transformations and Democratic Regimes." In *Elites and Democratic Consolidation in Latin America and Southern Europe,* ed. John Higley and Richard Gunther. Cambridge: Cambridge University Press, 1–37.

Cabaço, Jose Luis. 1995. "A Longa Estrada de Democracia Moçambicana." In *Moçambique: Eleições, Democracia e Desenvolviment,* ed. Brazao Mazula. Maputo: Inter-Africa, 78–113.

Cabanis, André, and Louis Martin. 1999. *Les Constitutions d'Afrique francophone: Evolutions Récentes.* Paris: Karthala.

Camp, Roderic Ai. 1999. *Politics in Mexico: The Decline of Authoritarianism.* 3rd ed. New York: Oxford University Press.

Cardoso, Carlos. 2001. "Liberal Transition and the Renovation of the Political Elite: The Case of Guinea-Bissau (1986–2000)." Paper presented at the Canadian Association for African Studies Meeting, Quebec City, May.

Carothers, Thomas. 1999. *Aiding Democracy Abroad: The Learning Curve*. Washington, D.C.: Carnegie Endowment for International Peace.

Carter Center. 2000. *Observing the 1999 Elections in Mozambique: Final Report*. Atlanta: The Carter Center.

———. 2002. "The Carter Center Final Statement of the Zambia 2001 Elections." Available at: http://www.cartercenter.org/documents/442.pdf. Accessed October 14, 2004.

Case, William. 1996. "Can the 'Halfway House' Stand? Semidemocracy and Elite Theory in Three Southeast Asian Countries." *Comparative Politics* 28, no. 4: 437–64.

Chabal, Patrick. 2002. "The Quest for Good Governance and Development: Is Nepad the Answer?" *International Affairs* 78, no. 3: 447–62.

Chabal, Patrick, and Jean-Pascal Daloz. 1999. *Africa Works: Disorder as Political Instrument*. Bloomington: Indiana University Press.

Charlick, Robert. 1991. *Niger: Personal Rule and Survival in the Sahel*. Boulder, Colo.: Westview Press.

Chazan, Naomi. 1994. "Between Liberalism and Statism: African Political Cultures and Democracy." In *Political Culture and Democracy in Developing Countries,* ed. Larry Diamond. Boulder, Colo.: Lynne Rienner, 67–97.

Chimgwede, Wisdom, and Don Kulapani. 2000. "Ministers in Another Scam." *The Chronicle* (Lilongwe, Malawi), December 18–24.

The Chronicle (Lilongwe, Malawi). 2001. "Editorial: Changing the Parliamentary Quorum— A Sure Way of Creating 'Single-Party' Multi-Party Rule." June 12.

Clark, Andrew. 1995. "From Military Dictatorship to Democracy: The Democratization Process in Mali." *Journal of Third World Studies* 12, no. 1: 201–19.

———. 2000. "From Military Dictatorship to Democracy: The Democratization Process in Mali." In *Democracy and Development in Mali*, ed. R. James Bingen, David Robinson, and John M. Staatz. East Lansing: Michigan State University Press.

Clark, John F. 1993. "Socio-political Change in the Republic of the Congo: Political Dilemmas of Economic Reform." *Journal of Third World Studies* 10, no. 1: 52–77.

———. 1994. "Elections, Leadership and Democracy in Congo." *Africa Today* 41, no. 3: 41–60.

———. 1997a. "Congo: Transition and the Struggle to Consolidate." In *Political Reform in Francophone Africa,* ed. John F. Clark and David E. Gardinier. Boulder, Colo.: Westview Press, 62–85.

———. 1997b. "Petroleum Income and Democratization in the Republic of Congo." *Journal of Democracy* 8, no. 3: 62–76.

———. 1998a. "Democracy Dismantled in the Congo Republic." *Current History* 97, no. 619: 234–37.

———. 1998b. "International Aspects of the Civil War in Congo-Brazzaville." *Issue* 26, no. 1: 31–36.

———. 2002a. "The Neo-colonial Context of the Democratic Experiment of Congo-Brazzaville." *African Affairs* 101, no. 403: 171–92.

———. 2002b. "Resource Revenues and Political Development in Sub-Saharan Africa: Congo Republic in Comparative Perspective." *Afrika Spectrum* 37, no. 1: 25–41.

Clark, John F., and David E. Gardinier, eds. 1997. *Political Reform in Francophone Africa*. Boulder, Colo.: Westview Press.

References

Collier, David, and Steve Levitsky. 1997. "Democracy with Adjectives: Conceptual Innovation in Comparative Research." *World Politics* 49, no. 3: 430–51.

Collier, Paul, and Anke Hoeffler. 1998. "On Economic Causes of Civil War." *Oxford Economic Papers* 50: 563–73.

Commission of the European Communities. 1996. "The European Union and the Issues of Conflicts in Africa: Peace-Building, Conflict Prevention and Beyond." Unpublished document, communication from the Commission to the Council, Brussels, Belgium.

Consumer Association of Malawi. 1997. "Study of the Distribution, Pricing, and Consumption of Sugar in Malawi." Unpublished paper, issued December 1997.

Coquery-Vidrovitch, Catherine. 1972. *Le Congo au temps des grandes compagnies concessionaires 1898–1930*. Paris: Mouton.

Cunha, J. M. Silva. 1959. "Missão de Estado dos Movimentos Associativos em Africa: Relatório da Campanha de 1958 (Guiné)." Centro de Estudos Políticos e Sociais da Junta de Investigações do Ultramar. Archival document, Center for the Study of Politics and Society, Overseas Investigative Institute, Lisbon.

Dahl, Robert. 1956. *A Preface to Democratic Theory*. Chicago: University of Chicago Press.

———. 1971. *Polyarchy: Participation and Opposition*. New Haven, Conn.: Yale University Press.

———. 1998. *On Democracy*. New Haven, Conn.: Yale University Press.

Daily Times (Blantyre, Malawi). Dates as listed.

Dale, Penny. 2001. "Voter Apathy in Rural Zambia." *BBC News Online*. November 26. Available at: http://news.bbc.co.uk/1/hi/world/africa/1676932.stm. Accessed September 15, 2004.

Decalo, Samuel. 1976. *Coups and Army Rule in Africa*. New Haven, Conn.: Yale University Press.

———. 1987. *Historical Dictionary of Benin*. 2nd ed. Metuchen, N.J.: Scarecrow Press.

———. 1990. *Coups and Army Rule in Africa*. 2nd ed. New Haven, Conn.: Yale University Press.

———. 1997. "Benin: First of the New Democracies." In *Political Reform in Francophone Africa*, ed. John F. Clark and David Gardinier. Boulder, Colo.: Westview Press, 43–61.

———. 1998. *The Stable Minority: Civilian Rule in Africa*. Gainesville: Florida Academic Press.

Decalo, Samuel, Virginia Thompson, and Richard Adloff. 1996. *Historical Dictionary of Congo*. Lanham, Md.: Scarecrow.

Decoudras, Pierre-Marie. 1994. "Niger: Démocratisation Réussie, Avenir en Suspens." In *L'Afrique Politique 1994: Vue sur le démocratisation à marée basse*. Paris: Karthala.

De Jorio, Rosa. 2003. "Narratives of the Nation and Democracy in Mali: A View from Modibo Keita's Memorial." *Cahier d'Etudes Africaines* 172, no. 4: 827–55.

Deng, Francis, Marcus Kostner, and Crawford Young, eds. 1991. *Democratization and Structural Adjustment in Africa in the 1990s*. Madison: African Studies Program, University of Wisconsin–Madison.

de Soysa, Indra. 2000. "The Resource Curse: Are Civil Wars Driven by Rapacity or Paucity?" In *Greed and Grievance: Economic Agendas in Civil War*, ed. Mats Berdal and David Malone. Boulder, Colo.: Lynne Rienner, 113–35.

Dhada, Mustafah. 1993. *Warriors at Work: How Guinea Was Really Set Free*. Boulder, Colo.: University Press of Colorado.

———. 2001. "Guinea-Bissau: Towards a Pluralism of Sorts." In *Africa Contemporary Record 1994–96*. Vol. 25: B86–B95.

―――. 2002. "Guinea-Bissau: Politics, Intrigues, and Vieira's Last Stand." In *Africa Contemporary Record 1996–98*. Vol. 26: B89–B97.

Diamond, Larry. 1988. "Introduction: Roots of Failure, Seeds of Hope." In *Democracy in Developing Countries,* ed. Larry Diamond, Juan J. Linz, and Seymour Martin Lipset. Vol. 2: *Africa*. Boulder, Colo.: Lynne Rienner, 1–32.

―――. 1999a. *Developing Democracy: Toward Consolidation.* Baltimore and London: Johns Hopkins University Press.

―――. 1999b. "Introduction." In *Democratization in Africa,* ed. Larry Diamond and Marc F. Plattner. Baltimore: Johns Hopkins University Press, ix–xxvii.

―――. 2002. "Thinking about Hybrid Regimes." *Journal of Democracy* 13, no. 2: 21–35.

Diamond, Larry, Juan Linz, and Seymour Martin Lipset, eds. 1988. *Democracy in Developing Countries: Africa.* Boulder, Colo.: Lynne Rienner.

Diarrah, Cheikh Oumar. 1996. *Le Défi démocratique au Mali.* Paris: L'Harmattan.

Dias, Eduardo Costa. 2000. "A Balantização da Guiné-Bissau." *Publico* (Lisbon), December 5.

Dickson, Bruce J. 1996. "The Kuomintang before Democratization: Organizational Change and the Role of Elections." In *Taiwan's Electoral Politics and Democratic Transition: Riding the Third Wave,* ed. Hung-mao Tiem. Armonk, N.Y.: M. E. Sharpe, 42–78.

DiPalma, Giuseppe. 1990. *To Craft Democracies: An Essay on Democratic Transitions.* Berkeley: University of California Press.

Dowd, Robert A. 2001. "Why Multiparty Politics Has Not Made Government More Accountable in Africa: Lessons from Kenya in Comparative Perspective." Paper presented at the forty-fourth annual meeting of the African Studies Association, Houston, Texas, November 15–18, 2001.

Duverger, Maurice. 1964. *Political Parties: Their Organization and Activity in the Modern State.* 1954. Reprint. Trans. B. North and R. North. London: Methuen.

Eboussi-Boulaga, Fabien. 1993. *Les Conférences Nationales en Afrique Noire: Une Affaire à Suivre.* Paris: Karthala.

Economist Intelligence Unit (EIU). 1996. *Country Report: Mozambique Malawi.* First Quarter. London: Economist Intelligence Unit.

―――. 1998. *Country Report: Mozambique Malawi.* First Quarter. London: Economist Intelligence Unit.

―――. 2001. *Country Report: Mozambique Malawi.* Annual Report. London: Economist Intelligence Unit.

Ekeh, Peter. 1975. "Colonialism and the Two Publics in Africa: A Theoretical Statement." *Comparative Studies in Society and History* 17, no. 1: 91–112.

Englebert, Pierre. 2004. "Mali. Recent History." In *Africa South of the Sahara.* London and New York: Europa Publishers.

Englund, Harri. 2002. "Winning Elections, Losing Legitimacy." In *Multi-Party Elections in Africa,* ed. Michael Cowen and Liisa Laakso. New York: Palgrave, 172–86.

―――. 2003. "Introduction: The Culture of Chameleon Politics." In *A Democracy of Chameleons: Politics and Culture in the New Malawi,* ed. Harri Englund. Uppsala, Sweden: Nordic Africa Institute, 11–24.

Faltas, Sami. 2001. "Mutiny and Disarmament in the Central African Republic." In *Managing the Remnants of War: Micro-disarmament as an Element of Peace-Building,* ed. Sami Faltas and Joseph Di Chiaro III. Baden-Baden: Nomos, 77–96.

Fatton, Robert. 1992. *Predatory Rule: State and Civil Society in Africa.* Boulder, Colo.: Lynne Rienner.

References

Fengler, Wolfgang. 2001. *Politische Reformhemmnisse und ökonomische Blockierung in Afrika: Die Zentralafrikanische Republik und Eritrea im Vergleich.* Baden-Baden: Nomos.

Field, G. Lowell, and John Higley. 1985. "National Elites and Political Stability." In *Research in Politics and Society: Studies of the Structure of National Elite Groups,* ed. Gwen Moore. Greenwich, Conn.: JAI Press, 1–44.

Forrest, Joshua B. 1987. "Guinea Bissau Since Independence: A Decade of Domestic Power Struggles." *The Journal of Modern African Studies* 25, no. 1: 95–116.

———. 1992. *Guinea-Bissau: Power, Conflict and Renewal in a West African Nation.* Boulder, Colo.: Westview Press.

———. 2002. "Guinea-Bissau." In *Lusophone Africa since Independence,* ed. Patrick Chabal. London: Hurst, 236–63.

———. 2003. *Lineages of State Fragility: Rural Civil Society in Guinea-Bissau.* Athens: Ohio University Press.

Forum de la Semaine (Benin).Weekly. Dates as listed.

Foundation for Democratic Process. 2002. "FODEP 2001 Draft Election Monitoring Report." Available at: http://www.fodep.org.zm/elecreport.htm. Accessed October 15, 2004.

Frank, Philippe. 1997. "Ethnies et partis: le cas du Congo." *Afrique Contemporaine* 182, no. 3: 3–15.

Freedom House. 2001. "Freedom in the World Country Rankings, 1972–73 to 2000–01." Available at: http://www.freedomhouse.org/research/freeworld/2001/tables.htm.

———. 2002. *Freedom in the World 2002.* New York: Freedom House.

———. 2004. "Essay." In *Freedom in the World 2004: The Annual Survey of Political Rights and Civil Liberties.* Available at: http://www.freedomhouse.org/research/freeworld/2004/essay2004.pdf. Accessed October 15, 2004.

Frelimo. 1991. "Relatório do Comité Central." Colecção Sexto Congresso, Maputo. Unpublished party documents.

———. 1997. "Relatório do Comité Central." Colecção Septimo Congresso, Maputo. Unpublished party documents.

Friedman, Kajsa Ekholm, and Anne Sundberg. n.d. "Ethnic War and Ethnic cleansing in Brazzaville." Unpublished manuscript, based on research conducted in May 1994 in Congo.

Fukuyama, Francis. 1995. *Trust: The Social Virtues and the Creation of Prosperity.* New York: Free Press.

Galli, Rosemary E., and Jocelyn Jones. 1987. *Guinea-Bissau: Politics, Economics and Society.* Boulder, Colo.: Lynne Rienner.

Galvan, Dennis. 2001. "Political Turnover and Social Change in Senegal." *Journal of Democracy* 12, no. 3: 51–62.

Geertz, Clifford. 1973. "Thick Description: Toward an Interpretive Theory of Culture." In *The Interpretation of Cultures: Interpretive Essays,* ed. Clifford Geertz. New York: Basic Books, 3–30.

Gertzel, Cherry. 1984. "Dissent and Authority in the Zambian One-Party State, 1973–80." In *The Dynamics of the One-Party State in Zambia,* ed. C. Gertzel. Manchester: Manchester University Press, 79–115.

Gervais, Myriam. 1995. "Structural Adjustment in Niger: Implementation, Effects, and Determining Political Factors." *Review of African Political Economy* 63, no. 22: 27–42.

———. 1997. "Niger: Regime Change, Economic Crisis, and Perpetuation of Privilege." In *Political Reform in Francophone Africa,* ed. John F. Clark and David E. Gardinier. Boul-

References

der, Colo.: Westview Press, 86–108. Glélé, Maurice. 1969. *Naissance d'un État Noir.* Paris: R. Pichon and R. Durand-Auzias.

Good, Kenneth. 2002. *The Liberal Model and Africa: Elites against Democracy.* New York: Palgrave Macmillan.

Government of Niger. 1979. *Résultats édifiants d'un sursaut national.* Niamey: Secrétariat d'Etat à la Présidence.

Green, Daniel. 1999. "Liberal Moments and Democracy's Durability: Comparing Global Outbreaks of Democracy—1918, 1945, 1989." *Studies in Comparative International Development* 34, no. 1: 83–120.

Green, Daniel, ed. 2002. *Constructivism and Comparative Politics.* Armonk, N.Y.: M. E. Sharpe.

Greif, Avner. 1994. "Cultural Beliefs and the Organization of Society: A Historical and Theoretical Reflection on Collectivist and Individualist Societies." *Journal of Political Economy* 102, no. 51: 912–50.

Gyimah-Boadi, E. 1998. "The Rebirth of African Liberalism." *Journal of Democracy* 9, no. 2: 18–31.

———. 1999a. "Institutionalizing Credible Elections in Ghana." In *The Self-Restraining State: Power and Accountability in New Democracies,* ed. Andreas Schedler, Larry Diamond, and Marc Plattner. Boulder, Colo.: Lynne Rienner, 105–22.

———. 1999b. "The Rebirth of African Liberalism." In *Democratization in Africa,* ed. Larry Diamond and Marc F. Plattner. Baltimore: Johns Hopkins University Press, 34–47.

Hanlon, Joe. 2000a. "Power without Responsibility: The World Bank and Mozambican Cashew Nuts." *Review of African Political Economy* 83: 29–45.

———. 2000b. *Mozambique Peace Process Bulletin* 24, no. 4.

Harbeson, John W., Donald Rothchild, and Naomi Chazan, eds. 1994. *Civil Society and the State in Africa.* Boulder, Colo.: Lynne Rienner.

Havik, Philip J. 1995–99. "Mundasson i Kambansa: espaço social e movimentos políticos na Guiné Bissau (1910–1994)." *Revista Internacional de Estudos Africanos* 18–22: 115–67.

Heilbrunn, John. 1993. "Social Origins of National Conferences in Benin and Togo." *Journal of Modern African Studies* 31, no. 2: 277–99.

———. 1994. "Authority, Property and Politics in Benin and Togo." Ph.D. diss., University of California at Los Angeles.

Herbst, Jeffrey. 2000. *States and Power in Africa: Comparative Lessons in Authority and Control.* Princeton, N.J.: Princeton University Press.

———. 2001. "Political Liberalization in Africa after Ten Years." *Comparative Politics* 33, no. 3: 357–74.

Hobbes, Thomas. 1985. *Leviathan.* New York: Penguin Books.

Horcasitas, Juan Molinar. 1996. "Changing the Balance of Power in a Hegemonic Party System: The Case of Mexico." In *Institutional Design in New Democracies: Eastern Europe and Latin America,* ed. Arendt Lijphart and Carlos H. Waisman. Boulder, Colo.: Westview Press, 137–59.

Horowitz, Donald L. 1991. *Democratic South Africa?* Berkeley: University of California Press.

———. 1996. "Comparing Democratic Systems." In *The Global Resurgence of Democracy,* ed. Larry Diamond and Marc Plattner. Baltimore: Johns Hopkins University Press, 143–49.

Human Rights Watch. 1997. "Zambia: Reality amidst Contradictions." *Human Rights Watch Report* 9: 3.

———. 1998. *Human Rights Watch World Report, 1999.* New York: Human Rights Watch.

References

Huntington, Samuel P. 1968. *Political Order in Changing Societies*. New Haven, Conn.: Yale University Press.

———. 1984. "Will Countries Become More Democratic." *Political Science Quarterly* 99, no. 2: 193–218.

———. 1991. *The Third Wave: Democratization in the Late Twentieth Century*. Norman: University of Oklahoma Press.

Ibrahim, Jibrin. 1999. "Transitions et successions politiques au Niger." In *Les Figures du politique en Afrique: Des pouvoirs hérités aux pouvoirs élus*, ed. Momar Coumba Diop and Mamadou Diouf. Paris/Dakar: Karthala/Codesria, 189–216.

Ibrahim, Jibrin, and Abdoulaye Niandou Souley. 1998. "The Rise to Power of an Opposition Party: The MNSD in Niger Republic." In *The Politics of Opposition in Contemporary Africa,* ed. Adebayo O. Olukoshi. Uppsala: Nordiska Afrikainstitutet.

Idrissa, Abdourahmane. 2000. "Aperçu sur les débats autour de la nature et de la forme du regime politique au Niger: 1989–1999." Unpublished mémoire de D.E.A., Faculté des Sciences Juridiques et Politiques, Université Cheikh Anta Diop de Dakar, Senegal.

Igue, John O., and Bio G. Soule. 1992. *L'Etat Entrepôt au Bénin: Commerce Informel ou Solution à la Crise?* Paris: Karthala.

Ihonvbere, Julius O. 1996. *Economic Crisis, Civil Society, and Democratization: The Case of Zambia*. Trenton, N.J.: Africa World Press.

Illiassou, Ali, and Mahaman Tidjani Alou. 1994. "Processus électoral et démocratisation au Niger." *Politique Africaine* 53 (March): 128–32.

Imperato, Pascal James. 1991. "Downfall of a Dictator." *Africa Report* (July–August): 4–27.

Indian Ocean Newsletter (Paris). Indigo Publications. Dates as listed.

Info-Matin (Bamako). Dates as listed. Available at http://www.info-matin.com.

Integrated Regional Information Network. Dates and titles as listed.

International Foundation for Elections Systems (IFES). 1998. *Les Lois Electorales d'Afrique Francophone*. Washington, D.C.: IFES.

Jackson, Robert. 1992. "The Insecurity Dilemma in Africa." In *The Insecurity Dilemma: National Security of Third World States,* ed. Brian Job. Boulder, Colo.: Lynne Rienner, 81–94.

Jackson, Robert, and Carl Rosberg. 1982. *Personal Rule in Black Africa: Prophet, Autocrat, Prophet, Tyrant*. Berkeley and Los Angeles: University of California Press.

———. 1985a. "Democracy in Tropical Africa: Democracy versus Autocracy in African Politics." *Journal of International Affairs* 38, no. 2: 293–305.

———. 1985b. "The Marginality of African States." In *African Independence: The First Twenty-Five Years,* ed. Gwendolyn Carter and Patrick O'Meara. Bloomington: Indiana University Press, 45–70.

Jeune Afrique (Paris). 2002. "J'ai survécu à sept putschs et j'ai toujours pardonné (Interview)." April 22–28.

Job, Brian. 1992. "The Insecurity Dilemma: National, Regime, and State Securities in the Third World." In *The Insecurity Dilemma: National Security of Third World States,* ed. Brian Job. Boulder, Colo.: Lynne Rienner, 11–35.

Joseph, Richard. 1992. "Zambia: A Model for Democratic Change." *Current History* 91, no. 565: 199–201.

———. 1997. "Democratization in Africa after 1989: Comparative and Theoretical Perspectives." *Comparative Politics* 29, no. 3: 363–82.

———. 1998. "Africa, 1990–1997: From Abertura to Closure." *Journal of Democracy* 9, no. 2: 3–17.

References

———. 1999. "Africa, 1990–1997: From Abertura to Closure." In *Democratization in Africa*, ed. Larry Diamond and Marc F. Plattner. Baltimore: Johns Hopkins University Press, 3–17.

Joseph, Richard, ed. 1999. *State, Conflict, and Democracy in Africa*. Boulder, Colo.: Lynne Rienner.

Kalck, Pierre. 1971. *Central African Republic: A Failure in De-colonisation*. London: Pall Mall Press.

———. 1974. *Histoire centrafricaine*. Paris: Berger-Levrault.

Kanjaye, Hazwell. 1999. "Politics—Malawi: Clergymen Speak Out on Escalating Violence." Inter-Press Service. July 14. Available at: http://www.oneworld.org/ips2/july99/14_40_067.htm. Accessed May 16, 2000.

Karatnycky, Adrian. 2003. *Freedom in the World 2003: Liberty's Expansion in a Turbulent World—Thirty Years of the Survey of Freedom*. Available at: http://www.freedomhouse.org/research/freeworld/2003/akessay.htm. Accessed April 30, 2004.

Karl, Terry Lynne. 1995. "The Hybrid Regimes of Central America." *Journal of Democracy* 6, no. 3: 72–86.

———. 1991. "Dilemmas of Democratization in Latin America." In *Comparative Political Dynamics: Global Research Perspectives*, ed. Dankwart Rustow and Kenneth Erickson. New York: Harper Collins Publishers, 163–65.

Kasfir, Nelson. 1976. *The Shrinking Political Arena*. Berkeley: University of California Press.

Kaunda, Jonathan Mayuyuka. 1998. "The Transition to a Multiparty System and Consolidation of Democracy in Malawi." *Il Politico* 63, no. 3: 425–48.

Kim, Byung-Kook. 1999. "Party Politics in South Korea's Democracy: The Crisis of Success." In *Institutional Reform and Democratic Consolidation in Korea*, ed. Larry Diamond and Doh Chull Shin. Stanford, Calif.: Hoover Institution Press, 53–85.

King, Gary, Robert O. Keohane, and Sidney Verba. 1994. *Designing Social Inquiry: Scientific Inference in Qualitative Research*. Princeton, N.J.: Princeton University Press.

Koyt, Michel, M'bringa Takama, Maxime Faustin, and Pierre-Marie Decoudras. 1995. "République Centrafricaine: Les vicissitudes du changement." In *L'Afrique Politique 1995*, ed. CEAN. Paris: Karthala, 235–51.

Krislov, Samuel, and David H. Rosenbloom. 1981. *Representative Bureaucracy and the American Political System*. New York: Praeger.

Kuhn, Thomas. 1972. *The Structure of Scientific Revolutions*. Chicago: University of Chicago Press.

Kulapani, Don. 2001. "Ministers Operating Illegally." *The Chronicle* (Malawi). March 19.

Laitin, David. 1986. *Hegemony and Culture: Politics and Religious Change among the Yoruba*. Chicago: University of Chicago Press, 1986.

La Nation (Benin). Dates as listed.

Le Citoyen (Bangui). Dates as listed.

Le Pape, Marc, and Pierre Salignon. 2001. *Une Guerre Contre les Civils: Reflexions sur les pratiques humanitaires au Congo Brazzaville (1998–2000)*. Paris: Karthala and Medecins Sans Frontières.

Les Echos. (Bamako). Dates as listed. Available at: http://www.cefib.com/presse.

Levine, Daniel. 1978. "Venezuela since 1958: The Consolidation of Democratic Politics." In *The Breakdown of Democratic Regimes: Latin America*, ed. Juan Linz and Alfred Stepan. Baltimore and London: Johns Hopkins University Press, 82–109.

Le Vine, Victor T. 2004. *Politics in Francophone Africa*, Boulder, Colo.: Lynne Rienner.

References

Levitsky, Steven, and Lucan A. Way. 2002. "The Rise of Competitive Authoritarianism." *Journal of Democracy* (April): 51–65.

L'Hirondelle (Bangui). Dates as listed.

Libération (Paris). 1998. "Patassé, main basse sur les diamants." April 9.

Lijphart, Arendt. 1977. *Democracy in Plural Societies: A Comparative Exploration*. New Haven, Conn.: Yale University Press.

———. 1996a. "Constitutional Choices for New Democracies." In *The Global Resurgence of Democracy,* ed. Larry Diamond and Marc Plattner. Baltimore: Johns Hopkins University Press, 146–58.

———. 1996b. "Double-Checking the Evidence." In *The Global Resurgence of Democracy,* ed. Larry Diamond and Marc Plattner. Baltimore: Johns Hopkins University Press, 171–77.

Lindblom, Charles E. 1977. *Politics and Markets: The World's Political-Economic Systems*. New York: Basic Books.

Linz, Juan. 1978. *The Breakdown of Democratic Regimes: Crisis, Breakdown and Reequilibration*. Baltimore and London: Johns Hopkins University Press.

———. 1996a. "The Perils of Presidentialism." In *The Global Resurgence of Democracy,* ed. Larry Diamond and Marc Plattner. Baltimore: Johns Hopkins University Press, 108–26.

———. 1996b. "The Virtues of Parliamentarianism." In *The Global Resurgence of Democracy,* ed. Larry Diamond and Marc Plattner. Baltimore: Johns Hopkins University Press, 154–61.

Linz, Juan, and Alfred Stepan. 1996. *Problems of Democratic Transition and Consolidation: Southern Europe, South America, and Post-Communist Europe*. Baltimore and London: Johns Hopkins University Press.

Lipset, Seymour Martin. 1959. "Some Social Requisites of Democracy: Economic Development and Political Legitimacy." *American Political Science Review* 53, no. 1: 69–105.

Lique, René-Jacques. 1993. *Bokassa 1er: La grande mystification*. Paris: Editions Chaka.

Lwanda, John. 1996. *Promises, Power, Politics, and Poverty in Malawi*. Glasgow: Dudu Nsomba Publications.

MacGaffey, Wyatt. 2000. *Kongo Political Culture: The Conceptual Challenge of the Particular*. Bloomington: Indiana University Press.

Magnusson, Bruce. 1991. "Antecedents to Political and Economic Reform in Benin." In *Democratization and Structural Adjustment in Africa in the 1990s,* ed. Lual Deng, Marcus Kostner, and Crawford Young. Madison: African Studies Program, University of Wisconsin–Madison, 178–87.

———. 1997. "The Politics of Democratic Regime Legitimation in Benin: Institutions, Social Policy, and Security." Ph.D. diss., University of Wisconsin–Madison.

———. 1999. "Testing Democracy in Benin: Experiments in Institutional Reform." In *State, Conflict, and Democracy in Africa,* ed. Richard Joseph. Boulder, Colo.: Lynne Rienner, 217–37.

———. 2001. "Democratization and Domestic Insecurity: Navigating the Transition in Benin." *Comparative Politics* 33, no. 2: 211–30.

———. 2002. "Transnational Flows, Legitimacy, and Syncretic Democracy in Benin." In *Constructivism and Comparative Politics,* ed. Daniel Green. Armonk, N.Y.: M. E. Sharpe, 175–93.

Mail and Guardian (South Africa). 1997. "Malawi Opposition Too Broke to Elect New Leader." April 4.

References

Mainwaring, Scott, and Matthew Soberg Shugart. 1997. *Presidentialism and Democracy in Latin America.* New York: Cambridge University Press.

Malawi News Online. 1997a. "Muluzi under Fire in Bribery Accusations." No. 23, February 2. Available at: www.sas.upenn.edu/African_Studies/Newsletters/mno23.html. Accessed October 14, 2004.

———. 1997b. "MCP Disputes Three By-Elections Results." No. 31, June 23. Available at: www.sas.upenn.edu/African_Studies/Newsletters/mno31.html. Accessed October 14, 2004.

———. 1998. "Kadzamira Gets Lions Share." No. 39, January 11. Available at: www.sas.upenn .edu/African_Studies/Newsletters/mno39.html. Accessed October 14, 2004.

Malawi Update. 2001. Issue 39. November.

"Malawi: National Assembly Debates (Hansard)." Sixth Meeting—Thirty-Fourth Session, January 12, 2001.

Mamdani, Mahmood. 1996. *Citizen and Subject.* Princeton, N.J.: Princeton University Press.

Mamdani, Mahmood, and Ernest Wamba-dia-Wamba, eds. 1995. *African Studies in Social Movements and Democracy.* Dakar: CODESRIA.

Mané, Ibrahima. 1997. "La démocratie malienne à l'épreuve." *Démocraties africaines* 11: 20–22.

Manning, Carrie. 1997. "Beginning at the End? Democratization in Mozambique." Ph.D. diss., University of California, Berkeley.

———. 1998. "The State of Democratic Transition in Mozambique." Paper presented at the University of Florida, Center for African Studies, November 6, 1998.

———. 2000a. "Elite Habituation to Democracy in Mozambique: The View from Parliament, 1994–2000." *Journal of Commonwealth and Comparative Politics* 40, no. 1: 61–80.

———. 2000b. "Conflict Management and Elite Habituation in Post-war Democracy: The Case of Mozambique." *Comparative Politics* 35, no. 1: 63–84.

Marchés Tropicaux et Méditeranéens (MTM) (Paris). 1993. "Congo-Brazzaville." May 21: 1321.

Marcus, Richard R. 2000. "Cultivating Democracy on Fragile Ground: Environmental Institutions and Non-Elite Perceptions of Democracy in Madagascar and Uganda." Ph.D. diss., Department of Political Science, University of Florida.

———. 2001. "Madagascar: Legitimating Autocracy?" *Current History* 100, no. 646: 226–31.

Marcus, Richard, and Adrien Ratsimbaharison. Forthcoming. "Political Parties in Madagascar: From Neopatriomonial Tool to Mechanism for Enhanced Democratic Action?" *Party Politics.*

Marcus, Richard R., and Paul Razafindrakoto. 2003. "Madagascar's New Democracy?" *Current History* 102 (May), no. 664: N.p.

Martin, François. 1991. *Le Niger du President Diori: 1960–1974.* Paris: L'Harmattan.

Marx, Karl. 1978. "The Eighteenth Brumaire of Louis Bonaparte." In *The Marx-Engels Reader,* 2nd ed., ed. Robert C. Tucker. 1852. Reprint. New York: Norton, 594–617.

Masquelier, Adeline. 1999. "Debating Muslims, Disputed Practices: Struggles for the Realization of an Alternative Moral Order in Niger." In *Civil Society and the Political Imagination in Africa: Critical Perspectives,* ed. John L. Comaroff and Jean Comaroff. Chicago: University of Chicago Press, 219–50.

Mazrui, Ali. 1984. "Africa Entrapped: Between the Protestant Ethic and the Legacy of Westphalia." In *The Expansion of International Society,* ed. Hedley Bull and Adam Watson. Oxford: Oxford University Press, 289–308.

Mbeko, Maurice Honoré. 1993. "Régimes issus des coups d'Etat militaires et transition démocratique en Afrique noire: Le cas de la République Centrafricaine." Ph.D. diss., Université de Laval.

References

Mbembe, Achille. 2001. *On the Postcolony.* Berkeley: University of California Press.

Mehler, Andreas. 1996. "Zentralafrikanische Republik." In *Afrika Jahrbuch: Politik, Wirtschaft und Gesellschaft in Afrika südlich der Sahara,* ed. Institut für Afrika-Kunde. Opladen: Leske & Budrich, 224–28.

———. 1997. "Zentralafrikanische Republik." In *Afrika Jahrbuch: Politik, Wirtschaft und Gesellschaft in Afrika südlich der Sahara,* ed. Institut für Afrika-Kunde. Opladen: Leske & Budrich, 219–22.

———. 1998. "Zentralafrikanische Republik." In *Afrika Jahrbuch: Politik, Wirtschaft und Gesellschaft in Afrika südlich der Sahara,* ed. Institut für Afrika-Kunde. Opladen: Leske & Budrich, 211–14.

———. 1999a. "Central African Republic." In *Elections in Africa: A Data Handbook,* ed. Dieter Nohlen, Michael Krennerich, and Bernhard Thibaut. Oxford: Oxford University Press, 205–20.

———. 1999b. "Meuterei der Armee und Tribalisierung von Politik in der demokratisierten Neokolonie Zentralafrikanische Republik (ZAR)." In *Unvollendete Demokratisierung in Nichtmarktökonomien: Die Blackbox zwischen Staat und Wirtschaft in den Transitionsländern des Südens und Ostens,* ed. Heidrun Zinecker. Amsterdam: G & B Facultas, 193–211.

———. 2000. "Zentralafrikanische Republik." In *Afrika Jahrbuch 1999,* ed. Institut für Afrika-Kunde and Rolf Hofmeier. Opladen: Leske & Budrich, 221–25.

———. 2002. "Structural Stability: Meaning, Scope and Use in an African Context." *Afrika Spectrum* 37, no. 1: 5–23.

Mehler, Andreas, and Vincent Da Cruz. 2000. "La démocratie n'est pas un vaccin: Politique formelle et informelle en République Centrafricaine." In *L'Afrique politique 2000,* ed. CEAN. Paris: Karthala, 197–208.

Meinhardt, Heiko. 1997. *Politische Transition und Demokratisierung in Malawi.* Hamburg: Institut für Afrika-Kunde.

———. 1999. "Malawi." In *Elections in Africa: A Data Handbook,* ed. Dieter Nohlen, Michael Krennerich, and Bernhard Thibaut. New York: Oxford University Press, 549–65.

Mendes, Pedro Rosa. 2001. "Guiné: A Ditadura dos Incompetentes." *Publico* (Lisbon). March 4.

Mercer International. 2003. "World-wide Quality of Life Survey; Personal Safety Rankings: Global. London." March 3. Available at: http://www.mercerhr.com/pressrelease/details.jhtml?idContent=1084615. Accessed April 30, 2004.

Midiohouan, Guy. 1994. *Du Bon Usage de la Francophonie.* Porto Novo: Editions CNPMS.

Mills, C. Wright. 1959. *The Power Elite.* New York: Oxford University Press.

Misser, François, and Olivier Vallée. 1997. *Les gemmocraties: L'économie politique du diamant africain.* Paris: Desclâee de Brouwer.

Mittelman, James H. 2000. *The Globalization Syndrome: Transformation and Resistance.* Princeton, N.J.: Princeton University Press.

Mkandawire, Thandika. 1999. "Crisis Management and the Making of Choiceless Democracies." In *State Conflict and Democracy in Africa,* ed. Richard Joseph. Boulder, Colo.: Lynne Rienner, 119–36.

Molteno, Robert, and Ian Scott. 1974. "The 1968 General Election and the Political System." In *Politics in Zambia,* ed. William Tordoff. Berkeley: University of California Press, 155–96.

Monga, Célestin. 1999. "Eight Problems with African Politics." In *Democratization in Africa,* ed. Larry Diamond and Marc F. Plattner. Baltimore: Johns Hopkins University Press, 48–62.

References

Moore, Barrington. 1966. *The Social Origins of Dictatorship and Democracy: Lord and Peasant in the Making of the Modern World.* Boston: Beacon Press.

Mozaffar, Shaheen. n.d. "Mali: a Two-Round System in Africa." Available at: http://www.idea .int/esd/case/mali.cfm. Accessed May 11, 2004.

———. 1995. "The Institutional Logic of Ethnic Politics: A Prolegomenon." In *Ethnic Conflict and Democratization in Africa,* ed. Harvey Glickman. Atlanta: ASA Press, 33–69.

———. 1998. "Electoral Systems and Conflict Management in Africa: A Twenty-Eight-State Comparison." In *Elections and Conflict Management in Africa,* ed. Timothy Sisk and Andrew Reynolds. Washington, D.C.: United States Institute of Peace Press, 81–98.

Mozaffar, Shaheen, James Scarritt, and Glen Galaich. 2003. "Electoral Institutions, Ethno-political Cleavages and Party Systems in Africa's Emerging Democracies." *American Political Science Review* 97, no. 3: 379–90.

Mphaisha, Chisepo J. J. 1996. "Retreat from Democracy in Post–One-Party State Zambia." *Journal of Commonwealth and Comparative Politics* 34, no. 2: 65–84.

Mwanawina, Inyambo, Kufekisa Mulima Akapelwa, Kalungu J. Sampa, and Justina Moonga. 2002. "Zambia." In *Budget Transparency and Participation: Five African Case Studies,* ed. Alta Folscher. Cape Town: Institute for Democracy in Southern Africa.

The Nation (Blantyre, Malawi). Dates as listed.

Ndegwa, Stephen. 2001. "A Decade of Democracy in Africa." In *A Decade of Democracy in Africa,* ed. Stephen Ndegwa. Leiden: E. J. Brill, 1–17.

Ndiaye, Babacar. 2000. "Repères sur la crise bissau-guinéenne." *Revue de la gendarmerie nationale* [France] 195: 123–28.

Ngongola, Clement. 2003. "Judicial Mediation in Electoral Politics in Malawi." In *A Democracy of Chameleons: Politics and Culture in the New Malawi,* ed. Harri Englund. Stockholm: Nordic Africa Institute, 62–86.

Nhane, Steve. 1997. "Banda's Assets." Africa Press Bureau, October.

Niandou-Souley, Abdoulaye. 1999. "Démocratisation et crise du modèle compétitif au Niger." In *Les Figures du Politique en Afrique,* ed. Momar-Coumba Diop and Mamadou Diouf. Dakar/Paris: Codesria/Karthala, 413–36.

Nohlen, Dieter, Michael Krennerich, and Bernhard Thibaut, eds. 1999. *Elections in Africa: A Data Handbook.* Oxford: Oxford University Press.

Noticias (Maputo). 1999. October 27.

Noudjenoume, Philippe. 1999. *La Démocratie au Bénin: Bilan et Perspectives.* Paris: L'Harmattan.

Nsafou, Gaspard. 1996. *Congo: De la Démocratie à la Démocrature.* Paris: L'Harmattan.

Nyambe, Lawrence. 1999. "Political Watch: Trail of Destruction." *Post of Zambia* (Lusaka). August 25.

Nyerere, Julius. 1992. "Statement at the Kampala Forum on Security, Stability and Development in Africa." In *Africa: Rise and Challenge,* ed. Olusegun Obasanjo and Felix N. Mosha. New York: Africa Leadership Forum.

Nzongola-Ntalaja, Georges, and Margaret C. Lee, eds. 1997. *The State and Democracy in Africa.* Harare: AAPS.

Nzunda, Matembo. 1998. "The Quickening of Judicial Control of Administrative Action in Malawi, 1992–1994." In *Democratization in Malawi: A Stocktaking,* ed. Kings Phiri and Kenneth Ross. Zomba, Malawi: Kachere Press, 283–315.

Obasanjo, Olusegun, and Felix N. Mosha, eds. 1992. *Africa: Rise and Challenge.* New York: Africa Leadership Forum.

Obenga, Théophile. 1998. *L'histoire sanglante du Congo-Brazzaville (1959–1997): Diagnostic d'une mentalité politique africaine.* Paris: Présence Africaine.

References

O'Donnell, Guillermo. 1994. "Delegative Democracy." *Journal of Democracy* 5, no. 1: 55–69.

———. 1996. "Illusions about Consolidation." *Journal of Democracy* 7, no. 4: 34–51.

O'Donnell, Guillermo, and Philippe Schmitter. 1986. *Transitions from Authoritarian Rule: Tentative Conclusions about Uncertain Democracies.* Baltimore: Johns Hopkins University Press.

Olokushi, Adebayo. 1999. "State, Conflict and Democracy in Africa: The Complex Process of Renewal." In *State Conflict and Democracy in Africa,* ed. Richard Joseph. Boulder, Colo.: Lynne Rienner, 451–65.

Organization of Economic Cooperation and Development. 2002. Creditor Reporting Service Online Database. Available at: http://www.oecd.org/dataoecd/50/17/5037721 .htm. Accessed October 14, 2004.

O'Toole, Thomas. 1986. *The Central African Republic: The Continent's Hidden Heart.* Boulder, Colo.: Westview Press.

Ottaway, Marina. 1999. *Africa's New Leaders: Democracy or State Reconstruction.* Washington, D.C.: Carnegie Endowment.

Ottaway, Marina, and Theresa Chung. 1999. "Toward a New Paradigm." *Journal of Democracy* 10, no. 4: 99–113.

Oyugi, Walter O., and Atieno Citango, eds. 1988. *Democratic Theory and Practice in Africa.* London: James Currey.

Pareto, Vilfredo, and S. E. Finer, eds. 1969. *Vilfredo Pareto: Sociological Writings.* New York: Praeger.

Parti Congolais du Travail (PCT). 1992. "La Verité sur les Raisons de l'Echec: Mémorandum sur la rupture de l'Alliance UPADS/PCT." Brazzaville: Editions du PCT.

Patel, Nandini. 2000. "The 1999 Elections: Challenges and Reforms." In *Malawi's Second Democratic Elections: Process, Problems and Prospects,* ed. Martin Ott, Kings Phiri, and Nandini Patel. Zomba, Malawi: Kachere Press, 22–51.

Phiri, Isaac. 1999. "Media in 'Democratic' Zambia: Problems and Prospects." *Africa Today* 46, no. 2: 52–65.

Pletcher, James. 2000. "The Politics of Liberalizing Zambia's Maize Markets." *World Development* 28, no. 1: 129–42.

Popper, Karl. 1968. *Conjectures and Refutations.* New York: Harper and Row.

Posner, Daniel. 1998. "The Institutional Origins of Ethnic Politics in Zambia." Ph.D. diss., Harvard University.

———. 2004. *Institutions and Ethnic Politics in Africa.* New York: Cambridge University Press.

Posner, Daniel M., and David J. Simon. 2002. "Economic Conditions and Incumbent Support in Africa's New Democracies: Evidence from Zambia." *Comparative Political Studies* 35, no. 3: 313–36.

Post of Zambia (Lusaka). Dates as listed.

Pourtier, Roland. 1998. "1997: Les raisons d'une guerre 'incivile.'" *Afrique Contemporaine* 186: 7–32.

Power, Timothy J., and Mark J. Gasiorowski. 1997. "Institutional Design and Democratic Consolidation in the Third World." *Comparative Political Studies* 30, no. 2: 123–55.

Przeworski, Adam. 1986. "Some Problems in the Study of Transition to Democracy." In *Transitions from Authoritarian Rule: Comparative Perspectives,* ed. Guillermo O'Donnell, Philippe C. Schmitter, and Laurence Whitehead. Baltimore: Johns Hopkins University Press, 40–63.

———. 1991. *Democracy and the Market: Political and Economic Reforms in Eastern Europe and Latin America.* Cambridge: Cambridge University Press.

References

———. 2000. *Democracy and Development: Political Institutions and Well-Being in the World, 1950–1990.* Cambridge: Cambridge University Press.

Przeworski, Adam, and Fernando Limongi. 1997. "Modernization: Theories and Facts." *World Politics* 49, no. 2: 155–83.

Przeworski, Adam, Michael Alvarez, Jose Antonio Cheibub, and Fernando Limongio. 1996. "What Makes Democracies Endure?" *Journal of Democracy* 7, no. 1: 39–55.

———. 1997. "What Makes Democracies Endure?" In *Consolidating the Third Wave Democracies,* ed. Larry Diamond, Marc F. Plattner, Yun-Han Chu, and Hung-Mao Tien. Baltimore: Johns Hopkins University Press, 295–311.

Publico (Lisbon). 2004. "Guinea-Bissau's Elections." March 9. Available at: http://www.jornal publico.pt/publico/2004/03/09/Mundo/I12.html. Accessed April 15, 2004.

Putnam, Robert. 1976. *The Comparative Study of Political Elites.* Englewood Cliffs, N.J.: Prentice Hall.

———. 1993. *Making Democracy Work: Civic Traditions in Modern Italy.* Princeton, N.J.: Princeton University Press.

Quantin, Patrick. 1997. "Congo: Transition démocratiques et conjoncture critique." In Jean-Pascal Daloz and Patrick Quantin, eds., *Transitions démocratiques africaines: Dynamiques et contraintes (1990–1994).* Paris: Kharthala, 139–91.

Radio France International. "Dossiers Politiques et Diplomatiques." Available at: http://www .rfi.fr/fichiers/MFI/PolitiqueDiplomatie.

Rakner, Lise. 1998. "Reform as a Matter of Political Survival: Political and Economic Liberalisation in Zambia." Ph.D. diss., University of Bergen, Norway.

Rakner, Lise, Nicolas van de Walle, and Dominic Mulaisho. 2001. "Zambia." In *Aid and Reform in Africa,* ed. Shantayanan Devarajan, David R. Dollar, and Torgey Holmgren. Washington, D.C.: World Bank, 533–623.

Rakotoarisoa, Jean-Eric. 2001. Editorial. *Dans les Medias Demain.* July 5.

Randall, Vicky, and J. Scarritt. 1996. "Sounding a Cautionary Note on Democratization: Lessons from India and Zambia." *Journal of Commonwealth and Comparative Politics* 34, no. 2: 19–45.

Raynal, Jean-Jacques. 1983. "L'Evolution politique et constitutionelle de la République Centrafricaine (1958–1983)." *Revue Juridique et Politique* 37, no. 4: 795–816.

———. 1993. *Les institutions politiques du Niger.* Saint Maur: Sépia.

Reno, William. 1999. *Warlord Politics and African States.* Boulder, Colo.: Lynne Rienner.

Republic of Madagascar. 1992. *Constitution de la République de Madagascar.* Antananarivo: Foie et Justice.

———. 1998. Loi Constitutionnelle no. 98–001 du 8 avril 1998.

Reuters News Service. Dates as listed.

Reynolds, Andrew. 1995a. "Constitutional Engineering in Southern Africa." *Journal of Democracy* 6, no. 2: 86–99.

———. 1995b. "The Case for Proportionality." *Journal of Democracy* 6, no. 4: 117–24.

Richburg, Keith B. 1997. "The More Things Change." *The New Republic.* June 16.

Rigger, Shelley. 1999. *Politics in Taiwan: Voting for Democracy.* London and New York: Routledge.

Risse, Thomas, Stephen C. Ropp, and Kathryn Sikkink. 1999. *The Power of Human Rights: International Norms and Domestic Change.* New York: Cambridge University Press.

Robinson, Pearl T. 1991. "Niger: Anatomy of a Neo-traditionalist Corporatist State." *Comparative Politics* 24, no. 1: 1–20.

References

———. 1994a. "Democratization: Understanding the Relationship between Regime Change and the Culture of Politics." *African Studies Review* 37, no. 1: 39–67.

———. 1994b. "The National Conference Phenomenon in Francophone Africa." *Comparative Studies in Society and History* 36, no. 3: 575–610.

Ronen, Dov. 1968. *Dahomey: Between Tradition and Modernity.* Ithaca, N.Y.: Cornell University Press.

Rosenstone, Steven, and J. M. Hansen. 1993. *Mobilization, Participation, and Democracy in America.* New York: Macmillan.

Ross, David. 2001. "Does Oil Hinder Democracy?" *World Politics* 53, no. 3: 325–61.

Roubaud, François. 2000. *Identités et Transition Démocratique: l'Exception Malgache?* Paris: l'Harmattan.

Rueschemeyer, Dietrich, Evelyne Huber Stephens, and John D. Stephens. 1992. *Capitalist Development and Democracy.* Chicago: University of Chicago Press.

Rustow, Dankwart. 1970. "Transitions to Democracy: Toward a Dynamic Model." *Comparative Politics* 2, no. 3: 337–63.

Sabanews Weekend Edition. 1998. No title. August 1. Available at: http://faramir.wn.apc.org/misa/articles/1998/aug/ips/6415–ips.html. Accessed September 19, 2001.

Sartori, Giovanni. 1991. "Comparing and Miscomparing." *Journal of Theoretical Politics* 3, no. 3: 243–57.

———. 1994. *Comparative Constitutional Engineering: An Inquiry into Structures, Incentives and Outcomes.* New York: New York University Press.

The Saturday Nation (Blantyre, Malawi). 1995. "Principles in Question." December 16–22.

Savana (Maputo). Dates as listed.

Schaffer, Frederic. 1998. *Democracy in Translation: Understanding Politics in an Unfamiliar Culture.* Ithaca, N.Y.: Cornell.

Schatzberg, Michael G. 2001. *Political Legitimacy in Middle Africa: Father, Family, Food.* Bloomington: Indiana University Press.

Schedler, Andreas. 1998. "What Is Democratic Consolidation." *Journal of Democracy* 9, no. 2: 91–107.

———. 2000. "Mexico's Victory: The Democratic Revelation." *Journal of Democracy* 11, no. 4: 5–19.

Schmitter, Philippe. 1995. "Organized Interests and Democratic Consolidation in Southern Europe." In *The Politics of Democratic Consolidation: Southern Europe in Comparative Perspective,* ed. Richard Gunther, Nikiforos Diamondouros, and Hans-Jurgen Puhle. Baltimore: Johns Hopkins University Press, 315–88.

Schmitter, Philippe, and Terry Lynn Karl. 1991. "What Democracy Is . . . and Is Not." *Journal of Democracy* 2, no. 3: 75–88.

Schumpeter, Joseph A. 1950 (1942). *Capitalism, Socialism and Democracy.* New York: Harper.

Seely, Jennifer C. 2001. "A Political Analysis of Decentralization: Coopting the Tuareg Threat in Mali." *Journal of Modern African Studies* 39, no. 3: 499–524.

Seligson, Mitchell, and John A. Booth. 1995. *Elections and Democracy in Central America, Revisited.* Chapel Hill: University of North Carolina Press.

Semu, Pilirani. 2000. "Protest: NGOs against Local Govt. Bill." *The Nation* (Blantyre, Malawi). October 20.

Simiyu, Vincent G. 1988. "The Democratic Myth in the African Traditional Societies." In *Democratic Theory and Practice in Africa,* ed. Walter O. Oyugi, E. S. Atieno Odhiambo, Michael Chege, and Afrifa K. Gitonga. Portsmouth, N.H.: Heinemann, 49–70.

References

Simon, David. 2002. "Can Democracy Consolidate in Africa amidst Poverty? Economic Influences upon Political Participation in Zambia." *Journal of Commonwealth and Comparative Politics* 40, no. 1: 23–42.

Sisk, Timothy, and Andrew Reynolds, eds. 1998. *Elections and Conflict Management in Africa.* Washington, D.C.: United States Institute of Peace Press.

Sklar, Richard L. 1987. "Developmental Democracy." *Comparative Studies in Society and History* 29, no. 4: 686–714.

Smith, Zeric Kay. 2000. "The Impact of Political Liberalization and Democratization on Ethnic Conflict in Africa: An Empirical Test of Common Assumptions." *Journal of Modern African Studies* 38, no. 1: 21–40.

Solinger, Dorothy J. 2001. "Ending One-Party Dominance: Korea, Taiwan, Mexico." *Journal of Democracy* 12, no. 1: 30–42.

Stepan, Alfred. 1990. "On the Tasks of a Democratic Opposition." *Journal of Democracy* 1, no. 2: 41–49.

Sundberg, Anne. 2000. "The Struggle for Kingship: Moses or Messiah—Ethnic War and the Use of Ethnicity in the Process of Democratization in Congo-Brazzaville." In *Ethnicity Kills? The Politics of War, Peace and Ethnicity in Sub-Saharan Africa,* ed. Einar Braathen, Morten Boas, and Gjermud Saether. New York: St. Martin's, 87–108.

Tag, Sylvia. 1996. "Mehr Demokratisierung durch Dezentralisierung? Analyse eines umstrittenen Reformvorhabens in der Zentralafrikanischen Republik." *Afrika Spectrum* 31, no. 3: 235–53.

Thiong'o, Ngugi wa. 1986. *Decolonizing the Mind: The Politics of Language in African Literature.* Portsmouth, N.H.: Heinemann.

Thystère-Tchicaya, Jean-Pierre. 1992. *Itinéraire d'un Africain Vers la Démocratie.* Genève: Éditions du Tricorne.

Tiangaye, Nicolas. 1991. "The Democracy Movement and Repression in the Central African Republic." *Africa Demos* 1, no. 4: 5.

Times of Zambia (Ndola, Zambia). Dates as listed.

Tordoff, William, and Robert Molteno. 1974. "Parliament." In *Politics in Zambia,* ed. William Tordoff. Berkeley: University of California Press, 197–241.

Touré, Amadou Toumani. 1994. "Comment j'ai pris le pouvoir. Pourquoi je l'ai quitté." *Jeune Afrique,* nos. 1753–1754: detachable supplement.

Tukula, Gracian. 1996. "Former MYPs Threaten War." *The Nation* (Blantyre, Malawi). November 25.

UNHCR Briefing Notes. 2001. "Afghanistan, Ministerial Meeting on Refugees, East/Horn of Africa, Central African Republic." December 4. Available at: http://www.reliefweb.int. Accessed December 15, 2001.

United Nations Development Program [UNDP]. 1998. *Human Development Report.* New York: UNDP.

United Nations Security Council. 2002. "Report of the [U.N.] Secretary-General on Developments in Guinea-Bissau." New York: United Nations Security Council, 1–12.

———. 2003. "The Situation in the Central African Republic and the Activities of the United Nations Peace-building Support Office in the Central African Republic." Report of the Secretary-General, June 20, 2003 (S/2003/661) and December 29, 2003 (S/2003/1209). New York: United Nations Security Council.

U.S. Department of State. 1997. "Madagascar Country Report on Human Rights Practices for 1996." Bureau of Democracy, Human Rights, and Labor, January 30. Unpublished report.

References

———. 2003. "Madagascar Country Report on Human Rights Practices for 1996." Bureau of Democracy, Human Rights, and Labor, February 25. Unpublished report.

van de Walle, Nicolas. 1997. "Economic Reform and the Consolidation of Democracy in Africa." In *Democracy in Africa: The Hard Road Ahead,* ed. Marina Ottaway. Boulder, Colo.: Lynne Rienner, 15–42.

———. 2001. *African Economies and the Politics of Permanent Crisis, 1979–1999.* New York: Cambridge University Press.

———. 2002. "Africa's Range of Regimes." *Journal of Democracy* 13, no. 2: 66–80.

van Donge, Jan Kees. 1995. "Zambia: Kaunda and Chiluba." In *Democracy and Political Change in Sub-Saharan Africa,* ed. John A. Wiseman. London: Routledge, 193–219.

———. 1998. "The Mwanza Trial as a Search for a Usable Malawian Past." In *Democratization in Malawi: A Stocktaking,* ed. Kings Phiri and Kenneth Ross. Zomba, Malawi: Kachere Press, 21–51.

Vansina, Jan. 1990. *Paths in the Rainforest: Toward a History of Political Tradition in Equatorial Africa.* Madison: University of Wisconsin Press.

Vengroff, Richard. 1993. "Governance and the Transition to Democracy Political Parties and the Party System in Mali." *Journal of Modern African Studies* 31, no. 4: 541–62.

———. 1994 "The Impact of the Electoral System on the Transition to Democracy in Africa: The Case of Mali." *Electoral Studies* 13, no. 1: 29–37.

Vengroff, Richard, and Moctar Koné. 1995. "Mali: Democracy and Political Change." In *Democracy and Political Change in Sub-Saharan Africa,* ed. John A. Wiseman. London and New York: Routledge.

Verschave, François-Xavier. 1998. *La Françafrique: Le plus long scandale de la République.* Paris: Stock.

———. 2000. *Noir silence: Qui arrêtera la Françafrique?* Paris: Les Arènes.

Villalón, Leonardo A. 1994. "Democratizing a (Quasi)Democracy: The Senegalese Elections of 1993." *African Affairs* 93, no. 371: 163–93.

———. 1996. "The Moral and the Political in African Democratization: *The Code de la Famille* in Niger's Troubled Transition." *Democratization* 3, no. 2: 41–68.

———. 1998. "The African State at the End of the Twentieth Century: Parameters of the Critical Juncture." In *The African State at a Critical Juncture: Between Disintegration and Reconfiguration,* ed. Leonardo A. Villalón and Phillip A. Huxtable. Boulder, Colo.: Lynne Rienner, 3–25.

———. 2000. "Constructing and Reconstructing Political Space: Africa in the Age of Democracy." Paper presented at conference, "Africa at the Turn of the Century," Centro de Estudos Africanos, Instituto Superior de Ciencias de Trabalho a da Empresa, Lisbon, Portugal, September 20–23.

Villalón, Leonardo, and Phillip A. Huxtable, eds. 1998. *The African State at a Critical Juncture: Between Disintegration and Reconfiguration.* Boulder, Colo.: Lynne Rienner.

VonDoepp, Peter. 2001. "The Survival of Malawi's Enfeebled Democracy." *Current History* 100, no. 646: 232–38.

———. 2002a. "Liberal Visions and Actual Power in Grassroots Civil Society: Local Churches and Women's Empowerment in Rural Malawi." *Journal of Modern African Studies* 40, no. 2: 273–301.

———. 2002b. "The Problem of Judicial Control in New African Democracies: Malawi and Zambia in Comparative View." Paper presented at the Annual Meeting of the African Studies Association, Washington, D.C., December 5–8.

———. 2003a. "Understanding Judicial Assertiveness in New African Democracies: The

References

Political Context of Judicial Behavior in Malawi and Zambia." Paper presented at the 2003 Annual Convention of the International Studies Association, Portland, Oregon, February 26–March 2.

———. 2003b. "The Battle for Third Term: Party Politics and Institutional Development in Namibia, Malawi, and Zambia." Paper presented at the Ninety-ninth Annual Meeting of the American Political Science Association, Philadelphia, Pennsylvania, August 28–31.

Weber, Max. 1958. "Science as a Vocation." In *From Max Weber: Essays in Sociology*, ed. Hans H. Gerth and C. Wright Mills. New York: Oxford University Press, 129–58.

Wehner, Joachim. 2001. "Zambia: What Is the Most Effective Role for Civil Society and Parliament in the Budget?" Institute for Democracy in Southern Africa, Africa Budget Project Research Report, April 2001. Available at: http://www.worldbank.org/wbi/publicfinance/publicresources/ZambiaCSandParlCaseStudy%5B1%5D.pdf. Accessed October 14, 2004.

Westebbe, Richard. 1994. "Structural Adjustment, Rent Seeking, and Liberalization in Benin." In *Economic Change and Political Liberalization in Sub-Saharan Africa*, ed. Jennifer Widner. Baltimore: Johns Hopkins University Press, 80–100.

White, David. 2003. "Comment and Analysis: Nigerian Elections." *Financial Times*, April 11.

Whitehead, Laurence. 1986. "Comparative Politics: Democratization Studies." In *A New Handbook of Political Science*, ed. Robert E. Goodin and Hans-Dieter Klingemann. Oxford: Oxford University Press, 353–71.

Whitehead, Laurence, ed. 1996. *International Dimensions of Democratization*. Oxford: Oxford University Press.

Widner, Jennifer. 1994. "Political Reform in Anglophone and Francophone African Countries." In *Economic Change and Political Liberalization in Sub-Saharan Africa*, ed. Jennifer Widner. Baltimore and London: Johns Hopkins University Press, 49–79.

———. 2001. *Building the Rule of Law: Francis Nyalali and the Road to Judicial Independence in Africa*. New York: W. W. Norton and Company.

Widner, Jennifer A., ed. 1994. *Economic Change and Political Liberalization in Sub-Saharan Africa*. Baltimore: Johns Hopkins University Press

Wildavsky, Aaron. 1987. "Choosing Preferences by Constructing Institutions: A Cultural Theory of Preference Formation." *American Political Science Review* 81, no. 1: 3–21.

Williams, David. 1977. *Malawi: The Politics of Despair*. Ithaca, N.Y.: Cornell University Press.

Wing, Susanna. 2002. "Questioning the State: Constitutionalism and the Malian Espace d'Interpellation Démocratique." *Democratization* 9, no. 1: 121–47.

Wiseman, John A. 1990. "Review: *Benin, the Congo, Burkina Faso: Politics, Economics and Society* by Chris Allen, Michael S. Radu, Keith Somerville, and Joan Baxter." *American Affairs* 89, no. 357: 605–606.

World Bank. 2001. *African Development Indicators 2001*. Washington, D.C.: World Bank.

Young, Crawford. 1976. *The Politics of Cultural Pluralism*. New Haven, Conn.: Yale University Press.

———. 1996. "Africa: An Interim Balance Sheet." *Journal of Democracy* 7, no. 3: 53–68.

———. 1999. "The Third Wave of Democratization in Africa: Ambiguities and Contradictions." In *State, Conflict, and Democracy in Africa*, ed. Richard Joseph. Boulder, Colo.: Lynne Rienner, 217–37.

Zakaria, Fareed. 1997. "The Rise of Illiberal Democracy." *Foreign Affairs* 76, no. 6: 22–43.

———. 2003. *The Future of Democracy: Illiberal Democracy at Home and Abroad*. New York: W. W. Norton.

References

Zambia Daily Mail (Lusaka). Dates as listed.

Zambia Today (Lusaka). 1996. No title. November 24.

Zartman, I. William. 1989. *Ripe for Resolution: Conflict and Intervention in Africa*. New York: Oxford.

Zartman, I. William, and Katharina R. Vogeli. 2000. "Prevention Gained and Prevention Lost: Collapse, Competition, and Coup in Congo." In *Opportunities Missed, Opportunities Seized: Preventive Diplomacy in the Post–Cold War World*, ed. Bruce W. Jentleson. Lanham, Md.: Rowman and Littlefield, 273–76.

Zoctizoum, Yarisse. 1983. *Histoire de la Centrafrique*. 2nd ed. Paris: L'Harmattan.

CONTRIBUTORS

MICHAEL CHEGE is Associate Professor of Political Science and former director of the Center for African Studies at the University of Florida in Gainesville. In 2004–2005 he served as a United Nations Development Policy Advisor to the newly elected democratic government of President Mwai Kibaki of Kenya. He has authored articles in such journals as *Foreign Affairs, Journal of Modern African Studies, Transition, Journal of Democracy, Current History,* and *Journal of Development Studies.* He is currently completing a book manuscript on governance in Africa.

JOHN F. CLARK is Associate Professor and Chairperson in the Department of International Relations at Florida International University. He is co-editor (with David Gardinier) of *Political Reform in Francophone Africa* and editor of *The African Stakes of the Congo War.* He has published numerous articles in such journals as *Journal of Modern African Studies, Studies in Comparative International Development, African Affairs, Journal of Democracy,* and *Comparative Studies in Society and History.*

JOSHUA B. FORREST is founding director of the Kerr Institute of African History, Culture and Politics at La Roche College in Pittsburgh, Pennsylvania. He is author of four books, including most recently *Lineages of State Fragility: Rural Civil Society in Guinea-Bissau* and *Subnationalism in Africa: Ethnicity, Alliances, and Politics.* He has also published numerous articles on Guinea-Bissauan and Namibian politics, on state collapse, and on the theory and practice of African democratization.

ABDOURAHMANE IDRISSA is in the Ph.D. program in the Department of Political Science at the University of Florida. A native of Niger, he holds two degrees in philosophy as well as a graduate D.E.A. degree in Political Science from the Université Cheikh Anta Diop in Dakar, Senegal, and an M.A. in Political Science from the University of Kansas. He has published articles on both philosophy and politics in journals in Senegal and Niger.

BRUCE A. MAGNUSSON is Associate Professor in the Department of Politics at Whitman College in Walla Walla, Washington. He has written on democratization in Benin for *Comparative Politics, l'Afrique Politique,* and (with John Clark) *Comparative Studies in Society and History.* He has also contributed chapters to such books as *Constructivist Comparative Politics* and *State, Conflict and Democracy in Africa.* His current research focuses on questions of justice and security in democratizing states in Africa.

CARRIE MANNING is Associate Professor of Political Science at Georgia State University in Atlanta. She is author of *The Politics of Peace in Mozambique: Post-Conflict Democratization, 1992–2000* and has published articles on democracy and conflict resolution in Mozambique and Angola in numerous journals, including *Democratization, Comparative Politics, Current History, Journal of Southern African Studies,* and *Journal of Commonwealth and Comparative Politics.*

RICHARD R. MARCUS is Assistant Professor of Political Science at The University of Alabama in Huntsville. His publications on democratization, local participation in democracy, and local environmental governance in Madagascar have appeared in *Current History, Afrika Spectrum, Journal of Asian and African Studies, Human Ecology, African Studies Quarterly,* and such edited volumes as *A Decade of Democracy in Africa* and *Achieving Sustainable Development.*

ANDREAS MEHLER is Director of the Institute of African Affairs in Hamburg, Germany. He has published extensively in English, French, and German, on conflict prevention, democratization, and elections in Francophone Africa. These include articles in *Africa Spektrum* and *l'Afrique Politique,* and several monographs, including (with Michael Lund and Céline Moyroud) *Peace-Building and Conflict Prevention in Developing Countries* and (with Claude Ribaux) *Crisis Prevention and Conflict Management in Technical Cooperation: An Overview of the National and International Debate.*

DAVID J. SIMON is currently Lecturer in Political Science at Yale University. He has published on economic conditions and voting patterns in Zambia in *Comparative Political Studies* and *Commonwealth and Comparative Politics.* In addition to democracy in Zambia, his current research focuses on the politics of aid and debt relief in Africa.

LEONARDO A. VILLALÓN is Director of the Center for African Studies and Associate Professor of Political Science at the University of Florida. He is author of *Islamic Society and State Power in Senegal: Disciples and Citizens in Fatick* and co-editor (with Phillip A. Huxtable) of *The African State at a Critical Juncture: Between Disintegration and Reconfiguration.* His articles have also appeared in such journals as *Comparative Politics, Democratization, African Affairs,* and *African Studies Review.*

PETER VONDOEPP is Assistant Professor of Political Science at the University of Vermont. His work on democratization and civil society has appeared in *Studies in Comparative International Development, Current History, Journal of Modern African Studies,* and *Commonwealth and Comparative Politics,* as well as such edited volumes as *Democratization in Malawi: A Stocktaking* and *A Democracy of Chameleons: Politics and Culture in the New Malawi.* He is currently working on a project comparing the role and effectiveness of judiciaries in new African democracies.

INDEX

Index

170–171; Malawi's courts and democratization, 176, 185–187, 192–193; Mali, role of the Constitutional Court in, 65

Da Costa, João, 253
Dabo, Baciro, 261
Dacko, David, 129, 131, 132, 134, 138, 143
Dahl, Robert, 155–156
Damara (CAR), 147
Democratic Front (FD) [Guinea-Bissau], 253
Dhlakama, Afonso, 226, 227, 239, 241, 242
Diaby, May Mamadou Maribatou, 65
Diallo, Ali Nouhoun, 63
Diallo, Djibril, 55
Dialogue National sans Exclusive (Congo), 102
Diata (Congo), 101
Dimbi (CAR), 144
Djalo, Sory, 260
Djermakoye, Moumouni Adamou, 35, 40, 42
Doe, Samuel K., 268
Dologuélé, Anicet Georges, 142, 145
Domingos, Raul, 226

Les Echos (periodical, Mali), 70
Economics: Benin, crisis in, 80; economic factors in democratization, 17–19; Guinea-Bissau, crisis in, 255–256; liberalization in, 52–53; Madagascar, crisis in, 157; Malawi, economic influences on elite in, 178, 180; Mali, crisis in, 53; neoliberal policies, 53, 61; Niger, crisis in, 30; Republic of Congo, crisis in, 108; Zambia, crisis in, 212–213
Elections, founding, 1, 7–8
"Electoral fallacy," 7–8, 11, 28
Electoral systems, 22–23; in Benin, 81, 83, 95n11; in Congo, 106–107; in Madagascar, 154, 161–162, 173n5; in Mali, 50, 57–60, 67; in Mozambique, 225–226; in Niger, 34–35, 42, 58
Electoral Union (UE) [Mozambique], 226
Elites: and consolidation of democracy, 12, 14, 20, 21; definition of, 12–14; factors shaping behavior of, 14–20; relations to institutions, 2–3, 9–10, 21–25. *See also individual country chapters*
Espace d'interpellation démocratique (Mali), 61
Ethnicity: in Benin, 80–81; in Central African Republic, 128, 130, 143; in Congo, 100–102, 103, 106, 111–113, 119, 122; in Guinea-Bissau, 261; in Madagascar, 159, 167; in Mozambique, 229; in Niger, 35–36

Farim (Guinea-Bissau), 249
FFKM (Council of Christian Churches or United Group of Churches) [Madagascar], 167, 169
Fianarantsoa (Madagascar), 159, 171
Financial Times, 271
Flambeau Centrafricain (FLAC) [CAR], 144
Fon (ethnicity), 81
Forces Spéciales de Défense des Institutions Républicaines (FORSDIR) [CAR], 138
Forum de la Semaine (periodical, Benin), 84
Forum for Democracy and Development (FDD) [Zambia], 203, 204, 205
Forum National de Renouveau Démocratique (Niger), 39
Forum sur la Réconciliation Nationale (Congo), 102
Foundation for Democratic Progress (FODEP) [Zambia], 214
Founding elections. *See* Elections, founding
France, 47n2, 52, 80, 99, 103, 110, 113, 114, 115, 119, 124, 128, 129, 136, 137
Freedom House, 273, 279, 285
Frelimo (Mozambican Liberation Front) [Mozambique], 221, 225–243 *passim*, 277, 278, 284
French Fifth Republic, 23, 33–34, 42, 43, 49, 57, 97, 280
Front Patriotique pour le Progrès (FPP) [CAR], 131, 132, 134, 139
Front pour la Restauration et la Défense de la Démocratie (FRDD) [Niger], 40–41
Fulani (ethnicity), 35
Fulbe (ethnicity), 255

Gbaya (ethnicity), 146
G-11 [CAR], 139
General Peace Accord of Rome, 238
Glélé, Maurice, 94n10
Gomes, Domingos Fernandes, 254
Goumba, Abel, 129, 130, 131, 132, 143, 148
Groupe d'Antananarivo [Madagascar], 167
Guebuza, Armando, 234, 236
Guinea-Bissau, 97, 154, 156, 246–266; army and democratization in, 256, 258, 263, 265; civil war in, 256; economic crisis, 255–256; ethnic issue in, 261; National Conference, 252; party system in, 253; Senegalese intervention in, 256–257

Haské (periodical, Niger), 30
Hausa (ethnicity) [Niger], 35
Haut Conseil de la République (HCR): Benin, 82, 84; Niger, 32, 42

Index

Index

Index

Index

Zafy, Albert, 154, 157, 158, 159, 160, 163, 169, 172

Zambia, 142, 199–220; constitutional manipulation in, 202; economic crisis, 212–213; electoral boycott, 203; electoral process in, 209–210; international donors' influence in, 213–215; neopatrimonialism in, 208, 210–213; opposition politics in, 205–206; political norms in, 210–212; Third Republic, 201, 208, 210

Zambia Democratic Congress (ZDC) [Zambia], 204, 205, 206

Zarma, Songhay (ethnicity), 35

Zimba, Newstead, 211

Zinder (Niger), 36

Zulu (militia, Congo), 116

Lightning Source UK Ltd.
Milton Keynes UK
UKHW020650080920
369340UK00019B/400